Mississippi Women

Mississippi Women

THEIR HISTORIES, THEIR LIVES

Volume 2

EDITED BY

Elizabeth Anne Payne, Martha H. Swain,

and Marjorie Julian Spruill

Bibliography by Brenda M. Eagles

The University of Georgia Press   *Athens and London*

© 2010 by the University of Georgia Press

Athens, Georgia 30602

www.ugapress.org

All rights reserved

Set in Minion by Graphic Composition, Inc., Bogart, Georgia.

Printed and bound by Thomson-Shore

The paper in this book meets the guidelines for
permanence and durability of the Committee on
Production Guidelines for Book Longevity of the
Council on Library Resources.

Printed in the United States of America

10 11 12 13 14   P   5 4 3 2 1

The Library of Congress has catalogued the first volume of this book as follows:
Mississippi Women : their histories, their lives / edited by Martha H. Swain,
Elizabeth Anne Payne, Marjorie Julian Spruill; associate editor, Susan Ditto.

xvii, 324 p. : ill. ; 23cm.

Includes bibliographical references (p.) and index.

ISBN 0-8203-2502-3 (alk. paper) —

ISBN 0-8203-2503-1 (pbk. : alk. paper)

1. Women—Mississippi—Biography. 2. Mississippi—
Biography. I. Swain, Martha H., 1929– II. Payne, Elizabeth Anne, 1943–
III. Spruill, Marjorie Julian, 1951–

CT3260.M57 2003

920.72'09762—dc21 2003008776

Volume 2 ISBN-13: 978-0-8203-3393-9 (alk. paper)

ISBN-10: 0-8203-3393-X (alk. paper)

ISBN-13: 978-0-8203-3394-6 (pbk. : alk. paper)

ISBN-10: 0-8203-3394-8 (pbk. : alk. paper)

British Library Cataloging-in-Publication Data available

To our sisters
Glenda Payne Rea
and
Bonnie Payne Davidson
Mary Elizabeth Swain Bacon
and
Margo Swain
E. Carol Spruill

Contents

Acknowledgments

This book and its companion volume of biographical essays began on a spring afternoon in 1997 at a café on State Street across from Millsaps College in Jackson. Martha Swain had recently retired from teaching at Texas Woman's University and moved back to Starkville, her hometown. Joanne Hawks was teaching in the history department at the University of Mississippi and directing the Sarah Isom Women's Center, which she had founded. I was moving from the University of Arkansas back to my home state to help launch the McDonnell-Barksdale Honors College at the University of Mississippi. It seemed an apt time for the three of us to explore more seriously our joint concerns about the lack of scholarship on Mississippi women's history.

Earlier in the decade, Joanne—Jan as she was fondly called—had surveyed archival sources dealing with Mississippi women's history. We knew that historical material existed, and we were eager to find scholars who would shape archival sources into inviting essays. We named ourselves the Mississippi Women's History Project.

Jan died unexpectedly in July 1998 but not before she had written her own contribution to volume 1. Shortly after Jan's death, Martha and I realized that so many scholars had agreed to write for our project that we needed to publish two volumes: the first dedicated to biographies and the second devoted to essays analyzing broader historical forces that shaped women's lives in Mississippi. Nicole Mitchell, the director of the University of Georgia Press, and Nancy Grayson, its editor-in-chief, boldly supported the idea of two volumes.

Marjorie Spruill, who was at that time (2000) teaching at the University of Southern Mississippi and writing an article for our first volume, volunteered to join us as an editor. In 2003, the first volume appeared with seventeen biographical articles of women who, except for Eudora Welty, Margaret Walker Alexander, and Fannie Lou Hamer, had not yet received scholarly attention.

Most of Mississippi's history has been written from the perspective of electoral politics and judicial decisions, making the study of our past male oriented and hierarchical—and white. The Mississippi Women's History Project was undertaken with the belief that when fully and expansively written, the history of Mississippi will be as compelling and as richly nuanced as are its native daughters' and sons' literary masterpieces. Eudora Welty and William Faulkner, Elizabeth Spencer and Richard Wright are read around the world.

The Mississippi Women's History Project is based at the University of Mississippi, and we are indebted to Robert Haws, former chair of the Department of History, and Joseph Ward, who presently heads the department, for their support of our work. Betty Harness, the department's administrative assistant, provided a steady hand throughout the preparation of the manuscript. Michelle Palmertree, Marie Baker Lloyd, Susan Nicholas, and Nichole Bourgeois assisted me cheerfully with diverse tasks. Susan Ditto was helpful at the beginning in suggesting authors. Elizabeth Jacoway, Sheila Skemp, and Charles Eagles did not read these essays, but they always welcomed and responded to my queries, gave me bibliographical tips, and on more than one occasion told me that I was outright wrong about a particular assertion. Anne Firor Scott, who is the inspiration for much that is presented here, cheered us on at all points. We thank Mary Beth Norton for her perspective on the history of organized women's petitions.

We are indebted to Mattie Sink, Betty Self, Jill Smith, Susan Tietz, Jeff Rogers, Diane Ross, Linda Breazeale, Laura Capell, and Terry Winschel for assisting us in our search for illustrations for this book. Dianne Walkup gave us permission to use the photograph of her Knight ancestors. Patricia Crosby shared the photograph she took of the Brownie group with Julia Jones, Claiborne County's first female African American circuit court clerk. Herbert Randall gave us permission to use his photograph of civil rights activity in Hattiesburg. Cora Norman provided us with the photograph of herself with Jessie Mosley. Phillip Barron helped us digitize images for this book. James Earl Price and Sue Moore shared information on the Elizabeth Female Academy, and we are especially indebted to them for giving me access to several documents vital to the history of women's education.

Bonnie Payne Davidson read several essays with a keen editorial eye. The two anonymous readers for the University of Georgia Press asked for greater specificity and clearer wording, and we are grateful for their unselfish service in carefully reading the manuscript. Most of these essays were edited by Brenda M. Eagles, whose innate gifts have been finely honed into an impressive capacity to transform awkward writing into smooth prose. Always with an eye toward the reader, she insisted that the authors write clearly. Both the history department at the University of Mississippi and at the University of South Carolina provided funds for the cost of this book.

The last stage of preparing the manuscript was completed while I was on leave at the National Humanities Center. I appreciate the encouragement of Geoffrey Harpham, the center's director, and the help of Kent Millikin and Lois Whittington, who gracefully guide the fellows who yearly work at the center. Joel Elliott understands computer malfunctions and nervous authors better than anyone I know. Marie Brubaker was helpful in multiple ways. Beth Snead, Courtney Denney, and Jon Davies were encouraging and efficient at the final stage of producing this book. We appreciate Barbara Wojhoski's pursuit of excellence in copyediting the manuscript. Robert Ellis skillfully indexed the book. Kenneth Rutherford, a fellow Mississippian, was patient with the clutter of essays spread across our dining-room table. I thank him for his support and companionship during the time I worked on these essays.

In writing histories of Mississippi women, scholars must often mine for material more expansively than those researching women's lives in other states. Mississippi established in 1902 the second state-supported archival depository in the country, the Mississippi Department of Archives and History (MDAH). Recently the MDAH has become aggressive in collecting papers, diaries, and journals that reflect the diversity of Mississippi's population, including its women. Scholars working on Mississippi women's history, nevertheless, must scout for material in private hands, snoop in county libraries, and dig for information that is not neatly organized in a single, large depository.

The editors offer this volume as an invitation to scholars to research and write on unexplored topics in women's history. We are pleased that our first volume inspired historians in Tennessee, Georgia, South Carolina, Louisiana, Texas, and Arkansas to begin work on similar projects for their states. There is, however, much to be done. We must, as the old hymn enjoins, "Come, Labor On."

Elizabeth Anne Payne
Oxford, Mississippi

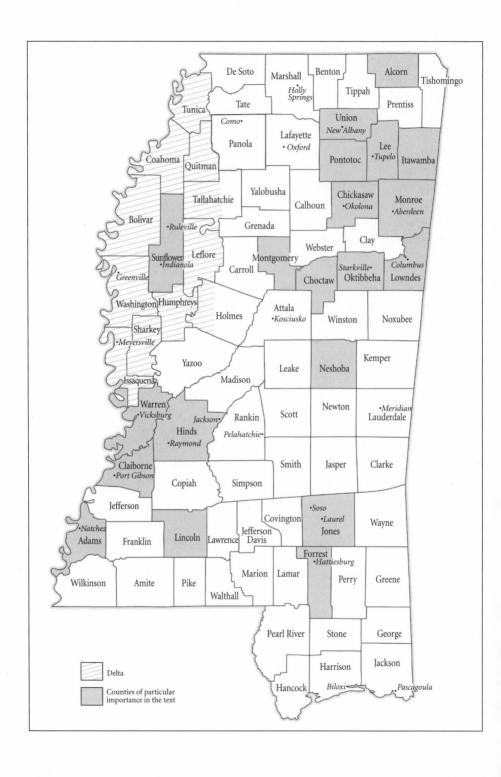

De Soto
Marshall
Benton
Alcorn
Tishomingo
Holly Springs
Tippah
Tate
Prentiss
Tunica
Como•
Union
New•Albany
Lafayette
Panola
•Oxford
Lee
•Tupelo
Coahoma
Pontotoc
Itawamba
Quitman
Tallahatchie
Yalobusha
Chickasaw
Monroe
Calhoun
•Okolona
•Aberdeen
Grenada
Bolivar
•Ruleville
Clay
Webster
Sunflower
Leflore
Montgomery
Starkville•
Columbus
•Indianola
Carroll
Choctaw
Oktibbeha
Lowndes
Greenville
Attala
Washington
Humphreys
Holmes
•Kosciusko
Winston
Noxubee
Sharkey
•Meyersville
Yazoo
Leake
Neshoba
Kemper
Issaquena
Madison
Warren
Newton
•Vicksburg
Jackson•
Rankin
Scott
•Meridian
Hinds
Lauderdale
•Raymond
Pelahatchie•
Smith
Jasper
Clarke
Claiborne
•Port Gibson
Copiah
Simpson
Jefferson
•Soso
Covington
•Laurel
Wayne
•Natchez
Jones
Adams
Franklin
Lincoln
Lawrence
Jefferson
Davis
Forrest
•Hattiesburg
Wilkinson
Amite
Pike
Marion
Lamar
Perry
Greene
Walthall
Pearl River
Stone
George
Harrison
Jackson
Hancock
Biloxi•
Pascagoula

Delta

Counties of particular
importance in the text

Mississippi Women

Part One

The Eighteenth and Nineteenth Centuries

ELIZABETH ANNE PAYNE

Native American groups who lived in the forests, bottomlands, and coastal areas of Mississippi first encountered Europeans in the sixteenth and seventeenth centuries. Choctaws and Chickasaws dominated most of the area that became the Mississippi Territory in 1798. From 1805 through 1832, treaties ceded land to the United States, which ultimately led to the removal of Native Americans as tribal people. However, an extremely important vestige of Indian law remained. Choctaw and Chickasaw women had exercised power and authority and served on tribal councils as a result of matrilineal land ownership. One of the most significant events in Mississippi women's history is the Mississippi Supreme Court's 1837 decree upholding the right of Betsy Love Allen, a high-ranking Chickasaw woman, to own her property. In 1839, the state legislature passed the Married Women's Property Act, the first such act of any state legislature.

James Taylor Carson in our first essay writes about the shape of power and gender in Choctaw and Chickasaw history. He maintains that Mississippi's property laws as well as its gender jurisprudence continue to bear the influence of generations of Chickasaw women. Painting women of both tribes as actors, he asserts that the differences, especially with regard to their interaction with Europeans, are more compelling than the similarities. Without sources written by tribal women themselves, Carson relies on ethnography to provide a richer and more complex understanding of women of both tribes.

Because there are few written sources by white women and none by enslaved women who moved into the newly opened frontier of North and East Mississippi, only generalizations can be made about the hardscrabble lives they endured in isolation or in scattered settlements. Memories like those of Macy Visor Ferrell, however, reveal compelling stories of families separated by bondage and harsh lives. Purchased in South Carolina, Ferrell's great-grandmother and her great-aunt were then brought "riding mules barefooted and barebacked" to Lafayette County.[1] Mattie Ivey Bruce remembers being told of her grandmother's riding from South Carolina to North Mississippi in a wagon full of enslaved women in an advanced state of pregnancy. The wagon stopped for a woman to give birth.[2] Betty Rutherford Wilson, daughter of parents who were also bought in South Carolina, harnessed herself to a mule and plowed alongside her husband as late as 1917.[3] Ruth Hawkins Payne, a white woman, remembers as a child seeing both black and white women plowing fields in her native Itawamba County.[4]

Much more is known about the women in affluent, cotton-rich towns such as Natchez, Columbus, and Holly Springs, where educational institutions for (white) girls flourished in the antebellum years even in small towns. Indeed, female academies and seminaries for white women were well established in Mississippi throughout the nineteenth century. In southwestern Mississippi near Washington, Elizabeth Female Academy, founded by the Methodist Church in 1818 and the first school for women chartered by a state legislature, was the equal of any school for women in the United States at the time. In fact, Troy Female Seminary in New York, usually described as the first institution offering a secondary education to women, was founded three years later.[5]

Elizabeth Female Academy's faculty and students were particularly devoted to the school. "Ladies" representing the academy petitioned the state legislature on behalf of the school in 1822, five years after statehood, when the population of Mississippi was just over seventy-five thousand. The petition calls for enlarging the "sphere of female ability and female usefulness." The "ladies" describe their academy as a "valuable institution" languishing "for want of funds." They inform the legislators that "the cultivation of mental improvements of the other half of the human species" has evoked "considerable interest" and close with a veiled threat: "Into their [the legislators'] hands, therefore the ladies simply commit to a cause, which interests all the fine feelings of their hearts, and in doing this, *they will not, they cannot* anticipate a disappointment." The signatures of 103 women follow. The document is the first petition to a state legislature by *organized* women on behalf of higher education in this country. Finally, in 1884, the Mississippi legislature created the Industrial Institute and College for the Education of White Girls (now Mississippi University for Women), the first state-supported college for women in the United States and a model for several schools in other states. A full history of Elizabeth Female Academy with its legacy of advocacy for higher education for white—and ultimately all—women is yet unwritten, but the institution's importance in state and national history is but one example of an incomplete story in Mississippi history.[6]

The territorial capital until 1802 and the largest town in Mississippi, Natchez was an early cultural capital as well. The richly recorded history of Natchez women, black and white, is especially well documented in the essays written by Joyce Broussard. She has drawn a picture of free black women who were dynamic and vital and who negotiated lives in slaveholding Natchez to carve out a sphere of influence and self-interest. Volume 1 of *Mississippi Women: Their Histories, Their Lives* includes an account of the founding of the Catholic church in Natchez by women of color. Two essays in the present volume follow that story into other avenues of Mississippi women's history. Randy Sparks provides a window through which we see the intense and self-sacrificing activity of white Protestant women as they helped to build Protestant churches in those frontier areas where little is known about women's lives.

In her essay "Naked before the Law," Joyce Broussard describes women's use of the courts in Natchez, illuminating why Mississippi became the first state to break with English common law in granting property rights to married women in the 1839 act. To those who interpret the measure as exclusively an extension of slavery and slaveholders' interests, Broussard acknowledges these conventionally interpreted realities. She nevertheless makes a more subtle and complicated argument insisting that women's use of equity law should also be read as a foundation of and legal preparation for the 1839 act. After passage of the Married Women's Property Act, according to Kevin McCarthy, women petitioned for myriad reasons. Furthermore, appellate judges consistently ruled expansively in interpreting the intent of the law. Taken together, the essays by Carson, Broussard, and McCarthy necessitate a reinterpretation of the intent and impact of the married women's property acts enacted in the South in the decade following 1839.

Much work remains to be done in seeking documents to augment our knowledge of the lives of Mississippi women in the early nineteenth century. Firsthand accounts of the lives of enslaved women and children can help us avoid relying too heavily on the prism of plantation mistresses, "belles," or other upper-class women. Among the latter accounts, the diaries of Amanda Worthington of Washington County, Susan Dabney Smedes of Hinds County, and Nancy Robinson of Holmes County, which depict the pleasantries of plantation life, have already been published and thus do not appear in this volume. There were few professional women in antebellum Mississippi other than teachers and principals employed by the private schools. The manuscripts describing the work of many of these women are available, however, and offer valuable descriptions of the social milieu in which they lived.

As the break between the North and the South loomed in the 1850s and the Civil War began, assertive women assumed a role in the debate. A rich legacy of diaries, journals, and correspondence document (mostly white) Mississippi women's wartime lives. After the war began in April 1861, Mississippi became a focal point in the western theater. Its railroads, arsenals, cotton, and most of all, the Mississippi River were targets of invading Union forces. In his essay, Michael Ballard places women at the center of the agony and terror of the long Vicksburg campaign, which began in Northeast Mississippi. The campaign swept from Corinth through Holly Springs and then to Vicksburg, the "Gibraltar of the Confederacy," where women made accommodations as cave dwellers and in refugee camps in the city's outlands.

For Mississippi, the Reconstruction Era, which lasted from 1866 through the "redemption" of the state by the Democratic Party in 1875, was a turbulent period of shifting forces that significantly affected the lives of women. Upper-class women suffered deprivation and humiliation, while lower-class white women, who had little before the war, owned even less afterward. Nancy Bercaw's essay takes us into the murky terrain of the unresolved legal issues of the Civil War and sees gender as the heart of the matter. Uncertainty left formerly enslaved women in limbo regarding their responsibilities for work in the field and at home. Almost all black women worked for meager wages whether in white households or in "light" industry. In 1866, female laundry workers in Jackson startled local leaders when they met to sign a petition for higher wages. This first known collective move of black working women in United States history begs for closer examination but is now only a fragmented story.

In "Hearth and Home," Susan Ditto offers readers an intriguing look at the transformation of material culture beginning around 1880. Until then, she insists, white women of both the middling and elite classes took little interest in the culinary arts. Yeoman women regarded themselves as independent because they with their husbands owned a small amount of property, and they performed multiple tasks that left little time for cooking. For elite women, cooking was designated as the task of African American women and not considered a proper undertaking for women of their standing. In the late nineteenth century, however, the kitchen emerged as central to the new domestic architecture of both dogtrot and Greek Revival homes. Elite as well as middling-class white women, partly in an effort to exert racial dominance, moved the kitchen inside and joined a domestic revolution that had occurred earlier outside the South. This racial consolidation across class lines, according to Ditto, significantly contributed to the creation of the Jim Crow South.

Women vitally engaged their civil and political culture at the local level, as is demonstrated by the petition to the state legislature signed by organized white women in early statehood, the important state court decision precipitated by a Chicakasaw woman, and the bold act of black women demanding higher wages a year after the Civil War ended. They knew their rights and defended them in gossip circles as well as through courts and petitions to legislative bodies and employers. Viewed from this perspective, we see a significantly different story from that of powerless women. Hierarchy existed, of course, but within a context in which women—white, Native American, and black—observed, often acted, and sometimes won.

NOTES

1. Macy Visor Ferrell, in *Makin' Do: Rural Women Coping with Difficult Times*, documentary film directed by Elizabeth Anne Payne, Department of History and Department of Media and Documentary Projects, University of Mississippi, Oxford, 2008.

2. Mattie Ivey Bruce, interviewed by Elizabeth Anne Payne, December 15, 2005, Center for Media Documentary Projects, University of Mississippi, Oxford.

3. Betty Wilson Rutherford, interviewed by Elizabeth Anne Payne, December 8, 2005, North Mississippi Women's History Project, copy in possession of author.

4. Ruth Hawkins Payne, quoted in personal journal of Elizabeth Anne Payne, June 12, 1996.

5. Randy J. Sparks, *Religion in Mississippi*, vol. 2, Heritage of Mississippi series (Jackson: University Press of Mississippi for the Mississippi Historical Society, 2001), 67.

6. Ladies' Petition to Mississippi Legislature, RG 47, Petitions, 1817–1908, series 2370, box 6815, School folder, Mississippi Department of Archives and History, Jackson. Letter to author from James Earl Price and Sue Moore, accompanied by copy of partially transcribed petition, June 12, 2008. Although the petition was deposited at the Mississippi Department of Archives and History, its faded quality and often illegible script present a challenge for modern readers. A portion of the document's content has been deciphered, thanks to James Earl Price and Sue Moore, two descendants of graduates of the institution who are devoted to the academy's legacy.

Choctaw and Chickasaw Women, 1690–1834

JAMES TAYLOR CARSON

In the second decade of the nineteenth century, a spate of witch killings cast a long shadow over Mississippi. The killings reflected in part the stresses on Mississippi's first peoples over two centuries of European contact. Choctaw and Chickasaw witches stood at the conjunction of forces that gave them powers beyond those available to normal folk. In daytime no one could distinguish a witch from anyone else, but at night they transformed into forest familiars or glowing apparitions. The most telltale sign of a witch's presence was disease, and it was a little girl's bout of sickness in 1819 that prompted missionaries among the Choctaws to write a detailed description of one of the witch killings that had been causing people to flee their homes.

The killing began with the death of the husband of Ellikee, a Chickasaw who had elected to leave her people to settle with her husband in the Choctaw Nation. Having forsaken the aid and protection of her Chickasaw clan, she was effectively among strangers, and the death of her husband left her alone and vulnerable. Perhaps that is why she took her son, two daughters, and two granddaughters to new lodgings near the recently completed missionary station at Elliot.

Ellikee apparently had a reputation as a healer because when a young girl in the neighborhood fell ill, the girl's family came to her for help. The cure that Ellikee fashioned from the roots, leaves, and other materials at hand worked, and grateful for her help, the family gave the widow a horse for her trouble. Unfortunately, the little girl took a turn for the worse and died a few days later. Her family immediately set out to find the witch who had caused the death. They consulted an old conjurer, who pointed his accusing finger at Ellikee, new in the neighborhood with neither husband nor clan to protect her.[1] The men of the little girl's family saddled up and rode twenty miles to Ellikee's house and hollered for her to come out. When she did, they claimed to have been

CHOCTAW WOMAN

Reproduced with permission of the National Anthropological Archives,
Smithsonian Institution (0622540), Washington, D.C.

worn out by a long day of cattle herding, and as was the custom, Ellikee offered them food. After they had eaten, the man who had given Ellikee a horse in exchange for her medicine stepped forward and declared, "I have bought your life. You are a witch, and must die." The old widow replied, "Others lie and you believe."[2]

The posse seized Ellikee because either her medicine had failed, or worse, she had deliberately caused the girl's death. She was an anomalous woman, an outsider without kin and clan protection. Women were dangerous even in the best of circumstances, for they alone commanded the chaotic and destructive powers of fertility, creation, and birth. When set against the male powers of order, killing, and death, the world held a tenuous balance. In Ellikee's case her dark work, at least for one family, showed a world out of balance and lethal to a young child. Order had to be restored through the old woman's compensatory death.

Ellikee is one of the few early Native women in Mississippi whose story has survived in the documentary record, and her story is part of an important larger one. Historians have only recently begun to consider Native American women as players in the larger history of colonial America and the early United States. Studies of Native women have shown that colonization affected men and women equally and that women often responded to the opportunities and impositions of the colonial order by drawing on their cultures to sanction both innovative behavior and resistance. In order to understand why Native women adapted to life in early America as they did, it is imperative to compare their experiences across cultures, thereby weighing the relative importance of culture, history, and happenstance. The experiences of Native women in Mississippi are most striking not for their similarities but for the different ways Choctaw and Chickasaw women adapted to life after European colonization.

Because so few historical sources reveal the world of Native wives, mothers, and daughters, comparison is difficult. Students of Native American history, however, compensate for gaps in the historical record by using theories to help explain the existing evidence. By weaving together insights from anthropology, sociology, linguistics, and history, ethnohistorians can construct theoretical interpretations of Native peoples' perspectives on events and their own reactions. Such a methodology can yield suggestive interpretations irrecoverable by more traditional historical and analytical methods.

Of particular theoretical importance is the way in which men and women in Native societies partitioned power and enacted the relationships among power, gender, and production. Because of their general association with warfare and diplomacy, men managed relations with outsiders, often controlled the scope and pace of trade, and occupied most political offices. Vested with official decision-making power in their communities, men held what scholars have defined as "authority." Women, according to the theory, often lacked access to such formal expressions of power as well as encounters with outsiders, but through their prominence in clans and households they were able to enjoy the "influence" that came with the control of land, household property, and children.[3]

Existing evidence for the early postcontact South suggests that Native women's exercise of power was more complex than discrete notions of either authority or influence allow. Reports of Spanish explorers, for example, make clear that women could govern Native societies. The Lady of Cofitachequi attempted to enlist Hernando de Soto as a military ally in 1540 when he marched through present-day Piedmont South Carolina. Some years later, Juan Pardo met the female chief of Guatari in present-day North Carolina. Female leadership may have been uncommon, but women could exercise authority as well as influence.[4]

The ancestors of the Choctaws and the Chickasaws may also have met de Soto, but the first sustained contact between Natives and Europeans began in the late 1690s, when the French and the English began staking claims to the Lower Mississippi Valley. Choctaw and Chickasaw women shared similar cultures and initially responded to contact in similar ways, but by the early nineteenth century their roles in the two nations appear to have diverged considerably. The Choctaw people, who numbered around twenty-one thousand at the time of contact, inhabited many villages clustered into three or four districts along the watersheds of the Pearl, Bogue Chito, and Chickasawhay rivers in present-day Neshoba, Kemper, Newton, Lauderdale, Jasper, Clarke, and Wayne counties. The Choctaw people had never been centrally organized, and it may be inaccurate even to speak of a "Choctaw nation" before the late eighteenth century. In spite of the chiefs' best efforts to build alliances and organize towns, factionalism rather than unity of purpose characterized their society throughout the eighteenth century.[5] Given the fractured nature of chiefly power, male leaders found it difficult to control their people's economic activity. Women could trade with settlers and achieved a degree of economic independence outside the scope of male authority. The decentralized political authority enabled Choctaw women to assert themselves far more freely and publicly than Chickasaw women apparently did.

The five thousand or so Chickasaws lived under a much more centralized political system. After enduring many Choctaw raids, they began in the 1720s to abandon their towns near the Choctaws and to concentrate their settlements in present-day Lee County.[6] As time passed, Chickasaw chiefs, unlike their Choctaw counterparts, became more powerful, so that by the early 1800s there was little room for women either to trade or to exert power publicly. By the time of removal in the 1830s, it appears that Choctaw women claimed economic and political authority for themselves while Chickasaw women relied on more-customary channels of influence to accomplish their goals.

Trade with the English and the French set in motion the chain of events that shaped the different histories experienced by Choctaw and Chickasaw women. In the 1690s, English factors from Charles Town began trading guns, cloth, tools, and other items to the Chickasaws for deerskins and war captives, which the English sold as slaves in the Caribbean. As the only nation in the Lower Mississippi Valley armed with guns, the Chickasaws terrorized what one official called their "Bow and Arrow Neighbours," and the Choctaws bore the brunt of their raiding activities.[7] Ten to twelve Chickasaw women typically accompanied their husbands and brothers on raids, where they sang songs of praise or ridicule depending on the engagement's outcome. On the opposing side of the battlefield, Choctaw women urged their warriors to defend their towns and "die like real men."[8] Upon the war parties' return, the women decided whether the captives would be executed, adopted into the community, or passed along to traders.[9]

Just as women participated in war, they also contributed to making peace. In 1731, for example, Chickasaw chief Imayatabé sought permission to settle in the town of Couëchitto in present-day Kemper County. It was home to a group of Choctaws that had sought trade ties with the English and shared kinship bonds with the Chickasaws. As a gesture of goodwill, Imayatabé presented the town chief, a French official wrote, with "a present of several Chickasaw women, figuring that by this present he would obtain more easily his good will and permission to settle at Couëchitto." Imayatabé received the chief's blessing to move into the town, and perhaps the women helped to tie together by marriage and kinship the Choctaw hosts and the Chickasaw arrivals, but there is no evidence of the move.[10]

Despite Imayatabé's efforts, enmity between the two nations persisted because the French opposed Choctaw involvement with English traders residing in the Chickasaw villages. In 1746, however, the chief delegated a Choctaw woman to broker a peace. Telling the Choctaws that the English offered a better trade than the French, the woman persuaded her audience to conclude an agreement with the Chickasaws that ended the fighting.[11] Having lost scores of kinfolk to the raiding, women were important diplomatic agents because only the ties of marriage and the power of kinship could stop the bloodshed.

Because Chickasaws and Choctaws traced kinship and status through the female rather than the male line, no man could hope to establish a firm claim to power without the support of clan matriarchs. At the end of the American Revolution, for example, when the United States government started meddling in the Lower Mississippi Valley, chiefs made clear the important influence of women on their chiefly careers. In 1796, Piomingo of Choukafalaya, a town situated in present-day South Tupelo, was the head warrior of the Chickasaws and a friend of the Americans. He and the leading civil chief, or "king," Minga-tushka, were to meet with federal treaty commissioners. Before they departed, the daughter of Piomingo's predecessor placed a medal around his neck, giving him the right to speak for his people. The daughter of the "great man" also bestowed her father's medal on Piomingo and reminded him that the medal and the power it represented belonged to her family.[12]

Choctaw and Chickasaw women's power was tied to land and horticulture, the basic patterns of which had been set several centuries before contact. By 1000 BCE women in some parts of the South had domesticated a variety of wild plants. The socioeconomic division between male hunting and fighting and female collecting and cultivation evolved into a complex belief system across the region. Men enjoyed a special relationship with the animal world, while women shared the same relationship with the plant world. The innovations women made in prehistoric horticulture peaked with the adoption of maize between 700 and 900 CE. The new crop played an important role in the rise of powerful chiefdoms encountered by de Soto and other early explorers.[13]

After contact, Native women tapped into what historian Daniel H. Usner Jr. has termed a frontier exchange economy, an exchange of foodstuffs, handicrafts, and services that was as important to the life of the Lower Mississippi Valley as was the trade in staples such as indigo, tobacco, and deerskins.[14] Choctaw women participated early and eagerly in the burgeoning economy. "We began our Traffic for Provisions," one soldier reported, "with the Women, who for Paint and Beads gave us Fowls, Eggs, Indian Corn & Caravanses."[15] Another visitor noted that the women engaged in a lively trade in pigs and chickens and that they "carried the spirit of husbandry so far as to cultivate leeks, garlic, cabbage and some other garden plants, of which they [made] no use, in order to make profit of them to the traders."[16]

Early nineteenth-century travelers also remarked on Choctaw women seeking to profit from trade. Benjamin Henry Latrobe deplored the dearth of free food and accommodation in Native towns: "Hospitality exists everywhere food cannot be bought or sold," he wrote of his trip through the Choctaw Nation along the Natchez Trace, but "a good market in the neighbourhood always puts an end to it."[17] "Almost every Indian we passed had something to sell," remembered the Reverend Jacob Young of his trip down the Trace through the Chickasaw towns, "especially corn at two dollars per bushel, corn blades at a bit, pumpkins for a quarter."[18]

As Choctaw and Chickasaw women entered the market revolution—the economic boom that altered the social, economic, and political structures of antebellum America—their traditional gender roles and responsibilities came into conflict with the world around them. Nowhere is the conflict clearer than in their relationship to livestock; men, not women, had always shared a deeply spiritual relationship with animals. The profusion of European animals on Native farms struck visitors to the Indian nations. Chickasaws raised "plenty of hogs and cattle." Beef and pork, wrote their agent, were two of their most important "articles for exportation."[19] Choctaw parents gave daughters, sons, nieces, and nephews a cow and calf, a sow and piglet, and a mare and colt so the children would have a sizable herd when they were grown and married.[20] "These people," one Choctaw agent remarked, "have stocks of horses, cattle, hogs, etc. some of them have *large* stocks, and appear to live plentifully."[21]

Most women raised chickens, pigs, cattle, and horses, but how they reconciled animal husbandry with their relationship to horticulture is unclear. Clues suggest that their languages may have enabled them to care for animals while maintaining their long association with the plant world. The Choctaw and Chickasaw languages belong to the Muskogee linguistic family, and they contain grammatical structures and vocabulary that distinguish in subtle ways the languages that men and women spoke. For example, most southern Indians called cattle *waka*, from the Spanish *vaca*, but the Choctaws had another word for cattle that suggested an altogether feminine relationship. *Alhpoa* meant "fruit trees such as are cultivated," and by constructing cattle as fruit trees Choctaw women and men could link the care, use, and sale of animals to that of the plum, peach, and persimmon trees featured in their town landscapes.[22] Whether Chickasaw women used similar words is unknown.

Cotton cultivation was by far the most important economic innovation women made because it tied them directly into the region's predominant pattern of staple crop production, and it afforded opportunities for manufacturing cloth for sale. In December 1801, a prominent chief requested that the federal government send weavers to the Choctaw towns to teach women how to spin thread and weave cloth. One year later, twelve families had begun to produce homespun cloth, and thanks to federal agents and the chiefs' regular requests for weeding hoes, cotton cards, and other necessary tools, the cotton economy took off.[23] In 1820, one federal investigator reported that Choctaw women had woven ten thousand yards of cloth.[24] According to federal subagent Stephen Ward, they produced such surpluses that they could sell to Natchez Trace travelers.[25] The racial and gender dynamics of southern society, however, impinged on their free market participation. One observer described how "unprincipled white men" "cheated" women out of the proceeds of their labors. Their alleged inferiority as Indian women undoubtedly encouraged such behavior.[26]

Chickasaw women avidly spun and wove, and in 1800 a chief asked the federal agent to hire a weaver to teach more women how to make clothing. The next year a chief demanded woodworking tools so that his people could build dugout canoes to carry their cotton crop to market. Chiefs also complained regularly to the federal government, probably at the behest of women, that the supply of cotton cards and spinning wheels was insufficient to keep up with production. By 1830, most Chickasaw women knew how to make cloth, and families proudly wore their finest homemade clothes to council meetings.[27] As sellers, however, there were limits to their entrepreneurial drive. As soon as they earned enough from weaving for their families' needs, according to the federal agent, "they converted their wheels into *play things for their children* and their looms into hen roosts."[28]

Why Chickasaw women shut down their weaving operations occasionally is an important question because it deals with an apparently fundamental difference between Choctaw and Chickasaw women. There is no evidence that Choctaw women ceased production once immediate needs had been met, so each nation's women appear to have followed different approaches to the market revolution, with Choctaw women entering it more fully. The differing degrees to which Choctaw and Chickasaw male chiefs controlled their people's economic activities may explain the difference.

Choctaw and Chickasaw chiefs had always tried to control the production and flow of goods to preserve their power and perhaps also to control women's contact with outsiders. When the French first arrived in the Lower Mississippi Valley, Choctaw chiefs sought to turn the French trade to their own advantage and to restore the balance of power that they had lost to the English-backed Chickasaws. Chiefs required French traders to visit them before peddling their wares. After smoking tobacco together, the chief would ask his guest, "You are come then?" Upon receiving an affirmative answer, the chief would tell the townspeople that a trader had arrived, what he had brought to trade, and what the exchange rates would be. In 1721, for example, Choctaws could purchase a foot-length of limbourg cloth for four dressed deerskins, while a musket cost twenty skins. To ensure the trader's complicity in their roles as brokers, chiefs often gave traders a portion of the gifts they had received from colonial officials, which the traders sold for their own profit.[29] While the Choctaw chiefs used trade to bolster their own authority and prestige, the French sought to use it to manipulate them. By consolidating the distribution of trade goods in the hands of a few leaders whom the French called "medal chiefs," colonial officials believed they could create a hierarchy of chiefs dependent on their largesse and amenable to following their orders.[30] The strategy failed, however, because some Choctaws preferred to trade with the English who frequented the Chickasaw towns. The resulting struggles over access to foreign trade goods destabilized Choctaw politics throughout the century and sparked both factionalism and civil war.[31] In the end, Choctaw leaders, while they continually aspired to the chiefly ideal of economic control, rarely achieved it.

Throughout most of the eighteenth century, Chickasaw chiefs traded almost exclusively with English factors, so their nation never experienced the deep-seated divisions and violent strife that characterized the Choctaws' struggles over trade with competing French and English agents. One English trader, James Colbert, who had lived in the nation since the 1730s, married into powerful families and put the English trade in the hands of a few leaders. In the early nineteenth century, the Chickasaw sons his wives bore, who would have belonged to their mothers' clans, built on the commercial and political ties he had created and continued to centralize economic and political power in the face of a rival faction equally committed to controlling trade. His son George Colbert expanded his family's power by marrying the daughter of a powerful chief, Wolf Friend. George, two of his brothers, and his father-in-law worked to prevent the United States from building a trading post at Chickasaw Bluffs (present-day Memphis) because he and his allies were, one observer remarked, "all Traders and [did] not wish a Store placed at that post to trade with individuals."[32] Unwilling to allow individuals to trade because it would undercut his authority, George Colbert went so far as to organize trading expeditions to Florence, Alabama, to oversee his people's market activities. "He did not permit them to come to town without him," one settler explained, "as he felt responsible for them."[33] However successful his strategy may have been, Colbert and his allies tightened their grip on Chickasaw trade in ways that the Choctaws could not. They skillfully used treaties they negotiated with the federal government to buttress their power. In one agreement signed in 1816, for example, the chiefs secured a provision prohibiting the federal agent from issuing trading permits to outsiders.[34] The treaty stipulation and the culture of strong chiefly leadership positioned the Colbert clan so well that in 1826 American officials remarked that the chiefs had created a "monopoly of the few."[35]

The incidence of slavery in each nation further suggests that wealth was more centralized among the Chickasaws than the Choctaws, but it also points to the success of each nation's women in pursuing their own economic initiatives. Although the Chickasaw population never exceeded five thousand, a federal census in 1839 counted more than one thousand slaves among them. Seventeen Chickasaw women owned slaves: Widow Emubby had three slaves, Patsey Camp had four, Sally Underwood had two, but Elizabeth Perry owned by far the most. Thirty-five chattels worked in her household and probably labored in her maize and cotton fields. The Choctaw population, almost four times larger than that of the Chickasaws, owned just over five hundred slaves. Of nine women slaveholders, only Delila Brashears, with sixteen, owned more than ten.[36] The more affluent Chickasaw chiefs who controlled trade more tightly appear to have afforded larger numbers of slaves. The Choctaws' relative lack of concentrated power and wealth militated against the formation of a large slave-owning class, despite clearly exceptional women like Delila Brashears.[37]

The adoption of slavery by Mississippi's first people represented a growing convergence between their societies and that of the surrounding settlers. Nevertheless, since entering the Union in 1817 the state government had complained that the Choctaws and the Chickasaws retarded economic growth and challenged Mississippi's control over land within its chartered boundaries. The two nations, however, had established through federal treaties the rights to occupy their land and to live under their own governments. To state politicians' chagrin, the administrations of presidents James Monroe and John Quincy Adams failed to secure the removal of the Choctaws and the Chickasaws from Mississippi, but with solid southern support Andrew Jackson swept into the presidency in 1828 and broke the "Indian question" impasse. Taking its lead from the president, who had publicly supported removal, the Mississippi legislature extended state jurisdiction over the two nations, abrogated their federal treaty rights, abolished their governments, and, except for marriage ceremonies, outlawed their cultures. In the eyes of the state government, Choctaws and Chickasaws ceased to exist as distinct persons and instead came to occupy a social position similar to that of free blacks.[38] Meanwhile, male chiefs in both nations tried to resist mounting federal and state pressure for removal. Choctaw chiefs sought to create a constitutional government to centralize political authority and enable them to defend more effectively their land and rights. They tried to model parts of Choctaw culture after Anglo-American culture, but their measures threatened women's authority and influence. The new laws replaced the matrilineal clans that had overseen traditional justice and retribution with a national court system presided over by male chiefs. According to new property laws, women had to forego claims to household property so that proceeds from estate sales could be applied to the extinguishment of their deceased husbands' debts. The new government also interfered with women's ability to choose marriage partners. One law required Choctaw women to obtain permission from their chief before marrying American men, as Greenwood LeFlore put it, "cordin to white Laws."[39] Because Chickasaw power was already centralized, they had no need to revise their government, so Chickasaw women experienced no curtailment of rights. In contrast to the Choctaws, Chickasaw chiefs continued to respect the longstanding rule of separate female property ownership.[40]

The Choctaws signed the first removal treaty negotiated under cover of the 1830 federal Indian Removal Act at a council held between two forks of Dancing Rabbit Creek in present-day Noxubee County. The negotiations reflected the extent to which the constitutionalists had been unable to overturn women's authority. On the morning of September 22, 1830, federal treaty commissioners John Eaton and John Coffee sat on a log before seven women and a broad semicircle of chiefs, all shaded by oak, pine, and mulberry trees. The first man to speak, Allen Wright, urged that "the Choctaws ought to sell everything they owned, land, cattle, horses, and hogs, and all in a body emigrate west." Land, however, lay outside his and the other men's authority, and in spite of the measures passed by the constitutional government, the chiefs were unable to silence the women, who asserted their rights. "Killihota," snapped one of the women, calling him by the name his mother had given him, "I could cut you open with this knife. You have two hearts." Though he survived the encounter, each subsequent speaker rebuked Killihota's advice and seconded the women's refusal to cede any land. The women had exercised authority and temporarily defended their land. The council broke up because the chiefs present felt confident that their refusal to treat had scotched the commissioners' plans. A few chiefs, however, lingered at the council ground, and after being threatened with destruction by Secretary of War Eaton, they relented and signed a treaty. Civil strife wracked the Choctaw Nation for the next several months.[41]

Chickasaw women played no visible role in either the 1832 Treaty of Pontotoc Creek negotiations or in the 1834 Treaty of Washington talks that amended the Pontotoc Creek document, but they influenced the chiefs' interpretation of them. The women worried about a provision providing reserves of land in Mississippi for heads of households, which could either be sold for profit or lived on by families that chose not to remove. The treaty made no mention of the gender of heads of households, but the federal government had presumed, consistent with Anglo-American culture, that only men would qualify. A group of Chickasaw women, however, persuaded their chiefs to make clear their own claims to reserves. After explaining in elaborate detail to President Jackson the Chickasaw customs of matrilineality and separate property ownership, the chiefs concluded, "It is an ancient and universal law . . . that the wife had a separate estate in all her property whether derived from her relations or acquired by her. . . . The home of each [wife] is regarded as her own, and is generally so known and distinguished by the community."[42] After the women had their wishes put to the president, it is unclear whether they got what they wanted, but they had drawn on their longstanding control of household property to seek redress.

In the end, neither Choctaw nor Chickasaw women could resist removal, but they played important roles in the history of their nations and ours. For example, without the ancestors of those Choctaw and Chickasaw women who first raised maize, corn might not be one of Mississippi's most important agricultural crops. Women's property and divorce law in Mississippi also traces its origins in part to a Chickasaw woman named Betsy Love. In 1837, she filed suit to prevent seizure of her slave to settle her American husband's debts. Before the state supreme court, Love argued in *Fisher v. Allen* that the Chickasaw custom of separate ownership of property entitled her to the slave, and the presiding justices found in her favor. Two years later, the state assembly codified the *Allen* decision by legislating that women's property owned before marriage could not be used to cover a husband's debts after marriage. Owing to Betsy Love's tenacity and intelligence, Mississippi's property laws and gender jurisprudence still bear the influence of countless generations of Chickasaw women.[43]

The histories of Choctaw and Chickasaw women diverge in their involvement in framing the possibilities and limits of each nation's response to colonization. In the absence of centralized political control, Choctaw women appear to have been able to carve out niches in the frontier exchange economy of the eighteenth century and in the market revolution of the nineteenth. Their economic success probably bolstered their claims to power, and they were able to voice their opposition to removal before a gathering of male Choctaw leaders and officials of the United States in spite of the constitutionalists' attempts to curtail their power. In contrast, eighteenth- and early nineteenth-century Chickasaw economic power became increasingly centralized in the hands of a few powerful male chiefs whose wives and female kin ran wealthier, slave-owning households. Chickasaw women had limited ability to buy and to sell for themselves. Lacking the independent economic wherewithal to exert political authority, they seem to have relied more on their personal influence to defend their places in society. Although the federal government ultimately succeeded in removing most of the Choctaws and all of the Chickasaws from Mississippi, the paths taken by each nation's women appear to have been different and to have reflected the particular confluences of culture, history, and happenstance.

Ellikee stood at such a confluence. It did not take long for the posse to batter her to death in front of her horrified children, and her daughter cradled her bloodied corpse and cried in grief to show her mother's spirit that she would be missed. The following day, Ellikee's family and friends watched as a missionary offered a prayer and lowered her body into the ground. Onlookers tossed in cloth and coins to speed her on her way before she was covered by the earth that had been the source of her womanly powers.

Ellikee is one of the few Mississippi women whose life bridged the Choctaw and Chickasaw nations, and while her story gives focus to an otherwise clouded history, we must beware. Ellikee was not even a proper name; it was the Choctaw word for witch or doctor. When the missionaries recorded her story, they did not realize that their Choctaw informants were speaking not necessarily of one woman but of a whole category representing those women who encapsulated their darkest fears and greatest hopes for shaping their own lives. The story of Ellikee sheds light on two terrible deaths but also cautions us that types and categories can sometimes be unsatisfactory tools for recovering the hidden pasts of Mississippi's first women.

NOTES

1. Elliot Journal, "Papers of the American Board of Commissioners for Foreign Missions," April 14, 1819, microfilm reel 755, Indian Archives, Oklahoma Historical Society, Oklahoma City; *Panoplist and Missionary Herald* 15 (October 1819): 460. All subsequent details for the story of Ellikee come from these two sources.

2. Horatio B. Cushman, *A History of the Choctaw, Chickasaw and Natchez Indians* (Greenville, Tex.: Headlight Printing House, 1899), 138.

3. Daniel Maltz and JoAllyn Archambault, "Gender and Power in Native North America," in *Women and Power in Native North America*, ed. Laura F. Klein and Lillian A. Ackerman (Norman: University of Oklahoma Press, 1995), 234.

4. Charles Hudson, *Knights of Spain, Warriors of the Sun* (Athens: University of Georgia Press, 1997), 174–84; Hudson, *The Juan Pardo Expeditions* (Washington, D.C.: Smithsonian Institution Press, 1990), 66–67.

5. Peter H. Wood, "The Changing Population of the Colonial South: An Overview by Race and Region, 1685–1790," in *Powhatan's Mantle*, ed. Peter H. Wood, Gregory A. Waselkov, and M. Thomas Hatley (Lincoln: University of Nebraska Press, 1989), 66–72; Patricia K. Galloway, "Choctaw Factionalism and Civil War, 1746–1750," *Journal of Mississippi History* 44 (November 1982): 289–327; Galloway, "'So Many Little Republics': British Relations with the Choctaw Confederacy, 1765," *Ethnohistory* 41 (Fall 1994): 513–38.

6. Wood, "Changing Population," 66–77; James R. Atkinson, *Splendid Land, Splendid People: The Chickasaw Indians to Removal* (Tuscaloosa: University of Alabama Press, 2004), 11; Thomas Nairne,

Nairne's Muskhogean Journals, ed. with an introduction by Alexander Moore (Jackson: University Press of Mississippi, 1988), 36–38.

7. Nairne, *Nairne's Muskhogean Journals*, 37–38.

8. Bernard Romans, *A Concise Natural History of East and West Florida* (Gainesville: University of Florida Press, 1962), 76.

9. "Discussion of Choctaw History by Nathaniel Folsom," Peter Perkins Pitchlynn Papers, Thomas Gilcrease Institute of American History and Art, Tulsa, Oklahoma.

10. Régis du Roullet to Perier, February 21, 1731, in *Mississippi Provincial Archives: French Dominion, 1729–1748*, ed. and trans. by Dunbar Rowland and A. G. Sanders, vol. 4, ed. Patricia Kay Galloway (Baton Rouge: Louisiana State University Press, 1984), 61–62; Atkinson, *Splendid Land, Splendid People*, 37.

11. Louboey to Maurepas, February 8, 1746, in *Mississippi Provincial Archives*, 4:260.

12. Hopewell Treaty Talks, January 9, 1786, *American State Papers: Class II; Indian Affairs*, ed. Walter Lowrie and Matthew St. Clair Clarke, 2 vols. (Washington, D.C.: Gales & Seaton, 1832), 1:51; Atkinson, *Splendid Land, Splendid People*, 12, 24–26, 132.

13. R. Douglas Hurt, *Indian Agriculture in America* (Lawrence: University of Kansas Press, 1987), 6–11; John H. Blitz, *Ancient Chiefdoms of the Tombigbee* (Tuscaloosa: University of Alabama Press, 1993), 33–39; John A. Walthall, *Prehistoric Indians of the Southeast* (Tuscaloosa: University of Alabama Press, 1980), chaps. 3, 4; Patty Jo Watson and Mary C. Kennedy, "The Development of Horticulture in the Eastern Woodlands of North America: Women's Role," in *Engendering Archaeology*, ed. Joan M. Gero and Margaret W. Conkey (Oxford: Basil Blackwell, 1991), 255–75.

14. Daniel H. Usner Jr., *Indians, Settlers, and Slaves in a Frontier Exchange Economy* (Chapel Hill: University of North Carolina Press, 1992).

15. Caravanses are legumes. Edward Mease narrative, 1770–1771, "Peter Chester, Third Governor of the Province of West Florida under British Dominion, 1770–1781," ed. Eron Opha Rowland, *Publications of the Mississippi Historical Society*, Centenary Series 5 (1925): 84.

16. Romans, *Concise Natural History*, 84.

17. Benjamin Henry Latrobe, *The Journal of Latrobe* (New York: Burt Franklin, 1971), 249.

18. Jacob Young, *Autobiography of a Pioneer* (Cincinnati: L. Swormstedt & A. Poe, 1857), 213–14.

19. Jesse D. Jennings, ed., "Nutt's Trip to the Chickasaw Country," *Journal of Mississippi History* 9 (January 1947): 41; John Allen, "Report of the Chickasaws," February 7, 1830, reel 136, M234, Chickasaw Agency, Letters Received, 1824–1881, Correspondence of the Office of Indian Affairs and Related Records, RG 75, National Archives Records Administration, Washington, D.C. (henceforth cited as NARA).

20. *Missionary Herald* 17 (April 1821): 110.

21. *Niles' Weekly Register* 38 (July 5, 1830): 345.

22. Mary Haas, "Men's and Women's Speech in Koasati," in *Language in Culture and Society*, ed. Dell Hymes (New York: Harper & Row, 1964), 228–33; Amelia Rector Bell, "Separate People: Speaking of Creek Men and Women," *American Anthropologist* 92 (June 1992): 332–45; Cyrus Byington, *A Dictionary of the Choctaw Language*, ed. John R. Swanton and Henry S. Halbert, Bureau of American Ethnology Bulletin 46 (Washington, D.C.: U.S. Government Printing Office, 1915), 77; James Taylor Carson, "Native Americans, the Market Revolution, and Culture Change: The Choctaw Cattle Economy, 1690–1830," *Agricultural History* 71 (Winter 1997): 13–17.

23. Minutes of the Fort Adams Treaty, December 12, 1801, reel 1, T494, Documents Relating to the Negotiation of Ratified and Unratified Treaties with Various Indian Tribes, 1801–1869, Records

Relating to Indian Treaties; James Wilkinson, Andrew Pickens, and Benjamin Hawkins to Henry Dearborn, December 18, 1802, reel 1, M271, Letters Received by the Secretary of War Relating to Indian Affairs, 1800–1823, Office of the Secretary of War; "Memorandum of Goods for Mushulatubbee's Dist. 1826," reel 169, M234; "Abstract of Articles Delivered to Chactaw Indians as a Part of Their Annuity for the Year 1828," all in RG 75, NARA.

24. Jedidiah Morse, *A Report to the Secretary of War of the United States, on Indian Affairs* (New Haven, Conn.: Howe & Spalding, 1822), 182.

25. *Niles' Weekly Register* 38 (July 3, 1830): 345.

26. L. R. Bakewell to James Barbour, September 2, 1825, reel 169, M234, NARA.

27. Samuel Mitchell to David Haley, January 23, 1800, David Henley Papers, Special Collections, William R. Perkins Library, Duke University, Durham, N.C.; James Wilkinson, Benjamin Hawkins, and Andrew Pickens to Henry Dearborn, October 25, 1801, *American State Papers*, 1:651; Benjamin Hawkins to Henry Dearborn, October 28, 1801, in *Letters, Journals and Writings of Benjamin Hawkins*, ed. C. L. Grant, 2 vols. (Savannah: Beehive Press, 1980), 1:387; Chinabu King to Secretary of War, February 10, 1817, reel 2, M271, RG 75, NARA; John Allen, "Report of the Chickasaws," February 7, 1830, reel 136, M234, RG 75, NARA.

28. Benjamin Smith to Thomas L. McKenney, October 6, 1825, reel 135, M234, RG 75, NARA, emphasis in original.

29. John R. Swanton, *An Early Account of the Choctaw Indians*, Memoirs of the American Anthropological Association 5, no. 2 (Lancaster, Penn.: American Anthropological Association, 1918), 56–57, 60; Memoir from the Council of Louisiana to the Council of the Company of the Indies, April 23, 1725, in *Mississippi Provincial Archives: French Dominion*, ed. and trans. Dunbar Rowland and A. G. Sanders, vol. 2 (Jackson: Press of the Mississippi Department of Archives and History, 1929), 461.

30. Galloway, "'So Many Little Republics,'"517–18; Vaudreuil to Maurepas, February 12, 1744, in *Letterbooks of Marquis de Pierre Rigaud de Vaudreuil*, LO 9, vol. 1, microfilm reel 1 (San Marino, Calif.: Huntington Library, 1994).

31. Galloway, "Choctaw Factionalism," 289–327.

32. Atkinson, *Splendid Land*, 24, 93 and James Robertson to David Henley, 22 March 1797, David Henley Papers.

33. Quoted in F. R. King, "George Colbert: Chief of the Chickasaw Nation," *Arrow Points* 7 (October 1923): 56.

34. Article 7, Treaty of Chickasaw Council House, September 20, 1816, *American State Papers*, 2:93.

35. Thomas Hinds and John Coffee to James Barbour, November 2, 1826, reel 135, M234, RG 75, NARA.

36. *Choctaw and Chickasaw Early Census Records*, comp. Betty Wiltshire (Carrollton, Miss.: Pioneer, n.d.).

37. Gregory Dowd, "North American Indian Slaveholding and the Colonization of Gender: The Southeast before Removal," *Critical Matrix* 3 (Fall 1987): 1–30.

38. James Taylor Carson, "State Rights and Indian Removal in Mississippi: 1817–1835," *Journal of Mississippi History* 57 (February 1995): 32–37.

39. Allene Smith, *Greenwood LeFlore and the Choctaw Indians of the Mississippi Valley* (Memphis: C. A. Davis Printing, 1951), 50–53; *Missionary Herald* 19 (January 1823): 10, and 25 (May 1829): 153; Greenwood LeFlore to Thomas L. McKenney, May 3, 1828, reel 169, M234, RG 75, NARA.

40. John Allen to Thomas L. McKenney, October 16, 1829, reel 135, M234, RG 75, NARA.

41. Henry S. Halbert, "The Story of the Treaty of Dancing Rabbit Creek," *Publications of the Mississippi Historical Society* 6 (1902): 374–77.

42. Ishtahotopa, Martin Colbert, Pistalutubbee, et al. to Andrew Jackson, 1835, reel 136, M234, M234, RG 75, NARA.

43. LeAnne Howe, "Talking Dirty to History: An Allegory on Betsy Love," paper excerpted in LeAnne Howe, *Evidence of Red* (Cambridge: Salt, forthcoming).

Stepping Lively in Place

The Free Black Women of Antebellum Natchez

JOYCE L. BROUSSARD

The multifaceted river town of Natchez, Mississippi, bustled with commerce in the generation prior to the Civil War, and its rough, infamous waterfront area, Natchez-under-the-Hill, was filled with brothels and taverns. Elite planters lived grandly in mansion estates in the surrounding countryside and in the garden area above the landing. Natchez also contained Forks-of-the-Road, one of the region's largest slave markets. The town's 4,100 whites resided alongside 2,100 enslaved people, and the immediate hinterland (Adams County, Mississippi, and Concordia Parish, Louisiana) featured dozens of large plantations on which thousands of blacks were held at hard labor in life bondage. Among the town's whites and enslaved blacks dwelled 214 free African Americans, about 59 percent of them female. Sixty-seven of the women were aged sixteen or older in 1860. This essay closely examines the lives of four of the women—Agnes Gordon Earhart, Fanny Leiper, Nancy Kyle, and Eliza Cotton—as they illustrate the experiences of the entire group.[1]

Who were these women? How did they cope, and what did they do? Obviously, gender, race, and class set their experiences apart from those of free black men, enslaved persons, and white men and women. They were black in a place and time when most people identified blackness with slavery and whiteness with freedom. They were women in a world dominated by males and by slaveholder authority. As free black women, moreover, they carried a color burden. No white woman in antebellum Natchez could be expelled from the state, whipped in punishment for crimes, or enslaved because she could not provide manumission documents. Neither did white women carry the social stigma of blackness, which often presumed sexual promiscuity of any black woman, whether enslaved or free.[2]

The free black women of Natchez in 1860 worked as seamstresses, dress-makers, and washerwomen in about equal numbers, and a few were cooks and nurses. They headed sixteen of the thirty-eight free black households of Adams County. Few lived with whites. Five of the households included neither chil-dren nor adult males, and in several a pair of sisters lived together. At least one household was probably a brothel. The census listed most of the women as mulattoes, and some were so light skinned that they could have passed for white. The wealthiest free black woman, Ann Johnson, was the widow of the prosperous free black barber William Johnson, who had been murdered in 1851. Among other properties, she owned several buildings, two barber shops, and seven slaves.[3]

During the decade before the Civil War, several dozen free black women in Natchez lived as the wives (common law or legally married) of free black men, at least eight of whom were relatively prosperous. Sixteen other women headed households with other women and/or children. The rest were young women living at home or as boarders in black households. Some of these wives, spinsters, widows, and mothers had lived in town for many years. Most of them were poor but not desperately so, and more than a few had acquired property by 1860.[4] They interacted frequently with one another, and they con-ducted their hard-working lives in households scattered widely throughout the municipality.[5]

The life experiences of Natchez's "free women of color" were shaped and defined substantially by sexual and familial relationships with local white men. Most of the women had white fathers, were or had been sexually involved with white men, or lived with free black men who were themselves the offspring of white fathers. The women were well known in the community because of their property holdings, length of residence, lighter skin color, and their familial or sexual relations with equally well-known white men. Moreover, because the "one-drop rule" seldom prevailed in the lower South before the Civil War, these free mulatto women escaped being relegated by the white community to the inferior status of their enslaved sisters. Biracial sexual and familial intimacy set free black women apart from white and enslaved women, and their special cir-cumstances affected their conduct as African American women.[6]

In 1859, Agnes Gordon Earhart petitioned the Mississippi state legislature for permission to remain in Natchez, where she had lived for over thirty-five years. She had nowhere else to go, but with civil war looming, legislators felt pressed to force free blacks to leave the state. Earhart posted a hefty five-thousand-dollar bond "for the good behavior of herself & family." At around fifty-six years old, she was the long-time consort of prosperous Natchez merchant

David Earhart, who had likely fathered at least eight of her eleven children. He was also legally married to—and still living with—Louisa Therese Chambers Earhart, the mother of his four white children. The legislature probably never acted on Earhart's petition because of the outbreak of the Civil War.[7]

Agnes's petition was one of many that year, including some by free blacks pleading to be re-enslaved rather than exiled.[8] It was not the first time whites had wanted free blacks excluded or expelled from Mississippi. In 1822, all free blacks had to be registered by each county's Orphans Court, and state law kept out-of-state free blacks from migrating into the state. By 1831 and again in 1842, the legislature enacted laws requiring free blacks to leave unless they could provide written, white-sponsored evidence for being allowed to stay; the Mississippi Code of 1857 reaffirmed such requirements. Complying with the law meant submitting petitions to the Board of Police signed by prominent whites attesting to the good conduct and moral character of the free black person.[9]

The birthplace and manumission date for Agnes Earhart—if indeed she had been manumitted—are unknown. Evidently she remained in Natchez for the rest of her life and died on January 27, 1909, at age 106.[10] David Earhart, who died on January 5, 1860, was buried in the Earhart family plot near his mother, Cassandra, a "free woman of color."[11] His will lists four children by his wife as well as "several natural (illegitimate) children," whom he instructs his wife and brother to "support" and protect "as they may need until they [should] be able to take care of themselves."[12] The 1850 census shows David living with his twenty-nine-year-old wife, Louisa, their infant daughter, and eight other children—all listed as free mulattoes with the surname Earhart—ranging in age from one to fifteen.[13] Land records list David Earhart's sale of a small house and lot to Agnes Gordon, a "free woman of color," in November 1841.[14]

David Earhart had almost certainly passed for white his entire life. He lived openly with a white wife as well as with a free black woman, although not always in the same house. There is no indication of his mixed racial heritage in public or private records. All four of David and Louisa Earhart's children appear in public records as white; only those children born to Agnes are designated mulattoes in the census. David Earhart's wife almost certainly knew about Agnes and her brood before she married David, and she surely knew later about their continuing relationship, but she never publicly protested.

A long history of misinformation about David Earhart's mother, Cassandra, runs through Natchez lore. Popular journalist Edith Wyatt Moore wrote of a runaway slave named Cassandra who fled from Tennessee in 1795 with a young Chickasaw slave.[15] Moore's story, based partly on the reminiscences of old-timers in 1930s Natchez, is romantic, intriguing, and dramatic but not easily documented. Evidently two runaways, Cassandra, a fifteen-year-old light-skinned mulatto girl, and an Indian slave named John Smith (who had allegedly kidnapped Cassandra in Tennessee), the "property of [a] General Colbert of the Chickasaw Nation," were arrested on the Natchez waterfront hiding in a flatboat. Cassandra's owner, James Bosley, sold her to wealthy planter Anthony Hutchins, who sold her in turn to young merchant Jacob Earhart. In 1803, Earhart manumitted Cassandra, noting that as long as she remained unmarried she would "pass by the name of Cassandra Bosley."[16]

Sometime during the next five years, Jacob Earhart's wife, Elizabeth, left him and moved to New Orleans.[17] Natchez records for 1809 show Jacob "along with his wife Cassandra" selling a house and lot in town.[18] There is no mention of their marriage, however. The couple had four children, and Cassandra also had a free black daughter, Julia Ann Hutchins, who was probably born while Anthony Hutchins still owned Cassandra and may, in fact, have been his daughter. Julia apparently was freed when Jacob Earhart manumitted her mother. Jacob and Cassandra had acquired plantation land and at least twenty-eight slaves by 1824. All their children, including David Earhart, married whites, and not one is identified as a mulatto or free person of color in local records. After 1803, Cassandra is never again characterized as free black in Adams County legal records. Jacob Earhart died around 1824, and Cassandra lived the rest of her life north of town in a small house purchased at auction in 1835.[19]

Natchez apparently took the complex black-and-white Earhart family in stride. No evidence suggests that Jacob or his son David were concerned about living openly with black women or with fathering their children. David likely paid or put up the security for the five-thousand-dollar bond for Agnes to remain in Mississippi. Although Elizabeth had probably left Jacob because of Cassandra, David's wife stayed with him and evidently accepted, or at least tolerated, Agnes's children. Neither father nor son seems to have suffered socially because of their open relations with black women, and David seems not to have been stigmatized for his partially black ancestry.

Fanny Leiper, a free black widow, took her surname from the free mulatto husband she was said to have married before 1831. She filed suit in 1847 in the Southern District Chancery Court of Adams County against four defendants: Malvina Huffman (aka Hoffman, Matthews), a frequently arrested, locally notorious woman who may have been partially black; Oliver L. Bemiss, Huffman's alleged paramour; James Walsh, Huffman's agent; and Joseph Winscott, a steamboat engineer in New Orleans who had once lived with Leiper in Natchez. Leiper charged the four with conspiracy and fraudulent possession of the property she had purchased in 1834. She had lived in the house she built there until she left for Ohio in 1845; a local agent, Samuel Hammett, kept the place rented during her absence. Leiper learned that her one-time friend and neighbor Huffman had somehow acquired the title to her house and lot and was renting it out herself and keeping the money. Leiper hired a white attorney, Lewis Sanders Jr., and took Malvina Huffman and her accomplices to court.[20]

The case eventually went to the state supreme court, where the entire story unfolded. The defendants argued that Leiper had never legally owned the house because she had bought it while still a slave, and she had no written evidence of her manumission. Fanny Leiper countered that she was free when she had purchased the house, having been manumitted by her owner, Margaret Overaker, in 1831 or 1832. Manumission papers had been filed in Natchez, according to Gabriel Tichenor, a prominent white banker. The papers were subsequently lost, and Overaker said she sent Leiper to Ohio to secure her freedom in 1834, before the property was purchased. Overaker said that Leiper's white father, wealthy planter J. S. Miller, had given her three hundred dollars to obtain Fanny's freedom. Leiper had returned from Ohio a free woman, and she bought the lot, built her house, and made improvements to the grounds.[21]

Leiper had not assumed sole ownership in clear title when she purchased the lot, however. Her attorney, Colonel Fleming Wood, had advised her to file for title jointly with Joseph Winscott, the white man with whom she had been living, because of "the temper of the times" (the public clamor for removing all free blacks from the state). For some reason, Leiper never informed Winscott that his name was on the deed, but she did confide the full details to her friend and next-door neighbor Malvina Huffman.[22]

Natchez constable Henry Dillon testified for Huffman and the other defendants. He claimed he had notified Leiper in 1843 that she would have to leave the state in twenty days or face arrest as an unlicensed free black person, but he dropped the matter when she told him she was owned by a wealthy planter named Miller, who had corroborated her story. Soon after Dillon's warning, Leiper moved to Cincinnati, worked as a washerwoman, and lived with or married Gustavus Howard, who may have been white.[23]

After Leiper left for Ohio, Huffman and Bemiss told Winscott about the joint deed. The three got the house keys from rental agent Hammett by telling him Leiper would not be returning and that Winscott had sold the property to Huffman. Employing rental agent James Walsh, the three then rented out the house.[24]

Malvina Huffman's criminal record suggests she was capable of fraud. She was arrested eight times from 1841 to 1860 on charges ranging from keeping a bawdy house to assault and battery and selling liquor without a license. In the 1850 census, she is listed as the single head of a household with four young white women. Deeds in Huffman's name show she owned many beds and dressers and all the accoutrements of a bordello.

During Reconstruction, Huffman (alias Matthews by 1860) was arrested for killing a Union soldier who had tried to break into her house on the bluff. Witnesses testified that she ran a brothel in her home and the dead soldier was a disgruntled customer. The Huffman/Matthews house was probably a brothel; Leiper's house next door may have been one, too.[25]

In 1854, the court, which found for Leiper, ruled that she had purchased the property with a white man who then held the property in trust for her. That she may have been a slave at the time was irrelevant because in that case the property would have belonged to Leiper's owner, Margaret Overaker. Leiper's white partner, James Winscott, held the property in trust either for Leiper or for her owner. Winscott could not have sold the property to Huffman without Leiper's, or the widow Overaker's, consent. Leiper could bring suit because having lived for several years in Ohio, she was a free woman. Her owner's intention to free her either in 1831 or 1834 by sending her to Ohio was all that mattered, even though there was no written record of manumission.[26]

Almost every stratum of Natchez society was represented in Fanny Leiper's case, including eleven wealthy, prominent whites who spoke for her, ranging from planters and lawyers to government officials and municipal employees. Their testimony confirmed for the court the story of Fanny's manumission in Natchez and again in Cincinnati. Also, the witnesses helped establish Leiper's paternal kinship ties to the Millers.

No witness was more important than Gabriel Tichenor, a regionally prominent businessman and banker who had close sexual and familial ties to black women. Just before Leiper filed her case, Tichenor had moved to Ohio, where he helped slaves achieve their freedom. In 1822, Tichenor had freed his own mulatto slave Harriet Battles, the future mother-in-law of free black barber William Johnson. Harriet's mulatto daughter Ann Battles, who married Johnson— who was himself the son of a white planter—may have been Tichenor's daughter. Tichenor sent Harriet and her young daughter Ann, who had remained Tichenor's slave under Louisiana law, to Cincinnati in 1826, where Harriet was formally emancipated and Ann was legally freed. After mother and daughter returned to Adams County in 1829, Tichenor sold a lot on State Street in Natchez to Harriet for two dollars. Around 1836, Harriet and her son-in-law, William Johnson, built a house on the property.[27]

Nancy Kyle, an unmarried free black woman, eighty years old or more in 1860, lived in a modest but stylish territorial-era townhouse on the northeast corner of High and Rankin streets, a few city blocks from the Johnson household. Located in a part of Natchez that had been known in the 1830s as "Kyle Town," the house featured four entrance bays, a gabled roof, a central chimney, and a front gallery. In 1850, Nancy shared the home with her middle-aged daughter Caroline and six other free black Kyle family members, including three males (Christopher, aged twenty; John, aged twenty-two; and Rufus, aged two) and three females (Frances, aged fourteen; Alzena, aged eight; and Sun, an infant).[28]

By 1860, the entire household except Nancy, Caroline, and Alzena Miller had left. Seventeen-year-old free black Angeline Morris had joined them, along with Nancy's infant great-grandson William. In the census, Nancy valued the residence at seven hundred dollars and her personal property at one thousand dollars, which probably included a slave Caroline reportedly owned.[29]

Kyle Town was situated north of Franklin Street, a shopping avenue that slave traders traveled to march their human cargo from the river landing to the Forks-of-the-Road slave market east of town. The area, known for small residences and a scattered free black population, was by no means a segregated, strictly working-class enclave. Next door to the Kyles lived an unmarried, thirty-seven-year-old white woman, Emily Balance, her eighteen-year-old daughter, and ginwright William Anderson and his wife and two children. Widow and dressmaker Margaret Link, also thirty-seven and white, lived with her five children, ages five to eighteen, on the other side of Nancy. Stanton Hall, Natchez's most impressive mansion, stood two short blocks north. It had been constructed in the 1850s for Frederic Stanton, one of the wealthiest planters and merchants in the lower South.[30]

Nancy's former owner, Christopher Kyle, a prosperous Natchez merchant, left the territorial-era house to Nancy in his will, which also freed Nancy and her three children—as of 1827: Caroline, John, and Christopher—by sending them to Ohio with one thousand dollars, even though Kyle may have already freed Nancy in 1819 by petition in Louisiana. Christopher and Nancy had likely lived together openly in the Kyle house, and Caroline and the other children were commonly recognized as their offspring. The house, moreover, remained in the hands of Nancy Kyle's descendants until the 1930s.[31]

The census identifies Nancy and Caroline as dressmakers and washerwomen, but their property made them equal to a handful of free black barbers and hack drivers who socially dominated the free black community.[32] The Kyle women were not above public scrutiny, though. In 1841, more than a decade after Christopher Kyle's death, local doctor Woodson Wren challenged the Kyles' lawfully filed petitions to remain in Mississippi. He claimed that the two women "Kept a House of ill fame, a House of asination [*sic*], a whore House, & c."[33] Such charges had been leveled at the Kyle women previously. In the summer of 1838, "various . . . respected citizens of the City of Natchez" had petitioned the Board of Police to revoke their licenses to stay. The board ordered the women to leave the state within ninety days and labeled them "dangerous members of Society." The order was suspended in January 1839, however, and their licenses were renewed in 1841.[34]

Board of Police hearings brought private lives into the public sphere. William Johnson's diary records that police board chairman Henry Connor shouted down the attacks on Caroline and Nancy Kyle made by "Old Dr. Wren" and threatened to jail him if he dared say "another word."[35] Wren, a local character, shows up earlier as the key witness against a white man for having sex with a black woman. He testified that he had watched the two through their window in the act of fornication. The arrested man sued Wren for malicious prosecution, and the court eventually awarded the plaintiff fifty dollars in damages and court costs.[36]

Support for the Kyle women came not only from Henry Conner but also from a "Great many [other leading members of the white community] that was very Glad of the old Fellows [Wren's] defeat."[37] If the prostitution charges had any basis in fact, the two women probably would have counted among their customers some of the very citizens who had sponsored their petitions to stay in Mississippi. A more flattering entry in William Johnson's diary tells of Nancy Kyle's 1843 visit to the nearby town of Rodney to minister to yellow fever victims. She was accompanied by "Lizor [Eliza] Cotton," another free black woman, who appears more than once in the public record as a woman who traded sex for money.[38]

That the town renewed their licenses despite the clamor from some whites who wanted to drive the Kyle women out of state reveals how the two unmarried women had made their way in the world. As well-known and even notorious free women of color, they enjoyed the patronage and support of white men who may have been their lovers, fathers, patients, or customers. The two women were tolerated—even accepted and welcomed—by some Natchez whites. In an honor bestowed on only a small handful of the town's free black residents, they were buried side by side in the local white cemetery.[39]

A grand jury indictment against Eliza Cotton on August 1, 1841, in Adams County Circuit Court charged Cotton (aka Eliza Holden or Eliza Bossack) with keeping a disorderly house where, day and night, "evil" men and women engaged in "tippling" and general misbehavior, including nudity, to "the great damage and common nuisance of all the good citizens of the state." Two months later she was indicted for selling spirituous liquors "to diverse Negroes," probably including slaves. Eliza posted over fifteen hundred dollars bail while the case proceeded for almost six months. The next year she was arrested again on identical charges.[40]

Eliza's first documented run-in with the law occurred in 1832, when she was indicted for fornicating with a white man, John Holden; in 1840 she was charged with harboring slaves, a serious offense for a free black person. No record exists of the cases going to trial. In 1832, the police board, despite the pending charge, judged her a person of "good character and honest deportment" and allowed her to remain in the state.[41]

Eliza Cotton/Bossack/Holden was born around 1802 in Washington, D.C. She may have been born a slave, brought to Natchez by slave traders, and then manumitted, but no manumission papers have been located, which strongly suggests that she was freed prior to coming to Natchez or granted freedom across the river in Louisiana, as often happened.[42] Or she may have been sent to a free state such as Ohio to be manumitted, a common practice after 1820.[43] She owned five slaves in 1840 as well as a lot and building on St. Catherine Street, a thoroughfare that passed the slave and free black hospital and terminated at the slave market. In the 1840s, she and three other free black women rented rooms in a downtown building across from the courthouse and next to the jail. According to the building's rental register, two of the women worked as washerwomen, but Eliza's occupation is not listed.[44]

Although she had avoided jail, Eliza Cotton was nearly driven from the state when the Board of Police revoked her license to stay on September 6, 1841. She immediately appealed to the circuit court, and six months later, even as she was under grand-jury indictment, the court granted her license to remain as a result of a "bill of exceptions" filed by her attorneys, Alexander Montgomery and Samuel S. Boyd.[45]

Eliza remained in Natchez despite the charges against her thanks to the many white men in her life. Five had routinely come to her aid by posting bonds (averaging about two hundred dollars each) or acting as security while she fought various indictments. Some of the best lawyers in town represented her either as friends or as paid counsel. Doing business out of her rented office on the courthouse square put Eliza in the middle of the Natchez legal community. Perhaps she did the washing for the jail or for the many lawyers who worked nearby, or maybe they knew her as a woman who offered sex for money.

The three men whose names she claimed—Holden, Cotton, and Bossack— may also help to explain her survival. Holden was probably John Holden, with whom she had been accused of fornication, but nothing is known of his background or occupation. Cotton may have been prominent slave trader William Cotton, who died in 1843. His probate records list two bad loans to Eliza Bossack for $280.00 and $666.50. Businessmen Peter Gemmell and Samuel Wakefield had endorsed the notes. The origin of her surname Bossack is unknown.[46]

William Cotton's probate records also list his young slave Eliza and her child, Merial, acknowledged to be Cotton's mulatto daughter in his 1843 will. Cotton paid the slave Eliza's steamboat passages, bought her calico dresses, and provided her lodging. He had instructed that she be freed upon his death. When settling Cotton's estate, however, his executor and business associate, Rice C. Ballard, petitioned the probate court in 1844 for the right to sell four of Cotton's slaves to pay his debts. Ballard sold twenty-four-year-old Eliza for $710.00 to wealthy planter J. S. Gillespie. All trace of the daughter Merial disappeared. She may have been Williams's child by the slave Eliza or his granddaughter by the free Eliza Cotton listed in the probate records. Perhaps the two Eliza Cottons were unrelated, but the favored status of the enslaved Eliza Cotton indicates a special link between her and William Cotton.[47]

Eliza Cotton's name appears in the municipal death records in 1854 and in the criminal court records in 1867, when she was arrested and jailed for petty theft, but no ages are given in either record. The woman arrested in 1867 was living in Under-the-Hill with another black woman, Eliza Smith, who was charged with Cotton as a coconspirator. She might have been Eliza Cotton/ Holden/Bossack or perhaps her mulatto daughter—the child and then lover of William Cotton.[48]

Each of the free black women profiled in this essay was intimately and sexually connected to prominent white men in the community. Agnes Gordon Earhart was the mother of at least eight mulatto children by merchant David Earhart. Fanny Leiper's father was probably a member of the Christopher Miller family, whose fortunes rested on cotton and slaves. The Kyles were the concubine and daughter of merchant Christopher Kyle. Eliza Cotton was linked to many white men, including John Holden, William Cotton, the unknown Bossack, and possibly several others. Excepting Agnes Earhart, the women shared a possible identity as prostitutes or brothel madams.

They were also fully engaged in the everyday reality of Natchez. Their fates were not solely determined by a rigid caste system, and they often found themselves the focus of public record. Most Natchez residents probably knew who they were and what they did. They were protected by their white male associates and too rooted in the local scene to be easily chased away: not one was "purged," when others were, from the community in the 1830s, 1840s, and 1850s.

The sometimes open sexual involvement of the women with white men linked them as well to most of the other free black women of Natchez. Free black barber William Johnson was probably the son of a prosperous but not wealthy white man (also named William Johnson), who had freed young William, his sister, and his mother, Amy. The white father had set up his mulatto son in business and provided the boy's mother with a house and property. Young William Johnson's wife, Ann, moreover, was the mulatto daughter of Harriet Battles, who had been freed and given property by banker Gabriel Tichenor.[49]

The most prominent free black families in Natchez—the Barlands, Hoggatts, Fitzgeralds, Winstons, McCarys, and Smiths—descended from prominent white men and enslaved, later freed, women. William Johnson's best friend, free black barber Robert McCary, had been freed along with his sister by their white father, who set him up with property and even slaves, including one thought to have been his own half-brother. Everyone in town knew the families' backgrounds and interrelationships.[50]

Adam Bingaman, one of the town's wealthiest planters, traced his Mississippi ancestry to the Spanish colonial era. He fathered several children with his beloved free black consort, Mary Ellen Williams, with whom he began a sexual relationship after the death of his white wife soon after they had married. Mary Ellen was Bingaman's slave at the time but was later freed by him. When his mother died in 1841, he took Mary Ellen and their children to New Orleans to live lavishly among the city's mixed free blacks. There his mulatto daughters, Charlotte and Elenora, formed a devoted friendship with the daughters of William Johnson that lasted until well after the Civil War. In 1859, Bingaman persuaded the Louisiana and Mississippi state legislatures to allow Mary Ellen and her children to remain as residents and keep their properties. At the end of the Civil War, Bingaman acknowledged both James A. Bingaman and Elenora Lucille Bingaman as his "natural Children." When he died in 1869, his entire estate passed to Elenora, the sole survivor of his black family.[51]

The sexual involvement of free black women with prominent white men set their lives apart from their free black brothers. The women's sexuality armed them with a gendered currency that enabled them to live in ways that would never have been tolerated in men. No free black man would have survived for long as the operator of a bawdy house. Except for those so light skinned that they could pass for white (like David Earhart), none would have been allowed to walk the streets of Natchez as the consorts or husbands of white women, and none would have been allowed to father their children. Such activities would have caused them to be arrested, exiled, enslaved, castrated, or killed. The key to success for free black males lay in their deportment and in the patronage of white protectors who were often their own fathers. As long as they did not threaten the system of slavery, free black males who were related to prominent whites were accepted and even valued for their services. Their proper deportment as faithful servants of the white social order mattered much more than the identities of their fathers.

William Johnson was applauded in the local press after his death for being a "most inoffensive man," a former slave who had earned "a respected position on account of his character, intelligence, and deportment."⁵² Similarly, the death in 1858 of Robert D. Smith, a free black carriage-business owner, led the *Natchez Courier* to write: "All of our old citizens—indeed—we may say—all our citizens—will regret to hear of the death of Robert D. Smith, a colored man of our city, but one who, by his industry, probity of life, correctness of demeanor and Christian-like character, had won the favor, and respect of the entire community. Every citizen knew him, and there are but few travelers, who frequented our city, who could not bear witness of his correct deportment and character."⁵³

For Fanny Leiper, the Kyle women, Eliza Cotton, Cassandra and Agnes Earhart, and others like them, deportment was not the key. They survived because of their sexual and familial links to white men, which enabled them to venture forth openly, even defiantly, as they "stepped lively in place" as free women of color. Even though free black people in Natchez did not enjoy citizenship or equality before the law or in society, free black women experienced life quite differently. Despite the ban on interracial marriages, some of the women considered themselves married to their white partners and often took their surnames. Society allowed them more latitude in their behavior than it did free black men and even white women, who appear in police records charged with crimes free black women usually managed to escape.⁵⁴

Amy Johnson, William Johnson's mother, provides a telling example of such relative freedom. Freed in 1819 by the white man who had probably fathered her two children, she was a town character until her death in 1849. Licensed as a retailer in the early 1820s, she acquired a house and slaves with the help of the William Johnsons, father and son. Just five feet tall, she was given to fighting real and imaginary enemies, and several of her battles wound up in court. She sued free black barber Arthur Mitchum in 1822 for damages after a fistfight. She claimed he had spit in her face, pulled her nose and hair, and ripped her dress and bonnet while beating her with brickbats. The court awarded her just $27.50 in damages and costs instead of the $500 she wanted. She was back in court one month later testifying against Mitchum on another assault-and-battery charge lodged by a free black woman named Delia Black. By 1837, Amy had become so uncontrollable that her son flicked his whip at her as "the quickest way to stop it." He estimated that his mother averaged three public quarrels a week and one nearly every day with her family.[55]

Despite her combative, irascible nature, Amy Johnson was never arrested, but she did publicly embarrass her son. Her identity as the mother of the most prosperous free black man in town probably helped shield her, along with the fact that her wrath was mostly aimed at free blacks, slaves, and working-class whites. Such conduct would never have been tolerated from a free black man, and indeed, no mention of disruptions by free black men appears in William Johnson's extensive diary. Occasionally enslaved women brawled in the street, but their owners or the slave patrol dealt with them quickly and severely. Only free black women with white male connections could get away with such behavior.[56]

The free black "stepping lively" women of Natchez were tolerated and embraced as relatively free spirits because their sexual, emotional, and familial connections complemented rather than threatened a prevailing social order held together by slavery, male patriarchy, and the servant ideal.[57] These women, though lively and demonstrative compared to free black males and enslaved women, mattered to the white men who loved them or regarded them as valued persons for whom they felt responsible. Their partially European ancestry trumped their partially African ancestry as long as they were family members or cherished objects of white affection and desire.[58]

NOTES

1. Ronald L. F. Davis, *The Black Experience in Natchez, 1720–1880* (Denver: Eastern National, 1999); William R. Hogan and Edwin A. Davis, eds., *William Johnson's Natchez: The Ante-bellum Diary of a Free Negro* (Baton Rouge: Louisiana State University Press, 1979); D. Clayton James, *Antebellum Natchez* (Baton Rouge: Louisiana State University Press, 1993).

2. There is a growing body of scholarship on free black women in the South, including David Barry Gaspar and Darlene Clark Hine, eds., *Beyond Bondage: Free Women of Color in the Americas* (Urbana: University of Illinois Press, 2004), to name but one of the most recent books on this subject.

3. Rosanne Welch, "A Family Affair: Emancipation and Slavery in the Old Natchez District, 1795–1860," MA thesis, California State University, Northridge, 2004; U.S. Manuscript Census (1840, 1850, and 1860), Adams County, Mississippi, National Archives Records Administration, Washington, D.C. (henceforth cited as NARA).

4. Nik Ribianszky, "'She Appeared to Be Mistress of Her Own Actions, Free from the Control of Anyone': Property Holding Free Women of Color in Natchez, Mississippi, 1779–1865," *Journal of Mississippi History* 67 (Fall 2005): 217–25.

5. U.S. Manuscript Census (1840, 1850, and 1860), Adams County, Mississippi, NARA; Death Records, Sexton Reports, Natchez, Adams County, Mississippi, Historic Natchez Foundation, Natchez, Mississippi (henceforth cited as HNF); Deed Records (1799–1870), Adams County Courthouse, Natchez, Mississippi,.

6. The "one-drop rule" refers to the cultural custom of defining as black anyone who possessed a "drop" of black blood. See especially Joel Williamson, *New People: Miscegenation and Mulattoes in the United States* (Baton Rouge: Louisiana State University Press, 1995), 1–2, 5–109.

7. Petition of Agnes Earhart, n.d., folder 1850–59, RG 47, vol. 26, 27, Legislative Records, Mississippi Department of Archives and History, Jackson (henceforth cited as MDAH); Marriage Records (1835–50), Adams County Courthouse Natchez, Mississippi; U.S. Manuscript Census (1850), Adams County, Mississippi, NARA.

8. Judith K. Schafer, *Becoming Free, Remaining Free: Manumission and Enslavement in New Orleans, 1846–1862* (Baton Rouge: Louisiana State University Press, 2003), 147.

9. A. Hutchinson, *Code of Mississippi: Analytical Compilation of the Public and General Statutes of the Territory and State with Tabular References to the Local and Private Acts from 1798 to 1848* (Jackson: Price and Fall State Printers, 1848), 510–42; William Sharkey, William Harris, and Henry T. Ellet, *The Revised Code of the Statute Laws of the State of Mississippi* (Jackson: E. Barksdale, 1857), 234–56; Charles Sydnor, "The Free Negro in Mississippi before the Civil War," *American Historical Review* 32 (July 1927): 769–88.

10. Death Records, Sexton Reports, Natchez, Adams County, Mississippi, HNF.

11. Ibid.

12. David Earhart, January 23, 1860, Will Book 3, Adams County Courthouse, Natchez, Mississippi.

13. U.S. Manuscript Census (1850), Adams County, Mississippi, NARA; Petition of Agnes Earhart, n.d., folder 1850–59, RG 47, MDAH.

14. David Earhart to Agnes Gordon (aka Earhart, f.w.c.[free woman of color]), November 5, 1841, Deed Records (1820–70), Adams County Courthouse, Natchez, Mississippi.

15. Edith Wyatt Moore, *Natchez Under-the-Hill* (Natchez, Miss.: Southern Historical Publications, 1958), 53–60.

16. James Hoggatt, for James Bosley, "claiming a slave," April 28, 1795, Book E, Spanish Records; Jacob Earhart to Cassandra Bosley (a slave), August 11, 1803, Deed Records (1799–1870), both at Adams County Courthouse, Natchez, Mississippi,.

17. Elizabeth Earhart to Isaac House, July 12, 1808, Deed Records (1799–1870), Adams County Courthouse, Natchez, Mississippi.

18. Jacob and Cassandra Earhart to Walter Irwin, July 1, 1809, Deed Records (1799–1870), Adams County Courthouse, Natchez, Mississippi.

19. Jacob Earhart and wife Cassandra to James J. Rowan, Trustee for David Earhart, et al., September 6, 1824; and William Shupan for John and Christiana Zeigline to Cassandra Earhart, March 22, 1836, Deed Records (1799–1870); Marriage Records (1826–45), Adams County Courthouse, Natchez, Mississippi; U.S. Manuscript Census (1820–60), Adams County, Mississippi, NARA; Terry L. Alford, "Some Manumissions Recorded in the Adams County Deed Books in Chancery Clerk's Office, Natchez, Mississippi, 1795–1835," *Journal of Mississippi History* 33 (February 1971): 39–50.

20. *Leiper v. Huffman et al.* (1851), 26 Miss. 622, MDAH.

21. Ibid.

22. Ibid.

23. Ibid.

24. Ibid.

25. John R. Wells to Malvina Huffman, February 27, 1834; Malvina J. Hoffman to Alfred Bemiss and Oliver L. Bemiss, April 29, 1841; and Joseph Winscott to Malvina Hoffman, September 27, 1845, Deed Records (1799–1870), Adams County Courthouse, Natchez, Mississippi; Criminal Justice Docket Books (1800–1870); *State v. Malvina J. Matthews* (alias Malvina J. Huffman), May 26, 1868, Natchez, Adams County, Mississippi, HNF; U.S. Manuscript Census (1850), Adams County, Mississippi, NARA.

26. *Leiper v. Huffman et al.* (1851), 26 Miss. 622, MDAH; see also Edwin Adams Davis, "William Johnson: Free Negro Citizen of Ante-bellum Mississippi," *Journal of Mississippi History* 15 (April 1953): 65.

27. Ibid. Curiously, Gabriel Tichenor's wife is also named in the deed of sale, Deed Records (1799–1870), Adams County Courthouse, Natchez, Mississippi; Emancipation Papers, Maria, Mary, Martha, and William Parker, December 23, 1843, Deed Records (1799–1870), Adams County Courthouse, Natchez, Mississippi; Hogan and Davis, *William Johnson's Natchez*, 33, 70, 115; Edwin Adams Davis and William Ransom Hoggan, *The Barber of Natchez* (repr., Baton Rouge: Louisiana State University Press, 1990), 27–28; James, *Antebellum Natchez*, 199–200.

28. See Davis, *Black Experience in Natchez*, 53; Kyle House files, Natchez, Adams County, Mississippi, HNF; U.S. Manuscript Census (1850, 1860), Adams County Mississippi, NARA.

29. U.S. Manuscript Census (1860), Adams County, Mississippi, NARA.

30. Ibid.

31. Christopher H. Kyle, 1827, Will Book 1; Deeds of Manumission: March 18, 1819, March 28, 1825, July 24, 1825, September 6, 1826, June 5, 1827, Deed Records (1799–1870), Adams County Courthouse, Natchez, Mississippi; Kyle House files, Natchez, Adams County, Mississippi, HNF; Hogan and Davis, *William Johnson's Natchez*, 345.

32. Davis, *Black Experience in Natchez*, 46–60; Winthrop D. Jordan, *Tumult and Silence at Second Creek: An Inquiry into a Civil War Slave Conspiracy* (Baton Rouge: Louisiana State University Press, 1993), 206–10.

33. Hogan and Davis, *William Johnson's Natchez*, 345.

34. March 1832, August 1838, January 1839, September 1841, Police Court Minutes, Adams County, Mississippi, MF roll 886352, Genealogical Society of Utah, Salt Lake City, Utah (henceforth cited as GSU).

35. Hogan and Davis, *William Johnson's Natchez*, 345.

36. *Thomas Smith v. Woodson Wren*, 1821, Natchez, Adams County, Mississippi, HNF.

37. Hogan and Davis, *William Johnson's Natchez*, 345.

38. Ibid., 453.

39. Death Records, Sexton Reports, Natchez, Adams County, Mississippi, HNF.

40. *State v. Eliza Cotton alias Eliza Holden, alias Eliza Bossack*, August 1, 1841; October 10, 1841; March 9, 1842, Adams County Courthouse, Natchez, Mississippi.

41. *State v. John Holden*, May Term, 1832, Criminal Justice Docket Books (1800–1870), Natchez, Adams County, Mississippi, HNF; June 1832, Police Court Minutes, Adams County Mississippi, MF roll 886352, GSU.

42. In Louisiana the state supreme court blocked legislative efforts to prohibit manumissions until the eve of the Civil War, often granting manumissions in individual cases, despite laws that otherwise barred such practices. This stance reflected the French and Spanish cultural heritage of the state regarding slavery. See especially Judith Kelleher Schafer, *Slavery, the Civil Law, and the Supreme Court of Louisiana* (Baton Rouge: Louisiana State University Press, 1994), 181–85.

43. C. G. Woodson, "The Negroes of Cincinnati Prior to the Civil War," *Journal of Negro History* 1 (January 1916): 1–22; and C. A. Powell et al., "Transplanting Free Negroes to Ohio from 1815–1858," *Journal of Negro History* 1 (January 1916): 302–17.

44. Account Journal—Rent Book, April 1841 to [1868], Pullen-Carson Family Papers, MDAH; U.S. Manuscript Census (1840, 1850), Adams County Mississippi, NARA.

45. Police Court Minutes, September 6, 1841, Adams County Mississippi, MF roll 886352, GSU; *State v. Eliza Bossack, a free negro*, October 1, 1841, Adams County Courthouse, Natchez, Mississippi; *Eliza Bossack v. Henry S. Conner*, December 1, 1841, Natchez, Adams County, Mississippi, HNF.

46. Will and Probate Records of William Cotton, Will Book 2, Probate Box 94, Adams County Courthouse, Natchez, Mississippi; Michael Tadman, *Speculators and Slaves: Masters, Traders, and Slaves in the Old South* (Madison: University of Wisconsin Press, 1989), 89.

47. Will and Probate Records of William Cotton, Adams County Courthouse, Natchez, Mississippi.

48. Death Records, Sexton Reports, Natchez, Adams County, Mississippi, HNF; *State v. Elizabeth Smith and Eliza Cotton*, July 19, 1867, Adams County Courthouse, Natchez, Mississippi.

49. Davis, *Black Experience in Natchez*, 56–59; Hogan and Davis, *William Johnson's Natchez*, 15–18, 33, 70, 115.

50. Will of James McCary, February 16, 1813, Will Book 1, Adams County Courthouse, Natchez, Mississippi; Daniel F. Littlefield Jr., *The Life of Okah Tubbee* (Lincoln: University of Nebraska Press, 1988).

51. Cecie M. Shulman, "The Bingamans of Natchez," *Journal of Mississippi History* 63 (Winter 2001): 285–315; Hogan and Davis, *William Johnson's Natchez*, 597; Virginia Meacham Gould, ed., *Chained to the Rock of Adversity: To Be Free, Black, and Female in the Old South* (Athens: University of Georgia Press, 1998), 36.

52. Hogan and Davis, *William Johnson's Natchez*, 262–72.

53. *Natchez Courier*, June 2, 1858.

54. Such assumed marriages were nothing unusual among enslaved blacks, who were legally prohibited from marrying. See especially Joyce L. Broussard, "Female Solitaires: Women Alone in the Lifeworld of Mid-century Natchez, Mississippi: 1850–1880" (PhD diss., University of Southern California, 1998), 226–55; John Hope Franklin, *From Slavery to Freedom: A History of Negro Americans*, 4th ed. (New York: Alfred A. Knopf, 1974), 173–74; H. E. Sterkx, *The Free Negro in Ante-bellum Louisiana* (Rutherford, N.J.: Farleigh Dickinson University Press, 1972), 243–45; and Charles S. Syndor, *Slavery in Mississippi* (repr., Gloucester, Mass.: Peter Smith, 1965), 63.

55. Hogan and Davis, *William Johnson's Natchez*, 15, 18–19, 44–45, 71, 76, 86, 89, 90, 102, 175, 183, 187, 189, 203, 211, 354, 641–42; *Amy Johnston, f.w.c., v. Arthur Mitchum, f.m.c.*, April 19, 1819; and *State v. Arthur Mitchum, f.m.c.*, May 25, 1819, Natchez, Adams County, Mississippi, HNF.

56. Hutchinson, *Code of Mississippi: 1798–1847*, 510–42; Sharkey, Harris, and Ellet, *Revised Code*, 235–256.

57. Broussard, "Female Solitaires," 1–59.

58. During the decade from 1850 to 1860, several hundred free black women are found in various public or private records as being present at one time or another in Natchez but do not show up in the 1850 or 1860 manuscript census records. See also Martha Hodes, *White Women, Black Men: Illicit Sex in the Nineteenth-Century South* (New Haven, Conn.: Yale University Press, 1997).

The Good Sisters

White Protestant Women and Institution Building in Antebellum Mississippi

RANDY J. SPARKS

In his landmark 1977 study of southern religion, Donald Mathews forcefully reminded us that "women made southern Evangelicalism possible." His statement can be extended to argue that women made southern Protestantism possible. Over twenty-five years have elapsed since Mathews first made that striking observation, but the full story of southern women's vital role in establishing southern Protestantism has yet to be told. Reconstructing women's roles in creating and sustaining southern churches is more difficult because the historical legacy—usually recorded by men—has largely obscured their involvement. Given the gap in the historical record, feminist scholars have urged historians to apply a "hermeneutic of suspicion" to religious history that overlooks or underestimates the critical role women played in the movement.[1]

The study of women and religion can also cast light on important issues confronting scholars of American women's history. Until the late 1970s, the dominant interpretation of antebellum women's history revolved around the concept of separate spheres. Historians such as Barbara Welter, Gerda Lerner, Carroll Smith-Rosenberg, Nancy Cott, and Anne Firor Scott explored the constraints imposed on women by the cult of domesticity that confined women to the home and celebrated their piety, purity, and submissiveness. Although the ideology of separate spheres subordinated women, it also contributed to the rise of a distinctive women's culture nurtured through close friendships among women, women's education, and the rise of women's benevolent associations. Religion played an important role in the formation of friendships, the establishment of religious schools for women, and the rise of women's organizations. Over the past decade, scholars have attempted to move beyond the concept of separate spheres to explore the ways in which women and men participated in creating their common culture and institutions.[2]

In a variety of ways and with important implications for the history of women and southern religion, scholars are broadening their understanding of the concept of separate spheres. Women made vital contributions to the rise of Protestantism in Mississippi; they actively joined in—and often led—the process of institution building and participated in the construction of gender relations generally. One way historians have broadened their understanding of separate spheres is by taking the concept more literally and by examining the physical spaces that women created themselves or that others defined for them. The use of the term "separate spheres" significantly enhances understanding of the early history of evangelicalism, the creation of churches, and the complex use of sacred space. Anthropologists have observed that public spaces have often been considered male preserves, while women were often relegated to the more private domestic settings that physically reflected their social subordination. The first eighteenth- and early nineteenth-century Protestant churches in Mississippi were Baptist and Methodist. The early evangelicals, with no meeting houses or available public spaces, often resorted to open-air meetings; indeed, celebrated camp meetings have come to typify early evangelicalism in the South. More often, however, before they had sufficient members and funds to construct meeting houses, evangelicals met in private homes for worship. For example, Methodist circuit rider William Winans preached on the Wilkinson Circuit from 1811 to 1812; his four-week circuit took him to twenty-four meeting places, most of them private homes. Women often opened their homes for worship; the first Baptist church in the Mississippi Territory met in the home of Margaret Stampley, while the first Methodist conference was held in the home of "Mother White." Ann Finley recalled that when she moved to Bachelor's Bend in Washington County in 1836, "there was no organized church until 'Mrs. Blanton, one of the first settlers, opened her home for worship.'" In such circumstances, private space—domestic space typically regarded as a part of the female sphere—became public, and women were instrumental in creating the new sacred space.[3]

In a few isolated cases, women organized churches themselves, even though they often met with opposition, ridicule, or condescension from husbands or fathers who resented the challenge to their patriarchy. Methodist itinerant Elijah Steele, who preached to Shiloh Church's three women members, praised their efforts and added, "God's presence was not entirely confined to great assemblies, but he condescends to meet with two or three." In 1832, the nine Presbyterian women who chartered Amite County's Unity Church used their own family names rather than their husbands' surnames, but there were limits to their spiritual autonomy. The Presbyterian church's patriarchal structure forced the women to appoint a temporary elder from another church until men joined later that same year. Similarly, a church in the Biloxi Baptist Association could not send delegates to the 1852 annual meeting because it had only ineligible women members.[4]

As evangelicals ventured aggressively into the marketplace of ideas and held out the possibility of conversion to everyone regardless of gender, race, or age, they challenged the control of white men over their households. Methodist itinerant Samuel Sellers recorded many such instances in his diary. At one particularly emotional camp meeting in 1816, he reported that "a considerable commotion took place." Some men "were taking away their wives" and others were carrying away their children because, according to the men, "they [the women and children] could be scared." Sellers knew that what the men actually feared was that their women and children would be converted.[5] Fortunately, few patriarchs went as far as John B. Fisher of Vicksburg, a young overseer who accosted the Reverend Peter E. Green, the preacher who had converted his wife. Fisher met Green on the street, "abused him terribly and finally pulled out a pistol and shot him." Green's assault at the hands of an angry husband testified vividly to the threat conversion posed to some southern patriarchs and warned ministers to carefully monitor the family relationships of the converted.[6] Some men dismissed the spiritual lives of their dependents with a smirk and a sneer, while others saw in such expressions of spiritual independence an inherent, unacceptable threat to their control.[7]

Crowded together in small log cabins, Christian bands with sporadically visiting ministers engaged in intimate, lay-oriented services. As one early member wrote, "It was not an uncommon thing for souls to be converted in night meetings in private houses."[8] Early evangelicals did not compartmentalize their religion, and they refused to confine their worship to Sunday-morning church services. At one point, Winans preached on his circuit every day except Monday. Services featured intensely personal and intimate rituals and practices such as Methodist love feasts and class meetings, where women spoke, testified, and served as class leaders, and Baptist foot-washing ceremonies, which were segregated by gender so that women washed only the feet of other women. Winans described an 1821 love feast where "old Sister Hamilton . . . spoke with an eloquence wholly irresistible for she spoke from the heart in the strong language of feeling."[9]

Evangelicals emphasized the importance of spiritual gifts that God bestowed on the faithful without regard to gender or race, and women were encouraged to exhibit their gifts in singing, public prayer, and exhortation. Hannah Swayze, daughter of the Mississippi Territory's first Protestant minister, was revered for her gifts; she was praised as "a wise and safe counselor in religious matters, but her greatest excellence, perhaps, was in the eloquence and power of her public prayers." Her daughter, Hannah Coleman Griffing, inherited her mother's spiritual power and "was also greatly gifted in . . . prayer, and was often called on . . . to exercise her gifts."[10]

Domestic worship services allowed women to exercise a greater role than might otherwise have been the case, and once empowered, some women were able to carry their involvement even further into the "public" sphere. Elizabeth Osteen, regarded as "one of the most influential and useful members of the [Methodist] Church," attended a camp meeting where preachers failed completely in their efforts to move the crowd. "Elizabeth Osteen arose. . . . She became inspired with the Spirit of God, and, turning to the congregation, gave a powerful impromptu exhortation, called for mourners, and soon had the altar crowded." William Winans described an 1851 revival meeting where "Sister Thomas came up . . . and gave an excellent talk on Sunday morning." A Methodist minister from Clinton praised an elderly parishioner as "verily a mother in our Israel! She was one of the nine that formed the first class that was ever organized in this State. She rejoiced aloud, and seemed as if on the very suburbs of heaven."[11] Revered as "Mothers in Israel," such faithful women asserted their spiritual authority with the encouragement of ministers who saw the efficacy of their labors and felt the power of their spiritual gifts. Winans's quote suggests that although it became increasingly difficult for women to exercise a public role in worship, they continued to do so throughout the antebellum period.[12]

Some ministers gave churchwomen deserved credit for advancing religion. Methodist Rev. A. C. Ramsey acknowledged the vital contributions of "the good sisters . . . in these great religious efforts of moral and religious reform" on his circuit. The women, he wrote, "were in great measure the more active and successful agents . . . especially in instructing, advising, encouraging and praying for the sin sick, and broken hearted; and by their many joyful shouts of praise to God." Though he did not use the word "ministry," the women, through their instruction, advising, encouragement, and prayers, were as deeply engaged in ministry as was Ramsey. He went on to compliment some of the younger church women, "whose piety, as evidenced by constant walking with God, their secret, and family devotions, frequently in their fathers [sic] family, their labors and public prayers at the church . . . gave them the character of the most devoted and exemplary members of the church in all that country." The zealous young women of the Vicksburg area were called the "Warren County Fire Company" for their success in saving souls from the fires of hell.[13]

Ministers, especially itinerants, depended on faithful women for their basic necessities. Ramsey gratefully recorded donations to him and his fellow Methodist preachers: "We had been the recipients of several presents in the matter of clothing & c. Particularly in socks from the good sisters. I never had as many pairs of socks at one time before; which I took to conference and after selecting from the bundle as many as I thought I would need, divided or gave the balance to the young preachers." Not all preachers were so fortunate, and those who earned women's displeasure could face severe consequences. Ramsey related the story of one unfortunate Methodist circuit rider who was too "elevated, in his thoughts and manners, for poor folks in the piney woods." The preacher "was very unpopular with some of the women for his standing by them and showing how he liked this thing and that cooked and served up." He so alienated the women that "he was not very useful on the circuit . . . and was expelled from the conference."[14]

While evangelical ministers often recognized their debt to women, encouraged gifted women converts, and preached the doctrine of the equality of all believers—a message that helped attract groups like women and slaves who were otherwise marginalized in society—women did not find complete equality in churches no matter how great their spiritual gifts. Churches did not ordain women and barred them from serving as deacons, presbyters, or other important officials, but women were not without influence in churches. Many Baptist and Methodist churches allowed women to vote in congregational business meetings, where important decisions, such as selecting a new minister or deciding cases of church discipline, were made. Baptist churches' rules of order usually stated that church governance "was equally the right and privilege of each member thereof." Some church rules more explicitly stated: "All male & female members shall have privileges in church government."[15]

Some women struggled to maintain their voting rights as men tried to restrict their privileges. Such conflicts underscore the fact that women took their rights and responsibilities very seriously and worked to protect them. Given the importance of voting in antebellum America, woman suffrage in churches took on added significance. Feminist scholars have found that the right to vote "was a key symbol of national and gender identity," and "the question of who had the right to vote transfixed mid-century Americans."[16] Given the substantial female majority in the typical evangelical church, the right to vote gave women some measure of authority within an institutional setting and provided a public example of women exercising a highly symbolic right generally reserved for white men. How actively women exercised their right to vote and whether they voted as a gender bloc are difficult to discern from sparse church records, though efforts to deprive women of their rights on the basis of gender suggest that men feared that women, given their numbers, could easily dominate church politics.

Women's right to vote and to participate in church governance could be especially important in the disciplinary process that lay at the heart of evangelical experience. Churches functioned as "moral courts" where members carefully monitored one another's behavior. In churches where women voted, their votes could be decisive. Even when women did not vote, they routinely took part in disciplinary deliberations and served on committees appointed to visit women charged in the church courts.[17] Conversion ushered men and women into a redemptive community in which members joined to struggle against Satan's many arts. In the context of church discipline, gender conventions would be defined and enforced.

A survey of over 1,150 disciplinary cases from Baptist, Methodist, and Presbyterian churches in Mississippi reveals striking gender differences. Most notably, churches disciplined white men in numbers far out of proportion to their membership. While white men made up only about 35 percent of church members, well over half of the disciplinary cases (55.9 percent) involved charges against white men. White women, by contrast, faced only 150 charges (12.8 percent) despite their overwhelming majority in the membership. By far the most common charge against white men was intoxication, ranging from over 45 percent of charges from 1820 to 1830, to about 20 percent of charges from 1860 to 1870. In part the decline represents the success of the antebellum temperance campaign. Evangelicals opposed drinking because it threatened the family, and church records reveal that in disciplinary cases alcohol consumption was often linked to violent and aggressive behavior.[18]

Churches insisted that southern patriarchs uphold their duties to their families; as Stephanie McCurry found in her study of discipline in Lowcountry South Carolina churches, "The arm of the church reached every corner of family life." Men were charged with adultery, wife and child abuse, fornication, rape, and bigamy. In 1850, for instance, George W. Bayles faced a charge of wife and child abuse. In keeping with standard practice, the church appointed a committee of three white men to visit him to investigate the charges. The committee found no evidence, but the issue refused to die. He was charged once again, and though he denied the charges before the church conference, other testimony proved his guilt, and the church excluded him. Such cases could be difficult; when the members of New Zion Baptist Church charged Brother Lopez with unchristian conduct toward his wife, the case became so acrimonious that they called in representatives from other Baptist churches to help settle the dispute.[19]

Women were also subject to charges of adultery and desertion. The Mt. Moriah Baptist Church conference heard two cases in 1860 alone in which women were charged with marrying men who had living wives, and Clear Creek Baptist Church excluded Sister Jane Wilkinson after she left her husband. As these cases suggest, evangelicals saw marriage as a holy institution with religious duties. Evangelicals encouraged companionate marriages; a Baptist circular letter, for example, maintained that "the husband and wife . . . must be considered as a joint head of the family." The power of the patriarch over his family, as such cases suggest, was not absolute; churches attempted to protect women and children from abusive husbands and defended the sanctity of the marriage vow.[20]

The number of women charged with violations of adultery or any other sexual offense was very low, well under 10 percent of the total. More men than women were charged with adultery, and an equal number of men and women (three) were charged with fornication. Whether or not women controlled the disciplinary process, it clearly worked to their advantage. As historian Frederick A. Bode writes, "There was little reason for them to oppose a standard of church discipline that provided even limited sanctions against male violence and disorder."[21] The disciplinary records suggest that the vast majority of women church members, unlike men, found it relatively easy to live within their churches' strict moral codes. Through their votes, their engagement in the deliberations, their service on visitation committees, and their sheer numbers, they helped shape religious gender conventions and, by extension, those of the entire region. A writer in the *Mississippi Baptist* "acknowledged the all controlling power of woman's influence" and observed that women established "the standard of morality in any community."[22]

In some ways, evangelical churches emphasized the spiritual equality of all members, but at the same time they reinforced the idea of sisterhood among white women. Again, the use of space was a significant reflection of the religious community's social vision. The Baptists and the Methodists in Mississippi and across the South segregated congregations by gender and race; men and women sat on different sides—men on the right, women on the left—and church roll books often separately listed men and women. Gendered seating in Baptist and Methodist churches marked a sharp departure from the Church of England's ranked seating in walled family pews. The Anglican seating plan reflected the order of society and the centrality of households governed by white men. The evangelical seating plan broke down the family unit and no longer assigned seating among whites by class. Drawn largely from the ranks of the yeomanry, early evangelicals bristled at social status distinctions and de-emphasized class and family. Their stress on the importance of the individual's relationship with God grew out of their faith's egalitarian nature while at the same time emphasizing gender and racial differences. Evangelicals typically referred to one another as "Brother" and "Sister," appellations that reflected their egalitarianism and also reinforced the concept of sisterhood and brother-hood. Many Baptist churches' rules of discipline even required members to use such familial terms of address, and church records, diaries, and letters indicate that the practice was commonplace.[23]

Scholars have debated the extent to which evangelicalism, with its empha-sis on spiritual equality and its attacks on elite culture, actually challenged patriarchy. Following Rhys Isaac's lead, historians have characterized the early evangelical movement as a vehicle through which plain folk challenged gentry domination and its supporting hierarchical, deferential social structure. The extent to which the evangelical revolt affected gender relations, however, is a particularly thorny issue. The relationship between spiritual and social equality in the evangelical message was obviously conflicted, and the evangelicals' egali-tarian rhetoric had definite practical limits in a slave society based on house-holds controlled by white men. Historians have increasingly turned their atten-tion to a more careful examination of those limits, the contradictory tendencies within evangelicalism, and the ways in which women's roles evolved.

Evangelicalism came of age in the years following the American Revolution, a period when the proper role of women was a subject of intense interest and debate. The revolution gave rise to the ideology of republicanism, which called into question the hierarchical social structure and gentry domination that characterized colonial southern society. Evangelicalism, with its emphasis on individual conversion, voluntarism, virtue, and the equality of believers, agreed with some of the most potent elements of republicanism. The revolution also challenged old assumptions about the proper role of women, and the emerging republican ideology ascribed new responsibilities to women as republican wives and mothers. Republican ideology emphasized marriage as the most impor-tant familial relationship and focused more on the bond between husbands and wives than that between parents and children. The ideal family was thought to be one in which husband and wife were conjugal equals, with women occupy-ing a central role. Women served as the guardians of male virtue, and through their beneficial influence within the family, they would ultimately reform the morals of the entire society. The very concept of virtue, central to republican ideology, became increasingly feminized.[24] Evangelicals took part in celebrating republican womanhood and spreading the emergent ideology among their rapidly growing membership.

Evangelical women understood the potential inherent in republican ideology for furthering their own goals and carving out a larger sphere for themselves in the churches and in society. The creation of Elizabeth Female Academy exemplified the process. In 1818, the Mississippi Methodist Conference established the academy in Washington, Mississippi, at the urging of Methodist women who first envisioned the school and then raised the necessary funds. One of the first such institutions in America, the academy opened at about the same time as Emma Hart Willard's Troy Female Seminary in New York. Like Willard, the academy's sponsors drew on the ideal of republican motherhood in designing the school and its ambitious curriculum. The school, wrote its founders, would confer "much benefit upon the state" by educating young women in the "principles of Liberty, Free government and obligations of patriotism." The academy did not focus on fashionable accomplishments but offered courses in chemistry, natural and intellectual philosophy, botany, Latin, mythology, and history.[25]

Evangelicals derided the frivolity and finery associated with elite women and enforced a strict moral code at the academy.[26] Students regularly attended religious services and were required to dress plainly without "beads, jewelry, artificial flowers, curls, feathers, or any superfluous decoration." They also were not allowed to attend "balls, dancing parties, theatrical performances, or festive entertainments." For evangelical women, the choice of a bonnet or a dress and the selection of hairstyles or jewelry were symbolically laden markers distinguishing them from the unconverted. Revolutionary patriots had imbued popular British imports with political meaning in order to launch a powerful moral critique of colonial society. In a similar vein, evangelicals used the language of goods to distinguish religious women from their worldly sisters. The language of goods linked women's personal decisions about dress and deportment to larger ideological and theological precepts.[27] The Elizabeth Female Academy, which operated for over twenty-five years until the state capital moved from Washington to Jackson, contributed to the emergence of women's culture and encouraged the establishment of other women's denominational colleges across the state.

Evangelicals took pride in their commitment to women's education; in 1860, for example, Methodists boasted: "Our church has been foremost in this country in urging and sustaining . . . Female Education." Women's schools played an important role in fostering close lifelong relationships among women outside the family circle. The institutions also contributed to the emergence of an evangelical women's culture. Increasing educational opportunities and higher literacy rates for women brought them into a larger literate culture and gave them access to the expanding religious press, where women's views could find their way into public print. Women who attended the institutions might spend part of their leisure time as did Sophia Hays, who filled pages of her journal with theological commentaries and lengthy scriptural discourses. For Hays, meditations were an important part of self-examination; she wrote, "Oh how much I desire to be enlightened in the truth by the Spirit." Maria Davies engaged in the same process of "self-fashioning" through her extensive diary filled with meditations on books she had read. The evangelical press, which encouraged women to read widely and keep abreast of the issues of the day, recognized the importance of its female audience with regular women's columns and prescriptive literature on proper women's roles. Through the evangelical press, Mississippi women were exposed to the ideas of national women reformers like Boston editor Sarah J. Hale.[28]

Evangelicalism also played a significant role in nurturing female literacy through Sunday schools and tract and Bible societies. Both Sophia Hays and Maria Davies took their love of learning and reading to others by teaching Sunday school classes for young girls. As people of the Word, evangelicals encouraged all converts to read and interpret Scripture for themselves, and the Bible was the most common book to be found in homes across the South.[29]

Learned, pious women sought ways to use their talents in the public sphere. Their churches supported their efforts to an extent; a Methodist newspaper, for example, favored women's education and encouraged the church to find outlets for talented women: "If we undertake to educate our women, let us also . . . see that they have a field for their energy." Women did not wait for others to find that field; they moved to create opportunities for themselves. The gender segregation so common in evangelical churches encouraged the creation of homosocial religious associations and benevolent societies. The Natchez Orphan Asylum was organized by an ambitious group of almost one hundred well-connected Protestant women in 1816 through the Female Charitable Society, which had as its objectives "supporting a Charity School, and . . . maintaining poor orphans and widows." The women elected a body of female officers and managers. Although education was the primary object of the society, orphan care quickly became their chief concern. Given the regular outbreaks of yellow fever and other diseases, high mortality rates, and a mobile population, children in Natchez were frequently orphaned. The society also hired a Baptist minister to teach a charity school, which opened with ten pupils.[30]

The chief difficulty confronting the society was financial instability, and the women endeavored through a variety of public means to put the society on firm financial footing. Anxious "to accumulate a steady and permanent fund" in order to build and support an orphan asylum, they purchased bank stocks and solicited the county to help defray the expenses that would have normally fallen on the local government. Cleverly employing many of the tenets associated with republicanism and republican motherhood to justify their work, the women asserted, "The object of the Society is to confer the benefit of moral and religious instruction, to arrest profligacy, to cherish virtue, to strengthen the feeble, as well as to bestow the tender guardianship of a parent on the bereaved orphan."[31]

After a few years, the society laid plans to construct an orphanage, and the women successfully sought a legislative act of incorporation in 1819. The society, with its female trustees and managers, was "created a body politic" by the legislature's act. The society's managers negotiated a property purchase and bought a building that was moved onto their lot in 1821. A year later they sold the property for a larger lot and contracted for the construction of a house for twelve orphans. In their continuing efforts to make the society solvent, the women petitioned the state legislature for funds: "For nearly nine years they have struggled with various difficulties & distress—they have begged & borrowed—bought and sold, and their sole object has been . . . to protect, sustain, & instruct the helpless and hopeless orphan." Presbyterian and Episcopal ministers wrote in their favor, and the legislature responded with a grant of five hundred dollars. The managers continued to invest in bank stocks, but dividends and the state grant proved insufficient to cover expenses. They raised additional funds through contributions, chiefly from Natchez women. They successfully solicited other state grants, and in 1830 the legislature appropriated all license fees and fines for billiard tables—which brought in four to eight hundred dollars annually—to the society. By the 1850s, the old building was crowded and needed repair. The society purchased "a very desirable location in the Northern suburbs of the city" in 1852 and later built a structure there.[32]

The women's impressive financial dealings led them to state incorporation; to service as managers, trustees, and fund-raisers; to property ownership; to a variety of contractual obligations; and to successful efforts to petition the state legislature for funding. The women maintained complete control over the society throughout the antebellum period, at a time when women in other parts of the South saw their authority in similar charitable enterprises diminish as men took more and more responsibilities from them. The significance of their independence was not lost on their contemporaries. In 1855, Presbyterian minister

Joseph B. Stratton delivered the annual address to the society, in which he observed:

> The most interesting fact connected with the Institution, is that, it was originally established and has always been conducted by the ladies of Natchez. It is strictly and emphatically their enterprise. It has been a successful one, and stands to-day, in the maturity of its usefulness, looking down upon the wrecks of many a scheme projected by the other sex, which, after promising golden profits to the country, and absorbing millions of dollars . . . has ended in a disastrous abortion. . . . The Orphan Asylum has been handed down from mother to daughter through three generations of the females of Natchez. There are members of the present board of Managers, whose grandmothers, served in the first board ever elected.[33]

A group of learned and pious women had established a benevolent enterprise that functioned for the larger community, but it also served as an important outlet for the energies and talents of three generations of antebellum Natchez women. The founders carved out a public space that future generations not only maintained but expanded at a time when such activity was becoming increasingly difficult. The orphanage, a monument to their efforts, continues to this day to be administered by Natchez women.

While the Natchez Female Charitable Society was the most ambitious women's benevolent society in the state, smaller women's religious groups appeared in towns and villages across Mississippi. Baptist women began to organize after the Baptist Board of Foreign Missions sent a missionary to the Mississippi Territory in 1816. By 1822, the Ladies Charitable Mission Society operated as an auxiliary to the Mississippi Baptist Missionary and Education Society. The Ladies Charitable Mission Society's constitution reflected evangelical hostility to ladies of fashion by opening membership to "any female who wishe[d] to do good . . . by subscribing to the constitution, and paying annually in advance, in money, or in articles of clothing, or even in superfluous ornaments." Methodist and Presbyterian women also organized in the 1820s, and women's societies were among the largest donors to the state Methodist Conference and to the Mississippi Baptist Convention.[34]

Other women's church groups raised funds to build churches and parsonages or to furnish buildings, and their annual suppers and fairs became regular activities across the state. Church women in Port Gibson, for example, "closed a bargain with Dr. Martin giving him $2500 for his residence." "The bargain is a pretty hard one," a male observer wrote, "but I think they have done well in making the purchase." The women paid $1,074 up front, the church donated $272, and the women planned to raise the balance through "sewing and suppers." The writer made it clear that the women made these decisions themselves, and given the paltry donation from the church, it is not surprising that they were able to do so. Methodist women in Columbus "set themselves to work to purchase a parsonage . . . a brick home surrounded with forest trees. . . . They [were] to pay $3500.00 for the house & lot—and ha[d] already raised a large portion of the money." They were so successful that the minister was able to move in within a couple of months. By the late 1830s, cotton towns like Columbus supported a wide variety of women's groups; women "maintained three Sunday Schools, three ladies' sewing societies, a Bible society, a foreign mission society, and a temperance society."[35]

Episcopal women organized later, but by the 1850s they were an active force in the small but influential denomination. The first Episcopal service in Aberdeen was held in 1839, and the parish was formally organized in the late 1840s. One of its members, Jane Martin Dalton, wanted to build a church and enlisted the women's sewing circle. The ambitious and capable Dalton had previously founded St. James Church in Livingston, Alabama, before moving to Aberdeen. The circle raised twelve hundred dollars, and the cornerstone for the church was laid in 1851. Dalton died before the church was completed, but a replica image of the building was chiseled on her tombstone. Bishop William Mercer Green later recognized her as the "chief founder" of the church. Women were also instrumental in organizing the Episcopal Church in Columbus in 1847; the church rector reported that the church had "only 12 communicants, the most of them women." Episcopal priest Edward Fontaine preached in the Masonic hall in Aberdeen and reported: "The ladies appropriated the proceeds of their sewing society towards putting the room . . . in good repair . . . the sum is something more than $100.00."[36] Women created societies that drew on the roles prescribed for them; sewing, for example, was clearly a domestic activity well within accepted boundaries, but they pushed the boundaries by raising substantial funds that made them important contributors to and even leaders in the larger process of institution building.

Jane Dalton's family attempted to perpetuate the memory of her church work by writing it in stone; that such an effort was necessary relates to a problem identified in Suzanne Lebsock's study of Petersburg, Virginia, women. She found that "the most striking feature of the records left by the men of the white churches is their persistent failure to acknowledge women's collective contributions." That yawning gap in the historical record has led many women's historians to underestimate the prevalence of women's religious organizations in the South. Scholars as diverse as Jean Friedman, Elizabeth Fox-Genovese, and Stephanie McCurry contend that the few women's groups in the antebellum

South were only in urban areas. The South's rural character and its slave-based, patriarchal society confined women to the household. Friedman, Fox-Genovese, and McCurry all have a larger, legitimate point: southern women did not take the same path as their northern sisters, and southern women's organizations did not follow a "feminist-Whig" trajectory leading from benevolence to the women's rights movement. As Lebsock notes, however, women's contributions to southern religion need not be downplayed to make the point.[37]

Ministers and other churchmen might well have attempted to limit women's public participation in worship services or to gain some measure of control over women's organizations, but there were limits to what they could do. Women were often instrumental in organizing churches and facilitating the preachers' work. Women carved out an important space for themselves in their organizations, and the significance of their role cannot be overestimated. Their public confessions of faith, their prayers and exhortations, their role as voting members, and their active participation in discipline were all part of the process of "representation," what philosopher Hannah Arendt termed "distinction": the ability to speak publicly for oneself, to lead, and to judge and be judged for one's words and actions. Self-representation, visibility, and active participation, Arendt claimed, were the hallmarks of a public life and a civil identity.[38]

Historians who characterize women's involvement in church life as highly circumscribed and lacking moral authority or a sense of a women's culture are slighting the fundamental realities of women's religious lives.[39] Women literally found a public sphere in churches, a physical setting for their interactions with other women and with men. As women immersed themselves in their faith, read and interpreted the Scriptures, and filled diaries and journals with their meditations on the weightiest theological questions, they engaged in a critical process of self-fashioning. Self-actualization naturally led them to seek the counsel and friendship of like-minded women outside the family circle and across generational lines. Pious, learned women gained the respect of other women, ministers, and male church members who prized their spiritual gifts. Over time, however, it became increasingly difficult for women to publicly exercise their gifts in worship services. Although early evangelicals challenged the gender conventions that confined women to the domestic sphere and assaulted fashionable accomplishments in favor of learning, piety, and a life of religious activity, as evangelicals moved up the socioeconomic ladder and embraced and defended slavery, they largely abandoned their attacks on prevailing gender conventions. Women's public role in services declined as ambitious ministers carved out larger roles for themselves and cemented their alliances with the planter elite. Women's more circumscribed roles in worship services may well have encouraged them to work more closely with one another. As they resisted men's attempts to reduce their roles in church work, they channeled their efforts in ways that contributed to an emerging women's religious culture.

Through the churches' homosocial prayer meetings, class meetings, and other segregated services, women forged a separate religious culture—a sense of Christian sisterhood—that propelled them into their work in benevolent and charitable societies. As Lebsock notes, uncovering the often hidden female organizations that proliferated throughout the antebellum South is essential to recreating the "public female sphere" that emerged. In such organizations, women could "connect purposefully" to the larger community while creating a community of their own. Benevolent and charitable organizations took women further into the public sphere, expanded the space they were able to occupy, and involved them in activities generally regarded as the preserve of men. Through their fundraising efforts, they literally built the churches and parsonages of Mississippi, and they helped sustain their ministers, churches, religious schools, and denominational bodies.[40] Women did indeed make Protestantism possible in Mississippi and across the South.

NOTES

1. Donald Mathews, *Religion in the Old South* (Chicago: University of Chicago Press, 1977), 102. For a survey of the ongoing efforts to put women's contributions to Christianity in proper perspective, see Cullen Murphy, *The Word according to Eve: Women and the Bible in Ancient Times and Our Own* (Boston: Houghton Mifflin, 1998), Elizabeth S. Fiorenza quoted on 16.

2. For an overview of the literature that discusses these changes, see Linda K. Kerber, "Separate Spheres, Female Worlds, Woman's Place: The Rhetoric of Women's History," *Journal of American History* 75 (June 1988): 9–39. For examples of recent works, see Nancy Isenberg, "'Pillars in the Same Temple and Priests of the Same Worship': Woman's Rights and the Politics of Church and State in Antebellum America," *Journal of American History* 85 (June 1998): 98–128; Christine Leigh Heyrman, *Southern Cross: The Beginnings of the Bible Belt* (New York: A. A. Knopf, 1997), esp. chap. 4.

3. Winans Autobiography, 33, Cain Archives, Millsaps College, Jackson, Mississippi (henceforth cited as Cain Archives); "An Old Letter," Recollections of Mrs. Ann Finlay, Eunice J. Stockwell Papers, Mississippi Department of Archives and History, Jackson (henceforth cited as MDAH); *New Orleans Christian Advocate*, March 31, 1855. A Spanish census of 1792 lists Margaret Stampley as head of her own household. Richard A. McLemore, *Mississippi Baptists, 1780–1970* (Jackson: University Press of Mississippi, 1971), 13.

4. Benjamin M. Drake, *A Sketch of the Life of Rev. Elijah Steele* (Cincinnati: Methodist Book Concern, 1843), 54; Unity Presbyterian records in Albert E. Casey, comp. *Amite County Mississippi,*

1699–1865 (Birmingham, Ala.: Amite County Historical Fund, 1948), 2:401–12; Jesse Laney Boyd, *A Popular History of the Baptists in Mississippi* (Jackson: Baptist Press, 1930), 145.

5. Samuel Sellers Diary, May 4, 1814; July 9, 1814; October 1, 1816, Cain Archives; Winans Autobiography, 172, Cain Archives.

6. *Mississippi Baptist*, October 28, 1858; Randy J. Sparks, *Religion in Mississippi* (Jackson: University Press of Mississippi, 2001), 58.

7. Timothy Flint, *Recollections of the Last Ten Years.* . . . (Boston: Cummings, Hilliard, 1826), 294; Heyrman, *Southern Cross*, 173–89.

8. Lorenzo Dow Langford Autobiography, 22, Cain Archives.

9. Winans Journal, February 18, 1821, Cain Archives.

10. John G. Jones, *Complete History of Methodism in the Mississippi Conference*, 2 vols. (Nashville: Publishing House of the M. E. Church, South, 1908), 2:295.

11. Ibid.; Winans to Benjamin Drake, August 25, 1851, Drake Papers, Cain Archives; *New Orleans Christian Advocate*, March 1, 1851.

12. For an example of the use of the term "Mothers of Israel," see Union Baptist Association, *Minutes of the Thirty-sixth Anniversary of the Union Baptist Association . . . 1856* (Jackson, Miss.: The Association, 1856), 12. See also Heyrman, *Southern Cross*, 146, 162, 168–70.

13. Jean Strickland, ed., *Autobiography of A. C. Ramsey* (n.p., n.d.), 56–57; Jones Autobiography, 217, MDAH.

14. Strickland, *Autobiography of A. C. Ramsey*, 106, 49; Jones Autobiography, 79.

15. Galilee Baptist Church Records, in Casey, *Amite County Mississippi*, 2:211; Rules of Decorum (1839), Enon Baptist Church Records, Special Collections, Mitchell Memorial Library, Mississippi State University, Starkville (henceforth cited as MSU). For other examples, see Line Creek and East Fork Baptist Church Records, in Casey, *Amite County Mississippi*, 2:54, 78. Bogue Chitto Baptist Church Records, September 1860, MSU.

16. On the importance of the vote in antebellum America, see Desley Deacon, "Politicizing Gender," *Genders* (Fall 1989): 1–19, quotations on 5; Jean H. Baker, *Affairs of Party: The Political Culture of Northern Democrats in the Mid-Nineteenth Century* (Ithaca, N.Y.: Cornell University Press, 1983), 261–316. On the prevalence of women voting, see Gregory A. Wills, *Democratic Religion: Freedom, Authority, and Church Discipline in the Baptist South, 1785–1900* (New York: Oxford University Press, 1997), 51–53.

17. East Fork records in Casey, comp., *Amite County Mississippi*, 2:53–55; Randy J. Sparks, *On Jordan's Stormy Banks: Evangelicalism in Mississippi, 1773–1876* (Athens: University of Georgia Press, 1994), 146–73; William Warren Sweet, "The Churches as Moral Courts of the Frontier," *Church History* 2 (March 1933): 3–21.

18. Sparks, *On Jordan's Stormy Banks*, 154–55.

19. Stephanie McCurry, *Masters of Small Worlds: Yeoman Households, Gender Relations, and the Political Culture of the Antebellum South Carolina Low Country* (New York: Oxford University Press, 1995), 184; Sparks, *On Jordan's Stormy Banks*, 156–57; Bethlehem Baptist Church Records, January 1845, June 1850, MSU; New Zion Baptist Church, July, August, September 1849, MSU.

20. Mt. Moriah Baptist Church, May, December 1860, MSU; Clear Creek Baptist Church, June 1837, February 1838, Southern Baptist Historical Collection, Mississippi College, Clinton (henceforth cited as SBHC); Fellowship Baptist Church, August 1839, SBHC; Mississippi Baptist Association, *A Republication of the Minutes of the Mississippi Baptist Association for One Hundred Years.* . . . (New Orleans: Mississippi Baptist Association, 1906), 164.

21. Synod of Mississippi and South Alabama, *Extracts from the Records of the Synod of Mississippi and South Alabama from 1829 to 1835* (Jackson: Clarion Steam, 1880), quotation on 423; Sparks, *On Jordan's Stormy Banks*, 161; Frederick A. Bode, "The Formation of Evangelical Communities in Middle Georgia: Twiggs County, 1820–1861," *Journal of Southern History* 60 (November 1994): 736–37.

22. *Mississippi Baptist*, June 24, 1858.

23. Sparks, *On Jordan's Stormy Banks*, 47–48; A. B. Amis Sr., *Recollections of Social Customs in Newton and Scott Counties, Mississippi: Fifty Years Ago* (Meridian, Miss.: Dement Printing, 1934), 5; Union Baptist Association, *Minutes*, 1856, 12; Rhys Isaac, *The Transformation of Virginia, 1740–1790* (Chapel Hill: University of North Carolina Press, 1982), 58–65; McCurry, *Masters of Small Worlds*, 176. Christopher Owen, in a study of Georgia Methodist churches, writes, "Methodist church design emphasized divisions of race and gender, but not those of class." Christopher H. Owen, *The Sacred Flame of Love: Methodism and Society in Nineteenth-Century Georgia* (Athens: University of Georgia Press, 1998), 20.

24. Ruth H. Bloch, "The Gendered Meanings of Virtue in Revolutionary America," *Signs: Journal of Women in Culture and Society* 13 (Autumn 1987): 37–58; Jan Lewis, "The Republican Wife: Virtue and Seduction in the Early Republic," *William and Mary Quarterly* 44 (October 1987): 689–72; Kerber, "Separate Spheres," 20.

25. Charles B. Galloway, "Elizabeth Female Academy—The Mother of Female Colleges," *Publications of the Mississippi Historical Society* 2 (1899): 169–78; *Natchez Gazette*, March 11, 1826, article transcript in Elizabeth Female Academy subject file, MDAH.

26. Galloway, "Elizabeth Female Academy," 169–78; Sparks, *On Jordan's Stormy Banks*, 55–57; Mathews, *Religion in the Old South*, 111; Catherine Clinton, *Plantation Mistress: Women's World in the Old South* (New York: Pantheon Books, 1982), 130–32.

27. Galloway, "Elizabeth Female Academy," 177; Mathews, *Religion in the Old South*, 111; T. H. Breen, "'Baubles of Britain': The American and Consumer Revolutions of the Eighteenth Century," *Past and Present* 119 (May 1988): 73–104.

28. *New Orleans Christian Advocate*, April 2, 1853; quotation from February 6, 1860; *Mississippi Baptist*, March 10, 1860; *Tennessee Baptist*, June 1, 1848; *Southwestern Religious Luminary*, December 1836; Sophia Hays Diary, March 15, 1858, 7, Hays-Ray-Webb Collection, MSU; Mary Kelly, "Reading Women/Women Reading: The Making of Learned Women in Antebellum America," *Journal of American History* 83 (September 1996): 415–16.

29. Sophia Hays Diary, March 13, 1858, 7; *New Orleans Christian Advocate*, May 5, 1855; Amite and Florida Auxiliary Bible Society Minutes, August 1, 1818, MDAH; Ryan, "Reading Women/Women Reading," 404; First Methodist Church Records, Fourth Conference of 1838, MSU. An agent of the Amite and Florida Bible Society reported that he visited 262 families and found only 37 without Bibles; another visited 292 families and found 51 without Bibles. See the society's report in the *Liberty Advocate*, September 11, 1839. The Reverend Benjamin Chase, an agent for the American Bible Society in Adams County, reported that one-fourth of the families he visited were without Bibles. See "The Life of the Reverend Benjamin Chase, As Recorded in His Own Hand. . . . ," Rev. J. Whitner Kennedy Papers, 7, 12, MDAH.

30. Natchez Orphan Asylum, *Annual Report of the Managers and Officers of the Natchez Orphan Asylum. . . .* (Natchez: Natchez Orphan Asylum, 1855), 9–13.

31. Ibid., 14.

32. "An Act to Incorporate the Female Charitable Society of Natchez," February 12, 1819; "Petition from the Managers of Female Charitable Society of Natchez," January 8, 1825, both in Official

Archives of the State of Mississippi Legislature, vol. 321, MDAH; Natchez Orphan Asylum *Annual Report*, 4, 15, 20–24. For example, seven of eighteen donors from 1855 were men. Natchez Orphan Asylum Records, Natchez Trace Collection, Center for American History, University of Texas, Austin; Sparks, *On Jordan's Stormy Banks*, 52.

33. Natchez Orphan Asylum, *Annual Report*, 25.

34. Mississippi Baptist State Convention, *Second Annual Report . . . 1824* (Natchez: Free Trader Office, 1825), 3; Mississippi Baptist State Convention, *Proceedings of a Meeting . . . December, 1836* (Natchez: Free Trader Office, 1837), 21; Woman's Missionary Union of Mississippi, *Hearts the Lord Opened: The History of Mississippi Women's Missionary Union* (Jackson: Women's Missionary Union of Mississippi, 1954), 13, 14–18, 21.

35. J. to "Dear Doctor," April 14 [1850s], Charles B. Dana Papers, MDAH; James Adair Lyon Journal, October–December, 1854, MSU; *Mississippi Baptist*, April 14 and 28, 1859; November 3, 1859; John Hebron Moore, *The Emergence of the Cotton Kingdom: Mississippi, 1770–1860* (Baton Rouge: Louisiana State University Press, 1988), 199–200; Sparks, *On Jordan's Stormy Banks*, 54.

36. James L. Sykes, "A History of Saint John's Parish, Aberdeen, Mississippi," undated manuscript in Rollins Collection; Fontaine Journal, January 30, April 21, July 5, and December 13, 1848; "The Folly and danger of the idolatrous love of The Praise of Men," Fontaine Sermons, all at MSU.

37. Suzanne Lebsock, *The Free Women of Petersburg: Status and Culture in a Southern Town, 1784–1860* (New York: W. W. Norton, 1984), 216–17, 224–25, 197; Jean E. Friedman, *The Enclosed Garden: Women and Community in the Evangelical South, 1830–1900* (Chapel Hill: University of North Carolina Press, 1985), 19–20; Elizabeth Fox-Genovese, *Within the Plantation Household: Black and White Women of the Old South* (Chapel Hill: University of North Carolina Press, 1988), 70, 80–81; McCurry, *Masters of Small Worlds*, 190–91.

38. Mathews, *Religion in the Old South*, 102. Historian Nancy Isenberg uses Arendt's ideas in "Pillars in the Same Temple," 102–3.

39. McCurry, *Masters of Small Worlds*, 171–207, see esp. 190–91; Friedman, *Enclosed Garden*, chaps. 1–3.

40. Estelle Freedman, "Separatism as Strategy: Female Institution Building and American Feminism, 1870–1930," *Feminist Studies* 5 (Fall 1979): 512–29, first quotation on 513; Nancy F. Cott, *The Bonds of Womanhood: "Woman's Sphere" in New England, 1780–1835* (New Haven, Conn.: Yale University Press, 1977), 200, 125, 70, 173–74, 197, 205, second quotation on 173.

Naked before the Law

Married Women and the Servant Ideal in Antebellum Natchez

JOYCE L. BROUSSARD

An old English folktale tells of "smock marriages" in which the bride, dressed in a white shirt or chemise or sometimes with no covering at all (*puris natu-ralibus*), takes her connubial vows symbolically unencumbered by any property or attachments. This ritual, for which there also exists some evidence in colo-nial New England, supported the belief that a fully clothed (indebted) bride rendered the groom liable for her indebtedness. Conversely, if a wealthy but symbolically naked woman married an indebted or impoverished man, his creditors could not use her property to satisfy their claims. A casual observer consequently could not tell whether the bride's nudity symbolized wealth or poverty.[1]

No such smock marriage ceremonies occurred in the antebellum Natchez District, perhaps the wealthiest enclave of slave-plantation agriculture in the lower South.[2] This is not to say, however, that the issue of indebted or wealthy brides, widows, and divorcees was of little importance to the free women and men of the area—or to the enslaved persons owned by them. Indeed, so many penniless bachelors on the make arrived in the wealthy frontier community of Natchez after 1800 that certain marriage practices emerged in custom, law, and judicial decisions to protect the real and personal property of Mississippi brides, many of whose birth families had acquired substantial estates and slaves during the late Spanish colonial and early U.S. eras.[3] In the early nineteenth century, these legal protections took the forms of pre- and postnuptial mar-riage contracts or settlements, dower rights—by which a widow claimed at least one-third of her husband's estate at his death—and divorce provisions in territorial and state law. In 1839, the state added the Married Women's Property Act, which allowed married women to register personal and real properties as separate estates, meaning that wives alone legally controlled the registered items.[4]

At least in theory, such legal provisions and practices afforded significant autonomy for married women at a time and in a region in which the basic "givens" reflected a patriarchal legal code rooted in English common law and reinforced by civil statutes, male privilege, and a slave-based social hierarchy. When free white married women (*femes covert*) in the Natchez environs went to court to divorce or to contest claims to properties held in dower or in separate estates, they were fully aware of the limitations imposed on them by societal constructions of gender as well as of their equity rights as married women in law and judicial precedent. Guardedly committed to the prevailing ideology of what can be called the "servant ideal," these married women honored a principle of social cohesion to which all members of society were expected to adhere.[5] The "servant ideal" placed male heads of households as protectors (paternalists) of those subordinate to them in the social hierarchy and encouraged women to expect proper consideration and just treatment from the men around them, especially spouses, fathers, and judicial authorities.

Although a significant number of free white married women used the available legal instruments and the prevailing legal culture to circumvent many of the disabilities of coverture (the legal condition of a married woman), they did so without challenging the servant ideal or by demanding outright equality with men. Instead, Natchez married women demanded equity rights as women socially and politically subordinate to their husbands but legally equal to them in certain specifically identified circumstances recognized in law (prenuptial contracts, dower rights, and the Married Women's Property Act) and judicial verdicts (divorce). The judicial system in Mississippi and much of the South provided the institutional means for addressing such equity rights in chancery courts, which adjudicated issues of fairness and justice for married women on a case-by-case basis.[6] This essay examines the ways women in the Natchez District of the lower South used prevailing laws and the legal climate of the day to strengthen their positions in a patriarchal, slaveholding society.

Of the various legal measures available to married women, prenuptial contracts provided the most effective means by which Natchez women could retain their family property after marriage. In the Natchez jurisdiction, eighty-two marriage contracts were listed from 1799 to 1860, over 70 percent of which were negotiated in the thirty-year period following statehood, 1818 to 1848. Without a prenuptial contract, the husband owned any assets his wife brought to the marriage. Prenuptial contracts, on the other hand, typically specified assets to be retained by the bride and usually presented detailed instructions as to the rights of the bride or her designated agents to manage properties in her interest.[7]

Some agreements limited the contractual stipulations to a term of years, typically ending with the birth of a second child, and were obviously predicated on the assumption that children and the passage of time would reveal the husband's worthiness. Often contracts constrained husbands from having any say over the wife's inherited or gifted properties. Others allowed husbands to manage the estates in trust, meaning that they would supervise but not profit from the estates. More than a few prenuptial settlements involved the assets of dead husbands, with the widows using the contracts to protect their children by separating inherited property from their new husbands' property. Almost all the contracts were between women of wealth (principally inherited from fathers) and less-well-to-do grooms. Only one appears to have been initiated by a husband, although some—usually cases involving second marriages—included stipulations protective of both parties.[8]

The law allowed married women a measure of equality with men in property matters by means of prenuptial settlements, but virtually all the contracts placed the power of managing their properties, especially slaves, in the hands of husbands or male agents. The issue was not one of absolute equality with the husband but rather one of safeguarding the wife's interests as defined by her male protectors. In no case did a wife with a living husband assume sole management of her own property, but most contracts, especially those arranged by fathers for their daughters, allowed for such a possibility.[9]

In the period under review, only twenty-eight married women released their dower rights—the provision in law that protects from creditors a widow's claim, usually one-third of the husband's holdings—in separate instruments before the court. Almost always they set aside dower claims in order for the property under dower to be used as collateral for loans assumed by both marriage partners or to clear title to lands in a property sale. In these instances, the wife signed a statement under oath asserting her free and willful choice in the matter as an independent woman. Frequently, too, widows released dower rights in selling properties as executrixes of their husbands' estates by written attachments to deeds of sale. Sometimes a widow released her dower claim—required by state law—in order to take the larger share of inheritance specified in her husband's will.[10]

Perhaps more importantly, married women who survived their husbands usually obtained their dower rights as widows regardless of the claims of creditors. State legislators in the early 1840s limited a widow's dower claim to a lifetime grant to prevent a surviving wife from willfully passing the properties on to her children or other heirs unmindful of her husband's wishes or the rights of his offspring to the property, but there were ways of getting around such strictures. Mary F. Dunbar, for example, resorted to a common maneuver in acquiring property in excess of that allowed her in dower by her wealthy husband, William Dunbar. In a complicated arrangement, the widow Dunbar, acting as her children's custodian, relinquished dower rights to unwanted properties in order to sell them. Then, acting again as custodian, she purchased at public auction full title for herself and her children to her home, Forest Plantation. She was the only bidder that day on the courthouse steps, and her brother acted as executor. No other bidder stepped up because Mary Dunbar would not have relinquished her dower rights to anyone but her children and herself, as their custodian.[11]

In other cases, women leased their dower holdings and lived off the rents. Sometimes they transferred their property directly to the children who would one day inherit it and then purchased the property back for themselves, thereby acquiring property not willed to them directly. Such cases usually occurred when husbands died unexpectedly without wills. Mississippi's dower law enabled women of property to survive as independent heads of households despite their husbands' business failures or the lack of male relatives to shoulder family responsibilities.[12]

The need for married women's property legislation emerged during the national banking crisis of 1837, which threatened household stability and the prevailing social order in the slave-based, speculative cotton economy of Mississippi. The Married Women's Property Act of 1839, passed in response to the wave of bankruptcies, may have been designed in part to enable bankrupt husbands to protect their assets by transferring them to their wives. In passing the bill, however, the legislature eliminated all such debt relief provisions, suggesting that the law's final character reflected principally the desire of wealthy fathers to shield gifts to daughters with less-than-successful husbands. Additional legislation in the 1840s and 1850s, which certainly weakened the legal hold of husbands over the inherited estates of their wives, enabled married women in Mississippi to sign contracts and deeds, manage their holdings independently, and retain profits earned from separate estates.[13]

Although the separate-estate law in Mississippi was not conceived to lift women to equality with men, its unsettling potential set off a clamorous debate that raised the dire specter of a gender revolution.[14] The Jackson *Southern Sun*, for example, saw its passage as the first step on the road to woman suffrage.[15]

In reality, the debate had less to do with liberating married women than with fear of throwing them to marketplace wolves. The law's principal critic, state senator Spencer Monroe Grayson, a Natchez lawyer and planter, attacked the bill for undermining the protected position of women in the social order.[16] He presented his senatorial colleagues with a clear choice: "If you degrade and disgrace all that is lovely in women, pass this bill; but if you would sustain them firmly in the high and exalted eminence which they now occupy in the eyes of the world and of men, spurn and reject this bill, as one of the most unholy and fraudulent devices ever presented.[17]

In Grayson's mind, giving married women unchecked say over their property might transform them into businesswomen not unlike those creditors resented by the bill's supporters. Rather than sheltering women from male-dominated market forces, the legislation would force them to abandon their femininity in order to compete with men in the rough and often abusive economic arena. For Grayson, females were ill equipped physiologically and temperamentally to function effectively as the masters of slaves or competitors with superior males; they stood little chance of surviving in the market and establishing security for themselves and their families.

The section of the bill enabling women to own enslaved people as separate personal property especially disturbed Grayson and his supporters; it introduced "a degree of indelicacy unheard of in any country."[18] Grayson shared the common commitment of southern whites to a race-based hierarchical social order in which the bottom rung (slaves) posed a pervasive danger to the upper rungs. In order for white women and children to live safely within the racial hierarchy, firm top-down discipline of the enslaved was required. Placing women, who were physically unable to enforce racial discipline, in charge of slaves threatened the community with social chaos. What is more, because of the ever-present sexual dynamics between women and men of both races, allowing women to function as masters exposed them to great personal danger from male slaves. In raising the issue, Grayson had invoked the cultural symbols of chivalry, white supremacy, and paternalism on which the ideology of southern mastery rested. He had also touched on the deep-seated sexual tensions used by masters to justify both the enslavement of blacks and the dependency of white women.[19]

The bill's supporters, led by Thomas Hadley, a down-on-his-luck planter and slaveholder, argued that the separate-estate law would strengthen protection for married women by securing "to man's dearest idol (his wife) the possession of the property which they have acquired by their own exertion or the liberty of a fond father." As they saw it, daughters and wives would be better protected from the masculine gyrations of the marketplace by separating them from it altogether. By shielding married women from the business errors of their husbands, the new law would provide wives a safe refuge, much as the widow's dower did for women whose husbands died without wills. It was also seen as the just thing to do, especially for women who had inherited or earned their own property. Supporters like Hadley, calling forth the full symbolic power of the South's commitment to a protective and benevolent social order, especially emphasized the paternalistic features on which the law was based: "Is there a wish of such gross injustice in the mind of any man that he would withhold from women the shield of protection which this bill proposes?"[20]

This defense of the bill as protecting the sanctity of the household by sheltering property owned separately by wives possibly tipped the scale of support in its favor. Nevertheless, the bill was quickly amended upon passage by the introduction of language that barred husbands from transferring any threatened or mismanaged properties to their wives. As a result, property held by husbands (pursued by creditors or not) could not be shifted easily or at all to spouses, except by subterfuge subject to court action. This amendment to the bill strengthened its appeal to those opposed to it as a means of defrauding creditors.[21]

The fear that separate estates might force married women to dirty their hands with slave management also produced quick results. State legislators added a clause requiring husbands of women owning slaves as separate estates to assume management and supervision of the slaves for their wives' benefit. It seemed a reasonable, practical step in view of the many widowed, divorced, and unmarried female heads of households whose slaves were managed by fathers, brothers, and sons. It certainly protected white women, both legally and actually, from the messy business of slavery.[22]

The much-weakened Married Women's Property Act found no takers of record in the Natchez District in the initial years after its passage in 1839. The legislature amended the law in 1846 by requiring married women to register their separate estate properties within six months of the amended law's enactment or the acquisition of new estates or assets. Only forty-six married women in Adams County, the heart of the Natchez District, completed the necessary circuit court paperwork between 1846 and 1860. Eighteen of them listed real estate, and thirty-five of them registered slaves. In most cases, the enslaved were house servants (usually women), and almost all the real properties registered came from parents setting up separate estates for their daughters. In a few cases, fathers of already married daughters used the separate-estate law to strengthen prenuptial marriage contracts; others used the law to transfer properties as

gifts in cases where no marriage contracts had been signed. For women about
to be married, the separate-estate law enabled fathers to forego the prenuptial
contract and to deed property later to their married daughters independent of
their husbands' consent, a distinctively new and potentially empowering feature. Those fathers of prospective brides who doubted the character or promise
of their future sons-in-law continued to use the marriage contract rather than
the separate-estate law as the best means for safeguarding family properties and
ensuring the welfare of married daughters and grandchildren.[23]

Personal items, many of sentimental value, comprised the majority of entries
listed in the registration books. China cabinets, bedroom furnishings, kitchen-
ware, silver, books, clothing, trinkets, jewelry, and other assorted household
materials overshadow (by their magnitude) the few listings of real property or
slaves. Under common law, wives held no claim to personalty after marriage,
and such items were not typically included in marriage contracts or agreements.
The registration of personal items appears to have been the major accomplishment of the law, although it is possible that women registered separate estates of
more substantial value in the years from 1841 to 1845, for which no records are
extant. The absence, however, of any legal challenges to such registrations by
creditors in the local courts or before the state high court of appeals suggests that
few women used the law as protection from creditors prior to the Civil War.[24]

Practically, the limited nature of the separate-estate law did little to empower
women, but it was a useful companion to pre- and postnuptial contracts, dower
rights, and inheritance practices and laws in protecting married women from
the vagaries of the marketplace and the business failures of their spouses. The
new law also strengthened a married woman's legal hold on property given to
her after marriage and registered without the consent of the husband—which
was not the case in marriage settlements. That so few women registered significant amounts of property as separate estates indicates that most families used
the traditional means of wills, dower rights, and marriage contracts to safe-
guard assets. In most cases those women who registered separate estates listed
personal, real, and chattel properties gifted (rather than earned) to them before
or after the marriage from doting parents. Although those women who registered separate estates stood fully clothed before the law in the sense that they
could dispose of the property as they wished, none used the law aggressively
to separate themselves from the men who had power over them. Most women
considered themselves partners with their husbands, and they freely used their
registered property to support their family's needs when required.

Separate estates as well as marriage contracts and dower rights were available to all married women, but those of the lower and middling classes seldom

used them because they had little property to protect, inherit, or secure. They looked instead to divorce laws to protect themselves and their assets and to secure their rights. Divorce differed, however, from the other legal devices protecting married women because it transformed them wholly into single women (*femes sole*) unconstrained by the legal disabilities of coverture. So great was the potential of legal separation and divorce for empowerment and autonomy that many free white women from all social strata in the district resorted to dissolving their marriages in the years after statehood, especially when their spouses had been abusive or unfaithful.

In the sixty years prior to the Civil War, Mississippi moved the power of granting divorce from the legislature to chancery courts of equity and expanded grounds for divorce.[25] Liberalization of divorce in Mississippi followed a pattern similar to that in other states.[26] By 1860, extreme cruelty, habitual drunkenness, penitentiary imprisonment for two years or more, insanity (or idiocy at the time of marriage), and incest had been added to the earlier list of bigamy, impotence, adultery, and desertion as legal grounds for dissolving a marriage. In those cases where judges suspected subterfuge or collusion between the petitioning couple, the court could uphold the marriage bond or grant legal separations—called divorces from bed-and-board—which prohibited remarriage. In a step that diminished the distinction between divorce and separation, the legislature in 1853 began granting permanent divorce after three years of bed-and-board separation as a matter of routine rather than of formal litigation.[27]

Did the Married Women's Property Act affect the rate or character of divorce? Since marriage with a dowry and the laws of coverture constituted an important means of capital formation for southern white males, husbands probably had less reason to wed once dowries and the family property of the wife's father no longer came under their total control. Divorce possibly became more attractive to married women after the separate-estate law was enacted because women could take their individual estates with them as divorced women. Husbands, too, had similar incentives for disrupting those marriages based principally on sentiment rather than on capital formation once the sentiment had waned and the wife's inherited property was registered separately. Perhaps men had less inclination to marry physically unattractive women once husbands could exercise less control of spousal properties and assets.[28]

An investigation of divorce proceedings for the Natchez District indicates that such conjecture about the impact of the Married Women's Property Act on the frequency of divorce is unsupported by evidence. In fact, fewer divorces were filed in the years after the law's enactment; in the twenty years prior to 1839, ninety-three divorce actions were presented compared to sixty-seven between 1839 and 1860. Even though the judicial district had become smaller over the years, the population had increased enough to offset the difference. When the beginning date is pushed back to 1801—the inauguration of the territorial era—115 divorces were filed between that date and 1839.[29]

In the two decades prior to 1839, more women than men claimed to be the aggrieved spouse in divorces: fifty-six women compared to thirty-seven men. For the twenty years after 1839, when the grounds for divorce were expanded, fifty-three women initiated divorce actions compared to fourteen men, meaning that the absolute number of women suing for divorce remained about the same in both periods. The real change came in the relatively small number of men who petitioned for divorce in the years after the Married Women's Property Act. Women of the Natchez District, in other words, were as likely to divorce their husbands in the later era as in the earlier years, whereas men backed away from court intervention over time. Husbands might have avoided divorcing wives who held property in separate estates, but the evidence that few women actually registered separate estates points to other factors.[30]

Divorces examined before and after the passage of the Married Women's Property Act make clear that married women in the Natchez District well understood their moral and legal rights and customarily approached the bench determined to protect themselves and their families. Of fifty-five Mississippi divorce cases between 1789 and 1817, twenty-three of them initiated by women, forty-two were granted. By the time of statehood, several dozen Mississippi women had sued successfully for divorce, and most of them had filed their petitions in the Natchez District, home to the lion's share of the state's white population.[31]

In an early suit for redress that might have ended in a divorce suit had the husband lived, the widow Sophia Elliott argued that her dead husband had attempted when living to defraud her of her property. Widow Elliott charged in 1823 that her husband, without her knowledge, had sold property in the 1790s jointly held under Spanish law. Local planter William Green purchased the contested land from Don Carlos De Grand Pré, a wealthy and influential Spanish government official who had acquired the property originally from James Elliot, "without the consent or concurrence of [the] said oratrix, or without her joining in the conveyance or being in any wise privy thereto." Sophia Elliot based her claim on her legal standing under Spanish law, which she argued provided civil rights to married women unavailable under Mississippi laws of coverture. She most likely had waited until her husband's death to confront the issue because defrauding one's wife of her property was not grounds for divorce in Mississippi. Although she settled out of court with the Green family, the fact that Elliot had confronted the issue at all indicates how mindful were some of the district's women of their moral if not legal rights to equity.[32]

The large majority of antebellum divorce cases in the Natchez District involved issues of desertion and adultery—the traditional grounds for divorce encoded in state law since 1820. These grounds were also used in petitions initiated by men. Many women sued by husbands for desertion had likely abandoned their spouses as the only means of achieving a (nonlegal) divorce for reasons not recognizable in law. Extreme cruelty was difficult to prove, for example, as was physical and mental abuse or lack of affection. Most but not all the divorces instigated by wives were filed by women of some property, who often sued for divorce to prevent their own financial ruin.[33]

Aggrieved wives sought divorces from the very beginning of the territorial era, but the language used changed noticeably over time. Once divorce petitions began to be adjudicated by an individual judge rather than by legislative committees, the need to personalize the issue and to address the judicial authority as the male protector of the servant ideal increased substantially. In most cases, women pleaded for independence from husbands for cause, contending that they had served their spouses faithfully. Their appeals typically spoke of the husband's failure to care for them in exchange for having shed the protective clothing of their birth families and their *feme sole* status through marriage. They pleaded for protection as faithful servants of the larger society by employing the language of servitude and speaking of equity and fairness. The female petitioners publicly solicited the court to acknowledge the injustice done to them as vulnerable, married women fully committed to the servant ideal, an ethos to which both spouses were expected to adhere.

Among the numerous divorces in the Natchez District were two telling examples. The petition filed by Susannah Sessions against her husband, William, involved prominent members of the plantation elite, a child bride, allegations of public humiliation, and mental instability. The case also contained the standard plea for justice by a woman who had dutifully embraced what amounted to the servant ideal in the most trying of circumstances. Married in 1830 at age thirteen or fourteen, Susannah Sessions, a member of the wealthy Bisland and Reucker families, gave birth to a son in 1838, a year before her divorce petition. Although no record of a prenuptial contract between the two parties can be found, she undoubtedly came to the marriage with a substantial dowry. Swearing under oath that she had always been a "dutiful and affectionate wife" who "fully regarded and obeyed the duties and obligations of the marriage state," the aggrieved Susannah petitioned for divorce in 1839 on the grounds that her husband, also a member of a prominent family, had "disregarded the peace and

happiness of the family" as well "as his own duty" as a husband by openly fre-
quenting "at diverse times Houses of ill fame and similar places of improper
resort, in the companionship of women of lewd and infamous character."[34]

Susannah testified under oath that her husband's dishonorable "disregard for
the solemnity of his marriage vows" had repeatedly occurred since the very
day of their marriage, and that he had committed adultery time and time again
with well-known prostitute and madam Elizabeth Lawrence, much to Susannah's public humiliation.[35] Because of his habitual public fornication with Lawrence and other prostitutes over two years, William's actions had, according
to the petition, "completely and entirely destroyed . . . the domestic peace and
happiness" as well as "blasted" all hope for future happiness.[36] Witnesses testified to William's immoral behavior, which he had exhibited openly and with no
thought of remorse. When William ignored his summons to court, Susannah's
divorce was granted. Although she had appealed to the court for "further relief
in the premises as [might] be agreeable to Equity," the divorce decree made
no mention of a property settlement, alimony, or custody of their son, Peter.
Susannah probably gained custody of the boy and retained lifetime residence
in their home, the typical resolution in uncontested divorces.[37]

Shortly after the divorce, the court, convinced that Susannah was mentally
incompetent, appointed her brother, James R. Bisland, as her legal guardian.
Although she probably had lost all her personal and jointly owned property
and profits to William, her net worth at the time of the divorce is not known
nor is the management role played by her brother. There is much more that
we do not know: to what extent William's open adultery contributed to Susannah's debilitated mental state, why eight years had elapsed between her marriage and the birth of her only child, the motivations of Williams Sessions, and
why Susannah's family allowed him to take her as his child bride.[38]

Susannah's divorce petition begged the court to restore the dignity of a
faithful, devoted, and obedient wife whose husband had continually refused
to uphold his family and community obligations. For Susannah, the issue was
public disgrace and the mental anguish caused by William's adultery. The production of witnesses, usually neighbors and relatives, meant that the abandonment and adultery had become public knowledge. Had William's dishonorable
actions been less visible, the court might have ignored them, but the public
hearings pressured the court to reiterate the responsibilities of husbands of the
master class to their wives.

Susannah Sessions requested her rights in equity without spelling out what
she wanted or detailing her husband's assets; her lawyers knew it would not be
good strategy to press, given the prominent social and economic status of both

families. It would be foolhardy to expect the court to punish William Sessions by depriving him of property that Susannah did not need for her own maintenance, and in fact the court passed over the equity issue altogether. Nor did the court act to punish the wayward husband (they could have forbidden him to marry again in Mississippi). Instead, the court granted Susannah's petition for divorce not because of the charges she made but because William Sessions had refused to answer the charges, which Natchez courts typically regarded as evidence of guilt.[39] Had she asked for property and alimony, William would likely have contested the divorce. Susannah petitioned for divorce because William had violated a basic tenant of the servant ideal: the right of devoted and loyal wives to enjoy at least the appearance of public respect due them as good and faithful servants.[40]

In contrast to Sessions, when Martha Tewksbury petitioned for divorce from her husband, Timothy, in 1835, she wanted all her own property that he controlled, including cash earned from her estate. An illiterate widow with two adult children, Martha had married Timothy, a skilled Irish carpenter with no assets of his own. She brought to the marriage a substantial widow's dower of property, slaves, and cash as well as her skills as a boardinghouse manager. Shortly after their marriage, Martha gave birth to a baby girl.[41]

In her petition, Martha charged that her husband committed adultery with a black woman and several prostitutes, sold two of her slaves without her knowledge, and plotted to sell the remainder of her slaves and real estate to cover his gambling debts. She complained that Timothy had misled her about his character: not a sober and industrious Christian man, he was instead "a worthless, trifling man possessed of the most abandoned moral habits, and inattentive alike to the comforts of his family, and his own respectability and character, of which he was wholly lacking in both." Martha also complained that her husband had infected her with a venereal disease one month after their wedding, a condition that she had concealed in shame from her most intimate female friends and acquaintances.[42]

Timothy denounced all the charges, countering that Martha herself frequently committed adultery in her boardinghouse, which was little more than a brothel. He charged that he had contracted syphilis from his wife, who had committed adultery on her former husband and against whom she had once filed a divorce petition with the same allegations now lodged against himself. She was a woman of such "wanton passions as to defile and degrade the very notion of femininity itself." In response to his wife's charges of indolence and lack of industry, Timothy claimed to have built two houses on her town lots, paying for most of the expenses out of pocket and doing most of the actual labor.[43]

To press their claims, Timothy and Martha submitted depositions of numerous witnesses, including her son and son-in-law, who swore they had seen Timothy in brothels in Under-the-Hill, including once when they had accompanied him on a night on the town. They also defended Martha's practice of entertaining men in her bedroom, saying she often used her bedroom as a sitting room while managing the boardinghouse. Another witness testified to seeing Timothy with an enslaved woman late at night in the town graveyard. His reputation as a lazy, no-account gambler supported the charge of adultery, even though no witness could actually testify that he had seen Timothy in carnal relations with other women.[44]

Timothy's witnesses spoke of his sound reputation and verified his statements. Some of the most convincing testimony came from lumber merchant Andrew Brown, a local nabob who had known the Tewksburys for years. Timothy, he said, was a hard-working, reliable carpenter with a solid reputation, though he lacked the best habits of industry. When asked his opinion of Martha, Brown described her as not a "virtuous woman" but offered no details.[45]

The Tewksbury divorce case continued for several years in the courts before the state supreme court granted Martha's petition on appeal. Its coldly worded opinion found Timothy guilty of adultery and unfit to be married, ordered that all properties acquired in the marriage be turned over immediately to Martha, and directed Timothy to pay all court costs. The ruling upheld the right of even a woman of questionable character to public respect and good conduct from her husband. Most importantly, it upheld the notion that women of property and industry who professed support for the servant ideal were—in defiance of the traditional strictures of coverture—entitled to the fruits of their own labor.[46]

These two cases demonstrate that women and their judicial advocates well understood the requirements for a successful divorce: language supportive of the servant ideal, which accepted the right of husbands to dominate their wives in return for fair treatment and public respect; creditable witnesses willing to verify the wife's allegations; evidence of adultery with disreputable or enslaved women; and restraint in asking for transfer of assets. When Natchez District husbands publicly abandoned their responsibilities and mocked the servant ideal, the courts ruled in a woman's favor almost every time. The married women of Natchez, and perhaps the larger South, understood the law to be an instrument of protection and fairness that they were not afraid to use in their own interests.

Many of the free married women of the antebellum Natchez District well understood the tradeoff available to them: protection, security, and substantial but limited equity rights in exchange for their equality as individuals in the eyes of the law. The significant degree of female autonomy reflected in the legal records actually strengthened and helped re-create existing gender roles and the social continuity of southern life. While claims by married women to equity rights based on the servant ideal did not challenge fundamentally the patriarchal order, the values of a slave-based social hierarchy, or the role of women within the social order, neither did the claims fundamentally disempower women. Embracing servitude ironically produced a degree of independence and empowerment within the social order that privileged male heads of household as the "rightful masters" (or first servants) of women, children, and the enslaved. This was true in practice—with divorce, dower, and marriage contracts, as well as in concept—with the law of separate estates.

When the married women of the Natchez District registered their properties as separate estates, filed marriage contracts, held firm to their dower rights, and sued for divorce, they hoped for male protection in a just and equitable social order. The words of Natchez widow Susan Conner in justifying her suit in the Louisiana courts for title to property owned by her husband but not willed to her reveals what was uppermost in the minds of those who fully understood their rights as married women: "There is a great hue & cry raised against me as a womans rights woman, ... but I am not one except where the U.S. and reason, give me a right to be a rights woman. I care not a copper to be a governor a Legislator, or any other 'or,' but if I can protect my own rights, and those of others, I hold it my duty to resist the united world, with my single Will."[47] Judicial authorities in antebellum Natchez often agreed with women such as Susan Conner and chose to view actions like hers as supporting a common value system and a society not opposed to patriarchal authority. Indeed, when the servant ideal and women's equity rights were upheld and sustained by judicial authorities, the prevailing social order, based as it was on slavery and patriarchy, was daily sustained and re-created.

NOTES

1. William Elwell to Hannah Thomas, May 12, 1772, Marriage Records, Friendship, Maine, reprinted in *Records of Maduncook Plantation and Friendship, Maine, 1762–1899*, ed. Melville Bradford Cook (Rockland, Maine: Shore Village Historical Society, 1985). The smock marriage may have allowed the bride some protection in a court of equity, where a judge could rule in the bride's favor as a matter of fairness, reflecting perhaps a kind of reciprocity arrangement wherein the bride's nakedness empowered her to some degree.

2. The Old Natchez District included in the French, British, and Spanish colonial periods much of the lower Mississippi River Valley from present-day Baton Rouge, Louisiana, to Memphis. In the American era, it encompassed several adjoining Mississippi counties and Louisiana parishes located along both sides of the Mississippi River and anchored by the wealthy town of Natchez

in Adams County, Mississippi. The wealth and influence of the Old Natchez District is well documented by historians. See especially Winthrop D. Jordan, *Tumult and Silence at Second Creek: An Inquiry into a Civil War Slave Conspiracy* (Baton Rouge: Louisiana State University Press, 1993); Morton Rothstein, "The Changing Social Networks and Investment Behavior of a Slaveholding Elite in the Antebellum South: Some Natchez Nabobs, 1800–1860," in *Entrepreneurs in Cultural Context*, ed. Sidney M. Greenfield et al. (Albuquerque: University of New Mexico Press, 1979), 65–84; Morton Rothstein, "The Natchez Nabobs: Kinship and Friendship in an Economic Elite," in *Toward a New View of America: Essays in Honor of Arthur C. Cole*, ed. Hans Trefousse (New York: Columbia University Press, 1977), 97–111; William K. Scarborough, "Lords or Capitalists: The Natchez Nabobs in Comparative Perspective," *Journal of Mississippi History* 54 (August 1992): 239–68; William Banks Taylor, "Southern Yankees: Wealth, High Society, and Political Economy in the Late Antebellum Natchez Region," *Journal of Mississippi History* 59 (Summer 1997): 79–122.

3. Jack D. L. Holmes, *Gayoso: The Life of a Spanish Governor in the Mississippi Valley, 1789–1799* (Baton Rouge: Louisiana State University Press, 1965); John Francis McDermott, ed., *The Spanish in the Mississippi Valley: 1762–1804* (Urbana, Ill.: University of Chicago Press, 1974); Cecilia M. Shulman, "The Bingamans of Natchez," *Journal of Mississippi History* 63 (2001): 285–315.

4. Bill "For the Protection and Preservation of the Rights and Property of Married Women," *Journal of the Senate of the State of Mississippi* 42 (Jackson: Price and Fall, State Printers, 1839), 99–100; A. Hutchinson, *Code of Mississippi: Analytical Compilation of the Public and General Statutes of the Territory and State with Tabular References to the Local and Private Acts from 1798 to 1848* (Jackson: Price and Fall, State Printers, 1848), 492–99, 523, 601, 605, 608–9, 614–17, 620–24, 637–38, 649–55, 670–80; William Sharkey, William Harris, and Henry T. Ellett, *The Revised Code of the Statute Laws of the State of Mississippi* (Jackson: E. Barksdale, 1857), 307–10, 313–16, 335–38, 358, 410, 432, 467–70, 487, 510.

5. The idea of an ideology of mastery, which engulfed free men, women, and children and slaves within a hierarchical order that had evolved over time into a culturally inclusive, paternalistic social order, is principally associated with the scholarship of Elizabeth Fox-Genovese and Eugene D. Genovese. See especially Elizabeth Fox-Genovese, *Within the Plantation Household: Black and White Women of the Old South* (Chapel Hill: University of North Carolina Press, 1988); Eugene D. Genovese, *The Political Economy of Slavery: Studies in the Economy and Society of the Slave South* (New York: Pantheon Books, 1965); E. D. Genovese, *Roll Jordan Roll: The World the Slaves Made* (New York: Pantheon Press, 1974); E. D. Genovese, *The Southern Tradition: The Achievement and Limitations of American Conservatism* (Cambridge, Mass.: Harvard University Press, 1994); and E. D. Genovese, *The World the Slaveholders Made: Two Essays in Interpretation* (New York: Pantheon Press, 1974). This essay argues that a key and overlooked component of this so-called ideology of mastery was the "servant ideal," which placed a premium on rewarding and promoting the notion of service as the highest calling in life regardless of one's standing in the social hierarchy. Indeed, the message of duty and service saturates the literature of the antebellum South. For elaboration on and discussion of this ideal as a means of domination and social cohesion in antebellum southern society in general and in the Natchez District in particular, see Joyce L. Broussard, "Female Solitaires: Women Alone in the Lifeworld of Mid-century Natchez, Mississippi: 1850–1880," PhD diss., University of Southern California, 1998.

6. The concept of equity rights versus equality rights is an emerging contention separating so-called radical feminists from liberal feminists in the modern women's movement. I do not mean to employ this idea full scale herein, but much of the contemporary discussion about the empowering advantages based on equity rather than equality is especially relevant for understanding the way women in traditional and slave-based societies have used equity to navigate a male-dominated

social order. For significant comment on this discussion, see Estelle B. Freedman, *No Turning Back: The History of Feminism and the Future of Women* (New York: Ballantine Books, 2002), 156–58; Joan Hoff, *Law, Gender, and Injustice: A Legal History of U.S. Women* (New York: New York University Press, 1991), 350–75; and Peter Karsten, *Heart and Head: Judge-Made Law in Nineteenth-Century America* (Chapel Hill: University of North Carolina Press, 1997).

7. Deeds, Liens, and Mortgage Record Books (1799–1870), Office of Records for Adams County, Natchez, Mississippi; Hutchinson, *Code of Mississippi*, 604–19, 637–38; Sharkey, Harris, and Ellett, *Revised Code*, 306–16, 331–38, 358, 487.

8. Seligman Schatz and Matilda Miles, Marriage Contract, May 26, 1849; Seligman Schatz and Meriam Wexler, Marriage Contract, September 14, 1866, Deeds, Liens, and Mortgage Record Books, Office of Records, Adams County, Natchez, Mississippi. In the one exception to this pattern, Seligman Schatz signed a marriage contract in 1849 agreeing to a separate estate in personal property, principally store goods and household items, for his bride, Matilda Miles. It is one of the few contracts involving personal rather than real property recorded in the district. Schatz appears in the records again in 1866, agreeing in a prenuptial settlement to deed to his new wife, Meriam Wexler, land and a house in Natchez as a separate estate under her control. The agreement also differed from other marriage contracts by a stipulation allowing Seligman to reclaim the property should his wife precede him in death. Schatz, a Natchez merchant, may have deeded the property to his second wife as a means of safeguarding it from creditors, a common practice after the Civil War in postnuptial contracts.

9. Chancery Court and Vice Chancery Court Records (1800–1870); Circuit Court Records (1820–70); Court Manuscript Cases, Briefs, Petitions, Testimony, Depositions, etc. (1799–1870); Records of Judgment (1820–70), all at Historic Natchez Foundation, Natchez, Mississippi (henceforth cited as HNF).

10. Deeds, Liens, and Mortgage Record Books (1799–1870), Office of Records for Adams County, Natchez, Mississippi; Hutchinson, *Code of Mississippi*, 614–22. For discussion of inheritance law affecting women from colonial times to the present but especially for nonsouthern states, see Carole Shammas, Marylynn Salmon, and Michel Dahlin, *Inheritance in American from Colonial Times to the Present* (New Brunswick, N.J.: Rutgers University Press, 1987).

11. Mary F. Dunbar to Thomas and Alex C. Henderson, February 28, 1853, Deeds, Liens, and Mortgage Record Books, Office of Records, Adams County, Natchez, Mississippi. Historian Michael Wayne notes a similar transaction of a widow buying property as the only bidder at a public auction, but he mistakenly interprets the action as a duplicitous and self-serving maneuver on the part of the widow's male agent instead of seeing it as a common device whereby widows used the law and dower rights to secure properties in their own names. See Michael Wayne, *Death of an Overseer: Reopening a Murder Investigation from the Plantation South* (New York: Oxford University Press, 2001), 124–31.

12. Deeds, Liens, and Mortgage Record Books (1799–1870), Office of Records for Adams County, Natchez, Mississippi; Hutchinson, *Code of Mississippi*, 523, 608–9, 614–17, 620–22; Sharkey, Harris, and Ellett, *Revised Code*, 337, 410, 432, 467–70. Similar maneuvers by widows have been documented for nineteenth-century Pennsylvania by Lisa Wilson in *Life after Death: Widows in Pennsylvania, 1750–1850* (Philadelphia: Temple University Press, 1992).

13. Hutchinson, *Code of Mississippi*, 495–99; Sharkey, Harris, and Ellett, *Revised Code*, 333–38; *Journal of the Senate of the State of Mississippi* 42 (1839): 99–107, 258–63. Several leading scholars, notably Bertram Wyatt-Brown and Michael Wayne, are confused about the separate estate law in Mississippi, suggesting in their scholarship that the law allowed husbands to transfer properties to

wives after marriage. In fact, the law specifically prohibited such transfers in order to prevent husbands from defrauding their creditors.

14. Richard H. Chused, "Late Nineteenth-Century Married Women's Property Law: Reception of the Early Married Women's Property Acts by Courts and Legislatures," *American Journal of Legal History* 29 (January 1985): 3–35; Chused, "Married Women's Property Law: 1800–1850," *Georgetown Law Journal* 71 (June 1983): 1359–1425; Hoff, *Law, Gender, and Injustice*; Suzanne Lebsock, "Radical Reconstruction and the Property Rights of Southern Women," *Journal of Southern History* 43 (May 1977): 195–216; Lebsock, *The Free Women of Petersburg: Status and Culture in a Southern Town, 1784–1860* (New York: Norton, 1985); Sandra Moncrief, "The Mississippi Married Women's Property Act of 1839," *Journal of Mississippi History* 67 (May 1985): 110–25; Carole Shammas, "Reassessing the Married Women's Property Acts," *Journal of Women's History* 6 (Spring 1994): 9–38; Elizabeth Bowles Warbasse, *The Changing Legal Rights of Married Women* (New York: Garland Press, 1987).

15. Moncrief, "Mississippi Married Women's Property Act," 122.

16. *Journal of the Senate of the State of Mississippi* 42 (1939): 99–107, 258–63. See also Bertram Wyatt-Brown, *Southern Honor: Ethics and Behavior in the Old South* (New York: Oxford University Press, 1982), 466–92; Colonel James Creecy, *Scenes in the South, and Other Miscellaneous Pieces* (Washington, D.C.: Thomas McGill, 1860): 54; David Crockett, *Col. Crockett's Exploits and Adventures in Texas, Wherein Is Contained a Full Account of His Journey from Tennessee and Thence across Texas to San Antonio* (London: R. Kennett, 1837), 63–68; and Michael Grossberg, *Governing the Hearth: Law and the Family in Nineteenth-Century America* (Chapel Hill: University of North Carolina Press, 1985). Grossberg argues that the "family [was] in many ways a legal creation," whose identity "in the eyes of the law" served to function as "the primary institution of American society," and hence was crucial to the maintenance of the American social order, especially so in the nineteenth century.

17. *Journal of the Senate of the State of Mississippi* 42 (1939): 99–107, 258–63. Although there is no way of knowing what was uppermost in the mind of the bill's detractors—its threat to creditor interests or to the patriarchal status quo based on the dependency of women on men—it is clear that the two ideas were not necessarily incompatible. Southern Whigs had long supported sound currency and procreditor politics in the interests of slavery as an economic and social system. On the other hand, wealthy planters could also favor strengthening their daughters' claims to independent estates as a means of safeguarding the patriarchal household from ne'er-do-well husbands and as a means of sheltering assets from their own creditors. Both sides, moreover, could support their stand on the issue by contending that their position best safeguarded the patriarchy and the place of women within the traditional social order of male-dominated households.

18. Ibid. The introduction of the slave issue in the separate estate laws of Mississippi and the South in general underscores the case for southern exceptionalism. Separate estate laws and most other laws of property and personality in nonfree states were always interpreted in the context of free labor, free markets, and an egalitarian ethos that ran counter to the nonegalitarian culture and society of slavery. Historians opposed to the idea of southern exceptionalism often focus on the similarities of legal institutions in the North and the South without taking into consideration the differences in judicial interpretations of the law in slave-based societies compared to those rooted in free labor.

19. On this subject, see especially Karen A. Getman, "Sexual Control in the Slaveholding South: The Implementation and Maintenance of a Racial Caste System," *Harvard Women's Law Journal* 7 (Spring 1984): 115–52; Martha Hodes, *White Women, Black Men: Illicit Sex in the Nineteenth-Century*

South (New Haven, Conn.: Yale University Press, 1997); Cynthia M. Kennedy, *Braided Relations, Entwined Lives: The Women of Charleston's Urban Slave Society* (Bloomington: Indiana University Press, 2005); Joel Williamson, *The Crucible of Race: Black-White Relations in the American South since Emancipation* (New York: Oxford University Press, 1984); and Kirsten E. Wood, *Masterful Women: Slaveholding Women from the American Revolution through the Civil War* (Chapel Hill: University of North Carolina Press, 2004).

20. Elizabeth Gaspar Brown, "Husband and Wife—Memorandum on the Mississippi Woman's Law of 1839," *Michigan Law Review* 42 (April 1944): 1110–21; Moncrief, "Mississippi Married Women's Property Act," 110–25. The bill's chief supporter, Thomas Hadley, a Hinds County businessman and planter who had fallen on hard times, owned a boardinghouse in Jackson, the state capital, in partnership with his wife, Piety Smith Hadley, the daughter of a Mississippi planter, Major David Smith, who had bequeathed slaves and land to her in a separate estate. Hadley probably introduced the bill in hopes of transferring the boardinghouse business and other properties to his wife, thereby removing them from the possibility of being seized by his creditors.

21. Brown, "Husband and Wife," 1110–21; Moncrief, "Mississippi Married Women's Property Act," 110–25; *Journal of the Senate of the State of Mississippi* 42 (1939): 99–107, 258–63.

22. Empowering husbands to manage the enslaved people owned by wives reflected a common practice in marriage-settlement contracts upheld by the courts. Courts of probate frequently endorsed similar provisions in settling estates when widows inherited slaves outright or held dower rights to them when husbands died intestate.

23. Deeds, Liens, and Mortgage Record Books (1799–1870), Office of Records for Adams County, Natchez, Mississippi; Chancery Court and Vice Chancery Court Records (1800–1870); Circuit Court Records (1820–1870); Court Manuscript Cases, Briefs, Petitions, Testimony, Depositions, etc. (1799–1870); Records of Judgment (1820–1870); Registry, Property of Married Women Separate from Husbands (1846–1860), all at HNF.

24. Registry, Property of Married Women Separate from Husbands (1846–1860), HNF.

25. Mississippi state laws (including those on divorce) for the antebellum period can be found in Hutchinson, *Code of Mississippi*, 495–99; Sharkey, Harris, and Ellett, *Revised Code*, 333–38; *Journal of the Senate of the State of Mississippi* 42 (1939): 99–107, 258–63.

26. Chancery Court and Vice Chancery Court Records (1800–1870); Circuit Court Records (1820–70); Court Manuscript Cases, Briefs, Petitions, Testimony, Depositions, etc. (1799–1870); Records of Judgment (1820–70), all at HNF; and High Court of Errors and Appeals, RG 32 (1832–69), RG 47 (1796–1865), Legislative Papers of the State of Mississippi; Superior Court of the Chancery Records, RG 8 (1821–57); Vice Chancery Court, Southern District (1850–60), all at Mississippi Department of Archives and History, Jackson, Mississippi (henceforth cited as MDAH). Among the most important secondary sources on the history of divorce in the United States, including the nineteenth-century South, are the following: Peter W. Bardaglio, *Reconstructing the Household: Families, Sex, and the Law in the Nineteenth-Century South* (Chapel Hill: University of North Carolina Press, 1995); Norma Basch, *Framing American Divorce: From the Revolutionary Generation to the Victorians* (Berkeley: University of California Press, 1999); Victoria E. Bynum, *Unruly Women: The Politics of Social and Sexual Control in the Old South* (Chapel Hill: University of North Carolina Press, 1992), 59–87; Jane Turner Censer, "'Smiling through Her Tears': Antebellum Southern Women and Divorce," *American Journal of Legal History* 25 (January 1981): 24–47; Grossberg, *Governing the Hearth*; Lebsock, *Free Women of Petersburg*, 15–86; Donna Elizabeth Sedevie, "The Prospect of Happiness: Women, Divorce, and Property in the Mississippi Territory, 1798–1817," *Journal of Mississippi History* 47 (Fall 1995): 189–206.

27. Hutchinson, *Code of Mississippi*, 495–97; Sharkey, Harris, and Ellett, *Revised*, 333–35.

28. Chused, "Married Women's Property Law," 1359–1425.

29. Chancery Court and Vice Chancery Court Records (1800–1870); Circuit Court Records (1820–70); Court Manuscript Cases, Briefs, Petitions, Testimony, Depositions, etc. (1799–1870); Records of Judgment (1820–70), all at HNF; and High Court of Errors & Appeals, RG 32 (1832–69); Legislative Papers of the State of Mississippi; RG 47 (1796–1865); Superior Court of the Chancery Records, RG 8 (1821–57), all at MDAH.

30. Registry, Property of Married Women Separate from Husbands (1846–60), HNF.

31. Sedevie, "Prospect of Happiness," 190.

32. *Sophia Elliott v. Wm. M. Green*, March 3, 1823, Superior Court of the Chancery, Western District, RG 32, MDAH.

33. Unfortunately, the outcome of the entire record of divorce petitions is unknown due to the scattered sources and the unorganized array of records. The majority of individual petitions have been located either in county records or state archives, but the final decrees in numerous cases have been lost. Of those fully researched, approximately 75 percent, the lion's share, were successful petitions at the chancery level or on appeal to the high court of appeals. See Chancery Court Docket Books (1830–70); Chancery Court & Vice Chancery Court Records (1800–1870); Circuit Court Records (1820–70); Court Manuscript Cases, Briefs, Petitions, Testimony, Depositions, etc. (1799–1870); Records of Judgment (1820–70), all at HNF; and High Court of Errors and Appeals, RG 32 (1832–69); Legislative Papers of the State of Mississippi, RG 47 (1796–1865); Superior Court of the Chancery Records, RG 8 (1821–57), all at MDAH.

34. *Susannah Sessions v. William B. Sessions*, April 16, 1839, Court Manuscript Cases, Adams County Circuit Court Records, HNF.

35. In the legal records of the Natchez District, the colorful career of the prostitute and madam Elizabeth Lawrence spans some forty-five years of documentation. See especially *The State v. Elizabeth Lawrence*, May 1, 1841, Criminal Court Docket Books (1840–70); *The State v. Elizabeth Lawrence*, October 11, 1833, Court Manuscript Cases, both in Adams County Circuit Court Records, HNF.

36. *Susannah Sessions v. William B. Sessions*, April 16, 1839, Court Manuscript Cases, Adams County Circuit Court Records, HNF.

37. Ibid.

38. Susannah Sessions, Probate Court Records, box 104 (October 1839–58), Adams County Courthouse, Office of Records, Natchez, Adams County, Mississippi.

39. *Susannah Sessions v. William B. Sessions*, April 16, 1839, Court Manuscript Cases, Adams County Circuit Court Records, HNF.

40. Historian Bertram Wyatt-Brown argues that southern judges generally found against women in adultery cases in upholding male self-image as a point of honor between males (*Southern Honor*, 285–91). This pessimistic reading of the divorce situation fails to understand that the judgment issue before the courts was almost always a question of the degree to which the aggrieved wife could attest to her morality and to her devotion to the servant ideal. In cases where wifely fidelity and commitment to dutifully serving the husband could be proven, southern courts had little choice but to grant the divorce petitions, especially when the husband showed no sense of respect for his familial responsibility (as the master of the household) for keeping his adulterous ways hidden from the public's eye. In these matters, appearances counted above all else because how one behaved in the public arena gave credence to the organic ideal in which benevolent, decent, and moral patriarchs took into consideration the feelings and public face of their dependents in

the interest of fairness. When they did not, courts of equity judged them offensive and unfair to their wives, men who had broken the unwritten rules of public conduct that underlay the marriage bond.

41. *Martha Tewksbury v. Timothy Tewksbury*, July 26, 1838, Court Manuscript Cases, Adams County Circuit Court Records, HNF; *Martha Tewksbury v. Timothy Tewksbury*, High Court of Errors and Appeals, RG 32, Case 183 (1839), MDAH.

42. *Martha Tewksbury v. Timothy Tewksbury*, July 26, 1838, HNF; *Martha Tewksbury v. Timothy Tewksbury*, High Court of Errors and Appeals, MDAH.

43. *Martha Tewksbury v. Timothy Tewksbury*, July 26, 1838, Court Manuscript Cases, Adams County Circuit Court Records, HNF; *Martha Tewksbury v. Timothy Tewksbury*, High Court of Errors and Appeals, RG 32, Case 183 (1839), MDAH.

44. *Martha Tewksbury v. Timothy Tewksbury*, July 26, 1838, Court Manuscript Cases, Adams County Circuit Court Records, HNF; *Martha Tewksbury v. Timothy Tewksbury*, High Court of Errors and Appeals, RG 32, Case 183 (1839), MDAH.

45. The fullest treatment of Andrew Brown's place in Natchez society can be found in John Hebron Moore, *Andrew Brown and Cypress Lumbering in the Old Southwest* (Baton Rouge: Louisiana State University Press, 1967).

46. *Martha Tewksbury v. Timothy Tewksbury*, July 26, 1838, HNF; *Martha Tewksbury v. Timothy Tewksbury*, High Court of Errors and Appeals, RG 32, MDAH.

47. Letter from Susan B. Conner to Alexander Farrar, 1852, quoted in Wayne, *Death of an Overseer*, 125–26. Original letter is in the papers of F. H. and Thomas P. Farrar, Center for American History, University of Texas at Austin.

Cautious, Conservative, and Raced

The Maternal Presumption in Mississippi Child Custody Law, 1830–1920

KEVIN D. MCCARTHY

On the day after Christmas in 1840, Frances D. Foster forcibly took her seven- and eight-year-old daughters from the home of their legal guardian, James Alston, in Tipton County, Tennessee, and headed for the safety of home in Holly Springs, Mississippi. In a horse-drawn carriage and accompanied by armed men, she requested people along the route to send those pursuing her in other directions. She fatigued the horses but successfully outran the small posse that followed her group. The tale has a certain lawless quality, but subsequent events and testimony suggest that rather than trying to avoid the law, Frances Foster sought a legal solution to questions concerning her custody of the children.[1]

Frances Foster gained the legal care and control of her daughters in 1842, when the Mississippi appellate court, called the High Court of Errors and Appeals, established doctrines supportive of maternal custody. Frances Foster's legal battle occurred during a period of significant change in Anglo-American domestic relations law. Over the course of the nineteenth century, an "emerging trinity of judicial discretion, maternalism, and child nurture" came to underlie "modern" child custody determinations in habeas corpus petitions and divorce actions.[2] Legal doctrine regarding child custody shifted from nearly unassailable paternal rights of custody to a presumption of maternal custody in the child's "best interest." This essay explores a conservative society's acceptance of doctrines once considered radical by focusing on cases that were appealed to the state's highest court. It also analyzes the experiences of a broad sample of Mississippians in the only legal venues in which they ever acted—their local county courts. In both arenas, Mississippi women, both black and white, shaped the law of child custody, just as they were, in turn, shaped by it.

Frances Foster had lost her daughters because of internal family matters—earlier marital tensions, questions of class status, and a bachelor's desires for patriarchal control—as well as traditional common-law and social assumptions. Though the majority of dying husbands both explicitly and implicitly assigned their children's custody—or guardianship—to their wives, common-law precedents up to the mid-nineteenth century "extinguished maternal guardianship" upon the widow's remarriage because the law assumed that "maternal responsibility would be superseded by the deference and affection she owed her new husband."[3] Yet when Frances Foster took her daughters to what she hoped was friendlier legal territory, she acted in the shadow of several nationally reported and formative cases in the late 1830s. She also knew about trends that suggested she could find a satisfactory solution in Mississippi's own courthouses.[4] The state's legal structure followed the English example of separate common law and equity courts. Circuit courts heard legal issues. Chancery courts dealt with matters of equity, which included protecting the interests of those who, like married women and infants, had no formal standing under the common law.[5] Chancery courts thus exercised jurisdiction in divorces and child-related habeas corpus cases. An 1822 enactment, for example, gave chancellors discretionary power to make all orders "touching the care and maintenance of the children of that marriage" as shall be "equitable and just." In 1840, the courts gained even greater authority when lawmakers ended the requirement of legislative confirmation of divorces.[6]

A pathbreaking piece of legislation heightened the significance of the legal moment in which Frances Foster acted. Mississippi in 1839 was the first state in the nation to pass a married women's property act. The new law weakened men's common-law vested rights in property. Though conservative in intent and interpretation, the act raised concerns from stalwarts of paternal rights, who feared that it would "destroy that confidence between man and wife which constitutes the greatest charm of the married state."[7] Many expressed similar suspicions that weakening men's custody rights would also extinguish domestic accord.

Previous opinions of the High Court of Errors and Appeal likely encouraged Frances Foster because the bench had shown a heightened interest in custody over the course of the 1830s. In 1831, the court remained indifferent and silent on custodial matters, but by 1839 it promoted judicial determination of custodial rights in *Tewksbury v. Tewksbury*. In this divorce case, which focused on issues of adultery and the distribution of marital property, the high court reversed the Adams County court's decision and instead rendered a verdict for the wronged wife. Justice James F. Trotter explained that because no question of custody had been raised in either court, "we shall . . . make no order touching that matter, but leave it to the future disposition of the law."[8] Given Trotter's support of Frances Foster's custody claims just over two years later, one suspects the justice was paving the way for the bench's right to assert power of discretion against paternal claims, if not even to assert claims more firmly in the mother's behalf.

By 1840, Mississippi's judges had clear discretion in matters of custody in their equitable jurisdiction; they showed an interest in employing those powers; and the legislature had started to modify the common law presumptions of coverture in regard to married women's separate property. Mississippi's appellate court was ready to consider questions of a husband's vested rights in the custody of his children.

Yet Mississippi entered the appellate arena of custody adjudication conservatively. The bench developed the majority of Mississippi's nineteenth-century custody precedents in cases that did not directly pit husband against wife. The Fosters' case, for example, set the claims of a mother against a "third party," Frances's former brother-in-law, who had been made the girls' guardian upon their father's death in November 1834. Consequently, the court avoided the hot-button issue of separating, divorcing, and battling spouses, which riveted audiences who followed sensational cases in the national press, emboldened maternal rights advocates, and struck fear in the defenders of patriarchy "that too many rights would tempt women to leave the family."[9]

The Mississippi high court sounded newer, maternalist notes that emphasized mothers' "natural" nurturing abilities in supporting Frances Foster's claims. Key to the court's consideration, however, was the fact that she was not simply Annie's and Mary's mother. Frances's most obvious legal status was as a wife: *Foster and Wife v. Alston*. Her 1839 marriage to Colley Foster had precipitated the loss of physical control of her daughters to their legal guardian. Yet Frances's attorneys and the court used her marital status to portray her as a fit custodian and as a better person to have custody than the "bachelor" Alston. Accolades for her parenting skills as *Mrs.* Foster countered testimony that questioned her mothering abilities as a single woman for four years after the death of her first husband. Indeed, after her removal to Mississippi, little separation was made between her marital status and her motherhood.[10] The Fosters' attorneys used the conflation of marriage and parenthood against Alston, eliciting testimony such as "I do not think that an unmarried man [is a] fit or proper person" to care for the girls.[11] A majority of the court agreed. Though marital status was not made a part of the formal law of child custody, evidence of its weight in determining custodial fitness adds to the conservative tinge of Mississippi jurisprudence.

Over three decades passed before the court again dealt with issues of maternal and/or parental custody rights against third parties, as well as matters of marital status. During the 1870s, a decade wracked by the upheavals of Reconstruction and "Redemption," the court heard two cases with decidedly different outcomes for women in Mississippi: *Maples v. Maples* (1873) and *Moore v. Christian* (1879). The *Maples* decision qualified the court's commitment to maternalism. When it declared that "for the welfare of the child" the court would do best to "let well enough alone" by leaving the child with his grandfather, it invalidated Violet Maples's projection of herself as a legally entitled person—as an African American, a woman, and a mother.[12]

The primary consideration for the court was whether Violet Maples was the rightful custodian of her fifteen-year-old son. She was not, according to Justice Jonathan Tarbell's opinion, which set forth a parade of particulars as to how she had forfeited her right to the care and control of her child. The court's indictment declared, "Violet Maples is the mother of seven children, by different fathers. She is the servant of, and lives in the kitchen of the father-in-law of her agent. . . . She has no other . . . means of supporting her children. Her position, employment, and character, offer no guaranty of the proper care and training of her son Boss. He is evidently wanted by her to be hired out to other parties."[13] Tarbell might very well have opened his opinion with what he found most troubling in Maples's character—that she had "seven children by different fathers." The sexual "sins" of women proved an obstacle to custody throughout the nation well past the nineteenth century. More broadly, "the court classified Violet as a dependent person, undeserving of even the most basic right to her child."[14] Finally, Maples inspired the court's disapproval because she hoped to hire her son "out to other parties."[15] Immoral, dependent, and exploitative did not make a fit female custodian.

The appellant in *Moore v. Christian* found the state supreme court of the late 1870s to be more supportive of parental and maternal authority than Violet Maples had experienced. Though Bettie Moore, a white woman, faced losing a son's services to a third party, which was similar to Violet Maples's plight, the court interpreted the circumstances differently and overturned the chancellor's decree with instructions for the child to be turned over to his mother's custody. In part, the court reached such a different decision from the *Maples* case by espousing a renewed commitment to parental rights that echoed the "Redemption" legislature's enactment of a bill "for the Protection of Parental Authority over their Minor Children" in 1876.[16] But issues of womanhood, motherhood, and marital status also distinguish the cases.

The court's initial identification of Bettie Moore as "the widowed mother" was pivotal.[17] Her motherhood was not neutral but was positively constructed by emphasizing her connection to her recently departed husband. The court, assuming that her husband's verbal transfer of their son's labor to Thomas F. Christian—an Itawamba County landowner for whom Mr. and Mrs. Moore had worked in the past—was valid to begin with, found the contract "must . . . have terminated at his death" for it could not "divest her of that right to the custody of her son."[18] Of special concern was the right to her thirteen-year-old son's services that went along with his custody. Not being a member of the propertied class, Bettie Moore would not benefit from dower rights, the common-law right of a surviving wife to a third of her husband's property during her lifetime, to help keep her and the rest of the family from becoming public charges. Her son's services, however, were a legacy that could aid in achieving family self-sufficiency. The court's reasoning was closely aligned to contemporary debates about inheritance law carried on by women's rights advocates. More accurately, the court's opinion fit with the conservative approach toward granting women better protections by invoking "the sanctity of women's place in the home" in contrast to an "equality agenda."[19] From this view, widows had an "entitled dependency" that required protection, especially if the husband could be shown to be cruelly indifferent to his wife's situation after his death. In correcting the husband's posthumous control of his wife by returning the custody of their son to her, the court based Bettie Moore's "independence" as head of the household and in control of her children's services on her dependence in marriage. In contrast, the court denied Violet Maples's "independence" because of her independence. Violet Maples sought control over her child from an intellectual position much more akin to the radical notions of sex equality. This was not a discourse with which the Mississippi bench was comfortable.

Mississippi's high court crafted much of its child custody precedents on the cases of individuals as diverse as Frances D. Foster, Violet Maples, and Bettie Moore, but none of these women was fighting for the custody of a child against a separated or divorcing spouse. The bench was consequently able to solidify its role in custody adjudication without stirring up many social fears. The Mississippi appellate courts also approached custody questions conservatively because contending parties arrived at the bench cautiously. Even though custody challenges between spouses slowly increased, the proportion of such cases remained low. Fewer than half of Mississippi mothers who appealed a chancery court's custody decision to the high court between 1817 and 1930 opposed a separated or divorced husband. In contrast, a significant majority of Alabama mothers who approached their own state's high court with custodial concerns faced their (ex-)husbands.[20]

The Mississippi Supreme Court's rules that derived from cases setting current or former spouses against each other followed a rational sequence toward the maternal preference found in other jurisdictions. The logic is especially apparent in the various versions of the annotated code that reference what the compiler(s) found to be the most significant judicial precedents regarding interpretation of the statute law. Mississippi's code cites *Cocke v. Hannum* (1860) as holding that the divorce and alimony "statute annuls the paramount right of the father as it existed at common law, to the custody of the children." Following from there, the annotations focus on what shall guide the court's decisions, referring to the rule in *McShan v. McShan* (1879) that "though the father by abstract right be entitled to the custody of his children yet such right is modified by the circumstances of each case and the court will be guided by the children's best interest." The final and most distinctive ruling arrived when the court held in *Johns v. Johns* (1879) that "if the children be so young as to need the mother's care and attention, they should, in granting the divorce, be given to her." This was the basis of the "tender-years" doctrine that presumed a young and/or sickly child's best interests were to be found in the care of his or her "naturally" nurturing mother.[21] Aside from the organizational imperatives of the annotated code, the court's interference with paternal rights, the best interest of the child, and maternal custody all played a role in each case.

The 1860 case of *Cocke v. Hannum* exhibited concerns with the antebellum southern social order and the role of the state within the private household. At the time of the couple's 1856 divorce (based on his adultery), the lower court made no specific order as to custody and silently allowed the couple's own solution. John Cocke kept the son; Louisa Cocke had charge of their young daughter. In 1860, the remarried Dr. Cocke petitioned for a writ of habeas corpus to gain custody of his daughter from his former wife, now Mrs. A. B. Hannum. Cocke's attorneys argued in support of wide-ranging patriarchal prerogatives and sneeringly predicted the effeminization of the social order if the court sanctioned a mother's claims.

The court's opinion showed no concern that this father's loss of custody might threaten the foundations of the social order. Indeed, Justice Alexander H. Handy counseled the inverse—that the errant husband's loss promoted social order. At issue were the boundaries of household authority. As with the law's protection of the system of slavery through the occasional interposition between a master and a slave, the Mississippi judicial elite was comfortable intervening in the domestic affairs of *a* husband in order to support male dominance of households generally.[22]

Justice Handy used the child as a means of strengthening marital bonds. The mother, though not of flawless character, "was entitled [to her child] by fidelity to the marriage vow." And if the law made the guilty husband responsible for his actions, the rule "would induce him to be faithful to his marriage vows in order not to lose the society and comfort of his children."[23] The judgment's logic was gender neutral. The companionship of children could and would be used both by courts and within households as incentives for and threats against one spouse or the other. More often than not, women found access to their children used as weapons of compliance.[24]

During the 1870s, as individuals and the state struggled with redefining household authority in postbellum society, issues of the child's "best interest" served as a vehicle to discuss the limits of domestic mastery under new conditions. At the end of the decade, Mississippi's supreme court heard the state's only custody cases of the nineteenth century between couples in the midst of separation or divorce.[25] *McShan v. McShan* (1879) witnessed a battle between married but separated parents for custody of their two young girls. Dr. F. A. McShan abandoned his pregnant wife and first child in 1875. After Fannie McShan had spent three years on her own, her father retrieved her from Arkansas and brought her back into his Mississippi household. Soon thereafter, Dr. McShan moved to an adjacent county and proposed shared custody or visitation arrangements. Denied both, he petitioned the local chancery court to gain custody of the children. The chancellor allowed the children's mother to keep the girls, a decision that the doctor appealed.[26]

As in *Cocke*, the court considered that "the hand of the law . . . would be cruel indeed" if it now took the children from the mother. Yet the mother also had to be a fit custodian, and the court found this to be the case. Fannie McShan, the court stated, had the "warmest maternal solicitude and affection" for her children "on account of their sex and tender years." She also had a stable existence living in her father's home, and because her father "promised to provide for them after his death," she could maintain her custody of the children.[27] The court's reasoning suggested both broad parameters for giving custody— innocence and maternal affection—and narrowing qualifiers—sex, age, and a (grand)father's support. The primary beneficiary of the broad/narrow mix was the court, for it left wide-open spaces for judicial discretion.

The parties' briefs to the court employed highly gendered contentions. Mrs. McShan claimed that "tender children cannot be wrested from a mother[']s care without suffering moral and religious detriment." Dr. McShan expressed a more sarcastic view of his wife's feminine influence, declaring, "If she should impart her own amiable qualities to the children, it will only make a lively time for their husbands if they ever marry." Dr. McShan's purported interest in his daughters' future womanhood was shallow in comparison to concerns with his current manhood. In his own brief, he revealed that although he had had difficulty as a husband in dealing with "a very stubborn ill-natured woman," he would nevertheless do well as a father "taking care of his own children too young to write insulting letters, or provoke him to kick them out of bed."[28] Dr. McShan sought to restore his own sense of self as well as his reputation in the community by gaining custody of his children. The supreme court's affirmation of the chancellor's decree favoring the children's mother would have been a blow.

Later in 1879, the court heard a case between divorcing parents. *Johns v. Johns* found a white mother of two appealing the Jefferson County chancellor's dismissal of her divorce bill and request for custody of her young boys. According to Mattie Johns, her husband had driven her from their home when he "threaten[ed] to kill her . . . and retained the children," after she had already endured hurt feelings, frequent cursing, and the two occasions on which he "struck and choked her!" She charged her husband with "habitual cruel and inhuman treatment" and declared "that she was devoted to her two little children with that love and affection that only a mother can know and feel."[29]

The court found Mattie Johns "to be affectionate, amiable and submissive."[30] She did not promise the same financial support that Fannie McShan's dependence on her father afforded, but Mattie Johns claimed to be "able and willing, and desirous . . . to maintain, support, provide for and cherish them." Most basically, the two- and four-year-old boys required Mattie Johns's "care and attention." Her claim added that they would have been with their mother but for "the breach of [James R. Johns's] marital duties."[31] The court remanded the case with instructions to render a divorce and to award custody of the children to Mattie Johns.

In the *Johns* case, the court enunciated the so-called tender-years doctrine in Mississippi law. All succeeding versions of the annotated code cite the holding: "If children be so young as to need the mother's care and attention, they should, in granting the divorce, be given to her."[32] Yet the precedent from *Johns* was not quite what it appeared to be. The irony of the case's authority is that Mattie Johns did not wind up with the custody of her two young children. In the summer of 1880, Mattie Johns, now a cotton-mill worker in adjacent Copiah County, headed her own household, which included her mother plus a widow and her four children. Clearly not present were Mattie Johns's own three- and five-year-old sons, Edmond and Joshua. The boys lived with their father and a ten-year-old mulatto servant girl named Cicero.[33] Why the children remained with, or returned to, Mattie Johns's ex-husband is left to speculation. The situation suggests that while Mississippi's appellate court tended to frown on unmarried mothers having custody in most late nineteenth-century cases, practical matters of society also made it a hardship if well-off fathers, upon whom a woman like Fannie McShan could depend, were unavailable.

Unlike Mattie Johns and Fannie McShan, exceptionally few Mississippi women, or men for that matter, brought issues of child custody to the state's high court. Instead, the vast majority of Mississippians engaged child custody law while they sought divorces in county chancery courts. The evidence from those venues offers an important basis for exploring how the law evolved and what meaning(s) the doctrines pronounced by the supreme court held for various parties in different locations and over time. As at the appellate level, the maternal presumption became more compelling in local trial courts. The shift was less linear than in the high court, however, and was more subject to rapid advance and reversal. It was also more clearly mediated by issues of race.

The unpublished records from these jurisdictions differ from the appellate sources in several important respects. Chancery court case files do not consistently mention children. Also, specific doctrinal arguments and reference to the supreme court precedents discussed above were exceedingly rare. Furthermore, transparent testimony such as "I think a mother is the proper person to care for the children" seldom appears.[34] Certainly no case reporters summarized the courts' significant holdings in convenient "headnotes" like those found in the *Mississippi Reports*. Yet even if the local sources were generally less explicit about child custody, one can trace legal developments in the courts where most people experienced the law. Data derived from chancery court divorce suits reveal that the maternal presumption became compelling in the county courthouses of Mississippi, albeit at a slower rate than nationally. Mothers, and the fathers who challenged the strengthening presumption, acted out their legal subjectivity even as shifting conceptions and perceived imperatives of race significantly influenced the legal context within which they performed.

One means of gauging the ascendance of the maternal preference in the county courts is to consider alterations in female and male roles in divorce cases based on the presence of children in a family. Victorian Americans feared that maternal privileges to custody would cause women to flee homes with their children. Turn-of-the-century figures collected by the Bureau of the Census as well as certain recent historical studies seem to confirm that the maternal presumption led to increased numbers of mothers filing for divorce relative to both wives without children and fathers.[35] A second line of inquiry is to explore how legal practitioners—the attorneys who drafted legal documents and argued their clients' cases and the chancellors who decreed the courts' orders—assisted and/or resisted the development of the maternal presumption. For the legal doctrine to mature, child custody had to be recognized formally in the daily workings of Mississippi's county courts via written pleas explicitly requesting custody and in chancellors' decrees clearly ordering custodial placement. In order for the maternal preference to become the common sense of legal culture, both the participants and the practitioners had to pursue and promote the doctrine. It could not exist simply as an edict from above, juridically speaking. At the county level, the legal recognition of custodial matters *developed* unevenly and through continuing negotiation.

Examining divorces generally and not just those involving children provides a benchmark for evaluating changes in the behavior of parents specifically. Divorce became increasingly common in Mississippi's chancery courts during the second half of the nineteenth century. In contrast to the broad assertion that "women won a customary right to file for divorce" during the last third of the nineteenth century, it was not until after 1910 that more wives than husbands entered Mississippi's courts as the complaining parties, with the exception of the 1860s, during and after the Civil War.[36]

The presence of children, however, changed spouses' behaviors. Even if Mississippi wives were less likely than husbands to file for divorce into the early twentieth century, Mississippi *mothers* were usually more likely to file for divorce than the state's fathers although proportions were close or equal in the 1880s and 1890s. Parental roles and custodial matters obviously influenced decisions to terminate marriage. Motherhood thus emboldened women to take charge of their legal relations. The maternal presumption rested upon actual mothers entering county chancery courts, thereby giving concrete meaning and experience to infrequently announced appellate rules.

Factoring race into analyses of divorce, however, illuminates different patterns among wives and husbands as well as between mothers and fathers and suggests variations in accepted gender roles. The reach of the maternal presumption differed between blacks and whites. Among white couples, wives initiated at least half of all divorces, and typically many more. Within this range, white women proved least likely to file for divorce during the last quarter of the century. Perhaps this pattern resulted from a renewal of male authority, or maybe white women increasingly pushed accepted boundaries in marriage and provoked the increased male activity. In any event, after 1900 white wives became more assertive, appearing as the complaining parties in divorce actions in almost seven out of ten cases. In contrast, among African American couples, husbands filed two-thirds of divorce complaints during the fifteen years following emancipation. Although the proportions dropped in later decades, black husbands continued to instigate a majority of the divorces prior to 1925. Divorce in Mississippi was therefore a solution primarily sought by and was perhaps a prerogative of white wives and black husbands.

Most pertinent for this essay, matters of race affected patterns of behavior between divorcing *parents* and the ensuing issues of child custody. When a white couple had children, women were even more prone than their spouses to file for divorce. Indeed, county records indicate that the maternal preference had made significant inroads in chancery court adjudication, at least for whites, prior to the supreme court's enunciation of the tender-years rule in the 1879 *Johns* case. By the second decade of the twentieth century, mothers were filing more than 90 percent of divorce bills between white parents.

Mississippi chancery court activity also shows that black mothers shared in the shift toward stronger maternal claims to their children. For African American women, however, rights to their children proved much more difficult to achieve, much less obvious in the public record, and ultimately more ambiguous in effect. In contrast to whites, black mothers sought a minority of marital dissolutions between parents during the nineteenth century, but this was a larger proportion of cases than those filed by black wives without children. Not until the second decade of the twentieth century did black mothers come to file the majority of divorce cases, a position white mothers had held since at least 1860. Even in the period after 1910, when fathers pursued less than 10 percent of divorces between white parents, black men still instigated more than 40 percent of the cases involving children.[37] Thus, as the maternal presumption became ascendant in the state, shades of black and white altered its appearance.

White parents' legal interactions best fit the conventional wisdom that as the maternal preference gained greater social acceptance, mothers sought a larger proportion of divorces in comparison both to the fathers of their children and to wives who had no children.[38] The percentage of white women's divorce cases in which custody was an issue rose from just over two-fifths in the years during and immediately following the Civil War to just under half in the twentieth century. This was a noticeable increase, but it did not match the fears of those who thought divorce and custody reform would cause an exodus of women and children from the home.

The experience of black mothers, however, challenges the direct association of the maternal presumption with seeking divorce and custody of the children.

After 1900, the percentage of divorce cases filed by black mothers fell relative to the cases filed by all black wives. During the first quarter of the twentieth century, the proportion of black mothers seeking divorce dropped from almost two-fifths to less than a third of all divorce claims of black women. These figures appear to go against the common sense of the maternal presumption and African American women's own nineteenth-century experiences. They also contrast sharply with white interactions with the law, thus widening a gap in racial experiences that had been closing.[39]

Explaining this difference in behavior is more difficult than observing it. Nevertheless, analyzing formal recognition and pursuit of the maternal presumption by the law's practitioners suggests that Mississippi's African American mothers acted in the shadow of a legal culture that regarded black maternalism unevenly but which showed a special disregard for it during the first decade of the new century.[40] As a consequence of their experiences, fewer black mothers made custody a "legal" issue than the ascendance of the maternal preference and its literature would suggest.

Fluctuating gender and racial statuses of parents interacted with the law's doctrinal abstractions to influence the shape maternal presumption took in Mississippi over time. Child custody was not immediately a transparent legal matter in the state's county courts, but white mothers best negotiated their way toward formal legal recognition of their custodial concerns. During the last four decades of the nineteenth century, only two-thirds of white mothers' original bills, the first petitions placed on record by the complainants, formally requested custody awards. Emma Railey of Adams County, for example, asked the court "that she be decreed the proper custodian of her said son, and charged with his nurture and support," for her husband was "entirely unfit . . . and [would] prove incapable, both mentally and morally[,] of properly discharging the duties of a father to his child."[41] More parties were to follow Railey's example. In the first quarter of the twentieth century, Mississippi's white mothers directly asked for the control of children in over four-fifths of their suits, supporting the strengthening sway of the maternal presumption. Emboldened by complainants' successes, other white mothers asked for the custody of their children when they filed cross-bills, or countercharges, as defendants contesting husbands' petitions for divorce. Some mothers as defendants sought the legal control of their children when a husband's bill for divorce failed to request custody of the couple's offspring or even to mention them in passing.

Black mothers' experiences in Mississippi's chancery courts tell a different story. For African Americans, formal legal recognition of custodial concerns developed much more unevenly and incompletely. At times, black and white women moved in the same direction, requesting that the care and control of the children of a marriage be awarded to them at divorce more frequently in the twentieth than in the nineteenth century. Nevertheless, black women's pleas for custodial control remained less common, at times significantly, than among those of whites from the 1860s to the 1920s.[42] The gender politics of the black household and the racial politics of the larger society, most prominently during the first decade of the twentieth century, interacted with the law's own logic to shape the development of this pattern.

If a black mother did seek custody in the nineteenth century, her request could be quite detailed. Ann Heron of Marshall County asked that she be awarded the custody of her children, who had been legitimized when the Mississippi Constitution of 1869 legalized the formerly enslaved couple's marriage. In addition to emphasizing her maternal qualities and employing the ideals of the tender-years doctrine by describing "most" of her nine children as "small and helpless," Heron challenged her husband's paternal nature. "On account of his improvidence, indecency and bad temper, [Charles Heron] is wholly unfit to have the care and custody of their said children, nor does she believe he desires to have such care and custody."[43]

But more common than the formality of Ann Heron's request was the indeterminacy of Margaret Payne's original bill. When she filed for a divorce against her husband, William, she claimed only that he deserted her. In his answer, William denied abandoning his wife and asked that the charges be dismissed. Margaret's mother provided the corroborating testimony that the couple had not lived nor slept together. Margaret received the divorce, but unmentioned throughout were the couple's children, eight-year-old Henry and four-year-old Mary, whom the census enumerator found living with their mother a week after she filed the bill.[44]

At times, black couples expressed a distinct legalistic sense of custody rights and the maternal presumption that blended detail and silence. For example, when Roxy Kimmons of Lafayette County sought a divorce from Elias, neither she nor witnesses nor the court referred in any manner to children. Yet three years later, after her ex-husband's death, a custody dispute erupted between Roxy and her former mother-in-law, Polly Kimmons. During that dispute, a shared-custody arrangement created and witnessed during the divorce was placed in the court record. The agreement gave each of the parents "absolute" and "individual authority" over the children granted and allowed each parent to visit the children awarded to the other. Along with authority went responsibility, the "duty of caring for[,] cherishing and supporting the particular children" devolved to each custodian. The document expressed an especially strong maternal entitlement, for Roxy stated, "I . . . hereby waive all my rights—except insofar as hereafter mentioned—to the following children . . . and do surrender the same to the care and custody of the said Elias Kimmons."[45] The father, the traditional holder of the common-law prerogative to custody, was only the recipient of rights in Roxy and Elias's settlement. Nevertheless, the agreement that framed the Kimmonses' understanding of child custody law left Roxy vulnerable because it lacked the chancellor's explicit sanction.

Through their attorneys, black mothers increasingly made formal requests for custody orders during each successive decade in the nineteenth century. Still, only three-fifths of the complainants asked for their children in the twentieth century. Not only did these figures remain below those achieved by whites in the nineteenth century; they represent a significant contrast to the more than four-fifths of white mothers' bills that directly sought custody after 1900. Black/white distinctions were clearest in the first decade of the twentieth century. Bills such as that of Texana Long, which claimed "her care and attention [was] necessary for the health and comfort of the child," cropped up much less frequently than earlier.[46] Explicit requests for custodial awards dropped from almost two-thirds of African American mothers' complaints in the 1890s to just over two-fifths in the next decade, before rising rapidly after 1910.

Clear pleas for custody contributed to how people interacted with the law. The greatest variation in experience by different groups of complainants, however, was due to the courts' own shifting application of formal decrees that awarded the care and control of children. The courts also moved toward greater formality, but the change in practice failed to match the heightened interest expressed by complainants and their attorneys. The bench's more conservative approach maintained and sometimes widened the disparity between white and black experiences and prolonged the less-formal adjudication of blacks' custodial concerns.

For white mothers, even modest developments bolstered already strong positions. In the twentieth century, five of six divorces granted to white women with children incorporated clear, if not necessarily eloquent, orders, such as when Chancellor I. T. Blount stated that in light of the evidence, the court was "satisfied . . . the relief prayed for should be granted as to the alimony, divorce and custody of the child."[47] In combination with the increasing proportion of mothers who sought divorce among white couples, legal formality suggests that the maternal presumption had become persuasive in Mississippi among whites.

Using chancellors' positive awards of custody to compare the formal legal recognition of black mothers' custodial interests during the nineteenth and twentieth centuries suggests only incremental change. Both before and after

1900, custodial orders appear in fewer than half of divorces granted to black mothers. After the turn of the century, the figures were slightly higher than they had been in the nineteenth century. The overall change between centuries, however, hides dramatic shifts from one decade to the next.

Orders awarding custody appear in over 40 percent of the divorces filed by African American mothers during the 1870s and 1880s. In the 1890s, a slight majority of women received such declarations. This gradual development came to a halt in the decade following the turn of the twentieth century, retreating by more than half to the lowest proportion, about a quarter, of formal orders received by black mothers in the sixty years following emancipation.[48] The reversal was important, for the lack of a chancellor's specific order meant that a mother's custodial rights, whether the product of her sole desire or agreed upon with her departing spouse, were not secure.

Custodial orders were only provisional and could be modified if circumstances changed, but they did provide prima facie evidence of a parent's legal right to custody. This might at least have forestalled the inconvenience and expense of future litigation, which was no small issue amid the poverty of Mississippi. Orders could also protect women's custodial rights from more-forceful actions of their children's fathers. In *State v. Powe* (1914), the Mississippi Supreme Court held that only an "award of the custody *by decree of the court*" was binding. In that case, the court ruled that a father could not be held criminally liable for "kidnapping his own child, where its custody was in the mother *solely* by virtue of an agreement with the father."[49] A chancellor's silence—his choice not to issue a custodial order—thus served as a serious derogation of a black woman's maternal identity.

At a time when white women and the courts were confirming white maternal interests in matters of custody, black mothers' interests, which had been slowly gaining official sanction, faced a significant reversal. The increased vulnerability of custodial control that confronted black mothers contributed to the falling proportions of African American mothers who sought divorce during the first quarter of the twentieth century. Even as the bench overtly recognized black maternal desires much more commonly after 1910, recognition of the maternal presumption remained noticeably white.

The retreat from formal legal recognition of custodial rights experienced by black mothers during the first decade of the twentieth century was not the unconscious product of Vardaman-era racist nonchalance. Rather, the advancement of formal legal recognition of black men's custodial concerns suggests a deliberate shift in juridical experience. While chancellors had ordered explicit custody awards when granting divorce in only a quarter of African American fathers' cases during the nineteenth century, in the twentieth century they made such orders in more than half the cases in which they granted divorces, and most frequently during the first decade.[50] Strikingly, in the years following disfranchisement's exclusion of black males from the sphere of electoral politics, black males sought and gained greater formal and public recognition of rights in the politics of family.

Even so, courts did not always grant custody to complaining black fathers. One-third saw awards going to defendants, either as part of shared-custody arrangements or to the mother as the sole custodian. Yet when chancellors ordered such decrees, they followed the requests of the fathers, rather than creating shared custodial arrangements on their own. This indicates that black fathers had a public voice, if not at the polls, in a much-discussed area of public policy. George Shaw, for example, wanted and was granted custody of the four eldest children, who would be of assistance on his farm, for which he had been unable to make a payment in two years. To assist his household economy, George requested that the four youngest children, who were economic liabilities, be placed with and cared for by their mother, Bevill Shaw, over her protest.[51] The courts' legal support for black fathers' claims to their children served as a further slighting of black maternal identity. In turn, motherhood in Mississippi law became more clearly, and consciously, associated with whiteness.

The courts also added to the whiteness of maternalism through their interactions with white fathers. Although a father could still request and be awarded the custody of sons and daughters in the early twentieth century, the successful complaint required a great deal of justification.[52] Much more common than a court's explicit award of custody to a white father was the court's silence in response to a father's plea. When white mothers desired and/or gained custody, the law treated the issues more formally and publicly, helping to construct the preference as both legal and social. Alternative scenarios, even when the children's best interests rested with a father, wound up muted. Courts might award custody to fit fathers, but they would not advertise the orders. In one of the few twentieth-century divorce cases in which a white father, George Gean, requested "custody by proper decree," the chancellor ignored him, dissolving the marriage and finding it more legally important to state: "It . . . appears to the Court the parties of the suit are White."[53] By the early twentieth century, whiteness implied that the maternal presumption was in effect. Silence showed not an undeveloped system of formality but the conscious choice not to recognize publicly a claim of rights, whether to white males, or black parents, and especially black mothers.

Yet even black women's experiences proved dynamic, the legal recognition of their custodial concerns rising and falling and rising again. After 1910, chancellors in Mississippi began to apply more consistently maternalist ideals of parenthood to black custodial situations as well as white, perhaps once again confident that the racial order had been sufficiently reestablished to allow less worry about confusion of identities. In the second and continuing into the third decade of the century, African American mothers and their attorneys requested custody in close to 90 percent of their divorce petitions, in contrast to the 41 percent in the preceding ten years. Chancellors treated black women's custodial claims with greater seriousness as well. They explicitly awarded custody in over 70 percent of divorces granted in cases brought to the bench by black mothers, nearly a threefold advance from the previous decade.[54] It should be emphasized, however, that of all black wives filing for divorce, a smaller percentage of black women with children brought custody issues to the court than in the nineteenth century. They either chose not to make their children a legal issue and found access to the law more limited than it had been, made their decisions regarding custody in the shadow of a legal culture that had given short shrift to their custodial concerns in the past, or both.

By 1910, seven decades after Frances Foster dramatically reunited her family and caused Mississippi's highest court to consider mothers' custodial rights, the maternal presumption to custody had set firm roots in Mississippi's local jurisprudence. The gradual maturation of the maternal presumption in court precedent and practice helps explain the acceptance of doctrines many initially found to be radically dangerous to household and social stability. The state's high bench also blunted the drastic potential of maternalist ideals by privileging the causes of women maintained in other status relationships and identities, especially as remarried wives, dependent daughters, or faithful widows. Likewise, Mississippi women approached the appellate courts cautiously. The majority of women appealed their cases against third parties and not their (ex-) spouses. Decisions in their favor supported parental rights generally, not just maternal rights.

In part, the conservative tinge of the appellate court was less obvious in the county courts, the legal venues where most Mississippi women pursued their custodial rights and, interacting with male attorneys and chancellors, caused the maternal presumption to assume concrete meaning. In the local chancery courts, the state's mothers overwhelmingly challenged the fathers of their children, not other relations or employers as they had in front of the high bench. And yet concerns with "proper" status played an important role at the local level as well. In particular, the dynamics of race influenced the manner in which the maternal preference gained acceptance in Mississippi law and among its citizenry. The maternal presumption was a component and product of gender relations in the state. It also helped to determine, and was determined by, conceptions of racial identity and status. The broad acceptance of the maternal presumption by 1910 suggests that rather than undermining stable social relations in a conservative state, the maternal presumption helped to maintain them.

NOTES

1. William Coward, Chloe C. Coward, William H. Wooten, and Philip W. Alston depositions transcribed into the record of the Superior Court of Chancery of the State of Mississippi case of *James J. Alston v. Colley A. Foster & wife*; transcript located in the file of the Mississippi High Court of Errors and Appeals, Case 706, *C. A. Foster, et al. v. James J. Alstine* [misspelling occurs in archive database], RG 32, Mississippi Department of Archives and History, Jackson (henceforth cited as MDAH).

2. Michael Grossberg, *A Judgement for Solomon: The d'Hauteville Case and Legal Experience in Antebellum America* (Cambridge: Cambridge University Press, 1996), 167.

3. On widow's custody, see Suzanne Lebsock, *The Free Women of Petersburg: Status and Culture in a Southern Town, 1784–1860* (New York: W. W. Norton, 1984), 40–41. Quotation and discussion of conservative common-law precedents in Michael Grossberg, *Governing the Hearth: Law and the Family in Nineteenth-Century America* (Chapel Hill: University of North Carolina Press, 1985), 243.

4. Grossberg, *Judgement for Solomon* and *Governing the Hearth*; Hendrik Hartog, "John Barry and American Fatherhood," in his *Man and Wife in America: A History* (Cambridge, Mass.: Harvard University Press, 2000), 193–217. See also Peter W. Bardaglio, *Reconstructing the Household: Families, Sex, and the Law in the Nineteenth-Century South* (Chapel Hill: University of North Carolina Press, 1995).

5. A. B. Butts, "The Court System of Mississippi," *Mississippi Law Journal* 3 (November 1930): 97–125, esp. 97–103.

6. "An Act, concerning Divorces and Alimony," *Laws of the State of Mississippi*, Fifth Session, Adjourned, 1822 (n.p.), 355; "An Act entitled an Act concerning Divorce," *Laws of the State of Mississippi passed at a Regular Session of the Legislature, 1840* (Jackson: C. M. Price, State Printer, 1840), chap. 18, sec. 1, p. 51.

7. From Robert Josselyn, conservative Mississippi legislator, quoted by the *Boston Post* and reprinted in the *Jackson Mississippian*, April 26, 1839, 3. See Elizabeth Bowles Warbasse, *The Changing Legal Rights of Married Women, 1800–1861* (New York: Garland, 1987), 138–55.

8. *Louisa Holmes v. William Holmes*, 1 Miss. 474 (1831); *Martha Tewksbury v. Timothy Tewksbury*, 5 Miss. (4 How.) 109, 112, 113 (1839).

9. Mary Ann Mason, *From Father's Property to Children's Rights: The History of Child Custody in the United States* (New York: Columbia University Press, 1994), 57.

10. See John Postlethwaite and Joseph Bretney depositions, *Foster* Chancery Trans., 32, 50, MDAH. Frances Foster's death notice in *Holly Springs (Miss.) Gazette*, January 3, 1845, 3.

11. Jane Bretney deposition, *Foster* Chancery Trans., 53, MDAH.

12. *Maples v. Maples*, 49 Miss. 393 (1873), quotations at 404; *Moore v. Christian*, 56 Miss. 408 (1879). On African American women's competing visions of citizenship and household, see Nancy D. Bercaw, *Gendered Freedoms: Race, Rights, and the Politics of Household in the Delta, 1861–1875* (Gainesville: University Press of Florida, 2003); Laura F. Edwards, *Gendered Strife and Confusion: The Political Culture of Reconstruction* (Urbana: University of Illinois Press, 1997); Noralee Frankel, *Freedom's Women: Black Women and Families in Civil War Era Mississippi* (Bloomington: Indiana University Press, 1999).

13. *Maples v. Maples*, 49 Miss. 393, 403 (1873).

14. Bercaw, *Gendered Freedoms*, 176, 177.

15. *Maples v. Maples*, 49 Miss. 393, both 403 (1873).

16. *Laws of the State of Mississippi, 1876*, chap. 30, pp. 32–33.

17. These were the third, fourth, and fifth words of the opinion. *Moore v. Christian*, 59 Miss. 408, 409 (1879).

18. *Moore v. Christian*, 59 Miss. 408, 412 (1879).

19. Ariela R. Dubler, "In the Shadow of Marriage: Single Women and the Legal Construction of the Family and the State," *Yale Law Journal* 112 (May 2003): 1641–1715, quotations at 1679.

20. See cases in *Mississippi Reports* and *Alabama Reports*, 1819–1930. Cases are also accessible on the Web via LexisNexis Academic Universe.

21. *John J. Cocke v. A. B. Hannum and Louisa his wife*, 39 Miss. 423 (1860); *McShan v. McShan*, 56 Miss. 413 (1879); *Johns v. Johns*, 57 Miss. 530 (1879). Citations in William Hemingway, comp., *Annotated Mississippi Code* (Indianapolis: Bobbs-Merrill, 1917), chap. 20, sec. 1415, p. 851; chap. 23, sec. 2001, p. 1092.

22. On slavery and the law, see Eugene D. Genovese, "The Hegemonic Function of the Law," in his *Roll, Jordan, Roll: The World the Slaves Made* (1972; repr., New York: Vintage Books, 1976), 25–49.

23. *Cocke v. Hannum*, 39 Miss. 423, 440 (1860).

24. See, for example, *Ex parte Boaz*, 31 Ala. 425 (1858).

25. Also see *Anonymous*, 58 Miss. 15, 18 (1880).

26. Information drawn from the chancery court record found in the supreme court files: *F. A. McShan v. F. E. McShan*, Bill of Exceptions, 14; Brief for Appellant, 4; and Final Decree [Lee County Chancery Court], copy in Bill of Exceptions, 25; Mississippi Supreme Court, case 2925, RG 32, MDAH. Frank Threlkeld's (Fannie's father) household in *1880 Census of the United States*, Lee County, Mississippi, pp. 168 A–B, http://www.familysearch.org.

27. *McShan v. McShan*, 56 Miss. 413, 417, 418 (1879).

28. *McShan*, Brief and Argument of Appellees, 11; Brief for Appellant, 10; Brief for Appellant, 5, SC files, MDAH.

29. *Johns v. Johns*, 57 Miss. 530, 530, 532, 530 (1879).

30. *Johns v. Johns*, 57 Miss. 530, 532 (1879). See also Jane Turner Censer, "'Smiling through Her Tears': Ante-bellum Southern Women and Divorce," *American Journal of Legal History* 25 (January 1981): 24–47.

31. *Johns v. Johns*, 57 Miss. 530, 530, 532 (1879).

32. *Annotated Mississippi Code* (1917), chap. 20, sec. 1415, p. 851.

33. See *1880 Census of the United States* database, http://www.familysearch.org: James R. Johns, Jefferson County, Miss., p. 139A; Mattie Johns, Copiah County, Miss., p. 117C.

34. *Adam Harden v. Inda Harden*, AdamsMsChnc2421 (1908), testimony, 35. Assertions regarding chancery cases are based on more than 1,300 divorce and habeas corpus cases filed in Adams, Lafayette, and Marshall counties from 1860–1924.

35. Bureau of the Census, Department of Commerce and Labor, *Special Reports: Marriage and Divorce, 1867–1906*, part 1: *Summary, Laws, Foreign Statistics* (Washington, D.C.: Government Printing Office, 1909), 41.

36. Grossberg, *Governing the Hearth*, 251. See also Norma Basch, *In the Eyes of the Law: Women, Marriage, and Property in Nineteenth-Century New York* (Ithaca, N.Y.: Cornell University Press, 1982), 102. Bureau of the Census, *Marriage and Divorce, 1867–1906*, part 1, 25.

37. Kevin D. McCarthy, "Fit Custodians: Gender, Race, and the Law in Lower-South Trial Courts, 1830–1925 (PhD diss., University of Mississippi, 2005), 287–90.

38. See, for example, Grossberg, *Governing the Hearth*, 251.

39. McCarthy, "Fit Custodians," 292–94.

40. Robert H. Mnookin and Lewis Kornhauser, "Bargaining in the Shadow of the Law: The Case of Divorce," *Yale Law Journal* 88 (1978–1979): 950–97.

41. *Emma M. Railey v. Charles R. Railey*, AdamsMsChnc180 (1866).

42. McCarthy, "Fit Custodians," 296–99.

43. *Ann Heron v. Charles Heron*, MarshMsChnc1547 (1881).

44. *Margaret Payne v. William Payne*, LafMsChnc1863 (1880); 1880 *U.S. Census*, Lafayette County, reel 652, p. 171.

45. *Kimmons v. Kimmons*, LafMsChnc1886(1881); *Kimmons v. Pegues*, LafMsChnc2053 (1884).

46. *Texana Long v. Willie Long*, LafMsChnc3199 (1902).

47. *Mrs. Emma Jones v. Jeff Jones*, LafMsChnc3837 (1908).

48. McCarthy, "Fit Custodians," 303.

49. *State v. Powe*, 107 Miss. 770, 775 (1914), my emphasis. This case arose from a dispute in a white family.

50. McCarthy, "Fit Custodians," 303–7.

51. *Shaw v. Shaw*, LafMsChnc3325 (1903).

52. *Walter Neill v. Bessie Neill*, AdamsMsChnc2413 (1908).

53. *George Gean v. Mrs. S. H. Gean*, LafMsChnc3794 (1908). See Albert Hall Whitfield, T. C. Catchings, and William H. Hardy, comps., *The Mississippi Code of 1906 of the Public Statute Laws of the State of Mississippi* (Nashville: Brandon Printing, 1906), chap. 37, sec. 1671, p. 540, on requirement to specify race.

54. McCarthy, "Fit Custodians," 331–32.

Yankees in the Yard

Mississippi Women during the Vicksburg Campaign

MICHAEL B. BALLARD

Studies of women in the Civil War have burgeoned since Mary Elizabeth Massey's pioneering 1966 book, *Bonnet Brigades.* Our understanding of the experiences of women, their behavior, and their relationships to soldiers and slaves is now considerably more complete. Women coped with the war in various ways, and drawing conclusions can be difficult, but scholarly studies have shown that white women generally kept the line drawn between themselves and their slaves, even though they sometimes felt they needed their slaves for protection. Some white women viewed female slaves as rivals when it came to running households. Yet, as Massey points out, "White women and their slaves often drew closer during the war; for when the mistress was left without a white man's protection, the Negroes often sensed they were needed." One mistress recalled that when she chose exile, two black servants "begged to join" her. Such circumstances did not erase racial lines, but they did show that common fears could produce camaraderie. Mistresses and slaves who had worked together for years must have also felt some bonds of friendship.

Some white women, taking as many slaves as possible with them, simply deserted their homes. Since Federal soldiers often burned abandoned houses, many women returned to find nothing but ashes. Even valuable items that were buried were not safe. Slave women sometimes did not hesitate to turn their backs on their mistresses when they aided Union soldiers searching for valuables. Many women were defiant in confrontations with Union soldiers. Although some men in blue found this amusing, others ransacked and burned the houses of resistant women. Slave women sometimes found themselves

SOUTHERN REFUGEES ENCAMPED NEAR VICKSBURG

Sketch from the *Illustrated London News*, August 1863.

VICKSBURG WOMEN AFTER THE SIEGE

Courtesy of Vicksburg National Military Park, Vicksburg, Mississippi.

sexual targets of Union soldiers, and although it is impossible to determine how often attacks occurred, many black women were raped. White women sometimes deplored the practice, but they also knew that many of the victims had borne their husbands' and sons' children. In these cases, they may well have felt that such wretched women got what they deserved; never mind that the slave women had little choice but to yield to their masters' advances.[1]

This essay examines the experiences of several white and black women in Mississippi during the Vicksburg campaign, which was a lengthy effort by Union forces to capture the Mississippi River city. It focuses on the women's encounters with Federal soldiers. Many studies touch on the subject, but few have analyzed the nuanced relationships between enemy soldiers and southern women of both races.

Civil War battles brought terror to the doorsteps of southern women. Upper-class white women went from comfortable circumstances to deprivation and humiliation; lower-class white women went from not having much to having even less; and slave women went from a structured if oppressive existence to a perilously uncertain one. Whatever their station, women endured, and in most cases survived, the chaos.

Sometimes they relocated to live with their extended families and wait out the war, hoping that it would not overtake them. More often, they refused to leave their homes and faced indignities, abuse, violence, and hunger. Those who could write left bitter accounts of their suffering with common themes of anger, frustration, and terror. At the mercy of an invading army and its deadly missiles, they could not always protect their homes, nor could they count on Confederate soldiers to save them.

Many women were treated kindly and humanely by Federal troops while suffering vandalism at the hands of Confederates. Positive encounters with Union soldiers and negative ones with Confederates did not dominate immediate perceptions and memories, however. Mississippi women in the widely scattered phases of the Vicksburg campaign of 1862–63 almost always blamed Yankees for the hardships that accompanied war.

Abraham Lincoln considered Vicksburg the key to Union victory in the lower Mississippi Valley. Situated high above a hairpin turn in the river, Vicksburg's geography provided the Confederacy with impressive defensive terrain where heavy guns placed at various levels from the river's edge to higher ground threatened Union vessels. The town also served as a supply distribution point; a rail line ran east, taking supplies by train from Vicksburg wharves to all parts of the Confederacy. The Federal attempt to take Vicksburg began early in 1862 with Union warships sweeping down from Illinois to Memphis and upriver from the Gulf of Mexico to New Orleans, Baton Rouge, and Natchez.[2] An advance detachment steamed upriver from the Gulf, and officers demanded the surrender of Vicksburg on May 18, 1862, but city officials and the Confederate military refused. The Union navy then began bombarding the town, and the assault lasted, with intermittent breaks, until July 27.

Vicksburg women had already experienced the realities of war when they watched the town's young men board trains bound east to the conflict, but they got their first personal taste of combat during the initial Union attempt to reduce the Confederate bastion on the bluffs. Many left town, either to stay with relatives and friends in safer areas or to camp out in the Warren County hills. For those women, the summer of 1862 proved more inconvenient than dangerous. Those who left town were displaced but not far away. Nonetheless, an artillery shell killed one woman who remained in Vicksburg, and others had narrow escapes.

For those who fled the town, caves provided some protection, and women and other civilians learned how to judge a shell's direction and its probable impact point. When the Yankee boats finally left, life returned to normal, but much tougher times lay ahead. Initially, the women treated combat almost like a game: let the enemy come, get out of their way, watch them leave, and then return to life as usual. Their attitudes reflected naive views of the course of the war, for just because danger had passed did not mean it would not return.[3]

Although many families had already experienced war during and after the battles of Shiloh in April and Iuka and Corinth in September and October, the first personal impact of the Vicksburg campaign on Mississippi women came in North Mississippi when General U. S. Grant's troops invaded the state in November 1862. Grant planned to march his army from the Tennessee-Mississippi line south down the Mississippi Central Railroad to the capital city of Jackson, turn right, and attack Vicksburg from the east. The plan ultimately had to be abandoned, but many women in the path of Grant's force lived through days they never forgot.

In Holly Springs, women warned the invading Yankees that the Confederates would make them pay, but as Grant's army penetrated south on either side of the railroad, Mississippi women, children, and slave servants were abandoned and left vulnerable. Farther south families often awoke to find Union soldiers all over their property, in their yards, farm outbuildings, and slave quarters and on their farmland.

North Mississippi resident Cornelia Lewis Scales recorded that the Yankees suddenly appeared, camped in her family's yard, and ordered the "secesh" women to churn and serve them buttermilk. The invaders took corn and

fodder, stole chickens, and raided and trampled the garden. They used pro-
fane language and roamed the house looking for hidden treasures, including
young women who might be concealed. Scales's mother did her best to protect
her daughter, but on one occasion while doing chores outside she found herself
surrounded by Federal soldiers. They asked for food, and she boldly told them
that their comrades had taken everything. The men asked if their predeces-
sors had paid for the loot. She said yes, but that she considered Yankee money
to be as worthless as leaves. She then debated the Federals over the merits of
soldiers in blue and gray, all the while, she thought, winning their admiration
for her refusal to show fear. The soldiers did seem to find her candid partisan-
ship refreshing; one told her, "I had much rather see you so brave than for you
to pretend Union sentiments." Another commented that she was the "damdest
little Secesh I ever saw."[4]

Such tactics could also be dangerous. Cornelia Scales remembered that Kansas soldiers in particular established a record for brutality. They ripped earrings
off ladies' ears, unceremoniously removed rings and broaches, and grabbed
women's hair and jerked them around. The Kansans, perhaps steeled to such
behavior by the 1850s Bloody Kansas violence, often got into trouble with officers and were disliked by many fellow Union soldiers. Their actions showed
women that while some Federal officers kept their men from harassment,
others ignored their troops' behavior.[5]

Looting by Federal troops became a normal practice. Whether families
stayed in their homes and faced the enemy or left with plans to return, the
results were usually the same. Lafayette County resident Ella Pegues recalled
watching Confederate General John C. Pemberton's soldiers retreat. Her family
went to the county seat of Oxford to stay with relatives until the danger passed.
Later her mother returned to check on their home and found that "bonfires
had been made of the books, most of the family china had been trampled under
foot, carriages and horses taken, provisions confiscated." Ella Pegues recalled,
"My little geranium was pitched out of the upstairs window, some of my dolls
carried off and the little trunk emptied of its contents by a Yankee, who said he
could use it himself."[6]

Some women were so shocked by the effects of enemy troops on their lives
that they stood still as statues while Union troops marched through the countryside. A soldier in the Ninety-ninth Illinois noticed that as his regiment
marched through the town of Byhalia, many women looked on in terror as soldiers ravaged crops, homes, barns, and smokehouses. To these women, it must
have all seemed like a bad dream.[7]

A Dr. Bowles's daughter and niece escaped south on a lame horse guided by a family slave, but Mrs. Bowles and her small children remained at home and watched Union soldiers torch the house. General William T. Sherman ordered the fire extinguished because he wanted to use the house as his quarters. He confined the Bowles family to one room in the house and ordered the door barricaded for their own protection. During their confinement, a slave eased their situation somewhat by smuggling food through a hole in the floor. White women could not count on the assistance of slaves, however, for many escaped with Union forces.[8]

It was not unusual for Union soldiers to request that Mississippi girls sing for them. Undoubtedly, the sounds of feminine voices reminded many of them of their own wives, daughters, and sweethearts back home and may have kept them from mistreating southern women. In Washington County, a Union sergeant rode up to a house and asked the girls there to sing for him. Amanda Worthington sang "The Stars of Our Banner" and looked into the sergeant's eyes when she got to the line, "The foe must be silenced forever." His comrades soon arrived to carry out routine raiding. Worthington later heard that her father had been arrested on the plantation property (he was eventually released). She recalled, "Oh what bitter hatred toward Yankees was in my heart."[9] The popular song "The Homespun Dress," sung to the tune of "The Bonnie Blue Flag," epitomized such girls' defiant attitudes and their determination to survive the harshness of war:

> Oh yes! I am a southern girl
>   And glory in the name.
> And count it of far greater worth
>   Than glittering gems or fame.
> We envy not the northern girl
>   Her robes of beauty rare,
> Though diamonds grace her snowy neck
>   And pearls bedeck her hair.
> Hurrah! Hurrah! For the Sunny South so dear!
>   Three cheers for the homespun dress
>   The southern ladies wear.[10]

Military developments eventually gave North Mississippi women a reprieve, but the end of large-scale campaigning left them with memories of devastation and lingering anger. Grant's men carried out more destruction as they retreated to Tennessee. Although women did not openly criticize Confederate officers for leaving them vulnerable, one can easily read in their writings disappointment and shock at being abandoned to the enemy.

Union expeditions in the early months of 1863 drove many more Mississippians from their homes. The banks of the Mississippi River between Memphis and Vicksburg became trails of chimneys as many deserted homes were torched, often in retaliation for Confederate guerrillas shooting from the riverbanks at Union boats. Not until Grant managed to get troops across the river below Vicksburg on the night of April 30–May 1 did Mississippi civilians, especially women, again encounter Union troops in large numbers.

Civilians soon found themselves suffering depredations by Union troops. One lady of the house looked on in horror as Union stragglers took turns raping a young woman slave. They seemed to suggest that the same could happen to her if she resisted their demands.[11] Rapes probably occurred often. Confederate soldiers, many of whom had forced women slaves into sex in antebellum days, probably continued the practice during wartime. Rapes of white women were probably rarer, for such attacks infuriated both sides. Nonetheless, threats of rape brought shared terror to white and black women. Slave women ran away when they could, for they often found little sympathy from white mistresses, who had been infuriated over the years by the birth of slave children fathered by their husbands, sons, and relatives.

As Grant's army moved toward the Jackson–Vicksburg corridor, incidents of civilian abuse multiplied. Letitia Miller recorded that two Federal stragglers and a mulatto accomplice roamed in the wake of Grant's march inciting slaves to revolt, tying an overseer to a tree, and terrorizing her family. After his two friends became intoxicated, the mulatto managed to get them on horses, and the three escaped just before Confederate scouts arrived.[12]

Although straggler incidents persisted, the main bodies of Union troops carried out major destruction. Port Gibson had been left relatively unscathed by Grant, but Raymond—a few miles southwest of Jackson—was not so lucky. The town, including the courthouse, became a huge hospital, and Grant left behind an occupying force. When the shooting started, many Raymond residents fled. On May 12, the day of the Battle of Raymond, a Mrs. Bankston recalled, "Many people left town, knowing that it might be shelled. My next door neighbor was driving by my house in her carriage with her husband and child, and in the wagon following were her faithful servants, all refugeeing to Georgia." One of the servants called to Mrs. Bankston, "You might as well go and get anything you want, it will be gone before we get back."[13]

Another Raymond lady learned just how intolerant Union soldiers had become. She stood at the front door of her home, Confederate flag in hand, and sang a chorus of "The Bonnie Blue Flag." In response, a group of soldiers broke ranks and burned the house. Some soldiers laughed off such southern taunts, but others did not. Women often learned the hard way that it was better to keep one's mouth shut.[14]

Staying out of the enemies' way and hoping for the best proved to be a more prudent approach than displaying defiance. One woman and her family retreated into their home and kept the shutters closed until the Yankees began to move on, but they could not keep soldiers from boxing up the family silver and china to ship north. The soldiers also took books, curtains, saddles, and corn and left spoiled food scattered over the property. A young woman mourned the loss of the family cow, taken despite pleas that her mother needed the milk to nurse her sister, ill with typhoid fever. Many officers directed that homes not be violated, but other officers, both high and low ranking, were unconcerned with such issues, and theft became commonplace.[15]

Many Raymond women pitched in to nurse soldiers on both sides. Letitia Miller noted that the town became one big hospital, with the wounded occupying the courthouse and most churches. "Antiseptic surgery had not been dreamed of, and flies abounded, nay literally swarmed! And they died, how those men died—pitiful boys of sixteen or seventeen." Many women worked long hours and sacrificed family food to succor the wounded and dying.[16]

Another white woman noted the sad plight of black women. In addition to the constant threats of physical abuse, the women who followed the Union army had to work just as they had for their Confederate masters. "Well, the [black slave] women," wrote this observer, "were put to washing for the hospital. They washed from daylight until dark on the filthiest of clothes and bandages and were never paid a cent, not even given a place to sleep, only their food." Federal soldiers hired them as seamstresses but refused to pay promised wages. Many slaves swallowed their disappointment and abandoned their desire "to experience the blessings of freedom." Many others bided their time until they could walk away.[17]

Combat came to Vicksburg again, and this time the outcome would be decisive. Until the end, when their hometown fell to the enemy, heroic Vicksburg women endured danger and deprivation, though they doubtless would have been allowed to leave if they had requested passage from harm's way. Some women, content to find the safest ground, lived in caves dug by slaves. Others assisted those around them. Cave life soon evolved into a unique society. Networks of caves developed, and the siege brought about a social democracy that had never before existed. Wealthy women, who had often snubbed the less fortunate, now had to share the rigors of cave life with them.[18]

Emma Balfour kept a diary that described much of the siege's human drama. She and her husband—a doctor—lived next door to Pemberton's headquarters. Her words captured Vicksburg's chaos: "I hope never to witness again such a scene as the return of our routed army! From twelve o'clock until late in the night the streets and roads were *jammed* with wagons, cannons, horses, men, mules, stock, sheep, everything you can imagine that appertains to an army." Residents passed out food and water to the downtrodden soldiers shuffling by on their way to the city's entrenchments.[19]

Many women, children, and other noncombatants tried to leave town, but many soon returned, fearful of encountering enemy troops. Soon everyone in Vicksburg would be trapped between the Union gunboats on the river and Yankee legions. Balfour wrote mournfully, "What is to become of all the living things in this place when the boats commence shelling—God only knows— shut up as in a trap—no ingress or egress—and thousands of women and children—who have fled here for safety." She worried at the strain the refugees would put on the city's food supplies.[20]

Confederate commanders advised citizens and refugees that caves would be the safest place for them during the fighting. As locals who had experienced the 1862 bombardment had learned, the loess soil and hilly terrain made construction of caves relatively easy, and the arching artillery shells from Grant's field artillery and Federal gunboats made underground lodging more inviting than vulnerable above-ground structures.

Grant did not want to give anyone in the city time to dig in. He ordered all-out assaults on Confederate lines on May 19 and 22. The sudden, violent attacks caught some citizens off guard. Emma Balfour recorded the tumult of battle on the twenty-second, noting that her maid reported hearing the commotion when some Confederates retreated. The fighting neither stunned nor frightened Balfour, and she was surprised that she had become so steeled to the dangers of war. She stepped onto her back porch, saw Confederate reinforcements pouring toward a contested area, and felt a measure of relief. She spoke words of comfort to her distraught maid.

Mortar shells from the Union navy that flew up and over the bluffs into town forced horseback riders to leap for the nearest ditches. Balfour saw the inside of a cave for the first time, just in time to avoid a nearby exploding shell. Pinned between Grant's artillery and Union navy mortars, she had a "sense of suffocation from being underground, the certainty that there was no way of escape, that [they] were hemmed in, caged."[21]

The experience convinced the Balfours to dig their own cave; though Emma Balfour preferred to sit out the fighting in their home, the risk was too great. A family cave meant less crowded conditions, but she determined nevertheless to "stay out" as long as she could.[22]

After the second assault failed, Grant resorted to siege operations. For Vicksburg women, the siege days were fraught with hourly uncertainty. For every lull, there were periods of heavy shelling that brought terror and extreme mental stress. Security could be found only in the caves.

In spite of the urgency, the caves were not always built pell-mell; much thought went into how they could be constructed for maximum safety. Mary Loughborough's lengthy account of siege life noted, "Our policy in building had been to face directly away from the river. All caves were prepared, as near as possible, in this manner. As the fragments of shells continued with the same impetus after the explosion, in but one direction, onward, they were not likely to reach us, fronting in this manner with their course." Because Union lines formed an arch from north of the city to the southern extremities, shells might come from any direction, causing Loughborough to mourn, "Really was there to be no mental rest for the women of Vicksburg." She noted that male slaves made good money hiring out to dig family caves. People who lived in caves in dangerous, less desirable locations often sold their places and moved elsewhere. Cave construction became a booming siege industry as citizens sought to make their underground life as comfortable and safe as possible.[23]

Despite their efforts, security was never certain. On one occasion, Loughborough was reading, seemingly in safety, when suddenly a rifled shell struck near the cave entrance moments after she had called in her servants. The shell penetrated the ground without exploding, but more shells were flying, and another fell to the ground inside, where it lay ominously still and smoking. For an eternal moment, she recalled, "our eyes were fastened upon it, while we expected every moment the terrific explosion would ensue." Loughborough hugged her child tightly. Suddenly her servant boy George ran forward, grabbed the shell, and pitched it outside. Fortunately it never exploded, but it had certainly terrified the cave's occupants. So it went, Loughborough wrote, "the long weary days—when we could not tell in what terrible form" death might arrive.[24]

Death often came, and quickly, leaving survivors numb and grief stricken. Loughborough shared the pain of a mother whose child had been killed in its sleep when a heavy mortar shell came through the top of a cave. She wrote with much anguish: "How very sad this life in Vicksburg!—how little security can we feel, with so many around us seeing the morning light that will never more see the night!" Loughborough sometimes paced back and forth near the entrance to the cave to relieve her tension as she listened carefully for approaching missiles.[25]

Not all cave-life stories are filled with the anguish, anxiety, and doom of the Balfour and Loughborough accounts. Despite the rain of terror falling so frequently outside, Jane Bitterman recalled that most of the time life underground "was exceptionally pleasant," remarking, "I think I have never known sounder or more refreshing sleep than I experienced in the cave."[26] Surely her cave was not located in a major impact area swept by Union guns.

While most women learned to cope as cave dwellers, others braved the streets to help in hospitals. One such volunteer nurse earned the admiration of a pastor who observed her dedication to a young soldier she knew. Often she spent full days at his side until she tired and had to find lodging and sleep at night. Her dedication made her oblivious to the iron and lead falling from the skies. Determined to remain faithful to her commitment to care for her friend, "week after week, with untiring diligence would she nurse & feed this young man." At times she looked ill, but she never wavered. We do not know the fate of the patient or his nurse, who embodied the raw courage of women who lived through the siege.[27]

Vicksburg women trapped within the Union lines wrapping around the outer reaches of the city could expect no more security than those in the shelled zone. Ida Barlow recalled a costly incident. One morning a company of Yankees asked if her father had seen any Rebels. Mr. Barlow responded honestly that he had not. The company marched down the road, where they were ambushed by a detachment of Confederates hiding in a ravine. Several Union men fell wounded, and their captain was killed. The enraged survivors, certain that Barlow's father had known about the ambush in advance, "at once put the torch to [their] home and told [her] father that if he was on the premises at sundown they would hang him." The family, carrying no possessions save what they wore, walked to the home of Barlow's grandfather, leaving Federal soldiers to take livestock, chickens, and all the garden produce.[28]

The siege went on day after day as more Union soldiers and supplies arrived via the Mississippi River. Citizens trapped between Confederate lines and the Union navy hoped just to survive. Women who had witnessed the 1862 attack knew, after forty-three days, that they could not endure much longer. When the end came on July 4, they shed tears and coped with disappointment, yet remained defiant.

Margaret Lord, wife of local minister William Lord, who served in a Mississippi regiment, left an account of her refusal to be cowed by defeat. A Union soldier, having some connection with St. Louis newspapers and doubtless hoping for a story, called at her home one evening before dusk to ask many questions about the experiences of Vicksburg residents. He expressed sympathy, "which," Lord remarked, "though kind in intentions, was hard to bear." They had neither candles nor kerosene, and Lord told the man, "It is hardly necessary for me to apologize for a want of light. We have none." He told her he had influence in the army and would see that they received what they needed. Lord recalled, "I felt the proud blood rush to my face and tingle in my veins as I said, 'Sir, we stand in need of everything, but you must excuse me, I can receive nothing from you.'"[29]

Many women harbored such pride and contempt. They had suffered privations and devastation, and they were in no mood to be congenial. One Union soldier wrote of Vicksburg women that no humans more deserved scorn and contempt. No matter how kind the conquerors tried to be, they were often refused in Margaret Lord's unyielding manner.[30]

With the surrender came scenes of plunder that Grant did his best to bring under control, but the stage had been set for more depredations against civilians who lived between Vicksburg and Jackson and in the capital city itself. Sherman issued instructions that there must be no pillaging, for the army had ample supplies. But the Union soldiers either never heard his orders or chose to ignore them. Furniture, books, bedding, and kitchen wares were broken, torn, ripped up, and scattered around yards. A physician in the Thirty-third Wisconsin, hearing bitter accounts, felt especially shamed when an elderly woman claiming to be ninety-five years old told him that she had experienced the American Revolution and the War of 1812, and she wondered why this war had deteriorated into attacks on the very existence of women, children, and the sick. She showed the doctor the bed where Federal soldiers had stripped the sheets and bedcoverings while her daughter lay seriously ill. Other bedding had been ripped open and feathers scattered around the house, mirrors had been cracked, and curtains torn.[31]

General Joseph E. Johnston retreated from Jackson for the second time, and again the town suffered many destroyed dwellings and myriad fires. Johnston's withdrawal marked the end of the Vicksburg campaign, but women in Mississippi would suffer through two more years of destructive war.

The loss of Vicksburg took the fight out of Mississippi civilians, particularly women. Some remained loyal to "the cause," which meant different things to different people, but they had practically no faith in the Confederate government. The fall of Vicksburg destroyed Mississippi's morale. As one woman stated, "The Yankees have ruined this country completely and I am afraid the Confederacy is gone also."[32]

The havoc of war brought long-lasting ramifications to women's psyches. African American women had to cope with the vagaries of freedom, overshadowed by violent white resistance to Reconstruction. As one historian has noted, "The image of black women as somehow not women lingered and took on new life with the reconstruction of the cotton plantation and of white womanhood in the postwar South."[33]

For many years after the war, southern white women, including many Mississippians, scorned any and everything northern. Undoubtedly a deep-seated hatred of the North stretched across the length and breadth of the former Confederacy. A few southern belles married northern beaux, but many more "closed the shades and doors to evade the eyes of Yankees passing their houses, crossed the street to avoid meeting them on a stroll, shunned all social contact, and swore never to receive a northerner in their homes." White women in Vicksburg became inflamed when they saw freedwomen walking arm in arm with Federal soldiers. Whatever notions their former mistresses had about black women's loyalty quickly evaporated. Beyond the scorn they felt for interracial coupling, the terror the white women had survived underscored their vulnerability, and they were generally unforgiving of Yankees. That Confederate soldiers and the Confederate government had likewise contributed to their insecurity was conveniently forgotten.[34]

In 1895, various women's organizations across the South, most of which had been involved in honoring and assisting Confederate veterans, came together under the name United Daughters of the Confederacy. In Article II of their constitution, these women included among their statements of objects and purposes, "to cultivate ties of friendship among our women whose fathers, brothers, sons (and in numberless cases) mothers shared common dangers, suffering and privations, and to perpetuate honor, integrity and other noble attributes to true Southern character."[35] The Daughters wanted to be sure that the deprivations suffered by Confederate women would not be forgotten.

As postwar years mellowed animosity among veterans North and South, they held joint reunions, but the sentiments of many women remained firm. Mississippi women and their sisters across the South played key roles in perpetuating positive aspects of Confederate memory and negative attitudes toward Yankee soldiers. The women worked to compel southern politicians to eliminate Reconstruction policies. The ultimate victory of "Redemption" owed much to the determination of white women in Mississippi and elsewhere in the South to ensure that their trials would never be forgotten. But in many respects the end of Reconstruction returned white and African American women to the structures—and indeed the limitations—of their wartime and prewar lives.

NOTES

1. Mary Elizabeth Massey, *Bonnet Brigades* (New York: Knopf, 1966), 274; Sara E. Gardner, *Blood and Irony: Southern White Women's Narratives, 1861–1937* (Chapel Hill: University of North

Carolina Press, 2004), 103; Drew Gilpin Faust, *Mothers of Invention: Women of the Slaveholding South in the American Civil War* (Chapel Hill: University of North Carolina Press, 1996), 60–61, 198–202; Lee Ann Whites, *The Civil War as a Crisis in Gender: Augusta, Georgia, 1860–1890* (Athens: University of Georgia Press, 1995), 25–27; Laura Edwards, *Scarlett Doesn't Live Here Anymore: Southern Women in the Civil War Era* (Urbana: University of Illinois Press, 2000), 80, 144–45. See also the following for a concise discussion of trends in scholarship on southern women and the war: Drew Gilpin Faust, Thavolia Glymph, and George C. Rable, "A Woman's War: Southern Women in the Civil War," in *A Woman's War: Southern Women, Civil War and the Confederate Legacy,* ed. Edward D. C. Campbell Jr. and Kym S. Rice (Richmond, Va.: Museum of the Confederacy; Charlottesville: University Press of Virginia, 1996), 1–27.

2. On the Vicksburg campaign, see Michael B. Ballard, *Vicksburg: The Campaign That Opened the Mississippi* (Chapel Hill: University of North Carolina Press, 2004).

3. Ballard, *Vicksburg*, 21; Peter F. Walker, *Vicksburg: A People at War, 1860–1865* (Chapel Hill: University of North Carolina Press, 1960), 93–120; John McKenzie to My Dear Uncle, July 13, 1862, Duncan McLaurin Papers, Perkins Library, Duke University, Durham, North Carolina (henceforth cited as Duke University).

4. Ballard, *Vicksburg*, 108; Cornelia Lewis Scales to Loulie W. Irby, October 29, 1862, in *My Darling Loulie: Letters of Cornelia Lewis Scales to Loulie W. Irby during and after the War between the States,* ed. Martha Neville Lampkin (Boulder, CO: privately published, 1955), 45–49, copy in Cornelia Lewis Scales Collection, Southern Historical Collection, Wilson Library, University of North Carolina at Chapel Hill (henceforth cited as UNC–CH).

5. Scales to Irby, 60.

6. Ella F. Pegues, "Recollections of the Civil War in Lafayette County," 3–4, Mrs. Calvin S. Brown Papers, Mississippi Department of Archives and History, Jackson (henceforth cited as MDAH).

7. George P. Metz Diary, November 26, 1862, entry, in George Metz Diaries, Duke University.

8. Maude Morrow Brown, "What Desolation! At Home in Lafayette County, Mississippi, 1860–1865," 102, Maude Morrow Brown Manuscript, MDAH.

9. Amanda Doughtery Worthington Diary, April 19 and 23, 1863, entries, UNC–CH.

10. Brown, "What Desolation!" 94–95.

11. Samuel Agnew Diary, vol. 7a, May 7, 1863, entry, Samuel Agnew Diaries, UNC–CH.

12. "Some Recollections of Letitia D. Miller," 9–10, Letitia D. Miller Collection, UNC–CH.

13. Rebecca Blackwell Drake, *The Battle of Raymond, and Other Collected Stories* (Raymond, Miss.: Friends of Raymond, 1999), 34. Neither Mrs. Bankston's first name nor that of her husband could be ascertained since many Bankstons are listed in the 1860 census of Hinds County.

14. Ibid.

15. Lavinia to Emmie, June ?, 1863, in Crutcher-Shannon Papers, MDAH; "Some Recollections of Letitia Miller," 10–11.

16. Drake, *Battle of Raymond*, 51.

17. Anonymous, "Written by a Lady in Raymond at the Time of the Battle There," clipping in Personal Accounts of Siege of Vicksburg file, Vicksburg Campaign Series, Journals/Diaries/Letters Subseries, Vicksburg National Military Park Archives, Vicksburg, Mississippi (henceforth cited as VNMP; different series/subseries will be noted).

18. Ballard, *Vicksburg*, 285.

19. Emma Balfour Diary, May 17, 1863, entry, MDAH.

20. Ibid.

21. Ibid.

22. Ibid., May 20, 1863, entry.

23. [Mary Ann Loughborough], *My Cave Life in Vicksburg with Letters of Trial and Travel, by a Lady* (New York: D. Appleton, 1864), 72–74, 76.

24. Ibid.

25. Ibid., 81.

26. Jane Bitterman, clipping, Cave Life file, VNMP.

27. Kenneth Trist Urquhart, ed., *Vicksburg, Southern City under Siege: William Lovelace Foster's Letter Describing the Defense and Surrender of the Confederate Fortress on the Mississippi* (New Orleans: Historic New Orleans Collection, 1987), 48–49.

28. A. A. Hoehling et al., eds., *Vicksburg: Forty-seven Days of Siege, May 18–July 4, 1863* (Englewood Cliffs, N.J.: Prentice-Hall, 1969), 120.

29. Ibid., 283–84. The general consensus of those who have studied the Vicksburg siege is that it lasted forty-seven days. These scholars count the May 19 and 22 attacks as part of the siege, though they clearly were not. The official records show that Grant did not mention beginning the siege until May 23, the day after the failed second assault. Thus the siege lasted forty-three days, not forty-seven.

30. Ballard, *Vicksburg*, 400.

31. C. R. Blackwell, "In the Tornado, Days of '62–'64: from the Diary and Letters of an Army Surgeon to His Family," pp. 103, 117–119, in Thirty-third Wisconsin file, Vicksburg Campaign Series, Regimental Files Subseries, VNMP.

32. Elizabeth Parkman to Mrs. Alexander F. McGahey, [July 1863], Forty-second Alabama Infantry file, Old Courthouse Museum, Vicksburg, Mississippi.

33. Thavolia Glymph, "'This Species of Property': Female Slave Contrabands in the Civil War," in Campbell and Rice, *Woman's War*, 71.

34. Ballard, *Vicksburg*, 419; Gaines M. Foster, *Ghosts of the Confederacy: Defeat, The Lost Cause, and the Emergence of the New South, 1865 to 1913* (New York: Oxford University Press, 1987), 29–33.

35. Mary B. Poppenheim et al., *The History of the United Daughters of the Confederacy*, 3 vols. in 2 (Raleigh, N.C.: Edward & Broughton, 1956–88), 1–2:10–11.

The Gendered Construction of Free Labor in the Civil War Delta

NANCY BERCAW

In the nineteenth century, any discussion of emancipation was laced with gender, or to be more precise, the language of manhood. "Put a United States uniform on his back and the *chattel* is a *man*," declared Henry Johns, a white Union soldier serving in South Carolina. Sergeant Prince Rivers agreed, "Now we sogers are men—men de first time in our lives. Now we can look our old masters in de face. . . . Now we ain't afraid, if they meet us, to run the bayonet through them."[1] Manhood, although conceived in different terms, served as the cornerstone of liberty for both North and South, black and white.

Historians, listening to their sources, likewise emphasize the importance of manhood in the negotiation over freed people's economic and political rights.[2] The many "rehearsals for reconstruction" during the war have been analyzed, at least in part, as northern attempts to transform former slaves into free working men. According to free-labor ideology, wage work taught masculine responsibility. Theoretically, it enabled men to provide for and protect their families, to learn the value of thrift and saving, and to delay gratification. As such, wage work provided the perfect school for masculine freedom.[3]

Despite this optimism, however, historians have noted that the leased plantation system took a cautious approach to emancipation. Former slaves were granted not property but simply the right to work for a wage.[4] Even that limited right, according to many Americans in the nineteenth century, needed to fall under the stewardship of white men. Investigating the conditions of free labor in the wartime South, General James S. Wadsworth commented, "When these people first come to the depots, you must take them, like children, get them on the plantations, and make the bargain for them, no matter whether it be for seven or ten dollars a month." He continued, "They are only too docile. . . . It is because of that docility, that we must exercise a certain guardianship over them and suspend reconstruction until we have thoroughly emancipated them, and

MARRIAGE OF A COLORED SOLDIER AT VICKSBURG
BY CHAPLAIN WARREN OF THE FREEDMEN'S BUREAU

From *Harper's Weekly*, June 30, 1866.

got the idea of freedom into their heads."[5] Wadsworth, like many others, saw the leased plantation system as a halfway house between slavery and freedom.

Why did many northern whites believe that freed people needed this degree of guidance, protection, and restraint? Typically historians interpret these actions as the product of northern ideologies regarding class and race, and their analyses are convincing.[6] Yet they overlook the obvious. Dependency was also a gendered language of womanhood. Coming south, northerners stumbled over the indisputable fact that any free-labor system devised during the war would consist not of virile men, but of women, children, the old, and the disabled. Could the nation build a system of free soil, free labor, and free men out of a workforce of women or, better yet, out of a workforce of black men who were like women because they were helpless and homebound? The army, caught in a bizarre web of contradictory gender, racial, and class ideologies, attempted to teach black women and dependents to be free and independent working men.

Historians largely ignore the role of womanhood in the construction of free labor in the South.[7] They agree that the wartime experiments with wage labor established longstanding models for the implementation of free labor in the South that held firm well into the twentieth century. Yet few have asked how the contingencies of war shaped the outcome of these experiments. Arguably, no wartime experiment touched as many lives and left as long lasting an impression in the Mississippi Valley as the leased plantation system. One year into the program, an estimated 21,500 freed people worked on leased plantations, and 8,094 of those labored in the Mississippi Delta.[8] Closely examining the development of the leased plantation system in the Delta, this essay will explore how a workforce of women, children, and the elderly influenced wage work at its inception.

The U.S. Army policy to recruit African American men into the army and to employ women as free laborers on leased plantations was not simply an imposition of free-labor ideology, but a negotiated response between northern perceptions of household and the actions of freed people themselves. It was a reaction to the first year of emancipation, when slaves freed themselves.

Emancipation came to the Delta in two stages. The first, initiated by slaves, occurred in 1862, when Union troops captured and controlled Memphis to the north and Helena to the west just across from some of the Delta's richest plantations. Escaping to Union lines or staying at home and defying their white masters, African Americans freed themselves without the official sanction of President Lincoln.

The first declaration of freedom exposed differences among southern blacks, revealing a gendered construction of liberty. As Union forces drew near, it was mostly young men—in their teens and twenties—who were willing to risk their lives in a mad dash for freedom. Making their way through Confederate defenses, young men gambled with their lives and with the very real possibility that they might never see family or friends again. Men like George Parker did not hesitate when the opportunity for freedom presented itself. Parker, who had been living on Leota Landing on the banks of the Mississippi River, slipped onto a Union gunboat one night and was never seen by his wife again. On the night that he left, George had been married to Maria for over five years. Maybe Maria chose not to go with George. Maybe he simply left her. We only know for certain that she "staid on the place during the war" despite the numerous opportunities she herself would have had to leave. Perhaps Maria and George simply defined freedom on different terms. Many men and women faced this same choice, and many, like Maria and George, went their separate ways. They experienced war and the first moments of freedom in radically different contexts.[9]

The young men who pushed their way through Confederate lines asserted their personal autonomy by stealing themselves and claiming their right to their own bodies. Often traveling great distances, they relied on force and the plantation communities along their way. Reports came in from Sunflower County that African Americans were arming themselves. "Som six of the Negros Rebeld & Armed them selves . . . with Dubel Barel guns," wrote John W. Boyd. "Since that Som 5 Moor Rebeld . . . & Even sinc that time the Negros one the Place has *cut* the throat of the overseer."[10] In Boyd's report, rebellion was a contagion spreading rapidly throughout the county. Seizing the opportunity, Turner Holts and his uncle John Ben traveled over eighty miles from Sunflower County to the Mississippi River to join the Union forces. They, like many others, must have counted on slave communities along their route for food, shelter, and information. Planters apparently were at a loss in trying to control these underground railroads. Howard Wilkinson, a planter along the Mississippi Gulf coast, complained, "Negroes in numbers are constantly coming here from the interior & are harboured by ours until a means of escape to the Fed's. is afforded them."[11] Unable to command his own plantation, Wilkinson called for state troops to halt the steady hemorrhaging of slavery.

Wilkinson's letter and many others like it indicate that by the spring of 1862 slavery no longer functioned on many plantations. Yet when provided a choice, most African American women, children, and older men did not run for freedom. Instead they chose to stay on the plantations with their families and lay claim to the land. They located the meaning of emancipation in the security of the land, the crop, and the community, not in individual autonomy. Yankee troops saw their stubborn refusal to leave the plantation as a demonstration of a cautious and dependent nature, but white southerners knew otherwise. Having built their own houses, tended the livestock, cleared the land, and planted the cotton, many freed people were not about to abandon the plantation. As Jonathan Pearce, a Washington County planter, explained, "I believe every negro on this place will go to the Yankees before they would go [with us] . . . and at the same time [I] think they have made up their minds to stay at home."[12]

Many African Americans had indeed "made up their minds to stay at home." They felt a proprietary interest. They defined freedom by staying at home, working the land together as a group of interdependent black households, and vigorously entering the active cotton trade. Ada Burton, like Maria Parker, chose to stay on the plantation when Peter, her husband of ten years, left to join the army. Like many women who stayed on the land, Ada had young children to feed and raise. It was a practical decision. Perhaps unwilling to gamble with the complete unknown, she chose to stay on the land where she knew she could provide for her children. Ada's actions after the war, however, suggest that more than security kept her at home. She and Peter remained in close contact after he left the plantation, and both considered themselves to be husband and wife for the rest of their lives. Yet they seldom lived together. Ada refused to leave the plantation, and Peter was too active in Republican politics to come home. Writing from St. Louis and finally Kansas, Peter begged Ada to join him, but she had formed an unbreakable bond to the community and the land.[13]

In their camps along the Mississippi River, Union forces observed a gendered response to emancipation in the black community and drew conclusions that would shape U.S. government policy toward the freed people for the duration of the war. The second wave of emancipation occurred on January 1, 1863, when Lincoln issued the Emancipation Proclamation. In response, U.S. Secretary of War Edwin M. Stanton ordered Adjutant General Lorenzo Thomas to the Mississippi Valley to investigate the possibility of recruiting former slaves into the military. Thomas quickly responded with a two-prong approach. First, he initiated the recruitment of all able-bodied black men into the armed forces. Second, he established a system of leased plantations on land abandoned by white slaveholders. Under the leased plantation system, venture capitalists rented confiscated rebel property from the United States government and hired former slaves to work the crop for wages.[14] In many ways, Lorenzo Thomas's two-part plan—to enlist black men into the military and to put black women to work on leased plantations—mirrored freed people's actions in 1862.

The actions of black men startled and confused the Yankees. According to popular belief in the North, slavery infantilized and feminized black men by

placing them in a childlike dependency on slaveholders.[15] How could northerners reconcile creating free and independent working men out of a workforce of
dependents? Yet as hundreds of freedmen made their way against great odds
through Confederate territory into Union lines, many Yankees were impressed.
"[They are] very shrewd in escaping their masters," reported U.S. Army chaplain J. Grant, and they "exhibit intelligence greater than has been attributed to
their race." By defying white southerners, black men demonstrated what northerners recognized as essential masculine virtues: individualism, independence,
and bravery.[16]

The army interpreted the actions of black women, on the other hand, as
essentially passive and dependent. By choosing to stay on the plantation, freed
women were perceived as helpless and defenseless. But here Yankee perceptions
became twisted and distorted yet again. Women may have stayed at home, but
they were scarcely dependent. Moreover, despite the army's rhetoric, those who
stayed at home were not all women. Women may have formed the majority of
the adults on the plantations during the war (ranging from 62 to 70 percent
of the "first class hands"), but many men chose to stay on the land as well.[17] Yet
the army persistently referred to plantation workers as women. The wording of
General Lorenzo Thomas is suggestive. "Men," he argued, "should be employed
with our armies . . . and the others with the women and children placed on
abandoned plantations to till the ground."[18] "The others" were no doubt men,
but Thomas simply saw them as dependents, or, more accurately, he hardly saw
them at all.

So why the leased plantation system? How did the "problem of dependents"
shape the parameters of free labor in the South? The leased plantation system
served two goals, one pragmatic and the other didactic. The practical purpose of this plan was to take wartime refugees off the government payroll by
encouraging them to return to the plantations and work for others. But the
leased plantation system also served higher, loftier goals. According to Brigadier General James S. Wadsworth, the successful implementation of the leased
plantation system would "inaugurate at once the regeneration of the African
Race, restore the productiveness of the Country, make the people of the South
homogeneous with those of the North, and give to the nation a Peace which
will be lasting." All this could be accomplished by grafting a northern wage-
labor system onto the plantation economy and by transforming former slaves
into free working men.[19]

Both North and South agreed that liberty rested securely on manhood.
Yet each society grounded the source of masculine liberty in a different set of
social relations. In the North, the transition to a wage-labor economy centered

masculine liberty in competitive individualism. Each man, through his right to work and his right to vote, had equal access, according to theory, to a free market of political and economic liberties.

In the South, on the other hand, masculine liberty centered on the social relations of household. The only free men in the antebellum South were those who could demonstrate their mastery over others as the heads of their households. White men, therefore, both rich and poor, stood in a kind of common equality with one another as independent people in a landscape dominated by their dependents (wives, children, slaves, and wage workers). This measure of independence awarded men citizenship and the right to vote not as individuals per se but as the heads of their households.[20] Unlike in the North, home was not separated from work and public not divided from private. Instead, they were openly and inextricably linked in the physical and ideological construction of household.

Northerners, therefore, faced what they perceived as a bizarre gender inversion when they confronted the plantation household. All blacks were workers and therefore men. Yet, on the other hand, all blacks worked in their masters' households and were therefore women. To confuse matters further, many of these workers were indeed women.

The leased plantation system responded to this constant slippage between class, gender, and race by offering freed people a dependent position within a free-labor system. As recent legal historians suggest, free-labor ideology in the North did not extend to all workers. Women, domestics, and many blacks, unskilled workers, and "heavy laborers" were not granted full autonomy or independence in their own domestic affairs. These workers were often subject to "masters" rather than "employers." By custom, masters exercised the right to oversee their servants' labor, leisure, and domestic arrangements. In contrast, laws and customs granted skilled workers greater spheres of independence from their employers' oversight.[21]

If northerners hoped to transform former slaves into free working men, why did they slip them into the leased plantation system to labor under "masters" rather than "employers"? Why did they strip freed people of their right to labor as free wage workers rather than as dependents?

In large part, the answers to these questions can be found in the actions of black women in 1862 and the spring of 1863, when the leased plantation system was still in the early stages of development. The "problem of dependents" was that the "dependents" were, in many cases, not dependent enough. Freed women's ability to enter the workforce and provide for their families startled northern men.

By April 1863, recruitment drives in the Mississippi Delta began in earnest stripping each plantation of its young men. Driving deep into the forbidding swamps laced with Confederate guerrilla troops, Union forces made their way from plantation to plantation declaring, "Boys put down your hoes & stop plowing—you are all free." The men simply dropped their plow lines, unhitched the mules, and rode off to join the Union army.[22] Left behind, women were scarcely dependent or helpless. A. W. Harlan, agent of the U.S. government, reported that a recruiting officer came through his region "and carried away twenty of the Best men [on the plantation] leaveing some families without any men to assist them. Some of those women thus left alone with little children seemed discouraged whilst others were quite cheerful." An amazed Agent Harlan continued, "I will give a single instance one Martha Thompson eighteen years old had a small Babe when asked where her husband was replied that he ran away the first chance and joined the union army. . . . I enquired how she made a liveing she replied that she left her baby with a neighbor and then went and piled cord wood."[23] Martha Thompson, like other African American women who called on the resources of the black community to share child rearing, food, and shelter, assumed mastery over herself and went to work.

Perhaps what was most disturbing about black women was not just their supposed "dependency," but also the fact that as dependents they were challenging the rights of property. With freedom, African Americans did not differentiate between cotton they grew on their own time and the cotton they grew for the planters. As the producers of the crop, they laid claim to all the cotton on the plantations.[24]

The rampant cotton speculation in and around the Mississippi Delta permitted freedpeople to enter the cotton market with ease. As Rear Admiral David D. Porter remarked, "I have scarcely ever yet met with a Negro who has not been able to support himself, they are naturally astute at making money, and when they are not it is an exception to the rule."[25] In 1862, freedpeople in independent settlements near the Mississippi River negotiated the harvesting and marketing of the cotton crop first among themselves and later with potential buyers and the ever-present U.S. Army. Many people made enough in one year to pay their passage north to Cairo or St. Louis.

By August 1862, the government began to crack down on what it saw as a usurpation of property. In the Delta, General Frederick Steele enunciated this new policy. As former slaves, Steele argued, black southerners legally owned no property. The land, cotton, and timber belonged only to whites who could be classified as loyal or disloyal. White loyalists were permitted to keep their property, while the U.S. government seized rebel property as contraband.

Significantly, not just slave status but also black skin exempted an individual from legal trade. Even if black southerners could establish a legal claim to the crop, they were not permitted to trade the cotton themselves.[26] This understanding of property ignored any rights the producer might have to the crop and undermined freedpeople's aggressive redefinition of themselves as free and independent.

The leased plantation system was a logical extension of this policy. It swiftly eradicated any claims by blacks to the plantation, the crop, and even to control of their own labor. Plantations abandoned by their owners could not be relinquished to the laborers. Permitting ownership of the self was one thing, but extending ownership to material goods was quite another. The leased plantation system killed two birds with one stone. It protected the rights of property while placing dependents, mostly women and children, back within the secure confines of a radically restructured plantation household.

But here the boundaries between race and gender slipped. While the government denied black men any *legal* claim over property, apparently many officials felt that, as men, freedmen could *manage* property. General Wadsworth in 1863 passionately argued for granting freedpeople greater autonomy. He suggested dividing the plantations and renting land to freedpeople to manage their labor themselves. "I would take one of those great estates . . . and divide it into ten, twenty, or fifty lots and go on the plantations . . . wherever there was a whole family at home—husband, wife, and children, (because you could not put a woman on a lot; she must go work the plantation for wages,) and I would say to the man—'Here are ten acres, you may have these ten acres for $10 an acre, payable in ten years.'"[27] Blacks may have been seen as dependent; laborers may have been seen as dependent; but with the critical component of manhood, this could be overcome. A woman, however, "must go to work the plantation for wages." The leased plantation system was necessary because the workers, from the military's perspective, were mostly women, and women needed to be provided for and protected.

The system of leased plantations was designed, in large part, to deal with free people who, in the eyes of northerners, were unfit for freedom. From the northern perspective, the demise of slavery threatened to unleash an unruly population represented most forcefully by women. As women without men, former slaves without masters, and workers without employers, the freedwomen were literally loose, unfettered by the discipline and order of hierarchy. As historian Sally Alexander suggests, the transition from a household economy to a free-labor system in Britain created enormous fears of social upheaval as traditional hierarchies were reconfigured. The transition to wage labor undermined the

authority of the head of the household. This tension, she argues, was manifested in fears of sexual anarchy. The head of household no longer controlled
the labor of his family as his family members became individual competitors in
the labor market. Men protested this loss of parental control through a popular
discourse of misogyny, accusing women of sexual depravity. While men represented labor, women represented sexuality, which must be harnessed to reproduction or threaten social chaos.[28]

In the South, emancipation and the demise of the plantation household
created, from the northern point of view, a similar lack of control that may
have influenced the leased plantation system's cautious approach to freedom.
The army's primary contact with freedwomen was in the camps that sprang up
around Union lines. "The evil is a most perplexing one," wrote Brigadier General
William Sooy Smith. "Whole families of them are stampeding and leaving their
masters. . . . Something should be done to shield our service. . . . Their presence
in the immediate vicinity of our troops is demoralizing in the extreme, giving
rise to licentiousness of the lowest and most degrading kind." Colonel F. W.
Lister agreed: "The immorality developed after last pay day required a strong
effort to repress it. Large herds of colored prostitutes flocked to Bridgeport from
both ends of the line." Yet these women were, for the most part, not prostitutes,
but wives attempting to reestablish their households by finding their husbands
in the Union army. As George Buck Hanon, a soldier under Lister's command,
explained, "Men's wifes comes here to see them and he will not allow them to
come into they lines. . . . After comg over hundred miles [to see him] a colard
man think jest as much of his wife as a white man dus of his." The breakdown of
the plantation household created a world of autonomous dependents—a world
where many women were free to control their own sexuality, but also a place
where wives without husbands were perceived as "herds of prostitutes."[29]

The Union soldiers' inability to conceive of women outside the domestic
relation led to abuse. Not belonging to another man, black women were denied
even the most basic right to ownership and control of their bodies. Soldiers
and officers sexually abused them, threw them out of camp, and denied them
access to their husband's rations or wages. A committee of chaplains protested:
"The wives of some have been molested by soldiers to gratify their licentious
lust, and their husbands murdered in endeavering to defend them, and yet the
guilty parties . . . were not arrested. . . . For the sake of humanity, for the sake of
christianity, for the good name of our army, for the honor of our country, cannot something be done to prevent this oppression & to stop its demoralizing
influences upon the soldiers themselves?"[30]

The destruction of slavery demolished the vast plantation household, unleashing not only women but also men theoretically feminized by their dependent relation on slaveholders. Northerners extended this fear of sexual anarchy and the inversion of gender relations over the entire race. Therefore, it is not surprising that whites, North and South, laced their discussions of emancipation with their visions of sexual deviance. The coining of the word "miscegenation" in 1864 is a case in point. Even though white Americans had outlawed sexual relations between black men and white women since the mid-seventeenth century, no specialized discourse developed to describe these relations until the moment of emancipation.[31] It was not until black southerners left their masters' households (just as white women had left their fathers' households a generation earlier) that their sexual autonomy required a distinct and separate vocabulary.

The leased plantation system securely placed these unruly women (and by extension this unruly race) back within the strict confines of household, but this time as wage laborers. As laborers, black women were neutered and neutralized. All the troublesome issues of sexuality, children, husbands, and parents were put to rest by the government as it attempted to strip away the female to find the worker. The negotiation of free labor, therefore, was skewed by gender. Freedwomen were workers, but not quite, just as black people were free, but not completely. The even playing field of the competitive labor market was noticeably upset.

Northern definitions of freedom presented black communities with a bizarre anomaly. Freedpeople were granted the right to work for others without any control of the resources or the final product. Northerners and southern blacks both spoke of "independence," "autonomy," and "liberty," but each assigned dramatically different meanings to these words. Freedpeople concentrated on establishing their own autonomy by extricating themselves as much as possible from northern control.

Using the resources of their household, freedpeople worked together to limit employers' control of their labor. On the leased plantations, freedwomen organized their work by distributing the resources of their household. They went to the fields when necessary to earn wages or rations but focused their energy on alternative means of livelihood—on fishing, livestock, and gardens. They avoided jobs that afforded them little control over the final product or required a long-term investment. They resisted repairing fences, clearing land, draining swamps, and building houses. In general, they refused to care for and maintain property not belonging to them. After the land was confiscated by the Yankees and after they were put to work for others, freedwomen gradually withdrew their labor. This was a dramatic reversal from their first response to emancipation in 1862, when they had carefully tended the land as if it were their own.

By 1864, many had abandoned the plantation altogether and moved to Memphis or Vicksburg, where they could achieve greater autonomy and control over their own lives in the unregulated markets that sprang up around the army camps. Courtney Burton and Harriet Phillips's experience provides a glimpse into how women maintained themselves outside the bounds of military or government authority. During slavery, Courtney Burton took in and raised Harriet Phillips from her infancy. After emancipation, when Harriet was sixteen, they stayed on the plantation until life became unbearable, and then they set off to find Courtney's son, Philip, serving with the Forty-seventh U.S. Colored Infantry in Vicksburg. After finding Philip, Courtney was told that she could not live with him in camp and that his rations could not feed the three of them. The family, pooling their contacts and skills, not only survived but saved money. Philip used his army wages to rent his mother a house. With this house, Courtney maintained a garden, took in laundry, and made pies and cakes. The young Harriet took the pies and cakes to the army camps to sell to the soldiers. Courtney counted on Harriet's youth to encourage sales and on Philip's presence to protect her.[32]

Women like Courtney Burton and Harriet Phillips unnerved the army. Major General S. A. Hurlbut commented, "Most of these say from two thirds to three fourths are women & Children [who are] incapable of army labor . . . [they] are not supported by the Government crowded into all vacant sheds and housing living by begging and vice."[33]

To restrain women, the Union command in Memphis enacted General Order 75 commanding that "every free negro . . . must within 20 days enter into the employment of some responsible white person." As the editors of the Freedom History Papers argue, this "virtually prohibited black people in Memphis from working for black employers or undertaking any form of self-employment."[34] At stake was really the concept of household. Unable to recognize the independent households of black Union soldiers and their wives or of alternative households made up of extended kin networks in the black community, the U.S. government relied on an enforced system of wage labor. To control the "unruly negroes," General Order 75 (much like the leased plantation system itself) limited southern blacks' access to property and firmly placed them under the control not of white masters but of white employers.

While freedmen fought for political and social equality on the battlefront, it was freedwomen who negotiated the transition to free labor in the Delta.

As black men returned home to the plantation, they found themselves placed within this gendered construction of free labor established during the war. A. T. Morgan, a northern lessee observing and participating in this system, did his best to try to unravel and explain the curious inversions between race, class, and gender in Yazoo County during Reconstruction. "The question," he observed, "is not altogether one of race or color, but, that back of the race question more stronger and more merciless & cruel than it is the question of capital and labor." Yet "the attitude or relation," he went on, "[is] that of 'keeper' & 'sweetheart' or 'mistress' and not of employer & laborer and of 'white' man and 'black.'" As Morgan understood, labor relations in the South were masked and twisted by the gendered relations of household—by "mistress," "sweetheart," and "keeper."[35]

The northern confrontations with freedwomen, therefore, carried enormous repercussions for all African Americans. Women, in essence, represented the crisis of emancipation—the unfettering of a whole class of dependents. Facing black women, northerners encountered their worst fears of the breakdown of the plantation household. Dependents were claiming the rights and privileges of free men. To re-create a semblance of stability, Yankees placed these disorderly women (and by extension this disorderly race) back in the firm grasp of white men, who were employers this time rather than slaveholders. Ignoring the eloquent actions of African Americans, northerners slapped assumptions of race, class, and gender developed in a free-labor society onto the complexities of the plantation household. The implications of this action would haunt the southern free-labor system long after the Union forces withdrew.

NOTES

1. Henry T. Johns, *Life with the Forty-ninth Massachusetts Volunteers* (Washington, D.C.: Ramsey & Bisbee, 1890), quoted in Leon Litwack, *Been in the Storm So Long: The Aftermath of Slavery* (New York: Vintage Books, 1979), 101; *Report from the Proceedings of a Meeting Held at a Concert Hall, Philadelphia, on Tuesday Evening, November 3, 1863, to Take into Consideration the Condition of the Freed People of the South* (Philadelphia, 1863), quoted in Litwack *Been in the Storm*, 64.

2. Heather Andrea Williams, "'Commenced to Think like a Man': Literacy and Manhood in African American Civil War Regiments," in *Southern Manhood: Perspectives on Masculinity in the Old South*, ed. Craig Thompson Friend and Lorri Glover (Athens: University of Georgia Press, 2004): 196–219; Laura F. Edwards, "'The Marriage Covenant Is at the Foundation of All Our Rights': The Legal and Political Implications of Marriage in Postemancipation North Carolina," *Law and History Review* 14 (Spring 1996): 81–124; Jim Cullen, "'I's a Man Now': Gender and African American Men," in *Divided Houses: Gender and the Civil War*, ed. Catherine Clinton and Nina Silber (New York: Oxford University Press, 1992): 76–91.

3. Willie Lee Rose, *Rehearsal for Reconstruction: The Port Royal Experiment* (New York: Oxford, 1964), 217–41, 272–96; Barbara Jeanne Fields, *Slavery and Freedom on the Middle Ground: Maryland during the Nineteenth Century* (New Haven, Conn.: Yale University Press, 1985), 131–208; Thomas Holt, *The Problem of Freedom: Race, Labor, and Politics in Jamaica and Britain, 1832–1938* (Baltimore: Johns Hopkins University Press, 1992); Frederick Cooper, Thomas C. Holt, and Rebecca J. Scott, *Beyond Slavery: Explorations of Race, Labor, and Citizenship in Postemancipation Societies* (Chapel Hill: University of North Carolina Press, 2000); Eric Foner, *Nothing but Freedom: Emancipation and Its Legacy* (Baton Rouge: Louisiana State University Press, 1983); Julie Saville, *The Work of Reconstruction: From Slave to Wage Laborer in South Carolina, 1860–1870* (New York: Cambridge University Press, 1994); Harold D. Woodman, "Economic Reconstruction and the Rise of the New South," in *Interpreting Southern History:* Historiographical Essays in Honor of Sanford W. Higginbotham, ed. John R. Boles (Baton Rouge: Louisiana University Press, 1987), 254–307.

4. In addition to the works cited in the preceding note, see Eric Foner, "Reconstruction Revisited," *Reviews in American History* 10 (1982): 82–100.

5. Testimony of Gen. Wadsworth before the American Freedmen's Inquiry Commission, January ?, 1864, quoted in Nancy Bercaw, *Gendered Freedoms: Race, Rights, and the Politics of Household in the Delta, 1861–1875* (Gainesville: University Press of Florida, 2003), 34–35.

6. W. E. B. Du Bois, *Black Reconstruction in America: An Essay toward the History of the Part Which Black Folk Played in an Attempt to Reconstruct Democracy in America, 1860–1880*, 2nd ed. (Cleveland: Meridian Books, 1962); Fields, *Slavery and Freedom*; Foner *Nothing but Freedom*; Foner, "Reconstruction Revisited"; Holt, *The Problem of Freedom*; Joseph P. Reidy, *From Slavery to Agrarian Capitalism in the Cotton Plantation South: Central Georgia, 1800–1880* (Chapel Hill: University of North Carolina Press, 1992); Armstead Robinson, "'Worser than Jeff Davis': The Coming of Free Labor during the Civil War, 1861–1865," in *Essays on the Postbellum Southern Economy* (College Station: Texas A&M University Press for University of Texas–Arlington, 1985), 11–47; Saville, *Work of Reconstruction*; Woodman, "Economic Reconstruction."

7. For exceptions, see Noralee Frankel, *Freedom's Women: African American Women in Mississippi, 1860–1870* (Bloomington: University of Indiana Press, 1999); Leslie Schwalm, *A Hard Fight for We: Women's Transition from Slavery to Freedom in South Carolina* (Urbana: University of Illinois Press, 1997); Bercaw, *Gendered Freedoms*.

8. Bercaw, *Gendered Freedoms*, 34n41.

9. Frankel, *Freedom's Women*; Bercaw, *Gendered Freedoms*, 26n13.

10. John W Boyd to Governor Pettus, August 1, 1862, John J. Pettus Papers, Mississippi Governors Papers (henceforth cited as MGP), RG 27, roll 38, Mississippi Department of Archives and History, Jackson.

11. Bercaw, *Gendered Freedoms*, 24n10, 26n15; Howard W Wilkinson to Dear Sir, January 1, 1862, Pettus Papers, roll 39, MGP.

12. Bercaw, *Gendered Freedoms*, 24n10, 26n15; Howard W Wilkinson to Dear Sir, January 1, 1862.

13. Bercaw, *Gendered Freedoms*, 29n22.

14. Ibid., 31–33.

15. Eric Foner, *The Story of American Freedom* (New York: Norton, 1998), 69–94; Elizabeth Fox-Genovese, "Gender, Class and Power: Some Theoretical Considerations," *History Teacher* 15, no. 2 (February 1982): 255–76; Amy Dru Stanley, *From Bondage to Contract: Wage Labor, Marriage and the Market in the Age of Slave Emancipation* (Cambridge: Cambridge University Press, 1998); Laura F. Edwards, *Gendered Strife and Confusion: The Political Culture of Reconstruction* (Urbana: University of Illinois Press, 1997).

16. Bercaw, *Gendered Freedoms*, 32n34; Dudley Taylor Cornish, *The Sable Arm: Negro Troops in the Union Army, 1861–1865* (1956; repr., New York: W. W. Norton, 1966), 144–45; Joseph T. Glatthaar, *Forged in Battle: The Civil War Alliance of Black Soldiers and White Officers* (New York: Free Press, 1990), 130–35.

17. Bercaw, *Gendered Freedoms*, 34n41.

18. Adj. Gen. L. Thomas to Hon. Edwin M. Stanton, April 1, 1863, in *The Black Military Experience*, ed. Ira Berlin, Joseph P. Reidy, and Leslie S. Rowland, Freedom: A Documentary History of Emancipation, series 2 (Cambridge: Cambridge University Press, 1982), 489.

19. Bercaw, *Gendered Freedoms*, 35.

20. Foner, *Story of American Freedom*; Stephanie McCurry, "Two Faces of Republicanism: Gender and Proslavery Politics in Antebellum South Carolina," *Journal of American History* 78, no. 4 (March 1992): 1245–64; Laura Edwards, *Gendered Strife and Confusion*; Elizabeth Fox-Genovese, "Antebellum Southern Households: A New Perspective on a Familiar Question," *Review* 7 (Fall 1983): 215–53.

21. Christopher Tomlins, *Law, Labor and Ideology in the Early American Republic* (New York: Cambridge University Press, 1993); Harold Woodman, *New South, New Law: The Legal Foundations of Credit and Labor Relations in the Postbellum Agricultural South* (Baton Rouge: Louisiana University Press, 1995); Laura Edwards, "The Problem of Dependency: African Americans, Labor Relations, and the Law in the Nineteenth-Century South," *Agricultural History* 72, no. 2 (1998): 313–40; Stanley, *From Bondage to Contract*.

22. Bercaw, *Gendered Freedoms*, 32n35–36.

23. Ibid., 33.

24. Ibid., 28–31; Earl J. Hess. "Confiscation and the Northern War Effort: The Army of the Southwest at Helena," *Arkansas Historical Quarterly* 44 (Spring 1985): 56–75; Court of Inquiry, Records of the Inspector General, RG 159, National Archives and Records Administration, Washington, D.C. (hereinafter NARA).

25. Bercaw, *Gendered Freedoms*, 29n25.

26. Testimony of Maj. W. D. Greene, May 4, 1863, Court of Inquiry, vol. 2, p. 99, Records of the Inspector General, RG 159, NARA.

27. Bercaw, *Gendered Freedoms*, 34.

28. Sally Alexander, "Women, Class and Sexual Differences in the 1830s and 1840s: Some Reflections on the Writing of Feminist History," *History Workshop Journal* 17 (Spring 1984): 125–49.

29. Bercaw, *Gendered Freedoms*, 42–44.

30. Ibid., 44.

31. See Martha Hodes, "Wartime Dialogues on Illicit Sex: White Women and Black Men" in Clinton and Silber, *Divided Houses*, 230–42.

32. Bercaw, *Gendered Freedoms*, 43. See also Frankel, *Freedom's Women*.

33. Bercaw, *Gendered Freedoms*, 36n48.

34. Ibid., 45.

35. A. T. Morgan to Gov. Adelbert Ames, September 24, 1875, pp. 46–48, Ames Papers, MGP.

Hearth and Home

Constructing Domesticity in Mississippi, 1830–1920

SUSAN DITTO

The kitchen as we know it did not exist in Mississippi until late in the nineteenth century. From the time the Mississippi territory was wrested from its native residents in the 1820s and 1830s until about a decade and a half after the Civil War, Mississippi's yeoman farmers built thousands of houses complete with any number of outbuildings, but almost none included a whole building or room just for cooking. On the other end of the socioeconomic spectrum, no self-respecting antebellum planter would have been without an outdoor kitchen staffed by a full-time slave cook. Neither yeoman women nor plantation mistresses spent much time or effort preparing food. After generations of disregard, when kitchens ultimately arrived inside the homes of rural Mississippians, they did so en masse, signaling a material shift in the domestic lives of Mississippi women.

Around 1880, ordinary white families, long accustomed to cooking and eating in the same room in which they also slept and carried on in numerous other ways, began to add substantial wings or ells onto their simple, two-room homes. These additions contained large kitchens and, in some cases, dining rooms. Whereas white southerners of modest backgrounds had traditionally placed little stock in the culinary arts, by the turn of the twentieth century they had identified cooking as an essential feature of white southern womanhood and had come to glorify and honor it above most other female pursuits. At the same time, elite whites, whose forbears had disdained virtually all cookery as labor unbecoming to respectable white women, shared in the new celebration of domesticity, embracing the kitchen as an integral part of the big house.

To borrow a phrase from a prominent American historian of race, white southerners at the turn of the twentieth century were "very much alike and becoming more so."[1] But why did southern yeoman farmers and planters alike shun kitchens until twenty years or so before the turn of the twentieth century, while New England dairy farmers, New York City tenement dwellers, and many other Americans had long been accustomed to them? And why, in the waning decades of the 1800s, did the domestic culture of both middle- and upper-class white southerners undergo such a rapid and marked change?

Studying kitchens allows us to think about both women's work and how women and men thought about that work. By the late 1800s, white women—both yeoman and planter—began not just to cook in kitchens attached to their homes but also to attach some special virtue to that practice. Parallel to the ways white men were coming together over various political, economic, and legal issues that united them against black men, white women were crossing class lines in a shared celebration of domesticity. Other historians of southern culture have observed the growing interest early twentieth-century white southerners took in reconstructing cultural memory and glorifying a largely imagined past, including the romanticization of female domesticity, through the study of politics, religion, law, film, literature, public monuments, and other sources.[2] The evolution of vernacular houses—in this case, the appearance of kitchens—provides another way of examining how ideas about gender, race, class, and history shaped what became known as the New South.

Yeoman farmers stood at the center of antebellum southern society, belonging neither to the ranks of elite planters nor to those of the poor and landless. Most importantly to them, they were free and independent, unlike slaves. Mississippi yeoman farming culture predominated in twenty-three counties in the northwest and central parts of the state: Alcorn, Attala, Benton, Calhoun, Carroll, Choctaw, Itawamba, Kemper, Lafayette, Lauderdale, Leake, Lee, Monroe, Montgomery, Newton, Pontotoc, Prentiss, Rankin, Tippah, Tishomingo, Union, Webster, and Winston.[3]

In the middle of the nineteenth century, in the yeoman-farming county of Monroe, Mississippi, a typical white landowner built a two-room, dogtrot-style house out of hewn logs. The dogtrot, also known as a "possum trot," "turkey trot," "dog run," or "two pens and a passage," was one of the most common house types in yeoman farming regions of the antebellum South. Like other dogtrots, this Monroe County farmer's home consisted of two rooms, about twenty square feet apiece, set parallel to each other with an open-air hallway, or "trot," about ten feet wide between them. Typical of its kind, the houses included both front and back porches, which, along with the trot, served as

KITCHEN PORCH AND YARD, POND HOUSE,
UNION COUNTY, MISSISSIPPI

Photograph by Jack Elliott.

Courtesy of the Mississippi Department of Archives and History, Jackson.

AFRICAN AMERICANS STANDING IN FRONT
OF A DETACHED KITCHEN AT
LOCHINVAR PLANTATION IN PONTOTOC COUNTY

Courtesy of the Mississippi Department of Archives and History, Jackson.

multifunctional working, entertaining, sleeping, and storage space. On the outside wall of each room stood a deep, wide fireplace.[4]

Mississippi's yeoman farmers in the early to mid-nineteenth century were
partial to two-room, rectangular houses like dogtrots with a fireplace in each
room. Both rooms were about the same size, had about the same number of
windows and doors, and were thus equally comfortable and accessible, yet one
room was used more extensively and put to a wider variety of uses than the
other. This room was the hearth room, the family room, the sitting room, or the
"room we lived in," the center of all indoor family activity.[5] The busy hearth—
surrounded by pots, tools, chairs, beds, and people—was both the physical and
the symbolic focal point of yeoman household life.

Household probate inventories, which were customarily prepared upon
a property owner's death for the purpose of administering his or her estate,
are extremely useful in recreating the hearth room's interior. For a space rarely
larger than four hundred square feet, the typical hearth room contained a collection of household items that was amazingly large in both quantity and variety, suggesting that the widespread use of two-room houses and of the hearth
room as the hub of household activity was not necessarily linked to poverty.
Nonetheless, virtually all the contents of a typical hearth room were utilitarian
rather than decorative in nature, and some items served multiple functions.

A pot rack suspended from the ceiling or wall bore a couple of frying pans, a
set of tongs, a sieve, and other utensils. A large kettle or "dinner pot" hung from
hooks within the fireplace, which also contained a pair of cast-iron "firedogs,"
or andirons, while a hunting rifle or shotgun hung from the wall above. In a
nearby cupboard sat a collection of tinware and a few pewter plates or mugs, a
pair of glass tumblers, a set of wooden bowls, a jumble of tin forks and spoons,
and perhaps a set of silver teaspoons. The typical cupboard also housed a coffee mill and coffee, jars filled with preserved fruits and vegetables, and various
other small tools and containers.[6] Margaret McMacklin's cupboard contained a
set of candle molds, some mousetraps, screws and a screwdriver, twenty empty
bottles, a pair of glass decanters, some glass dishes, a teapot, a jug, eight cups
and saucers, and a tureen.[7]

In a cool, dark corner of most hearth rooms stood a safe that held perishables
such as a ceramic crock of butter, a basket of eggs, and freshly baked bread.
Nearby sat barrels, sacks, or other containers of staples like brown sugar or
molasses, rock salt, pepper, corn, and lard. Many households also kept stores of
potatoes, wheat flour, and fruit. In the center of the room stood a cherry drop-
leaf table, used for dining at meal times or for work such as laying out cloth for
sewing at other times. When not in use, it could be folded and pushed aside to

make room for other pursuits like a loom or quilting frame. Not far away sat a spinning wheel next to which lay a basket filled with deseeded cotton, two pairs of cards for straightening the fibers in preparation for spinning, and a reel on which to wind newly made yarn.

Other items in the hearth room were related to the space's personal functions. For morning or mealtime hand washing, a pewter or ceramic basin and a pitcher filled with water rested on a communal washstand. If the washstand itself or an adjacent dresser did not contain a mirror, a framed looking glass might hang nearby. Against the wall a walnut wardrobe, a dresser, and a couple of trunks or chests held winter clothing, quilts, and counterpanes during summer or mosquito netting, sun hats, and bonnets during winter. On a small side table made of cherry or pine rested the family Bible. In some cases the Bible was joined by other devotional books, for instance, a hymnal or *The Doctrines and Discipline of the Methodist Episcopal Church, South*, or histories like the *Life of Washington* or *Life of Jackson*, or spellers and readers for the children.

Still more items indicated the importance of the hearth room as the center for social activity. The table, when not in use as a work space, was surrounded by chairs. Some were ladder backed or Windsor style with wooden seats; many had seats of woven cane. A few of the more comfortable households had chairs with horsehair cushions. Even fewer listed rustic chairs with seats of animal hide, but most estate administrators did not even bother to count, much less describe, chairs, listing only a "lot chairs" or "sett chairs," implying both great quantity and variety.

The homes of most yeoman families contained far more seating space than household members, which suggests the frequent presence of neighbors or extended kin for visiting, work sharing, or entertainment. Although the average family in Rankin County, Mississippi, had fewer than six members, the otherwise quite humble home that William Pallie and his wife shared in 1854 contained six cane-bottom chairs, nine "common chairs," a rocking chair, and a lounge.[8] In 1867, the widow of Major T. P. Ware of the same county was able to accommodate the many callers she no doubt entertained upon her husband's death with her four cane-bottom chairs, twelve "dining chairs," a lounge, and a "second hand sofa."[9]

The largest and most valuable articles of furniture in the homes of middling farmers were their beds. Virtually every frontier farming family had at least one sturdy bedstead in its main room, which could double as workspace or couch. Other "beds" were often just mattresses, which could be rolled up during the day and pulled out at night, converting the hearth room into the home's primary sleeping space. Featherbeds, which were worth up to twenty-five dollars, compared to about two dollars for a mattress stuffed with straw or cornhusks, were prized possessions that may have remained on display at all times.

Although cooking was almost exclusively a female pursuit, the hearth was not perceived as a feminine space. In a southern version of the idea of separate spheres, the evangelical values of prayer, quiet, harmony, and self-control were associated primarily with women and "identified the home as a counterpoint to and rejection of the aggressive, self-indulgent pleasure seeking of male recreation."[10] However, the angelic qualities of warmth and light, which were later ascribed to Victorian womanhood, were not visited to any great degree upon the women of the southern yeomanry or upon the hearth itself. Typically, yeoman women prepared food out on the porch, in the dogtrot, or in the hearth room, and cooked it over the same open fire that served many other functions. As the site where families gathered for prayer or recreation, a major source of light by which to work or read, and the only source of heat in winter, the hearth was the functional center of the home, but it was associated more with the household as a whole rather than with mother or domesticity. Household heads, who were usually male, preferred to sleep nearest the hearth. This preference may have stemmed from an understanding of the hearth as the center of household productivity, or the hearth may have derived some of its symbolic significance from the centrality of authority embodied in the patriarch. Likely, the relationship was dialectical.

Another reason why the hearth was not closely identified with women may be that women did not particularly identify with the hearth. The women of yeoman farming families ordinarily did the cooking for their families, laborers, and guests, but for most of the nineteenth century neither typical white women nor those they fed appear to have placed much stock in the culinary arts. Ordinary white farming women were first and foremost workers in the household economy, and cooking assumed no special place among the plethora of other activities necessary for the family's basic subsistence. The production-oriented landscape—their smokehouses, barns, corncribs, and hen houses—meant independence and sometimes survival for yeomen and their families. One would not therefore expect them to venerate cooking or any other exercise primarily aimed at consumption.[11]

Travelers through the antebellum South repeatedly indicted yeoman menus for lack of variety and poor preparation. As was the case in other frontier regions, pork and corn seem to have been the main choices at the tables of ordinary folk during much of the year.[12] Disappointed travelers and their historians have typically attributed such uninteresting fare to the unavailability of many ingredients in rural backwaters. Although pigs outnumbered people in

Mississippi by as much as two to one for most of the nineteenth century, the prevalence of pork over other meats, as well as for corn bread over wheat bread, and corn liquor or water over milk, may have been a matter of convenience or preference rather than availability. The frontier yeomanry had a tremendous variety of foodstuffs at their disposal virtually year round.

Travelers to the antebellum South seem to have missed wheat bread and dairy products the most, yet household inventories of the time frequently mention "milch cows," butter churns, and barrels of flour. Ordinary white women also kept chickens and other fowl, which could offer a fairly regular supply of fresh eggs, poultry meat, and broth. Although mutton and beef were distinctly minor foodstuffs among all but the wealthiest families, some yeoman farmers kept sheep and cattle, which they sometimes slaughtered for food or trade.[13]

Household gardens also yielded fresh vegetables like peas, yams, turnips, Irish potatoes, and a variety of greens. The growing season in Mississippi averages between 200 and 240 days per year. Since most garden vegetables take only 60 to 110 days from seed to harvest, one could have planted several gardens per season, ensuring fresh produce for seven or eight months out of the year.[14] A number of yeoman farmsteads also contained orchards. Those families who remained settled long enough for fruit trees to bear could count on apples, pears, peaches, plums, and apricots, as well as grapes. Fruits and vegetables that were not consumed right away could be dried, pickled, or jellied, providing continued dietary variety beyond the growing season. Household inventories of the period indicate that many families kept exactly this kind of food store on hand. Some, like Margaret Cromwell of Lafayette County, who sold "six lots of peaches from her orchard" for twelve dollars in 1838, also used produce for barter or sale.[15] Since the technology involved in canning sterile preserves for long-term storage was little known and cost-prohibitive due to the expense of sugar—not to mention that of handblown glass jars—much excess fruit was converted to hard cider or brandy.

Even if, as some observers have suggested, poultry keeping, gardening, and food preservation were too much work for the leisure-oriented common folk of the region, one could have lived off the land and eaten like nobility.[16] The preindustrial rivers and streams that eddied through the region brimmed with fish, turtles, and bullfrogs. Mississippians without poles or hooks learned to poison fish with crushed walnut shells or to "muddy" the water, depriving it of oxygen, thereby forcing fish to the surface. Nineteenth-century farmers, who cultivated relatively small plots of land using a combination of man power, animal power, and controlled burning, without chemical herbicides or pesticides, created an environment conducive to even larger populations of birds and small mammals

than did virgin forest. Quail, wild turkeys, raccoons, opossums, skunks, squirrels, and especially rabbits were an important part of the diet of rural Mississippians in the nineteenth and early twentieth centuries. Deer were less available
to nineteenth-century yeomen than smaller game but were hunted whenever
possible.[17] Despite such readily available alternatives, the bland repetition of
daily fare for most yeomen is evidence of the low priority that this class of
white southerners assigned to cooking and serving food in the first three quarters of the nineteenth century.

Spoilage probably played a role in yeomen's lack of enthusiasm for cuisine.
Any meat that was not consumed soon after slaughtering was heavily salted
and smoked—a process that left most meat tasting more or less the same, but
for which pork is particularly well suited. The cooking methods most often
employed by yeoman women—boiling and frying—also tend to give foods a
relatively consistent flavor and texture, furthering yeoman indifference to varied ingredients. The preferred techniques of yeoman cooks—and the material
and cultural basis for them—warrant further consideration. The typical yeoman household in the first three quarters of the nineteenth century contained
little in the way of cookware. Although the men who usually recorded household inventories seldom itemized cookware in detail, those who did listed a
"big pot," a "dinner pot," or a "kettle" more often than any other item used for
preparing food. About half as often, they listed a frying pan or skillet. Slightly
fewer than half recorded ovens. Only about 5 percent of inventories indicated a
"lot pots" or "lot cookware," suggesting any kind of variety.[18] Extensive investment in specialized cooking implements would have violated a yeoman's practical, multifunctional approach to goods. Hence, boiling and frying were ideal
because each required only one simple pot or pan.

Elaborate recipes required another luxury uncommon to yeoman women—
time. Women with no or few slaves worked their fingers to the bone just to
keep up with the demands of daily life. Producing soap, starch, and candles;
preserving food; and carding, spinning, and weaving textiles were all labor-
intensive tasks, although these jobs were necessary only a few times a year.
Other jobs such as sewing and mending clothing, laundering, ironing, gardening, and tending to small livestock warranted more frequent attention. During
the peak agricultural cycles, women also labored in the fields.[19]

Rural farming women, whose families tended to be large by modern standards, suffered perhaps the greatest drain on their attention and stamina simply
by bearing and caring for their children. The frequency and gravity of childhood illnesses made nursing one of a mother's principal duties. When a child
was seriously sick, all-night vigils at his or her bedside could last for weeks,

during which time the aggrieved mother would have little time or energy for other pursuits.[20] Panfried dishes were quick and required little advance preparation, while boiled meals could be allowed to simmer all day if necessary, enabling the cook to attend to other matters.

Besides limited utensils and insufficient time, another compelling reason for Mississippi farm women's lack of enthusiasm for complex cooking methods may have been the heat the process generated. On an average summer day in Mississippi, the temperature inside one room of a dogtrot house, without a flame of any sort in its quiet hearth, could top eighty degrees around noon and might not dip below eighty degrees again until after nine in the evening.[21] In such an environment, any activity that would generate additional warmth would have been dispatched as expeditiously as possible.

To say that yeoman women lacked enthusiasm for cooking is not to say that they did not use skill and ingenuity. Generations of women, accustomed to preparing dinner over their home's central hearth amid countless other demands, developed methods of cooking that utilized the tools and products at hand and demanded a minimum of time and attention while generating as little heat as possible. Women learned to soak dried beans and peas in water overnight to reduce the need for lengthy boiling and simmering. Their knowledge of how to preserve vegetables and meats was a crucial contribution to the household economy, while pickled vegetables and cured meats require very little, if any, time on the fire before serving. Women baked several loaves of bread at a time, further reducing the need to heat the house every day. Better yet, they learned that cornmeal could easily be transformed into corn cakes, which could be crisp and delicious in only a matter of minutes. In contrast, wheat bread required hours to knead and bake and was less filling. Corn cakes could also be made without yeast, baking powder, or milk.

Women also sought, within their means, to provide their families with the greatest possible dietetic benefit. A widespread nineteenth-century belief held that fatty foods were among the healthiest.[22] Perhaps yeoman mothers and wives learned from experience that a high-fat, high-carbohydrate diet provided much-needed fuel for hard-working bodies. By this standard, a diet rich in corn, pork, and fried foods would be nearly ideal. Also, many nineteenth-century Americans favored salted or dried meat over fresh protein, which they believed unwholesome.[23]

As with many aspects of farm work, cooking among the yeomanry seems to have been most valued as part of communal activity. Communities seized on demanding but necessary jobs like log rolling, corn shucking, and house and barn raisings as opportunities for recreation and socialization. While the men worked, their mothers, wives, and daughters prepared a feast of regal proportions. One man recalled a typical Mississippi work-sharing meal as consisting of "baked sweet potatoes, corn pone . . . big pans of chicken pie, egg custard, turnip greens, backbone and rice, home-made cake, huckleberry pie, etc."[24] Other meals fixed especially for work sharings included burgoo (a soup made with squirrels or other small game), dumplings, boiled ham, crackling or shortening bread, Irish potatoes, biscuits, pumpkin custard, apple pie, and grape pie.[25]

Barbecue was particularly popular at large gatherings, and fish fries were also a favorite. Good food was also valued at harvest celebrations, Christmastime, and for special church events such as all-day singings and other church gatherings accompanied by "dinner on the ground." A reminiscence of traditional Sacred Harp singings in Mississippi, penned during the Great Depression, recalled food of "great quantity and variety" featuring every possible way to prepare chicken including "crisp fried," "country fried" with gravy, broiled, chicken giblets, chicken pie, and hard-boiled eggs.[26]

Most yeoman women did their cooking either at these large communal events or in the hearth rooms of their own small houses. The vast majority of yeoman farm women in Mississippi did not set foot in a room called a kitchen until the last two decades or so of the nineteenth century. Of the houses surveyed for this study that were likely to have been built by middling farmers, less than 2 percent (3 of 158) included a kitchen in their original design. Just 12 percent of yeoman families (19 of 158) appended kitchens onto their existing homes before 1880.[27]

Not far from the Monroe County dogtrot house described earlier, at about the same time, another landowner constructed a very different house. For one thing, this home had a name: Lenoir. In some ways, Lenoir and its more humble neighbor appear rather similar. Like the dogtrot house, Lenoir had a wide hallway running right down its middle—with the not insignificant addition of exterior doors on the front and back. Like the dogtrot, Lenoir's rooms were arranged symmetrically, although the latter house had two stories and two rooms on each side of its central hall, instead of only one. Lenoir, when originally constructed, was likely inspired by the Greek Revival style, the preferred fashion of planters and aspiring planters in the three decades or so preceding the Civil War. To advertise their social pretensions, the Lenoir family opted to ornament their home with a two-story colossal portico instead of a front porch. But the homes of slaveholders and the homes of yeomen differed not only in scale and accoutrements. Behind Lenoir, near the other working buildings of the plantation, sat a structure almost the size of the yeoman house down the road. This building too had a name: the kitchen.

Detached kitchens, like other plantation outbuildings, were considered primarily a part of the slaves' realm. The idea of a segregated space for servile domestic labor gained prominence among the planter elite in the late seventeenth to early eighteenth century—at precisely the same time that laws defining inheritable, race-based, chattel slavery were codified in the tobacco colonies.[28] Thus, the detached kitchen was a physical manifestation of the emerging caste system in which the lines between masters and servants, and particularly those between whites and African Americans, were becoming increasingly distinct. Once these separate domains were established, the great many footsteps and the many fruits of slave labor that passed between big house and kitchen built a strong link between cooking and involuntary servitude in the space they shared.[29]

Besides its proximity to the planter's home, little else but the chimney differentiated some antebellum detached kitchens from other outbuildings. Some plantation kitchens were designed to complement the big house in style and scale.[30] None, however, resembled the "cozy family gathering place" preferred by northern farming families of the same period, nor the wholesome site of female production and "family-centered domesticity" envisioned by romantic theorists and Victorian advice givers.[31] The sweaty, often backbreaking toil of preparing large meals over a huge open fireplace in an uncomfortable outbuilding placed plantation cooking squarely in the camp of all the other disagreeable tasks that were ubiquitously classified as "Negro work."

When it came to dispensing meals for their slaves from detached kitchens, some slaveholders, it would seem, took pains to make the process resemble as much as possible the feeding of livestock. In the 1930s, a former Mississippi slave told an interviewer for the Federal Writer's Project: "The way they fed the children, they took pot-liquor or bean soup or turnip liquor or the juice from anything they boiled and poured it out in a great big wooden bowl and let all the children get 'round it like so many cats and they would just tip their hands in it and eat what they wanted."[32] Another Mississippi slave remembered, "Cook had a big wooden tray and she'd come out and say 'Whoopee!' and set the tray on the ground. . . . We'd fall down and start eatin."[33] For some plantation owners, it would appear, feeding one's slave "family" was akin to slopping hogs.

It is hardly surprising then that the elite white women of the antebellum period did not exhibit much interest in plantation cooking. It was within the responsibilities of a planter's wife to "order" breakfast, lunch, and dinner and to dole out supplies from the plantation storehouses, but most women of the planter class knew little and cared less about cookery beyond the odd specialty dish or dessert.[34]

In the late 1800s, the views of white southerners toward women's culinary skills, cooking as labor, and domesticity in general took a significant turn. The most prominent material evidence of growing reverence for some domestic skills is the vigorous rise of kitchens as a functionally distinct yet wholly integrated part of most white rural households beginning around 1880. The remains of rural homes in Mississippi and bordering states indicate that, from the last couple of decades of the nineteenth century through the second decade of the twentieth, houses both large and small were being enlarged or built anew with kitchen or kitchen/dining combinations.

Although some homeowners, like most in the Bay Springs community in Tishomingo County, Mississippi, chose to construct their kitchens by adding, in their words, a "lean-to" to the rear of the house or "boxing in" part of the back porch, most kitchen expansions came in the form of an "ell," a rectangular wing attached behind and perpendicular to the existing house.[35] Kitchen ells almost always contained a full-length porch on their inward-facing side where women could sit and do food-related work, like shelling peas or peeling potatoes, in a partially enclosed space out of easy view of neighbors or passersby.

As scholars have noted about the dooryards of New England farmsteads, the kitchen yards created by ell additions to Mississippi's rural homes provided a "spatial and experiential focus to life on the family farm."[36] Also, most ell kitchens had a coal-burning stove, eliminating the chore of gathering or chopping wood to keep a hearth fire burning, and many had built-in wells or cisterns that provided ready fresh water for domestic tasks, putting an end to the ritual labor of carrying water from a distant source. Thus, kitchen ells drew the center of the house—physically, visually, and functionally—into a more private realm and encouraged a more home-centered focus for women's work. After the establishment of state Cooperative Extension Services beginning in 1914, male agents exhorted rural men to take control over traditionally female farmyard chores like poultry keeping and dairying, further defining the outer limits of women's daily activities.[37]

By the second decade of the twentieth century, the L-shaped house had become the single most prevalent vernacular house type in rural Mississippi. Of the 151 rural Mississippi houses surveyed for this study that were likely built by ordinary farmers between 1880 and 1910, over a third included a kitchen as an integral part of their design. At the same time, almost two-thirds of the surveyed houses that had been constructed prior to 1880 were expanded with kitchen additions so that, by the end of the first decade of the twentieth century, over 60 percent of all the farmhouses studied contained integrated kitchens.[38]

In 1910, the owners of Lenoir Plantation in Monroe County, Mississippi, replaced their old detached kitchen with a new one connected to the rear of the big house. Other former slaveholders reached out with hallways, pantries, or dining rooms to bridge the gap between their houses and existing plantation kitchens, transforming what were essentially agricultural outbuildings—in the manner of a smokehouse or dairy—into domesticated space. Many kitchens ells added onto more humble homes were similarly composed of two parts, one of which was used as a dining room.

Some historians of late nineteenth-century manners consider the dining room the "heart of the home," linking the space to the increasing importance of domesticity.[39] Like formal parlors, proper dining rooms were expected to display "elegance and the appearance of lady habitancy."[40] The dining table itself, carefully set with china, silver, and linens, and a matching sideboard with a display of other valuable domestic items such as candelabra and fancy serving dishes, "revealed the household's social position and devotion to domestic ritual."[41]

Sarah Elliott, a late nineteenth-century domestic-advice columnist, cookbook author, and pulp novelist from North Carolina, made an almost obsessive connection between dining rooms and whiteness. According to Elliott, proper dining rooms or kitchens should have "snow-white" tablecloths or at least a "clean white table," "pure white china," white napkins folded in crystal goblets, and a "salt-cellar with fine sifted salt by each plate." Housewives who deviated from this lily white scheme, Elliott implied, were presumed to be lacking in character.[42] Such gleaming rooms with their carefully chosen contents provided a marked contrast to the sweaty and dirty plantation kitchens or cluttered, utilitarian hearth rooms of yore.

Although the transformation in white southern attitudes toward domesticity took decades to mature, one can begin to see the seeds of that change in the 1860s. During and after the Civil War, white southern women, particularly those of the planter class, found themselves standing on shifting ground with regard to their customary roles and responsibilities in the absence of the labor and stewardship of their husbands, sons, brothers and, in some cases, slaves.

For elite white women, whose role in farm labor had once been virtually nonexistent and whose relationship to domestic labor had been largely managerial, the exodus of household servants introduced new domestic frontiers. After obtaining freedom, African American women resisted domestic servitude along the antebellum model, largely refusing to live in the homes of white families or to put the desires of their employers' families over the needs of their own, and resisting low wages and dictatorial treatment.[43] As a result, all but the most fortunate former slaveholding women faced the dilemma of either lending their own hands to much of the labor formerly done by slaves or doing without.

One former slaveholding woman who waged a constant struggle to retain and enforce authority over servants complained, "I get up every morning at six o clock and wake up Jim . . . and then we have to hurry the cook frequently in order to get breakfast by 8 o clock. . . . For the last four days we have had buckwheat cakes, but these we make in the house."[44] That this lady of the house (itself a telling term) preferred to cook inside when she made her own breakfast suggests that, although she may have assumed more responsibility for cooking, she continued to reject the detached kitchen. Also, contrary to common practice prior to the Civil War, this mistress required her cook to help with the housework. The cook, she wrote, "only makes up the beds, and would give this up, but I insist upon her coming in," suggesting some awareness on the part of both servant and employer that distinctions between big house and kitchen, domestic work and cooking were beginning to erode along with many other institutions on which white southerners had once relied.

While wealthy women were working more with their hands, once-independent yeoman households were gradually abandoning subsistence farming and household economy in favor of cotton and at least hopes of cash. The post–Civil War period saw many middling whites slip from self-sufficient farming into tenancy or sharecropping. The mobility of tenant farming life, greater competition and less cooperation among neighboring farmers, smaller nuclear families, and fewer extended families or complex households all contributed to the deterioration of many of the communal work activities that had perpetuated much of yeoman culture. Further, both African American and white renters were commonly required to plant virtually all their allotted acreage in cotton and to procure their necessities from plantation stores, a practice that discouraged activities like dairying, curing meat, or producing other staples at home.[45] Whereas there had once been over a million and a half head of swine in the state compared to a human population of less than 800,000, by 1900 people outnumbered pigs by 85 percent.[46] This shift could suggest growing interest in a diet that was more diversified than the once ubiquitous hog meat and hoe cake, but it also indicates the disappearance of a self-sufficient way of life and less diverse forms of labor in and around the home.

Beginning around 1880, growing numbers of Mississippians, especially white women, started visiting stores more often and buying a much greater variety of goods than they had earlier in the century.[47] By the early 1900s, household inventories in Mississippi counties that had once been heavily populated with yeoman farmers contained comparatively few implements of household production like spinning wheels, butter churns, bee hives, or grind stones.[48] The absence of such tools, along with the near eradication from the landscape of smokehouses, corn cribs, chicken coops, and other material remnants of rural self-sufficiency—all of which had been nearly universal among farming households a few decades earlier—directly resulted from and perpetuated the abandonment of subsistence farming and household economy in favor of increasing reliance on staple crop production and commercially available goods.

By the second decade of the twentieth century, Mississippi state home economists were roaming the countryside advocating a return to rural self-sufficiency and promoting skills that had once been taken for granted among ordinary white farming women. Home demonstrations and the distribution of leaflets on topics like vegetable gardening, home canning, dairying, poultry keeping, and making clothes suggest that the cooperative labor networks through which rural women had traditionally learned and passed down such skills from one generation to another had broken down.[49]

In their place arose an idealized view of white women and romanticized notions of female domesticity. Despite the fact that, prior to the late 1800s, neither elite nor middling white women had ever been significantly interested in domesticity, especially with regard to cooking, the drive for social stability and the desire for continuity with a heroic past imbued the "Lost Cause" myth of the southern lady with the belief that the home arts had always had a valued place in southern women's lives. Further, in order to free work in the kitchen from the stigma of servile labor and separate it from the surfeit of duties incumbent upon farm women, "Lost Cause" mythmakers lauded cooking as an esteemed occupation worthy of an honored place within a righteous society.

In 1899, the Spinning Wheel Club of Woodville, Mississippi, an organization whose name alone implied a long-standing connection to domesticity, published one of the earliest cookbooks produced for southern women by southern women. That these women produced a cookbook at all is significant evidence of the growing importance that the region's women afforded to cooking skills in the late nineteenth century. But these Mississippi women went one step further, beginning every section of the book with quotes from classical or Renaissance literary figures such as Pericles, Horace, Seneca, and Shakespeare, thereby tying the domestic aspirations of Mississippi women to a glorious past.[50]

A few years later, another Mississippi Ladies' Aid society connected domesticity to "Lost Cause" mythology much more overtly, beginning their cookbook with a poem:

We read of Knights and Ladies fair
In days of chivalry
Of bold and daring exploits
And deeds of bravery

. . . .

We sigh to emulate them,
Their glory we would share
But lend me now your ear for I
A secret would declare.
Each hero needs must dine and sup
In present days or past,
They're all dependent on the cook,
Men cannot eat and fast.
With due consideration
All people must concede,
The cook who cooks the dinner
Makes possible the deed.
So scan these pages carefully
And learn to boil and bake
For who can tell what deed depends
On how to stir a cake.[51]

Women who may not have participated in voluntary organizations like the Spinning Wheel Club received the word on "home heroism," as a preacher from Columbus, Mississippi termed it, in church.[52] Another preacher told the women of his congregation that they needed to "resuscitate [the South's] faded life and rebuild [its] fallen greatness" through housework. "Every day there goes on in the world's homes labor . . . that would put to shame all the heroism which history emblazens and all the martyrdom which the church exalts," he claimed. This reverend made no bones about the reason why white women needed to stick close to home. The abundance of freedmen, which he referred to as "the peculiar condition of the South," necessitated extra vigilance if their "race-standard, ordained by God," was "to be kept pure; if the social contest of races" was to "maintain the dignity of Anglo-Saxon blood." Home heroism, and the perpetuation of white female virtue, were vital not only to the family but to "our national life and future glory."[53]

Many kitchen additions constructed in Mississippi through the first decade of the twentieth century contained their own hearth, perhaps indicating the homeowners' desire to continue some kinds of open-hearth cooking or the reluctance of other families to part with the custom of placing a fireplace at the center of every important room in the house. Most often, however, the integration or addition of a kitchen coincided with a family's acquisition of a cookstove. A 1906 advertisement for the Majestic Range company—contained, not coincidentally, inside a Mississippi Ladies' Aid Society cookbook—called its stove a "Happy Home Builder," joining together white women, cooking, kitchens, and household appliances as symbols of domestic bliss.[54]

Amid the various ways that white southerners idealized white womanhood and domesticity, the proliferation of integrated kitchens takes on particular significance. The emergence of kitchens in the homes of white Mississippians signaled the demise of a utilitarian worldview that enabled rural farming folk to conceptualize many spaces within one and to conceive of women's role as similarly multifunctional. At the same time, integrated kitchens helped elevate cooking from servile labor to heroic virtue. As the physical and emotional center of rural home life literally shifted toward the kitchen, the strong association between kitchens and an idealized view of white womanhood helped to diminish the image of the home as dominated by a male household head in favor of a more female-centric understanding of domestic space.

NOTES

1. Joel Williamson, *The Crucible of Race: Black-White Relations in the American South since Emancipation* (New York: Oxford University Press, 1984), 438.

2. W. Fitzhugh Brundage, *The Southern Past: A Clash of Race and Memory* (Cambridge, Mass.: Belknap Press of Harvard University Press, 2005); Laura Edwards, *Gendered Strife and Confusion: The Political Culture of Reconstruction* (Chicago: University of Illinois Press, 1997); Glenda Gilmore, *Gender and Jim Crow: Women and the Politics of White Supremacy in North Carolina, 1896–1920* (Chapel Hill: University of North Carolina Press, 1996); Grace Elizabeth Hale, *Making Whiteness: The Culture of Segregation in the South, 1890–1940* (New York: Pantheon, 1998).

3. For this study, counties that, according to aggregate census data from 1860, conformed to at least four of the following seven categories were deemed predominantly yeoman: the average farm in the county included between 75 and 225 improved acres; the countywide slave population amounted to less than 30 percent of the total population; at least 60 percent of slaveholders owned fewer than ten slaves; less than 3 percent of slaveholders owned more than fifty slaves; countywide corn production was at least thirty bushels per capita; average yearly cotton production did not exceed thirty bales per square mile; and the county was rich in at least two different varieties of staple foods such as pigs, peas, or sweet potatoes. Eighth Census of the United States, 1860, Agriculture and Population.

4. "House 095-GRS-7521," Historic Resources Inventory, Monroe County, Mississippi Department of Archives and History, Historic Preservation Office, Jackson (henceforth cited as MDAH HPO).

5. Michael Ann Williams, *Homeplace: The Social Use and Meaning of the Folk Dwelling in Southwestern North Carolina* (Athens: University of Georgia Press, 1991), 42–43, 77–79.

6. This list and the descriptions of household contents that follow, except where noted, are composites created from numerous inventories of households of median wealth that listed few or no slaves in predominantly yeoman Rankin County (1854–72), Monroe County (1858–61), Lafayette County (1837–70), and Pontotoc County (1845–48), Mississippi.

7. Edward F. McMacklin Estate, September 14, 1839, Lafayette County Chancery Court Records, Oxford, Mississippi.

8. Estate of Wm. Pallie and Wife, November 28, 1854, Inventories and Appraisements, Rankin County, Mississippi.

9. Major T. P. Ware and widow, 1867, Inventories and Appraisements, Rankin County, Mississippi.

10. Ted Ownby, *Subduing Satan: Religion, Recreation, and Manhood in the Rural South, 1865–1920* (Chapel Hill: University of North Carolina Press, 1990), 104.

11. LuAnn Jones, *Mama Learned Us to Work: Farm Women in the New South* (Chapel Hill: University of North Carolina Press, 2002); Stephanie McCurry, *Masters of Small Worlds: Yeoman Households, Gender Relations, and the Political Culture of the Antebellum South Carolina Low Country* (New York: Oxford University Press, 1995); Rebecca Sharpless, *Fertile Ground, Narrow Choices: Women on Texas Cotton Farms, 1900–1940* (Chapel Hill: University of North Carolina Press, 1999); Melissa Walker, *All We Knew Was to Farm: Rural Women in the Upcountry South, 1919–1941* (Baltimore: Johns Hopkins University Press, 2000).

12. Sam B. Hilliard, *Hogmeat and Hoecake: Food Supply in the Old South* (Carbondale: Southern Illinois University Press, 1972), 92–111; W. J. Rorabaugh, *The Alcoholic Republic: An American Tradition* (New York: Oxford University Press, 1979), 113–18; Joe Gray Taylor, *Eating, Drinking, and Visiting in the South: An Informal History* (Baton Rouge: Louisiana State University Press, 1982), 21–26.

13. Household inventories from Rankin, Monroe, Lafayette, and Pontotoc counties (1837–72); Hilliard, *Hogmeat and Hoecake*, 44–46.

14. Sam Bowers Hilliard, *Atlas of Antebellum Southern Agriculture* (Baton Rouge: Louisiana State University Press, 1984), 13–17.

15. Lafayette County, Mississippi, Chancery Court Records (1838).

16. On the perception of common white southerners as disinclined toward work, see Grady McWhiney, *Cracker Culture: Celtic Ways in the Old South* (Tuscaloosa: University of Alabama Press, 1988), 43–49; David Bertleson, *The Lazy South* (New York: Oxford University Press, 1967).

17. Wiley Charles Prewitt Jr., "The Best of All Breathing: Hunting and Environmental Change in Mississippi, 1900–1980" (MA thesis, University of Mississippi, 1991), 113–14, 53, 103–5, 54–56.

18. Household inventories from Rankin, Monroe, Lafayette, and Pontotoc counties (1837–72).

19. Jones, *Mama Learned Us to Work*, 5–9; McCurry, *Masters of Small Worlds*, 78–83.

20. Sally G. McMillan, *Motherhood in the Old South: Pregnancy, Childbirth, and Infant Rearing* (Baton Rouge: Louisiana State University Press, 1990), 135–41.

21. Arnold J. Aho, *Neo-Dogtrot Mississippi: A Low-Cost Passive Solar House for Rural Mississippi* (Starkville: Mississippi State University, 1981), 16.

22. Hilliard, *Hogmeat and Hoecake*, 58.

23. Susan Strasser, *Never Done: A History of American Housework* (New York: Pantheon Books, 1982), 14.

24. Ownby, *Subduing Satan*, 95.

25. Frank L. Owsley, *Plain Folk of the Old South* (Baton Rouge: Louisiana State University Press, 1982), 110; Ownby, *Subduing Satan*, 95.

26. Anon., "All Day Singing," *Mississippi Folklife* (Winter/Spring 1997): 20.

27. Based on analysis of all Historic Resources Inventories of rural houses with an estimated construction date prior to 1880 from all 23 of Mississippi's yeoman counties, MDAH HPO.

28. John Michael Vlach, *Back of the Big House: The Architecture of Plantation Slavery* (Chapel Hill: University of North Carolina Press, 1993), 43; Winthrop D. Jordan, *White over Black: American Attitudes toward the Negro, 1550–1812* (Chapel Hill: University of North Carolina Press, 1968), 71–82.

29. Elizabeth Fox-Genovese, *Within the Plantation Household: Black and White Women of the Old South* (Chapel Hill: University of North Carolina Press, 1988); Jennifer L. Morgan, *Laboring Women: Reproduction and Gender in New World Slavery* (Philadelphia: University of Pennsylvania Press, 2004); Kirsten Wood, *Masterful Women: Slaveholding Widows from the American Revolution through the Civil War* (Chapel Hill: University of North Carolina Press, 2004).

30. Vlach, *Back of the Big House*, 45.

31. Sally McMurry, *Families and Farmhouses in Nineteenth-Century America: Vernacular Design and Social Change* (New York: Oxford University Press, 1988), 145; Gwendolyn Wright, *Building the Dream: A Social History of Housing in America* (Cambridge, Mass.: MIT Press, 1981), 77.

32. Mississippi Narratives, Federal Writers' Project, vol. 9, pt. 3, 216.

33. Ibid., pt. 4, 136.

34. Elizabeth Fox-Genovese, *Within the Plantation Household*, 118.

35. Jess Watson House, Historic Resources Inventories, MDAH HPO.

36. Thomas Hubka, *Big House, Little House, Back House, Barn: The Connected Farm Buildings of New England* (Hanover, N.H.: University Press of New England, 1984), 77.

37. *Helps for Mississippi Poultry Raisers*, Extension Bulletin no. 5, Mississippi State College Extension Department, vol. 1, September 1917, 3.

38. Based on analysis of all Historic Resources Inventories of rural houses with an estimated construction date prior to 1910 from all 23 Mississippi yeoman counties, MDAH HPO.

39. Mary Titus, "The Dining Room Door Swings Both Ways: Food, Race, and Domestic Space in the Nineteenth-Century South," in *Haunted Bodies: Gender and Southern Texts*, ed. Anne Goodwyn Jones and Susan V. Donaldson (Charlottesville: University Press of Virginia, 1997), 244–45; John F. Kasson, *Rudeness and Civility: Manners in Nineteenth-Century Urban America* (New York: Hill & Wang), 187.

40. Architect Calvert Vaux, quoted in Clifford Edward Clark, *The American Family Home: 1800–1960* (Chapel Hill: University of North Carolina Press, 1986), 40.

41. Titus, "Dining Room Door," 245.

42. Elliott, *Mrs. Elliott's Housewife*, quoted in Edwards, *Gendered Strife and Confusion*, 140.

43. Nancy Bercaw, *Gendered Freedoms: Race, Rights, and the Politics of Household in the Delta, 1861–1875* (Gainesville: University Press of Florida, 2003); Jacqueline Jones, *Labor of Love, Labor of Sorrow: Black Women, Work and the Family from Slavery to the Present* (New York: Basic Books, 1985); Leslie A. Schwalm, *A Hard Fight for We: Women's Transition from Slavery to Freedom in South Carolina* (Urbana : University of Illinois Press, 1997).

44. Anna to Margaret Butler, February 6, 1867, Margaret Butler Correspondence, Louisiana and Lower Mississippi Valley Collection, Louisiana State University, Baton Rouge.

45. Edward Ayers, *The Promise of the New South: Life after Reconstruction* (New York: Oxford University Press, 1992); Steven Hahn, *The Roots of Southern Populism* (New York: Oxford University Press, 1983); Gavin Wright, *Old South, New South: Revolutions in the Southern Economy since the Civil War* (New York: Basic Books, 1986).

46. Eighth Census of the United States, 1860, Agriculture and Population; Twelfth Census of the United States, 1900, Agriculture and Population.

47. Ted Ownby, *American Dreams in Mississippi: Consumers, Poverty, and Culture, 1830–1998* (Chapel Hill: University of North Carolina Press, 1999), 82–95.

48. "Inventory Records of Estates," Monroe County, Mississippi (1884–1906); "Accounts and Reports of Probate," Rankin County, Mississippi (1872–94).

49. Mississippi State College Extension Department, *Extension Bulletins*, vol. 1 (June 1916–October 1924).

50. Spinning Wheel Club of Woodville, Mississippi, *The Spinning Wheel Cookbook* (Woodville, 1899).

51. Ladies Aid Society of the Presbyterian Church, *Tried and True Cook Book* (Gulfport, Miss., 1906).

52. "Women—Her Characteristics," Meek (Samuel M.) & Fly Papers, Louisiana and Lower Mississippi Valley Collections, Louisiana State University, Baton Rouge.

53. Galloway Papers, Louisiana and Lower Mississippi Valley Collections, Louisiana State University, Baton Rouge.

54. Ladies Aid Society, *Tried and True Cookbook*.

Part Two

The Twentieth Century

ELIZABETH ANNE PAYNE

AND MARTHA H. SWAIN

Giving birth for most Mississippi women—and over 90 percent in the twentieth century did—remained an at-home experience until midcentury. As late as 1947, 58 percent of Mississippi's babies were born at home, and a third were delivered by black midwives.[1] We were unable to secure an article on childbirth, midwifery, and public health for this volume, so we offer here a detailed explanation of the need for further research and writing on the subject. From our perspective, a fuller history of state-sponsored public health care for Mississippi mothers and their infants is vital. It is also necessary to assess historically the state's priorities regarding women's medical and health needs over the course of the century.

The story of the role of African American women in upgrading the state's public health is compelling. In 1921, Laurie Jean Reid, a nurse from the United States Public Health Service, traveled the eighty-two counties of Mississippi counting midwives. Her goal, as she told the (white) Mississippi Medical Association, was to emphasize that the United States lagged behind European countries in terms of maternal and infant care. She found four thousand midwives; the state later identified one thousand more.[2]

Reid proposed a strategy of using registered nurses, almost all of whom were white, to train midwives, 99 percent of whom were black. She found an eager supporter in Felix Underwood, head of the Mississippi Board of Health from 1924 to 1958 and a Nettleton, Mississippi, native who would become a national public health reformer.[3] Midwives were highly regarded in the African American community. Among the five thousand midwives, for example, was

MILLIE SIMPSON, HATTIE STONE, LOUANNA BELL,
RHODA MORRIS, AND MAGGIE VENZANT,
MIDWIVES OF UNION COUNTY, 1942

Courtesy of the Union County Historical Society, New Albany.

Kate Baker Price, mother of Leontyne. Once the initial fear of not becoming certified subsided, the midwives eagerly learned techniques of sterilizing scissors and sheets. They proudly carried the bags that marked them as state certified and therefore informed about modern medical techniques of birthing. They also learned how to recognize and combat infectious diseases, and they became the vehicle of the state's assault on syphilis. Their role in carrying out the reforms of the Department of Health at the local level is an incomplete story that, when more elaborately written, will attest both to the commitment of the midwives and to a public health program that few associate with the state. In 1937, the maternal death rate had dropped 47 percent from that of 1921.[4]

Midwife Hattie Stone (see opposite page) made a profound impression on Sherra Owen, a white woman who grew up in rural Union County. From her childhood days, Owen recalls seeing the midwife travel daily to New Albany, where she waited in front of the courthouse for anyone who needed her to "bring babies," in the meantime offering lemon drops to children. When her mule died, the midwife walked the ten miles into town each weekday.[5]

In 1946, Congress passed the Hospital Survey and Construction Act, popularly known as the Hill-Burton Act. Its purpose was to modernize hospitals, especially those in rural areas. The act also required uncompensated services from the hospitals for twenty years after accepting the funds. In order to practice in a Hill-Burton hospital, a physician was required to attend a certain percentage of patients who could not pay.

No Mississippi midwife under the state certified program was ever found incompetent in her work. Even medical authorities conceded that physicians and midwifes were equally effective at delivering babies. Yet, in 1947, a year after the passage of the Hill-Burton Act, the state certification program began a movement to "retire" midwives. This resulted in a major transfer of power, prestige, and money from black female midwives to white male physicians. Connecting the story of Mississippi's midwives and the upgrading of public health with the consequences of the Hill-Burton Act and the retiring of midwives is a book that begs to be written.

Factories in Mississippi did not hire black women until the late 1960s, but white women began working in significant numbers in the 1920s and 1930s. Mostly married women, the female factory workers were typically wives of men who continued to farm. In some cases, they were widowed or had ill or alcoholic husbands. Jack Herrington, who worked in his father's garment factory in New Albany, called the husbands of these factory women "gophers" (go-for-her) because the men drove the women to work in the morning and returned home to work on farm tasks. In seasonal downtimes, some played dominoes with other men in the afternoon at country stores. In order to understand the importance of women's work in factories, we need to comprehend its impact on the family economy. To what extent did families in which a wife, mother, or daughter worked in a factory prosper more than other families, given the same circumstances? How much did spending extensive time away from the home in the company of nonkin womenfolk blunt patriarchal power? Take, for instance, the ability to drive a car. After working in a factory for some time, a woman often learned to drive a car and in time bought one. She then picked up other women along the way to work who paid her, increasingly reducing the need for male drivers. This farm-to-factory transition of women raises cultural, social, gender, and economic questions that have not been addressed in a Mississippi context.[6]

New Deal programs opened up good jobs for white women as secretaries, receptionists, and bookkeepers throughout the South. In Mississippi, a smart high school graduate could work in the local office of the Soil Conservation Service, for example, and have medical and retirement benefits. In many cases, this allowed a woman who referred to herself as "independent" and who wanted to remain single to buy a modest but inviting brick house, in which she entertained her friends with crystal and sterling flatware.[7]

Missing from women's history in Mississippi is a solid monograph on women and World War II that documents their role in the military and in munitions and garment factories. I. G. Schwabe Factories in North Mississippi provided enough shirts during World War II to put one on each soldier's back. Milam Manufacturing Company in Tupelo, founded and owned by a woman, transformed itself from making baby clothes to sewing parachutes with flares, the kind used in the invasion of Normandy. A woman from New Albany served as one of Eisenhower's top assistants and was one of the five people to take notes at the Casablanca Conference, where the strategy for ending the war was developed. Thousands of Mississippi women poured into Washington, D.C., to work as secretaries, clerks, and accountants.

In the second part of this volume, Karen Cox gives us the cultural trajectory of memory and the subsequent creation of the Mississippi United Daughters of the Confederacy (UDC). She balances the UDC's transmission of the "Lost Cause's" negative influence in perpetuating racial segregation with the UDC's positive contributions of preserving important historic sites and the benevolent care of aging veterans. In contrast, Victoria Bynum offers the haunting case of Anna Knight and her sisters as they traversed the boundaries of race and gender during the long era of Jim Crow from the late nineteenth century well into the twentieth. The story of the Knight sisters is that of growing up poor, black or mixed race, and female in rural Mississippi and yet transcending those limitations.

Because so little attention has been given to farm women and factory workers in Northeast Mississippi, it is refreshing to read the essays by Sara Morris and Ted Ownby. The austere lives of farm and small-town women became even more desperate during the economic downturns of the 1920s and the Great Depression of the 1930s. Morris explores the benefits that women derived from home-improvement programs of the late 1920s and 1930s, particularly the electrical power created by the Tennessee Valley Authority and subsequent rural electrification. As avid consumers of available appliances, white Northeast Mississippi women enjoyed greatly improved lives as homemakers. In a companion essay, Ted Ownby explores the ways in which two women of diverse backgrounds, factory worker Gladys Smith Presley of Tupelo and social scientist Dorothy Dickins of Mississippi State College, faced the limits of female agrarianism in their approach to the consumerism that came with the modest prosperity of the post–New Deal era.

Moving to the civil rights movement of the 1950s and 1960s and a time when there was greater social change than at any other, Emilye Crosby and Todd Moye expand our understanding of the work of both black and white women activists. Both show that women's work in the movement was complex and diverse. Crosby looks at black women's work in Claiborne County in Southwest Mississippi, and Moye adds to his study of black women's political activity an exploration of the coterie of white upper-class and professional women who formed the Wednesdays in Mississippi program to promote acceptance of civil rights work and workers. He also notes the role of a national board of Methodist women who financed and published Pauli Murray's state-by-state analysis of discriminatory law, an important resource for lawyers and scholars preparing the *Brown v. Topeka* court case. Localism is the major theme of both essays.

In two essays, Martha Swain and Marjorie Spruill examine the quest for an expansion of women's rights after the end of the suffrage movement, which concluded in 1920 without a victory because the Mississippi state legislature refused to ratify the Nineteenth Amendment. Swain describes the work of five organizations of white women as they sought to define their concepts of women's rights from the early 1900s through at least the 1980s. Although most of the groups agreed that educational and professional opportunities for women should be expanded, there was also bitter conflict among them regarding appropriate legislation to advance women's status, including the proposed Equal Rights Amendment. Spruill shows how, even as white women activists in Mississippi united behind the ERA in the 1970s, the amendment still failed.

In 1977 white feminists came together with African American women veterans of the civil rights movement in support of feminist goals during the International Women's Year (IWY) conferences, but the women were defeated by a coalition of white conservatives who opposed feminism as a threat to traditional values. In 1984 the Mississippi legislature made a symbolic gesture by ratifying the Nineteenth Amendment, affirming women's right to vote, long after women had become active in politics, served in the legislature, even if in disappointing numbers, and one woman, Evelyn Gandy, had been elected lieutenant governor.

Just as an earlier essay provides the rich history of a Jones County, Mississippi, family, so does the final essay by Elizabeth Anne Payne, Hattye Raspberry-Hall, Michael de L. Landon, and Jennifer Nardone demonstrate the value of looking at family and local history to understand women's lives. The article describes the storytelling and recollections of an African American family from the Northeast Mississippi town of Okolona and the Raspberry family's triennial pageant, in which each family member reports back to an "unknown grandmother" and recommits to a life of service.

The editors offer this collection of essays as a testament to the richness and variety of Mississippi women's history. We trust that reading these essays will inspire other and especially younger scholars to explore unmarked terrain. Our fondest hope is that these essays will be regarded as an invitation to continue beyond our offering.

NOTES

1. James H. Ferguson, "Mississippi Midwives," *Journal for the History of Medicine* 5 (May 1950): 85.

2. Susan L. Smith, "White Nurses, Black Midwives, and Public Health in Mississippi, 1920–1950," *Nursing History Review* 2 (1994): 30–32.

3. See L. R. Bridforth, "The Politics of Public Health Reform: Felix J. Underwood and the Mississippi Board of Health, 1924–58," *Public History* 6, no. 3 (Summer 1984): 5–26.

4. Ferguson, "Mississippi Midwives," 85.

5. Sherra Owen, interviewed by L. Lane Noel, April 5, 2006, in *Makin' Do: The North Mississippi Women's History Project*, Department of History and Department of Media and Documentary Projects, University of Mississippi, Oxford, http://www.outreach.olemiss.edu/media/documentary/women_history/main.html (accessed September 21, 2008).

6. Jack Herrington, interviewed by Elizabeth Anne Payne, September 15, 2005; Eloise Conley Newell, interviewed by Elizabeth Anne Payne, January 23, 2006, both in *Makin' Do* (accessed September 21, 2008).

7. See, for example, the case of Robbie Ray, interviewed by Elizabeth Anne Payne, September 8, 2005, in *Makin' Do* (accessed September 21, 2008).

Mississippi's United Daughters of the Confederacy

Benevolence, Beauvoir, and the Transmission of Confederate Culture, 1897–1919

KAREN L. COX

During the Civil War, Mississippians were greatly affected by the destruction, deprivation, and defeat that came to their state. White men in particular were morally devastated by their failure to defend their homeland successfully. Many of Mississippi's white women sought to ease the emotional suffering of their men in the years immediately following the war by joining a movement to preserve the memory of Confederate veterans, most specifically through Ladies' Memorial Associations (LMAS). Each April 26, in towns across the state, white women memorialized the Confederate dead in a spring ritual in which they decorated the graves of their fallen heroes with flowers and Confederate flags. Beginning in the 1890s, however, the ways in which women commemorated the Confederacy expanded dramatically, and some of the most prominent women in the state led the way.[1]

Women calling themselves "Daughters of the Confederacy" organized in Mississippi in 1893. What became the United Daughters of the Confederacy (UDC), the organization that brought together in one body all southern women's Confederate organizations, was founded the next year in Nashville, Tennessee. Almost immediately afterward, UDC affiliate chapters formed in Vicksburg, Meridian, and Baldwyn, Mississippi. On April 26, 1897, members of the three chapters met at the Meridian Public Library to form the Mississippi Division, making it the third division formed in the South.[2]

MISSISSIPPI DELEGATION TO THE UNITED DAUGHTERS
OF THE CONFEDERACY CONVENTION, NEW ORLEANS
From the *Confederate Veteran* 10 (December 1902): 536.
Reprint edition by Broadfoot Publishing, Wilmington, North Carolina.

Mississippi women who joined the UDC in the period between 1890 and 1930 continued the tradition begun by memorial associations of commemorating the Confederacy and its heroes—a commemoration integral to the regional effort to preserve the values of the Old South, which many white southerners believed had made it a superior "civilization." Chief among those values was the commitment to the constitutional principle of states' rights. UDC members sought to honor these values as well as those who had fought for them during the Civil War. This commemorative tradition, known to contemporaries and later to historians as the "Lost Cause," already included decorating graves and building monuments and was essential to what historian Charles Reagan Wilson has called the South's "civil religion." Accordingly, the Daughters regarded both the southern past and the Confederate generation as "sacred." Like other UDC members throughout the South, Mississippi's Daughters were also determined to honor veterans by perpetuating Confederate values into the future, and they did so with much success. They built monuments, founded museums, wrote "true" histories of the war and its aftermath, and monitored textbooks used by children in the public schools.[3]

Teaching children pro-southern history was, in fact, the UDC's most important mission, because the organization placed its hopes for the state's and the region's future on the younger generation of white southerners. If the young minds of the South learned to revere and respect their Confederate ancestors and adopt as their own the principles of states' rights and white supremacy, the Daughters reasoned, then the cause for which the South went to war was not and would not be "lost."

Indeed, this effort was remarkably successful. The UDC was instrumental in creating a New South that in many ways resembled the Old. Despite their frequent insistence that they were neither "a political body" nor "shrewd and wily politicians," the Mississippi Daughters accomplished many of their objectives through adroit use of political connections and strategy. And in Mississippi as elsewhere in the South, other Lost Cause organizations, including the Sons of Confederate Veterans (SCV), found themselves having to turn to the Daughters for assistance.[4]

After its founding in 1897, the Mississippi Division experienced phenomenal growth. Within six years, there were 48 chapters in the state representing 1,627 members. Two years later, in 1905, there were 65 chapters and 2,347 members. By World War I, chapters of the UDC in Mississippi numbered 124 with a membership of almost 4,300. Margaret Kinkhead Thompson, president of the Jefferson Davis Chapter in Yazoo City, commented that the success of her chapter was due to its good leadership, "the officers being women of unusual executive ability." UDC members in Mississippi had a strong sense of mission. As Lizzie George Henderson of Greenwood argued, the organization had grown quickly because "God" wanted the Daughters to "do great things" for their country— "their country" being the South.[5]

The rapidly growing organization attracted a variety of women from all regions of the state. Some had experienced the Civil War firsthand, while others grew up in its aftermath, but the women who joined the UDC were literally "daughters" of the Confederate generation. The men and women they sought to honor, often referred to as the "generation of the sixties," were their fathers and mothers.

The Mississippi UDC was very popular among white upper-class women in the late nineteenth and early twentieth centuries, and its members included a host of women from the state's elite. Many were connected to leading men in their state through blood or marriage. For example, Lucy Yerger, longtime state division president, came from an elite planter family in the Delta, as did Mary Southworth Kimbrough, a close friend of Jefferson and Varina Davis. Kimbrough was instrumental in the effort to save Davis's last home, Beauvoir, as a Confederate soldiers' home and was married to a state judge, Allen Kimbrough of Greenwood.[6]

Many who joined the Daughters were also women of achievement. Most were well educated and active in several women's clubs. Okolona native Josie Frazee Cappleman, one of the founders of the Mississippi Division, was an important leader in the Mississippi Federation of Women's Clubs. Cappleman also served as a correspondent for a variety of publications including the *Memphis Commercial Appeal*, the *Detroit Free Press*, and *Harper's Weekly*. Eron Rowland, born in Chickasaw County near Okolona, was an equally productive writer, publishing pieces in the *Nation* and the *Chicago Tribune*. She also authored a two-volume book on the wife of the Confederate president, titled *Varina Howell: Wife of Jefferson Davis*. Born Eron Moore, she married Dunbar Rowland, long-time director of the Mississippi Department of Archives and History, and was an active preservationist in her own right.[7]

Two of Mississippi's Daughters achieved the UDC's highest honor when they were elected "president-general" of the general organization. The first, Lizzie George Henderson, was president-general from 1905 until 1907. Henderson, who lived in Greenville, came from a family with a long tradition of service to the Confederacy and the cause of states' rights. Her mother, Elizabeth Brook George, had organized a Ladies' Sewing Society in Carrollton during the war. Lizzie's father, James Z. George, was a United States senator and the author of the "Mississippi Plan," which allowed the state to avoid adherence to the Fifteenth Amendment to the Constitution, which guaranteed black men the right to vote, a maneuver that was emulated by several other southern states. The plan was part of a larger disfranchisement movement that included violence, intimidation, and the overthrow of the Republican Party in Mississippi. Lizzie George worked as his secretary in Washington, D.C., between 1887 and 1890, when the Mississippi Plan was developed. Returning to her home state, she became president of her local chapter of the UDC in Greenville before becoming president of the state division in 1902, and subsequently president-general of the UDC.[8]

The second Mississippi woman to attain the UDC's highest office was Daisy McLaurin Stevens of Brandon. She, too, had important political ties. The daughter of the state's former governor and later United States senator, Anselm McLaurin, Stevens rose through the ranks of the state division, eventually becoming its president before being elected UDC president-general in 1913. Through UDC appearances throughout the region, she became well known as one of the South's leading orators.[9]

With few exceptions, Mississippi's Daughters came from the same race and class. They were drawn to the UDC by a set of common goals: to honor the generation of the 1860s, the men and women whom they believed had made personal sacrifices for the region; to control how the Civil War was regarded and remembered; and most importantly, to do what they could to ensure that future generations of southerners were instilled with a respect for their Confederate ancestors and the principle of states' rights. Of these goals, Mississippi's Daughters made it their first order of business to assist the poor and indigent Confederate veterans in their state.

After its formation in 1897, the Mississippi UDC initially focused its efforts on building an annex for veterans at the State Charity Hospital in Vicksburg. Though the regional movement to build soldiers' homes had begun in the 1880s, no such movement had emerged in Mississippi. The UDC's plan was to remove veterans from the locally managed poorhouses in which they were currently living and place them in an institution where they could be properly cared for by the state. The Daughters insisted that honoring Confederate veterans was an obligation that could not be met simply by Lost Cause rhetoric. They believed that the State of Mississippi owed these men something far more concrete for their wartime sacrifices and diligently promoted government care for the generation of the sixties.

The efforts by the Daughters to assist those less privileged and to insist on state support for veterans place their activity within the bounds of the national reform movement known as Progressivism. It was through the Daughters' lobbying efforts that southern state legislatures eventually provided pensions (through state taxes) and built soldiers' homes. This activity formed a unique strain of southern Progressivism that was not simply "for whites only" but rather "for Confederates only."[10]

In 1900, the Mississippi UDC's statewide campaign for a veterans' annex at the State Charity Hospital at Vicksburg was successful. Owing largely to the Daughters' lobbying, the state legislature appropriated two thousand dollars to build the annex, making the hospital the only such institution in the state. Though pleased with this accomplishment, UDC members wanted more aid for the veterans and soon set out to assist the SCV in its bid to purchase Beauvoir, the last home of Jefferson Davis, for a soldiers' home.[11]

The Mississippi Daughters formed their own Home Committee, whose members worked to acquire the beautiful home, located on the Mississippi Gulf Coast near Biloxi. Lizzie George Henderson, whose days as her father's secretary in Washington, D.C., had equipped her with the political acumen she now needed, headed the committee. Henderson's report to the annual state meeting in 1902 offers evidence of her executive ability. As she noted, she had written to every chancery clerk in the state to obtain the names and addresses of Confederate veterans living in poorhouses or on private charity. She had also attended the veterans' reunion in Memphis, Tennessee, spending two days soliciting signatures on a petition to establish a veterans' home in Mississippi. She sent circulars to members of the state's press corps urging them to use their influence with the legislature to garner support for a home. The state senate passed the bill by a large majority, but as Henderson reported, the house killed the bill in committee. Undaunted, she took the detailed information she had gathered regarding the number of destitute Confederate veterans in Mississippi and used it to publicize the need for a home and boost the Daughters' own fundraising campaign to assist the SCV in its purchase of Beauvoir.[12]

In October 1902, the Sons purchased Beauvoir from Varina Davis for ten thousand dollars. They still needed funds to pay the balance of the mortgage on the home before they could move forward on the project. They also needed money to maintain the property and convert the home into a suitable living space for veterans. For help, the SCV turned to the UDC.[13]

The UDC, which was already sending a substantial donation to the hospital annex in Vicksburg, again came to the SCV's aid. In 1903, the organization donated five thousand dollars to prepare the home for veterans. Afterward, however, the Daughters resolved to "desist from work" so that the SCV could raise its share of funds without "interference" from the UDC. The reality was that the Daughters were ready to take independent action; however, they did not want to join the SCV's effort nor be blamed in the event that the Sons failed. According to Lizzie Henderson, if the UDC were involved in the home's development it would give the Sons a "very good reason to lay their failure . . . at our door," adding, "Even the most chivalrous of men are eager to lay all their failures at some woman's door."[14] By remaining independent from the SCV's efforts, Mississippi's Daughters maintained control over the funds they raised, giving them power and influence over the direction of the soldiers' home at Beauvoir.

Ironically, in an era when the ideal southern woman was apolitical, trusting men to rule wisely for her sake, the SCV and other southern men often turned to women for help with their public endeavors. In fact, many projects initiated by all-male Confederate organizations, whether construction of monuments or homes for soldiers, were not fully successful until the men called upon the Daughters to help with the fundraising. This is a powerful testament to the effectiveness and power of this southern women's organization, and the Daughters often used that power to influence a monument's design or a home's management. This was definitely the case at Beauvoir.

While the UDC portrayed itself as a "helpmeet" to the SCV, UDC members often became impatient with a behind-the-scenes approach and stepped forward to take the initiative. Indeed, Home Committee chairwoman Lizzie Henderson proclaimed in January 1903 that Mississippi's Daughters had "waited on the Sons long enough" and began publicly soliciting funds to furnish Beauvoir. O. L. McKay, commander of the Mississippi SCV, asked that the UDC instead turn its attention to paying the balance due on Beauvoir. The Daughters agreed, but when they met with Beauvoir's board in February 1903, they not only helped pay off the mortgage but also provided additional funds they had raised to furnish and equip the home.[15]

Still, the Sons were unable to furnish the home fully and take in veterans as promised, and the Daughters placed the blame for leaving the revered veterans in destitute conditions squarely on their shoulders.[16] Reporting to the Mississippi Division about this "terrible delay," Lizzie George Henderson lamented that, because the Daughters were "powerless to do anything to someone else's property . . . the poor, old men in the poor houses must wait. . . until the Sons [were] ready to do something." If women were fully in charge, she implied, the soldiers' home would have already opened. Her frustration with the SCV was palpable and highlights the situation in which women in the UDC found themselves. Even though many of their activities made them "New Women," they had to comply with traditional ideas about womanhood when working with their Confederate male counterparts.[17]

When the home finally opened on December 1, 1904, however, the UDC's contribution to buying the property and equipping the home was well recognized, and the Daughters were in a position to continue to influence Beauvoir's future. While the state legislature differed over the issue of appropriations to support the home, the UDC footed the bill for Beauvoir's expenses. As a result, Beauvoir had a "Home Board of Lady Managers" made up of UDC members. Stephen D. Lee, a former Confederate general from Columbus, Mississippi, hailed the Daughters' efforts in opening the home. Addressing the UDC's annual meeting in 1904, he stated: "When the men could not persuade our Legislature to build a home for the helpless Veterans who were needy, you, with your brothers, the Sons of the Confederacy, put your shoulders to the wheel." He further remarked that if the men of the state had the faith of Confederate women (referring to the UDC), then together they could "move mountains."[18]

For three years after its purchase, as the state's legislature continued to debate the issue of support for the home, the Daughters continued to try to persuade the state's representatives. UDC leaders met directly with Governor James K. Vardaman in 1905 seeking his support, and eventually funds were forthcoming.[19]

In time, the wives and widows of Confederate veterans would also be cared for at Beauvoir, one of the few homes in the South that allowed women to live with their husbands. UDC members across the South argued for the care of Confederate women, because they regarded their sacrifices on behalf of the South as having equal merit with those made by Confederate veterans. Yet not all UDC efforts to include women were successful, and Mississippi's home for veterans and their wives or widows was significant as an indication of the power of the Daughters in the state.

Having provided for Mississippi's Confederate veterans and widows, whose days were numbered, the UDC turned to its next—and more enduring—projects. These included establishing an approved version of the history of the Civil War and its aftermath and educating the state's white youth to revere and respect the principles for which, they believed, the South had gone to war: preservation of states' rights and white supremacy.

In 1900, Josee Frazee Cappleman, who had helped organize the Mississippi Division, gave a critical speech to the UDC state convention. In her address, titled "The Importance of Local History of the Civil War," she argued for proper documentation of the state's Confederate past, declaring this a "sacred duty" and one for which the UDC was well suited. Indeed, she argued, there was "no agency for the preservation of the Southerner's view of the Civil War to be compared with the Daughters of the Confederacy."[20]

Cappleman, like many of her contemporaries, was concerned that, as the numbers of surviving veterans dwindled, their stories would be lost. She suggested to her fellow Mississippians that they should collect the stories "as they [were] told by [Mississippi's] veterans" for use in southern school history books. By collecting these "reminiscences"—today known as oral histories—the Daughters saw themselves as preserving a "truthful" history of the former Confederacy, useful in keeping their promise to the Confederate generation to instill "into the descendants of the people of the South" a respect for the Confederate past.[21]

This effort to create a usable past involved preserving not only the memories but also the material culture of the war, and the Daughters set to work gathering documents and artifacts that they deemed sacred "war relics" for placement in archives and museums. UDC state historian Ida May Hardy of Hattiesburg recommended in 1902 that "all historical papers, or data of historic nature, collected by the State Historian and accepted, be delivered to the Secretary to the State Historical Society [later, the Department of Archives and History]," which had been established as a branch of government for that purpose. Such activity helped to preserve the Confederate past, including the Lost Cause narrative about Civil War history, which championed the South's "just cause."[22]

To perform the "sacred duty" in regard to history and historic preservation, each UDC state division and local chapter elected its own historian. Women who held these positions, including Ida May Hardy, were expected to lead the efforts to collect, monitor, and promote Confederate history. For UDC members, the task of collecting this material was highly personal, and this personal connection fueled their activity. It had been their mothers and fathers, after all, who participated in what the Daughters referred to as "the greatest struggle of modern times." President-General Helen Bell of Hattiesburg emphasized this in her address to the division, reminding UDC members that it was the personal stories of their parents that they must gather and preserve.[23]

It was not enough, however, to collect this material; it could not have the desired effect unless displayed before the public. For that goal the Mississippi Division also had a plan, and it lobbied successfully to attain its objectives. The Mississippi UDC collected war relics to be displayed at the Confederate Museum in Richmond, Virginia, which had opened in 1896. Each state of the former Confederacy had its own room at the museum, housed in the "White House of the Confederacy." Included among the items exhibited in the Mississippi Room was a saddle used by Jefferson Davis during the Mexican War, and a suit of clothes worn by Davis when he was captured at war's end.[24] Mrs.

Pinckney Morrison Moody reported to the 1901 national convention that the plans for the construction of Mississippi's new capitol building included a large room to be designated the "Hall of History," to be under the control of the Mississippi Daughters. This room, like the Mississippi Room at the Confederate Museum, would exhibit Civil War artifacts.[25]

The most visible remaining example of the Daughters' successful guardianship of history in Mississippi is the Old Capitol, a building preserved as a result of UDC efforts that began in 1908. The building was a particularly important symbol of Confederate history: the state legislature met in it prior to the Civil War and had passed Mississippi's Ordinance of Secession there. President-General Laura Martin Rose of West Point, Mississippi, who later served as historian-general for the national UDC, reported in 1909 that the division was "using its influence in every way" to secure an appropriation from the legislature to ensure the Old Capitol's preservation. The legislature defeated the appropriation bills for several years, but the division was on a mission to save the building and continued to push for state funding.[26]

Year in and year out, the Daughters campaigned to preserve the Old Capitol by seeking state appropriations. President-General Lucy Yerger, who once claimed that the UDC was "not a political body," told the state convention in 1910 that she had "talked to a number of Representatives and Senators of [the] State during the session of the last Legislature" about supporting the UDC's preservation effort. Two years later, in 1912, Eron Rowland, whose husband was director of the Mississippi State Archives and History, organized a highly successful petition drive to restore the Old Capitol. Indeed, members of many of the state's most active organizations, including the Colonial Dames, the Daughters of the American Revolution, the Daughters of 1812, the Mississippi Federation of Women's Clubs, the Mississippi Woman's Christian Temperance Union, the state's woman suffrage association, the United Confederate Veterans, and the SCV signed the petition.[27] Chairwoman of the Old Capitol Committee Laura Martin Rose also lobbied state representatives and in a 1914 circular "begged" state leaders "to vote for this bill, which [would] save the building—part of the State's history—for coming generations."[28]

Each year, the Daughters saw the gap close between votes for and against the appropriation. Eventually, on April 8, 1916, the state approved an appropriation of $125,000 to restore the Old Capitol, bringing to a successful close the UDC's eight-year struggle for the preservation of Confederate history.[29] It was an important victory for the Daughters, who saw historic preservation as a means not only to honor past generations but also to educate future ones about their "glorious heritage."

In Mississippi, and indeed across the South, the UDC was responsible for nearly every Confederate monument to appear on the southern landscape. Their lobbying efforts with local and state governments successfully garnered thousands of dollars for the monuments, many of them stone representations of Confederate soldiers that still stand guard in town squares and on courthouse lawns around Mississippi. Yet while UDC members are best known for building monuments of marble and stone, their least known but most important achievement was to create "living monuments" out of white southern boys and girls. The Daughters were determined to instruct southern children to respect and defend Confederate heroes, to know the "true" history of the South, and to uphold what were regarded as the "sacred" principles of states' rights and white supremacy. According to Mary Goodwin, Mississippi Division historian in 1917, the state's pride and patriotism were at stake if the organization failed to instruct children about the sacrifices and heroism of their ancestors. Southern white children, they believed, benefited from a proud—not shameful—image of their forbears. "We owe it to them [the children]," she said, "to keep them in touch with the record of our Confederate deeds."³⁰

To achieve its goals for children, Mississippi's Daughters engaged in a variety of activities. They wrote books for children, placed books on Confederate history and literature in public schools and libraries, and lobbied the governor and the state textbook commission to adopt books that reflected favorably on the South. UDC members also visited schools, sponsored essay contests for students and teachers, and spoke to schoolchildren about the "War Between the States," their official term for the Civil War. Within their communities, they also formed "Children of the Confederacy" chapters, which became official auxiliaries to the UDC.

Laura Martin Rose, who was responsible for saving the Old Capitol, also authored a children's primer celebrating the Ku Klux Klan (KKK). The book was published under the auspices of the UDC, which used the book's profits to finance a monument at Beauvoir. State UDC members pledged to educate children about the KKK so "that the truth of history is taught our children, many of whom are ignorant as to the Ku Klux, some believing them to have been demons and cut-throats." That "truth" according to Rose was that the Klan of Reconstruction was an honorable organization made up of chivalrous men who sought to protect the women and children of the South from rapacious black men. Speaking before the Daughters at a convention in Meridian, Rose pleaded, "Let me beg each of you to teach the children who the Ku Klux were and what was their high mission and permit them to think that you are not ashamed of being connected with the Ku Klux."³¹

Mississippi's Daughters were highly selective about which books should be read by children in the state's public schools. They considered it their duty to promote textbooks written by "loyal Southerners" until "every public school in Mississippi" was using them. At their state meeting in 1904, they resolved to lobby the governor of the state to select textbooks that would not "inculcate false ideas as to the issues of the struggle" or about the "motives which prompted [their] people [to war]."[32] In a second resolution, the Daughters also made it clear that their preference was "for such books as do not use the term 'civil war.'"[33] These included books written by Virginian Mary Williamson, who authored primers on Robert E. Lee and Stonewall Jackson, as well as works by more famous authors such as Thomas Nelson Page, also of Virginia, who wrote pro-Confederate novels and plantation stories that were known for using black dialect.[34]

In their efforts to get their message across through the public schools, Mississippi's Daughters were aided by superintendents, principals, and teachers. In 1903, they wrote Henry L. Whitfield, superintendent of public education for Mississippi, asking him to use his power to exclude history texts that "covertly misrepresent or insolently ignore the achievements of Southern statesmen and soldiery."[35] It is clear that many Mississippi officials were eager to cooperate. As members of the Winnie Davis Chapter of Meridian reported in 1905, "We are glad to again chronicle renewed expressions of interest in our work from our City Superintendent for Public Schools, Mr. J. G. Fant, and an expressed desire to have the pupils always represented in our exercises."[36] A few years later, Daughters from Yazoo City made a similar report: "One of the most pleasing features [of Confederate celebrations] is the part taken on all public occasions by children of the high school. . . . This unusual interest manifested by the children is due to the encouragement and influence of Superintendent M. Rose and his able faculty, who are always in hearty cooperation with the Daughters of the Confederacy."[37]

Also, according to Virginia Redditt Price's report in the division newspaper, *Our Heritage*, many Mississippi Daughters themselves were teachers. Interviews conducted with Mississippians who attended public school between 1910 and 1930 confirm this statement. Jones County native Katie Smith, who attended school in Ellisville in the second decade of the century, recalled that her teacher was a member of the UDC who held lessons on the War Between the States. During the lessons, her teacher "asked every student to tell something about his [Confederate] ancestor," Smith remembered.[38]

The Daughters' influence in the public schools was inescapable. It was evident in the thousands of portraits of Robert E. Lee they caused to be placed in white southern classrooms. Lizzie George Henderson argued that it would be a wonderful tribute to Lee's life if "the Daughters of the South determine[d] to place in every Southern schoolhouse an engraving of General Lee beside that of the 'Father of his country,' which the Mt. Vernon Association of women [were] placing in the public schools!"[39] In Mississippi, students were also likely to have a portrait of Confederate president Jefferson Davis on the wall. Such portraits were intended to serve as visual reminders of the importance of Confederate history.

The Daughters also organized commemorative activities in public schools across the state, again with the full blessing of teachers, principals, and school superintendents. UDC member Frances Thornton Smith recalled how, in the 1920s, her class commemorated Robert E. Lee's birthday in her hometown of Hattiesburg: "We'd have programs on him, and have his picture up all around." To commemorate the day, students might also have to write an essay on Lee. Smith, whose mother was a member of the UDC, explained that Lee's portrait was not the only one in her school. "We had all the southern generals we studied about."[40] The UDC also lobbied to have schools renamed after Confederate heroes.

As the centennial of Jefferson Davis's birth approached, the Mississippi Division spearheaded a regional celebration of the Confederate president to be held on June 3, 1908. The Winnie Davis Chapter of Meridian passed resolutions that were adopted by the state division formally requesting that the superintendent of instruction "introduce the supplementary study of the life of Jefferson Davis" in the schools. Indeed, by the time of the celebration, hundreds of portraits of Davis had been placed in schools throughout the South, and white children, especially in Mississippi, studied his life. The Daughters carefully chose a portrait of Davis that depicted him "as he looked when he assumed the administration of the Government of the Confederate States" and not of Davis "when worn with defeat, disappointment, imprisonment, and sorrow."[41]

Not only portraits but other items of Confederate material culture were used by the Daughters to inspire and instruct southern children. The UDC chapter in Greenwood, Mississippi, announced at the 1910 national convention that the state's Ordinance of Secession had been hung on the walls of its public-school building and suggested that other chapters do the same. Having the ordinances of secession of all states prominently displayed, they argued, would be "useful to students of southern history."[42]

The UDC also promoted the display of Confederate flags in the public schools. Virginia Redditt Price, the division's historian in 1914, argued that providing schools with a Confederate flag was very "patriotic," and she encouraged chapters in the Mississippi Division to donate flags to accompany portraits of Lee and Davis. She rebuffed the idea that it kept alive feelings of "strife and bitterness," saying that the flag was "merely a piece of bunting." The flag's visibility, said Price, would "have no baleful effect upon the minds of the growing generations," and students would be "elevated by contact with that which recall[ed] Davis, Lee and Jackson."[43]

The UDC clearly intended the placement of Confederate symbols in classrooms to influence children; it was part of their larger plan to vindicate the Confederate generation.[44] Building monuments to honor Confederate heroes was part of that plan, but educating children to revere the southern past, honor the generation of the sixties, and value the principles of southern nationalism—states' rights included—served the purpose of vindication in very important ways. It helped validate the southern version of the Civil War among a new generation of southerners as well as perpetuate the ideals of southern nationalism well into the future.

The UDC's contact with southern youth was far reaching. The effort to instill in southern children a reverence for Confederate values went on outside the schools as well. Local chapters of Daughters established chapters of the Children of the Confederacy (C of C) as auxiliaries to the adult chapters of both the UDC and the SCV. Mississippi was one of the first states to organize children's chapters, and boys as well as girls were eligible to join. Some children were made members the day they were born since the Daughters were quick to enroll their children and grandchildren. Most active members of children's chapters were between the ages of six and sixteen.[45]

In Mississippi, as in other states, children played prominent roles during Confederate holidays including Robert E. Lee's and Jefferson Davis's birthdays and Confederate Memorial Day, when they decorated the graves of soldiers with flowers and flags. C of C members also assisted the UDC in raising money to build monuments and competed for prizes in essay contests sponsored by the parent organization. At their meetings, the children studied history, wrote essays about Confederate heroes, and sang Confederate songs such as "Dixie" and the "Bonnie Blue Flag." Children in Mississippi made visits to Beauvoir to greet veterans and their wives or widows. They were also encouraged to meet with aging veterans in their own communities.[46]

The Mississippi UDC often employed a Confederate catechism to teach children about the Confederacy. Modeled after religious catechisms, the Confederate version was an appropriate tool for an organization that regarded the southern past as "sacred." It was written in 1904 by a Daughter from Texas, and like religious catechisms, it was designed as a call-and-response activity in which the chapter leader would read questions to students, who then responded with the appropriate answer. "What causes led to the War Between the States, from 1861 to 1865?" was a common question to which the appropriate response was "the disregard, on the part of the States of the North, for the rights of the Southern or slaveholding States." The catechism offered children a ready supply of pro-Confederate responses regarding southern history and principles.[47]

A primary activity of the children was to study history so that they would be able to recognize and "correct the errors" of northern historians. To assist children with this task, the UDC's historian-general devised a schedule of study, including a list of suggested reference works approved by the Daughters, for every month of the year. The Dixie Children's Chapter of Hazlehurst was perhaps typical in its schedule of activities. Following a program prepared by the Mississippi Division, the chapter held discussions about history, sang "old Southern melodies" at meetings, and observed "Lee and Jackson Days with appropriate ceremonies." During Confederate Memorial Day rituals, they decorated the graves of soldiers with flags and flowers. The Sunflower Guards Chapter of Itta Bena studied the lives and celebrated the birthdays of UDC founder Caroline Meriwether Goodlett, Robert E. Lee, and Thomas "Stonewall" Jackson. The W. C. Boyd Chapter of Gunnison studied the Confederate catechism, read southern stories, wrote essays, sang songs, and performed recitations.[48]

Laura Martin Rose became the UDC's historian-general in 1916 and developed the 1917 *Historical Yearbook* used to guide children's monthly activity throughout the South. According to her plan, C of C groups studied the reasons for secession in January, while in December they focused on the KKK, the reason for its existence, and its founder, Nathan Bedford Forrest. Rose's primer on the KKK, of course, was to guide their study. Later UDC historians added to the core of subjects for children's study such topics as the women of the Confederacy, Confederate secretary of state Judah P. Benjamin, and stories of faithful slaves.[49]

Through these combined efforts, the Daughters sought to instill in southern youth a belief in an orthodox Lost Cause narrative. That narrative reflected the patrician outlook of UDC leaders and was inherently racist. The Old South was idealized as a place where a benevolent planter class worked in harmony with its faithful and contented labor force. Women were refined "belles," loyal to their husbands and to the Confederacy. Confederate soldiers were celebrated as heroes in spite of military defeat, because they fought to defend a superior "southern civilization" that upheld states' rights and sought to maintain white supremacy. This venerated image of the Old South implicitly served as a model for race, gender, and class relations in the New South.[50]

The UDC invested its energy and resources in shaping children's views of the Confederacy, believing that boys and girls who learned the "truth" about the Civil War would become future defenders of the honor of their ancestors and the values for which the war had been fought—most importantly states' rights and white supremacy. Indeed, Mississippi's president-general Lucy Yerger emphasized that point in her report to the 1910 division meeting held in Columbus when she noted that the "very principles the South ha[d] ever held most precious" were "White Supremacy" and "Racial Integrity and Purity."[51]

Madge Burney of Waynesboro, who served as state director of children's chapters from 1919 to 1928, stumped the state to encourage the UDC's work with children. It was of utmost importance, she said, to teach the children to "love and honor the Stars and Bars" and to love and revere Confederate veterans "living or dead." Through the UDC, she insisted that the Daughters not only kept alive the "virtues and honors of the men and women who suffered and sacrificed in behalf of [their] rights during the War Between the States" but also created a base from which the adult organizations, the UDC and the SCV, could recruit new members. The UDC, therefore, saw itself as a link between a Confederate past and a future guided by Confederate values.

The enduring influence of the Daughters' in the state of Mississippi is abundantly evident. It is seen in the many monuments that appear in towns throughout the state. The Old Capitol they helped to save now houses the state's museum of history. After serving its purpose as a home for soldiers and widows, Beauvoir continues to be operated by the SCV as a "shrine" to Jefferson Davis, and despite the massive destruction caused by Hurricane Katrina, the home is being restored. Still, Beauvoir owes its existence as a shrine to the work of UDC members in the early twentieth century.

The Department of Archives and History houses several manuscript collections gathered by the Daughters, and Confederate Memorial Day, April 26 in Mississippi, continues to be commemorated in towns across the state. Students still attend schools named for Confederate heroes, and for decades, public-school textbooks continued to promulgate a pro-Confederate interpretation of history. In his book *Local People: The Struggle for Civil Rights in Mississippi*, historian John Dittmer suggests that, as recently as the 1970s, most whites in Mississippi still regarded Reconstruction as the "Tragic Era" of corrupt carpetbaggers and Negro rule, an "interpretation drilled into the minds of generations of schoolchildren." This, too, is part of the Daughters' legacy.

It is clear that through the transmission of Confederate culture to new generations, Mississippi's Daughters contributed to the longevity of racial segregation in the state. Politicians, educated under the watchful gaze of Lee and Davis, whose portraits hung in their classrooms, perpetuated Jim Crow schools and engaged in massive resistance against the civil rights movement in the 1950s and 1960s. The successes of the self-described "apolitical" Daughters of the late nineteenth and early twentieth centuries had profound implications for Mississippi well into the twentieth century.

NOTES

1. For a discussion of the history of Confederate Memorial Day, see Karen L. Cox, *Dixie's Daughters: The United Daughters of the Confederacy and the Preservation of Confederate Culture* (Gainesville: University Press of Florida, 2003). The literature on the Lost Cause is vast, yet two important works still influence thinking on the subject: Charles Reagan Wilson's *Baptized in Blood: The Religion of the Lost Cause, 1965–1920* (Athens: University of Georgia Press, 1981); and Gaines M. Foster's *Ghosts of the Confederacy: Defeat, the Lost Cause, and the Emergence of the New South, 1865–1913* (New York: Oxford University Press, 1988).

2. The history of the Mississippi Division can be found in "It was Fifty Years Ago," typescript, Estelle B. Heiss, Historian, Mississippi Division (1947), United Daughters of the Confederacy jumbo subject file, Mississippi Department of Archives and History, Jackson (henceforth cited as MDAH). See also Annie Wright Duncan, "Mississippi: A Short History of an Interesting State Division of UDC, *Lost Cause Magazine* (July 1898): 30.

3. Wilson, *Baptized in Blood.*

4. Quotation from *Mississippi Division Minutes* (1910), McCain Library, University of Southern Mississippi, Hattiesburg (henceforth cited as USM). Unless otherwise noted, all Mississippi UDC Minutes cited are from the McCain Library, University of Southern Mississippi, Hattiesburg.

5. Thompson quotation from *Mississippi Division Minutes* (1910), 65. Figures on chapters and membership from *Mississippi Division Minutes* (1903, 1905, 1914); "United Daughters of the Confederacy," *Confederate Veteran* (October 1907): 440.

6. Mary H. Southworth Kimbrough, subject file, MDAH.

7. Josie Frazee Cappleman, subject file, MDAH; Mrs. Eron Rowland, Miscellaneous subject file, MDAH; *Varina Howell, Wife of Jefferson Davis* (New York: Macmillan, 1927, 1931).

8. Cox, *Dixie's Daughters*, 38.

9. Daisy McLaurin Stevens, subject file, MDAH.

10. For a discussion of public welfare in the South, see Dewey Grantham, *Southern Progressivism: The Reconciliation of Progress and Tradition* (Knoxville: University of Tennessee Press, 1983). On Confederate Progressivism, see Cox, *Dixie's Daughters*, 73–92. Regarding the history of Confederate soldiers' homes, see R. B. Rosenburg, *Living Monuments: Confederate Soldiers Homes in the New South* (Chapel Hill: University of North Carolina Press, 1993).

11. *Mississippi Division Minutes* (1900), 5.

12. Ibid.; "Report of the Home Committee," in *Mississippi Division Minutes* (1903), 40–41.

13. *Taylor-Trotwood Magazine*, June 1908, 237.

14. *Mississippi Division Minutes* (1903), 48.

15. Ibid. 48.

16. Ibid., 49–50.

17. Ibid., 50.

18. Ibid. (1904), 99.

19. Ibid. (1905).

20. "The Importance of Local History of the Civil War," *Mississippi Division Minutes* (1900), 12–13. The objectives of the UDC were established in the organization's constitution and included the passage "to instruct and instill into the descendants of the South"; see *Minutes of the First Annual Convention, United Daughters of the Confederacy* (1894), 1–3.

21. *Minutes of the First Annual Convention* (1894), 1–3

22. *Mississippi Division Minutes* (1902), 43.

23. Ibid. (1903), 11.

24. "Museum Committee Report," *Mississippi Division Minutes* (1904), 73–75.

25. Cox, *Dixie's Daughters*, 99–100.

26. "Report of the Mississippi Division," *Minutes of the Annual Convention of the UDC,* 7.

27. "The Restoration of Mississippi's Old Capitol," *Our Heritage*, souvenir edition, 1952, 12; report of the Mississippi Division, *Minutes of the Twenty-third Annual Convention of the UDC,* 366.

28. Mississippi Division Minutes (1910), 13; (1914), 86.

29. Mississippi Division Minutes (1914), 86–87; (1915), 69; report of the Mississippi Division, Minutes of the Twenty-third Annual Convention of the UDC, 366. The Old Capitol today serves as the state's Museum of History.

30. *Mississippi Division Minutes* (1904), 90.

31. Ibid. (1914), 111.

32. Ibid. (1904), 90.

33. Ibid. (1905), 104.

34. "The Restoration of Mississippi's Old Capitol," *Our Heritage*, souvenir edition, (1952), 12; report of the Mississippi Division, *Minutes of the Twenty-third Annual Convention of the UDC,* 366.

35. *Mississippi Division Minutes* (1903), 59.

36. Ibid. (1905), 35.

37. Ibid. (1910), 66.

38. Virginia Redditt Price, "Our Historical Department," *Our Heritage*, March 1915, 3; Mrs. P. E. "Katie" Smith, interviewed by the author, February 29, 1996, Mississippi Oral History Program (henceforth cited as MOHP).

39. "United Daughters of the Confederacy," *Confederate Veteran*, March 1907, 103.

40. Frances Thornton Smith, interviewed by the author, February 14, 1996, MOHP.

41. Resolutions presented by the Winnie Davis Chapter, *Minutes of the Fourteenth Annual Convention of the UDC*, 48–50; Report of the Mississippi Division, *Minutes of the Fifteenth Annual Convention of the UDC*, 315–17.

42. Quotation from Lizzie George Henderson recorded in the *Minutes of the Seventeenth Annual Convention of the UDC*, 110–11.

43. Virginia Redditt Price, "Our Historical Department," *Our Heritage*, December 1914, 3. While Mississippi's schools placed portraits of Lee and Davis in the classrooms, Price's mention of Stonewall Jackson was typical in Lost Cause rhetoric, which often mentioned the three Confederate leaders together.

44. For a discussion of vindication as a UDC objective, see Cox, *Dixie's Daughters.*

45. Madge Burney Papers, McCain Library, University of Southern Mississippi, Hattiesburg.

46. *Mississippi Division Minutes* (1917); Burney Papers, USM.

47. Cox, *Dixie's Daughters*, 138–39.

48. *Mississippi Division Minutes* (1917), 50.

49. Mrs. S. E. F. Rose, UDC *Historical Yearbook* for 1917. For information on Laura Rose, see Mrs. S. E. F. Rose, subject file, MDAH; Rose's essays appeared in the *Confederate Veteran* and were published as pamphlets. Her book for children was titled *The Ku Klux Klan or Invisible Empire* (1913).

50. This definition of Confederate culture is derived in part from Raymond Williams, *Keywords: A Vocabulary of Culture and Society* (New York: Oxford University Press, 1983), 91; and Clifford Geertz, *The Interpretations of Cultures* (New York: Basic Books, 1973), 193–233.

51. *Mississippi Division Minutes* (1910), 11.

Negotiating Boundaries of Race and Gender in Jim Crow Mississippi

The Women of the Knight Family

VICTORIA E. BYNUM

The multiracial Knight families of the Jones County region of Mississippi have long confounded notions about race in the United States. Descended from white southerners, former slaves, and Native Americans, they did not fit the discrete categories of racial identity demanded by Jim Crow laws in the aftermath of the Civil War and Reconstruction. Furthermore, many of them refused to abide by the South's "one drop" rule, which demanded that white persons with African ancestors identify themselves as black.

White men who fathered the children of black women were common in southern society, but Newt Knight's behavior differed in that he openly embraced both his "black" and "white" families. Newt was not only the leader of Mississippi's most famous guerrilla band of Civil War Unionists; he was the patriarch of this mixed-race community. More shocking than his own crossing of the color line with his grandfather's slave Rachel were the interracial weddings that followed between two of his and two of Rachel's children. In 1878, Matt and Molly Knight, Newt's children by his white wife, Serena, married Fannie and Jeffrey, Rachel's children by a white man. From that point forward, the interracial Knight community, which grew larger every year, was an open secret. Everyone knew that white and black Knights who lived in the vicinity of Soso, on the borders of Jones and Jasper counties, were kin to one another, although few people publicly said so.[1]

Many of the Knights, called "white Negroes" by their white neighbors because of their light complexions, refused to consider themselves black. Other Knights considered themselves people of color but did not mix with people defined as "Negroes." Still others considered themselves African American despite their mixed ancestry. Marriage patterns among these three groups best indicated their senses of identity: some Knights married only whites; others married cousins or acquaintances who were as light skinned as they were; and still others affirmed African American identities by marrying partners whose skin shades were darker than their own.

The lives of mixed-heritage Knight women reveal various strategies by which conventions of gender, class, and marriage might be manipulated to escape the worst effects of racial discrimination. The three daughters of former slave Georgeanne Knight—Anna, born in 1874; Grace, born in 1891; and Lessie, born in 1894—learned early in life that a poor "mulatta" living in the Piney Woods of Mississippi could hope for little better than the economic support of a white man in exchange for sexual favors. Neither the mother nor the grandmother of the sisters ever married, but both gave birth to numerous children fathered by white men. To the dominant white society, such women were little more than prostitutes whose behavior reinforced a common stereotype that women of color lacked morals.[2] Yet through travel, education, or unconventional personal choices, Anna, Grace, and Lessie escaped the fate of their female forebears.

The oldest sister, Anna, joined the legion of educated middle-class black women who, between 1890 and 1930, worked tirelessly to uplift African Americans by opening the doors to education and health care.[3] Before she could join the ranks of elite African American women, however, she first had to uplift herself. Her struggle to escape her mother's fate began early in life. Described as having "blue, blue eyes," Anna had every reason to anticipate the sexual advances of white men as she approached her teen years. Sexual activity would likely result in pregnancy, at which point all avenues to social respectability would close. Had Anna followed the paths of her mother and grandmother, she too would have become just another mulatta concubine, bringing more unwanted "white Negroes" into their world. As late as 1963, her grandmother Rachel was remembered as a white man's "concubine."[4]

Of course, Anna might also have married a man of color and raised a family, but instead she never married at all. While still a teenager, she embraced Seventh-Day Adventism much as a drowning person would grasp a life jacket. She believed with all her heart that God had lifted her from a life of poverty and degradation. No amount of physical risk or intellectual challenge deterred her from following a religious path that simultaneously relaxed the grip of gender conventions and racism.

Anna's steely determination shaped the course of her kinfolks' lives as well as her own. In 1898, she established an Adventist-sponsored school and two

FAMILY OF JEFFREY AND MOLLIE KNIGHT, CIRCA 1908
Seated in the front row are Jeffrey Early Knight, son of Rachel Knight, and his wife,
Martha Ann (Mollie) Knight, the daughter of Newt and Serena Knight.
Standing behind them, left to right, are their children: Altamira, Otho (the father
of Davis Knight, tried for miscegenation in 1948), Leonard Ezra, Charlie,
Ollie Jane, and Chances Omar. Photograph from the collection of Dianne Walkup,
Monterey, California.

Sunday schools in the Knight community. Under her tutelage, most of her relatives gained educations and converted to Seventh-Day Adventism. Anna's impact on her sisters' lives was especially profound. Yet despite the influence of their older sister, Grace and Lessie followed divergent paths in life. Like Anna, Grace never married and became a schoolteacher. Unlike Anna, however, she lived her entire life within the community of her birth. Sister Lessie, on the other hand, followed yet another path by leaving Mississippi, marrying, and living as a white woman.

In taking the paths they did, all three sisters avoided much of the social harassment that plagued their kinfolk, particularly those who refused to be defined as "Negroes" and who engaged in illegal marriages or illicit relationships across the color line. The harshest punishment of such Knights occurred in 1948, when their cousin, twenty-three-year-old Davis Knight, was convicted of miscegenation and sentenced to five years in the penitentiary. During his trial, the private affairs of the Knight sisters' long-dead grandmother, mother, and several of their aunts were paraded before the public.[5]

On November 14, 1949, Davis Knight's trial again made national headlines when the Mississippi State Supreme Court overturned his conviction. In reporting the historic decision, newspapers recounted not only the facts of the case but also rehashed one of Mississippi's most famous legends, that of the "Free State of Jones." Davis, readers learned, was the great-grandson of Newt Knight, a white man and the infamous "captain" of a band of deserters in the Jones County region who had held the Confederacy at bay during the final two years of the Civil War. It was Newt's wartime collaboration with Davis's slave ancestor, Rachel, that publicly exposed intimate relations between black and white Knights in the Jones/Jasper County region of Mississippi. Newt was reputed to be the father of several of Rachel's children, as well as those of Rachel's oldest daughter, Georgeanne, mother of Anna, Grace, and Lessie.[6]

The absence of published material about the Knight community before the Davis Knight trial is particularly striking given that the legend of the Free State of Jones has long been a vital part of Mississippi folklore and history. Before the Knight trial, historians and folklorists ignored Rachel's role in the Civil War uprising, covering only those aspects of Newt's wartime behavior that pertained directly to his resistance to the Confederacy. In 1951, however, Ethel Knight, a pro-Confederate member of a white branch of the family, broke that silence in *The Echo of the Black Horn*, her version of the uprising. Unlike previous authors, Ethel extended the history of the Free State of Jones well beyond the war, providing readers with detailed accounts of the descendants of Newt and Rachel, whom she repeatedly labeled a "strange" people.[7]

Ethel's depiction of the Knight community reflected a common disdain and fascination that many whites felt toward racially mixed people. Her portrayal of Knight women drew freely on popular literary stereotypes of seductive black "Jezebels" who led white men to personal destruction and "tragic mulattas" who attempted to escape their inferior racial status by "passing" as white. She merged these images in Rachel and Georgeanne, who appeared as dangerous, desperate women, almost comically craven with desires for the same white man—Newt Knight. Ethel portrayed one of Rachel's younger daughters, Fannie, as a more conventionally "tragic" mulatta. In daring to marry Newt's white son Matt, Fannie transgressed what Ethel considered to be boundaries decreed by God. Interracial marriages, besides being illegal in Mississippi after 1878, created "white Negroes," who, she believed, had no place in segregated society. "There must be two races," she wrote, "a black, and a white, for a mixed race will always be a people without 'place.'"[8]

Long before Ethel Knight published her vitriolic history of the Free State of Jones, descendants of Rachel endured social ostracism and racial discrimination. Her granddaughters came of age around the turn of the twentieth century, during the height of white supremacy campaigns throughout the South. Their view of themselves and of their appropriate position in society reflected not only their genealogical descent from Newt, a white man, and Rachel, a woman likely of European, African, and Native American ancestry, but also their descent from Serena, Newt's white wife. Serena was the mother of Matt, who married Rachel's daughter Fannie, and Molly, who married Rachel's son Jeffrey. As a result, many second and third generations of Knights knew *both* their white grandparents on intimate terms.[9]

Serena moved out of her husband's household sometime between 1880 and 1900, yet she did not move out of the interracial neighborhood. Instead, this white woman lived in the mixed-race household of her daughter Molly despite having three white sons who by 1895 were all married to white women. Serena apparently rejected Newt because of his philandering, but she did not reject their two children who married across the color line, nor did she reject her grandchildren. Molly and Jeff's children never knew their enslaved grandmother, Rachel, but they grew up with Serena's daily presence.[10]

Third-generation Knight women, defined by white society as black despite their mixed ancestry and light skin, faced difficult choices. Segregation and violent repression of blacks actually increased throughout the South after 1889, the year of Rachel's death.[11] To elevate themselves and overcome limited social mobility, many of Rachel's twentieth-century descendants blended into white society, sometimes sporadically, sometimes permanently. Those with darker skin and curlier hair focused on achieving middle-class status through religious training and education. In either case, to be raised in a neighborhood that included white kinfolk meant that many Knights "performed" whiteness simply by being themselves. And because southern norms of middle-class behavior were white defined, familiarity with white culture aided their efforts to achieve gentility. To achieve social mobility was no easy task in the Jones County region, however, since most local whites identified "Knight Negroes" by their dark eyes, olive skin, and the neighborhood in which they lived. As Davis Knight's trial later demonstrated, many of these Knights found it necessary to leave Mississippi in order to live as whites or achieve middle-class status.

Given the Knight community's strong Euro-American heritage, it is not surprising that many members declined to identify themselves as black, despite the South's "one drop" rule. The presence of a white mother and grandmother in the household further influenced the children of Molly and Jeffrey to identify as white and later to leave the state. After Jeffrey's death in 1932, his son Chances Omar moved his family to Oklahoma, where he made his whiteness official. Chances's brother, Otho, took a more defiant route by marrying his cousin Addie and remaining in the Soso area, where he too raised his children as white.[12]

Whether or not they left Mississippi, Knights who refused to be labeled "Negro" defended their olive skin by claiming Native American ancestry. In Oklahoma, Chances Omar's descendants erased their enslaved ancestor, Rachel, from their family history and attributed their Indian ancestry to their white grandmother, Serena, who they claimed was descended from the Cherokees relocated via the "Trail of Tears." Descendants of Chances's sister Ollie Jane Smith offered yet another version of their ancestral roots. They did not deny descent from Rachel but suspected that she was a Sioux Indian who had been kidnapped, transported to Mississippi, and enslaved sometime before the Civil War.[13]

Like many of Molly and Jeff's children, several of Fannie and Matt Knight's children left Mississippi and identified as white rather than resign themselves to the bleak future they faced as Mississippi blacks. A legal challenge in 1914 to their right to inherit their deceased white father's property may have hastened that decision. That year, several of Fannie and Matt's adult children filed suit to inherit shares of Matt's meager estate. On January 27, 1914, fifty-year-old Fannie stood before the chancery clerk, W. H. Bufkin, and provided testimony that defended her children's claims. Whether the children could legally inherit their late father's property depended on whether Fannie was black, and thus whether her marriage to Matt, which had been performed by a white Methodist minister and recorded in the county court's "white" marriage book, was legally valid. The matter was further complicated because, around 1894, Matt had abandoned his wife and eight children. As Fannie explained to her lawyer, he "just went off and left me [for] this other woman." Assuming that his marriage to Fannie was no longer valid under Mississippi law, Matt had married that "other woman" (a white cousin) in 1895 without bothering first to obtain a divorce.[14]

Matt's decision to end his marriage to Fannie created problems for her beyond the obvious one of being left alone to raise eight children. On the one hand, if she conceded that her marriage to Matt was invalid, she would admit that she was nothing more than a kept black woman with a slew of illegitimate children. On the other hand, if she insisted on its validity, she could not legally marry again. Barely thirty years old when Matt left her, Fannie neither obtained a divorce nor remained single. On December 20, 1897, she gave birth to a child (presumably not fathered by Matt), who died before the age of two. In 1904, she married Dock Howze, a minister of the gospel.[15]

Marriage to Dock promised greater economic security and renewed respectability for Fannie. During the era of segregation, however, Mississippi courthouses did not extend the traditional courtesies of womanhood to black women. At the hearing for her children's suit, Fannie was peppered with humiliating questions by defense attorney Goode Montgomery. How many children did she give birth to *after* Matt left her, he asked? Why did she marry Dock Howze if she believed that her marriage to Matt was legal? Fannie answered with logic that made perfect sense in her world, but that played into the hands of the defense: "Well, he went off and married and left me," she answered. "I stayed single about ten years; I thought it was all right [to marry again]."[16]

Fannie's admission that she had remarried without first obtaining a divorce from Matt allowed Montgomery to deliver the defense's coup de grâce: "G. M. [Matt] Knight was a white man . . . and you are a negro woman." This Fannie denied. "I am Choctaw and French," she countered. When Montgomery asked her if Dock Howze was not also a Negro, she replied that Dock was Choctaw and Irish. Montgomery then cited evidence commonly used by whites to determine whether people as light skinned as Fannie and Dock were in fact black. Did not Fannie and Dock live among "niggers," he asked? Like the tragic mulattas of so many novels, Fannie was forced to admit that she and Dock "lived on that side." She was thus stripped of her dignity and her children labeled bastards because of her "sin" of attempting to cross over into white society.[17]

Such were the experiences that encouraged many Knights to leave Mississippi. By 1920, at least three of Fannie and Matt's children were living as whites in Texas. Like their Oklahoma cousins, they erased their African ancestry and told spouses and children that their olive skin and curly hair were the legacy of Native American ancestry. One son, George Monroe Knight, changed his last name and told his children that their grandmother, Fannie, was a "full-blooded Cherokee." Also like their cousins, not all the children of Fannie and Matt moved away. Their son Henry remained in the Soso region and married light-skinned Ella Smith. Henry and Ella's daughter, Addie, married her cousin Otho and became the mother of Davis Knight.[18]

The humiliation that Addie Knight experienced at her son's 1948 trial was no less than that suffered by her grandmother Fannie in 1914. Forced to listen to Tom Knight, her white cousin, testify in court that her son was a Negro, Addie endured worse insults outside the courtroom in the immediate aftermath of the trial. There, in the streets, Tom mingled with the crowd, freely labeling the family of Davis Knight as "nigger Knights." He did not recognize Davis's mother as she stood nearby listening to him, however. Assuming Addie was a white woman, Tom kindly asked her who she was. Addie spat back, "I'm the nigger mammy of that white boy you are trying to [im]prison."[19]

Addie and Otho Knight's determination to have their family accepted as white, which included refusing to send their children to Anna Knight's Adventist school, alienated them from some of their kinfolk. In the aftermath of Davis Knight's conviction, his "copper colored" cousin Nancy Knight, for example, told a reporter that she personally had no use for "white niggers." Neither, apparently, did Nancy's sister, Allie. Almost twenty years earlier, Allie had used her position as midwife to the Knights' family physician to report Otho and Addie's daughter, Louvenia, as a Negro on her birth certificate. Louvenia struggled against the consequences of Allie's act in 1960, when she sought to enroll her two sons in a white school. During an investigation conducted that year into the boys' racial status, Louvenia claimed that midwife Allie Knight had labeled her a Negro at birth "for spite," since Allie knew that her parents "considered themselves white." To Allie and her sister, Nancy, however, Otho and Addie's determination to be white was the problem. Descended from Rachel Knight's son Hinchie, they came from a branch of the family whose members either could not or chose not to identify as "white."[20]

In contrast to the family of Otho and Addie Knight, Lessie Knight attained a white identity, while avoiding ugly public scenes and family schisms, by moving out of Mississippi. She enjoyed a successful career as Mrs. Leslie Robertson, the manager of a Hilton Hotel in Beaumont, Texas. No longer burdened by the Knight surname or notoriety, she did not seem unduly concerned that her African ancestry might be discovered. She made regular trips back to Mississippi and remained on good terms with her sisters. As a middle-aged woman, she even sat for a portrait with her "black" sister Grace. When she died of kidney disease in Beaumont on February 20, 1944, her other "black" sister, Anna, was at her side. Lessie's death certificate listed her parents as Newton Knight and George Ann Knight and her race as white.[21]

Not all the Knights who left Mississippi did so to blend into white society. Anna Knight, who had left the state decades ahead of her cousins and her sister, represented the other route to social elevation: through attainment of education and middle-class mores. While still a child during the 1880s, Anna yearned for knowledge and respectability. Her intense love of reading led to her discovery of the Seventh-Day Adventist Church, which was proselytizing throughout the South during the late nineteenth century. When an Adventist salesman visited the Knight home, fifteen-year-old Anna convinced her mother to subscribe to the *Home and Fireside Magazine*. Soon afterward, she established contact with other Adventists by placing an ad requesting that subscribers send her reading material. She soon received a flood of Adventist literature and began an important correspondence with Edith Embree, who worked for the Adventist *Sign of the Times*. Under the tutelage of "Miss Embree," Anna became a devout believer in Adventist doctrine. Before long, her association with the church became her ticket out of Mississippi.[22]

After Anna announced her desire to be baptized in the church, Elder L. Dyo Chambers, secretary-treasurer of the Southern Missionary Tract Society and Book Depository in Chattanooga, Tennessee, invited her to attend the Graysville Seventh-Day Adventist Academy. Apparently impressed by Anna's religious devotion, determination, and self-discipline, Elder Chambers and his wife brought Anna to Chattanooga and took her under their wing. At critical points in her religious development, the couple housed her, subsidized her schooling, and arranged for her training as an Adventist missionary nurse.[23]

The Chamberses' investment in Anna Knight proved a wise one on their part, for Anna gave as much to the church as she received, working at various times as a missionary, nurse, teacher, and administrator. As a foreign missionary, she spent six years in India, and as a domestic missionary, she worked in Mississippi, Georgia, and Alabama to improve the health and education of southern black children. In 1971, one year before her death at the age of ninety-eight, the Adventist Church awarded her its thirteenth Medallion of Merit Award for "extraordinary meritorious service" to Adventist education.[24]

Despite her work on behalf of the church, Anna maintained strong ties with the Knight community her entire life. Because of the school she founded near Soso, generations of Mississippi Knights received excellent educations. As late as 1963, Quitman Ross, the white attorney who defended Davis Knight in 1948, commented that mixed-race Knights "have an elementary education quite superior to that possessed by the ordinary graduate of backwoods grammar schools."[25]

Because of Anna's long career, no one in the Knight community—not even Newt Knight—left behind as extensive a paper trail as she, including a church-sponsored autobiography, *Mississippi Girl*, published as a testimonial to Seventh-Day Adventism in 1952. Anna's religious work and devotion dominate the text. She wrote nothing about the anti-Confederate uprising led by Newt Knight, nor did she mention the relationships and marriages that evolved out of Newt's wartime alliance with her grandmother Rachel. Yet, in explaining how she became an Adventist and her subsequent efforts to uplift her kinfolk, she provided tantalizing glimpses into the Knight community as well as insights into her own character.

Anna only hinted at the interracial household in which she was raised, and which emerged simultaneously with the Mississippi legislature's mandate for racial segregation. She did not identify either her mother, Georgeanne, or her grandmother Rachel by name, but referred to her mother as a "slave born in Macon, Georgia." Her autobiography alluded to Newt Knight as "one of the younger Knights who did not believe in slavery," but did not identify him—or any white man—as her father. Although Anna's death certificate named Newt Knight as her father, her autobiography referred to both her parents as former slaves.[26]

Anna's reluctance to name her notorious Knight forebears in her autobiography or admit that she grew up in an interracial household is not surprising when one reflects on the course of her life. As the oldest of three sisters, she was also the most publicly visible. Like most black female reformers during this era of intense racial oppression, she was pious, impeccably groomed, and scrupulously chaste. Given the times, she dared not appear otherwise. From within black churches and women's clubs, women such as Anna countered dominant media images that presented the ideal white woman as genteel, sexually pure, and domestic, while stereotyping women of color as seductive Jezebels or maternal Mammies.[27]

By 1952, the year Anna's autobiography was published, Davis Knight's miscegenation trial and Ethel Knight's sensational exposé of the interracial Knight community had made the names of Newt, Rachel, and Georgeanne Knight synonymous with sexual scandal and racial amalgamation in Mississippi. Since Anna could not keep her family's story out of the public eye, she obscured her own connections to it. Rather than provide more grist for the gossip mills, she emphasized her personal triumph over multiple forces of adversity. A subtle subtext of her story is not only her escape from the worst effects of racism but her shunning of "feminine" characteristics that would have impeded her professional success. Though religiously pious and unfailingly neat and proper in appearance, as a foreign missionary Anna risked illness, loneliness, and physical assault rather than live the life of domesticity prescribed for proper ladies of the era. Clearly, many conventions of white womanhood held no more attraction for her than those assigned to women of color.

The other striking feature of Anna's personality was her asceticism. In large part, this reflected her conversion to Adventism, a conversion that fulfilled her deep desire for order and self-control. Development of Spartan habits enabled Anna to dramatically transform her life, achieve professional success, and gain social respect. It also left her with little tolerance for human weaknesses that led to vice and addictions—especially those involving sexual promiscuity, alcohol, and tobacco.[28]

Anna's rigid standards were most evident during her tenure at Oakwood College, an African American Adventist School in Huntsville, Alabama, established in 1895 to accommodate racial segregation. Oakwood students remembered Anna as a stern, exacting teacher whom they feared as well as respected. Tiah M. Graves described her as a "very intimidating individual," while Rosetta Baldwin recalled that students would walk on tiptoe and "shush" one another when they heard her approaching. Although Rosetta came to emulate "Miss Knight," she never forgot her first encounter with the teacher who barked, "What little girl is that; she can't teach school." Similarly, Natelkka Burrell remembered Miss Knight as a "lady with a commanding voice," whose reprimands earned the "great deference" of her students.[29]

Too many people were "enslaved" by their senses, Anna lamented, because of their unbridled individualism and lack of respect for authority. Like a good seventeenth-century Puritan, she justified her own youthful rebellion against earthly authorities by attributing it to God's will, which overrode the commands of parents. She believed, however, that Adventist leaders and parents drew their authority from the true God; therefore, their will must not be thwarted. Known at times to "correct" students with her black cane, she urged "strict order in the family, the school, and the public assembly." Parents, she counseled, must carefully train their children to resist becoming "the willing slaves of every foolish fashion and disgusting habit that ha[d] become popular."[30]

Anna's stern disapproval of unchaste behavior indicated her determination to distance herself from the sexualized images to which many of her female kin were subjected. Twice in her autobiography she condemned "card parties and dancing" as "questionable forms of amusement" from which Jesus had saved her. As a teacher, she not only forbade such activities, but also occasionally counseled amorous students not to sit too close to each other lest they crowd out the Holy Spirit.[31]

Yet Anna displayed no romantic illusions about marriage either and expressed a decided preference for remaining single rather than risking marriage with the wrong man. When questioned by another missionary about why she worked late into the night rather than socialize more, she replied, "I really am in love with my work." Anna's attitude allowed her to sidestep making the marital choices common among her kinfolk by the early twentieth century. To maintain their light skin, third-generation Knights generally married partners as light skinned as themselves—often their cousins—or like Davis, they thwarted the law and married whites. Anna chose instead to supplant marriage and motherhood with service to the Adventist Church. Her life as an Adventist professional spared her from ever becoming the sexual property of a white (or black) man or from enduring the public insults suffered by her aunt Fannie Knight Howze or her cousin Addie Knight.[32]

Although Anna obscured her kinship ties in her autobiography, she emphasized the struggle of growing up poor, black, and female in rural Mississippi. Poverty dictated that females work in the fields *and* the house. "There was no rest for women," she lamented. Interestingly, she did not long for a more "feminine" childhood, only a more just one. Given the choice, she preferred masculine work and play over feminine chores, stating emphatically that she "liked fieldwork better than housework." Far more distressing to her than the fact that she never owned a doll was that she was denied schooling on the basis of her race.[33]

Of course, racial discrimination did not end when Anna left Mississippi. Even within the Adventist Church, some objected to Anna's attending a white school. Although white and black Adventists still worshiped together in some regions of the South during the 1890s, increasingly the church was forced to adhere to southern standards of segregation, particularly within its schools. As a result, Anna's attendance at Graysville Academy in Chattanooga, Tennessee, was halted after the first day of school when several children reported to their parents that they suspected she was black. A group of citizens immediately complained to school administrators that a "nigger" had been admitted to a white school. Anna was identified as a "mulatto," a term which, according to her, she had never heard before that moment.[34]

Until this event, Anna may have hoped to escape the label of "Negro" altogether. Although that was not to be, and she could no longer attend classes at Graysville, administrators stood by her and arranged for the school's matron to privately house and tutor her. Small wonder she returned home after a ten-week semester a "dyed-in-the-wool Seventh-Day Adventist." For the rest of her life, she remained grateful that the Adventist Church, and especially the Chamberses, had helped a "poor colored girl" to obtain an education.[35]

Far less overt racism confronted Anna after the Chamberses sent her to Mount Vernon, Ohio, to complete her education and then to the American Medical Missionary College in Battle Creek, Michigan, where she obtained training as a nurse. In the urban North, being a country girl from the South stimulated prejudices more than did her olive skin and curly hair. Anna, self-described as "truly a child of the forest" before she discovered Adventism, worked hard to overcome stereotypes about rural backwardness. Mrs. Chambers helped her in her transition, symbolically covering Anna's "country dress" with a fine "broadcloth cape with a quilted satin lining" and replacing her "old feathered hat" with one that was more suitable for a Seventh-Day Adventist. Anna also learned class-appropriate behavior, at one point vowing to overcome all the "odd sayings" that marked her as a "green girl from the South." Her successful adjustment to northern middle-class culture made it increasingly unlikely that she would ever live in rural Mississippi again—at least not permanently.[36]

At the American Missionary Medical College, Anna earned the respect of Dr. John Harvey Kellogg, the famous Adventist health expert who developed the first cereals that bore his family name. In 1898, Kellogg approved Anna's request to return to Mississippi and found a school for her community as fulfillment of the required field medical missionary work. That year, under the auspices of the college, which paid Anna's transportation costs and provided teaching materials, she returned to the Jones County area to perform her first missionary work in the service of her own kinfolk.[37]

Anna's return to the Knight community precipitated a turbulent period in her life. She devoted almost an entire chapter of her autobiography to describing how a gang of white men reacted violently to her establishment of a school for her Knight kin. She claimed that the men were local "moonshiners" who objected to her teaching temperance in the name of Adventist morality, and to women preachers in general. Curiously, she said nothing about their likely feelings about an African American woman who proposed to educate children of African ancestry *and* teach them new religious ideas.

Armed with a revolver "and sometimes a double-barreled shotgun," Anna struggled to maintain order, but the men continued to menace her, forcing her one day to close the schoolhouse and escape through the woods on horseback. Later that same day, a raucous fight ensued between her drunken attackers and two unnamed Knight males. According to Anna, one or more of the men subsequently filed a lawsuit against the Knights, which cost them "a little money." She succeeded nonetheless in keeping the school open, albeit with protection from hired watchmen and by carrying guns with her to class.[38]

Anna's harrowing ordeal with the moonshiners tested her faith in God's protection and may have influenced her decision to accept a call from her church to travel to India as a medical missionary. After agonizing over the decision, in May 1901 she left her fledgling school in the hands of Julia Luccock Atwood and her husband, Parker Atwood, two trusted white Adventist missionaries from Iowa. While she was in India, however, the Atwoods were driven from the school by renewed attacks. Anna was deeply disappointed but too immersed in her duties as a missionary to return home.[39]

Several years passed before Anna returned to Mississippi, during which time her kinfolk were without a school. Finally, her conscience was pricked by a letter from home that asked, "Why don't you come back and teach us yourself? You understand us, and you are not afraid. Why would you stay over there, trying to convert the heathen while your own people here at home are growing up into heathen?" Those words convinced Anna that she could fulfill her dream of bringing Adventist principles, both practical and spiritual, to Mississippi as well as India. She now committed herself to battling the "evils of liquor and race prejudice" that motivated those who attacked her school.[40]

Although foreign missionary work provided Anna an escape from the unremitting pressures of American racism, around 1908 she returned to the Knight community to educate and preach Adventism to her kinfolk. Building a new school was clearly a collective effort among the Knights. Records show that on March 31, 1909, Jeff and Molly Knight sold one square acre of land to the Southern Missionary Society of Tennessee for $150 for "church and school purposes." Anna's brother John Howard Knight and his wife, Candis, conveyed forty acres to Anna on April 13, 1909. Two days later, Anna, her mother, Georgeanne, and Newt Knight jointly signed a security bond.[41]

As the Knight family rebuilt its school, Anna also worked to improve black health and education throughout the state. More than one black Mississippian told her that she should never return to India, arguing, "We need you here. Let the white folk go to India, and you stay here and work with us." Anna viewed her calling differently, however. Although she engaged in several Adventist projects dedicated to racial uplift in the South, she ultimately concluded, "While I could see that the colored work in America really did need workers, to me, the needs of India were greater by far."[42]

Despite her feelings, Anna did not return to India but continued to work on behalf of Southern blacks. In 1910, after reestablishing the Knight school and training her sister Grace to take over the teaching, she moved to Atlanta, Georgia, to become medical matron of a sanitarium for colored people. There, she joined a successful interdenominational effort to create a "colored" branch of the YWCA. By 1922, Anna was teaching summers at Oakwood College in Alabama, which enabled her to aid the Knight community without returning to Mississippi. Oakwood soon became a mecca for her relatives, who traveled there to obtain educations not available to most blacks in Mississippi. Van Buren Watts, the son of Anna's beloved Aunt Augusta, later thanked her for her dedication: "[You] stuck with our family all the way. Nothing was too good for you to do for us." Former Oakwood students expressed similar sentiments: "There was never a time that we could say there was no Knight there."[43]

Anna's ability to serve the needs of her relatives and simultaneously carve out a career for herself elsewhere was greatly facilitated by her sister Grace's willingness to remain in the Knight community. Despite the years and geographical distance that separated the sisters, they remained close all their lives. Grace Knight usually lived alone, farming her land and operating the Adventist school founded by Anna. As her community's schoolteacher, she became a pivotal point of contact between Knights who lived great distances from one another and who often assumed opposite racial identities.

Communications in 1948 between Grace and T. B. Corley, a Laurel oil man, demonstrate this. Intending to drill for oil, Corley sought to lease farmland from the heirs of Newt Knight, whom he described as having "scattered to the four corners of the country." Unlike in 1914, when Fanny Knight was labeled a "nigger" in a court of law for trying to claim marital property rights, in 1948 Corley gained the right to drill on property willed by a white man to his descendants of color by first convincing the heirs to lease their lands to him and then proving the legitimacy of their land claims.[44]

It was Grace who contacted those descendants and assured them that the lease would serve their interests as well as Corley's. In a letter dated May 21, 1948, Grace wrote Ardella Knight Bramwell, her cousin's daughter, "Personally, I don't think there is any harm in signing a lease. . . . You might get something. This fellow doesn't want your minerals just a lease." Ardella took Grace's advice but worried that her right to inherit from Newt Knight was compromised by the illegality of her grandparents' interracial marriage. In a subsequent letter to Ardella, Corley admitted that "there [were] forces at work trying to eliminate the children of Fanny Knight, who was the first wife of Matt Knight, because of a mixed blood marriage." Corley assured Ardella, their granddaughter, that the descendants of Matt and Fanny Knight were "legitimate and therefore rightful heirs to an interest in the old Newt Knight farm," and that she would receive a "small income" from the lease "for many years to come."[45]

Grace's ability to contact and influence the far-flung descendants of Jeffrey and Molly Knight and Matt and Fannie Knight, many of whom were living as whites, made her as central a figure from within the Knight community as Anna was from outside it. As Anna acknowledged when she dedicated *Mississippi Girl* to Grace, her sister's willingness to confine her power to the circumscribed world of family, despite the fact that she was an educated single woman, assisted Anna's own escape from that world. Perhaps feeling a bit guilty, Anna thanked Grace: "[She] stayed at home and carried on there, making it possible for me to travel among our people from place to place, doing the work I have tried to describe in this little story."[46]

Although Anna, Grace, and Lessie led very different lives, and although none of them openly challenged the racial and sexual imperatives of the segregated South, all three escaped the fates of their mother and grandmother. In choosing careers that marked them as "old maids," Anna and Grace avoided poverty, numerous childbirths, and the degraded status routinely assigned to African American women throughout much of the twentieth century. Unlike her sisters, Lessie did marry, but she did so as a white woman. Her life embodied the fear of many white supremacists that numerous "white Negroes" were "passing" for white, while it simultaneously contradicted literary images of the "tragic mulatta." No "tragic" discovery of Lessie's African ancestry ever brought misery and shame to her or her children, nor did being white force her to abandon completely her ancestral roots. It was Anna Knight, however, who most successfully manipulated conventions of race and gender to gain that which was routinely denied to black women: respectable social status and professional work.

NOTES

1. Victoria E. Bynum, "'White Negroes' in Segregated Mississippi: Miscegenation, Racial Identity, and the Law," *Journal of Southern History* 64, no. 2 (May 1998): 247–76.

2. Nell Painter, *Southern History across the Color Line* (Chapel Hill: University of North Carolina Press, 2002); Kent Anderson Leslie, *Woman of Color, Daughter of Privilege: Amanda America Dickson, 1849–1893* (Athens: University of Georgia Press, 1995); Mary Bullard, *Robert Stafford of Cumberland Island: Growth of a Planter* (Athens: University of Georgia, 1995); Adele Logan Alexander, *Ambiguous Lives: Free Women of Color in Rural Georgia, 1789–1879* (Fayetteville: University of Arkansas Press, 1991).

3. Glenda Gilmore, *Gender and Jim Crow: Women and the Politics of White Supremacy in North Carolina, 1896–1920* (Chapel Hill: University of North Carolina Press, 1996); Evelyn Brooks Higginbotham, *Righteous Discontent: The Women's Movement in the Black Baptist Church, 1880–1920* (Cambridge, Mass.: Harvard University Press, 1993).

4. Eva B. Dykes to Anna Knight, scrapbook, March 10, 1964, Anna Knight Collection, in the possession of Dorothy Marsh, Washington, D.C.; Erle Johnston Jr. to Honorable Jack Tubb and

Honorable F. Gordon Lewis, December 12, 1963, Mississippi Sovereignty Commission Papers, Faulkner Civil Rights Collection, University of Southern Mississippi, Hattiesburg.

5. *State of Mississippi v. Davis Knight*, December 13, 1948, case no. 646, court record and transcript of the Circuit Court, Jones County, Mississippi, on file at Clerk's Office, Mississippi Supreme Court, Jackson; Bynum, "'White Negroes' in Segregated Mississippi," 247–76. The verdict was reported in many newspapers, including the *New York Times*, December 19, 1948.

6. U.S. Federal Manuscript Census, 1900, Jasper County, Mississippi; *St. Louis Post-Dispatch*, December 18, 1948; December 19, 1948; December 20, 1948; January 9, 1949; January 10, 1949; November 14, 1949.

7. Ethel Knight, *The Echo of the Black Horn: An Authentic Tale of "The Governor" of "The Free State of Jones"* (n.p., 1951), 315.

8. Ibid., 250, 265, 283–87, 302–9; Suzanne Bost, *Mulattas and Mestizas: Representing Mixed Identities in the Americas, 1850–2000* (Athens: University of Georgia Press, 2003).

9. Victoria Bynum, *Free State of Jones: Mississippi's Longest Civil War* (Chapel Hill: University of North Carolina Press, 2001), 144–45.

10. After Molly's death in 1917, Serena lived with her son Tom. U.S. Federal Manuscript Censuses, 1900, 1910, 1920, Jasper County, Mississippi.

11. On increased legal and extralegal persecution of interracial marriages, see Martha Hodes, *White Women, Black Men: Illicit Sex in the Nineteenth-Century South* (New York: New York University Press, 1999), 176–97; Gilmore, *Gender and Jim Crow*, 71.

12. Frances Jackson, e-mail message to the author, April 30, 2000, McCain Library, University of Southern Mississippi, Hattiesburg (henceforth cited as ML-USM).

13. Ibid.; Dianne Walkup, e-mail message to the author, May 31, 2005; Anna Knight, *Mississippi Girl* (Nashville: Southern Publishing Association, 1952), 16, 23.

14. *Martha Ann Musgrove et al. v. J. R. McPherson et al.*, January 27, 1914, Chancery Court of Jones County, Laurel, Mississippi. My thanks to Kenneth Welch for providing me with a copy of Fannie House's deposition.

15. Ibid.

16. Ibid.

17. Ibid.

18. Rhonda Benoit, e-mail message to the author, January 14, 2000, ML-USM. Addie Knight was first cousin one generation removed to her husband, Otho, a son of Molly and Jeffrey Knight (Bynum, "'White Negroes' in Segregated Mississippi," 251–58).

19. Quoted in F. A. Behymer, "The Tragic Story of Davis Knight," *St. Louis Post-Dispatch*, January 9, 1949. On Tom Knight's estrangement from his African American kin, see Bynum, *Free State of Jones*, 178–88.

20. Nancy Knight quoted in F. A. Behymer, "The Remote No-Man's Land of Soso," *St. Louis Post-Dispatch*, January 10, 1949; Florence Knight and Annette Knight, interviewed by the author, Soso, Mississippi, July 22, 1996, ML-USM; report, West Jasper County School Board, Bay Springs, Mississippi, August 18, 1960, Sovereignty Commission Papers.

21. Lessie Robertson, death certificate, February 21, 1944, Texas Department of Health, Bureau of Vital Statistics, Austin; Obituaries, Beaumont *Enterprise*, February 21, 1944.

22. Knight, *Mississippi Girl*, 20–24; Tiah M. Graves, "A Historical View of the Life of Anna Knight," 2–3, http://www.oakwood.edu/history/Faculty/knight.

23. Knight, *Mississippi Girl*, 29–32, 39–47, 52–57.

24. Medallion of Merit Award for Anna Knight, brochure, Oakwood College, November 17, 1971, Oakwood College Archives, Huntsville, Alabama.

25. Johnston to Tubb and Lewis, December 12, 1963, Sovereignty Commission Papers.

26. Knight, *Mississippi Girl*, 11.

27. Darlene Clark Hine, "Rape and the Inner Lives of Southern Black Women: Thoughts on the Culture of Dissemblance," in *Southern Women: Histories and Identities*, ed. Virginia Bernhard, Betty Brandon, Elizabeth Fox-Genovese, and Theda Purdue (Columbia: University of Missouri Press, 1992), 177–89.

28. Anna Knight, "The Great Contest," undated, unpublished essay, Anna Knight Collection.

29. Graves, "Historical View," 1; Rosetta Baldwin and Natelkka E. Burrell letters, March 4, 1964, scrapbook, Anna Knight Collection.

30. On Anna's family's resistance to Adventism, see Knight, *Mississippi Girl*, 33–37; Graves, "Historical View," 2–4; Knight, "Great Contest."

31. Knight, *Mississippi Girl*, 27, 165; Graves, "Historical View," 2.

32. Knight, *Mississippi Girl*, 147–48, 153.

33. Ibid., 18.

34. Ibid., 31.

35. Ibid., 32, 43.

36. Ibid., 40, 42, 46.

37. Ibid., 75–76.

38. Ibid., 82–87.

39. Knight, *Mississippi Girl*, 88–91, 108–9; "Miss Anna Knight," 3, unsigned, unpublished, undated biography, Oakwood College Archives.

40. Knight, *Mississippi Girl*, 90, 108–9, 159, 163.

41. Miscellaneous records, Anna Knight Collection.

42. Knight, *Mississippi Girl*, 168.

43. Ibid., 168, 171, 176–80. Quoted passages from Van Buren Watts to Anna Knight, March 2, 1964, scrapbook; *North American Regional Voice*, April 1988, 15, Oakwood College Archives.

44. T. B. Corley to George and Sylvia, June 29, 1948, Ardella Knight Barrett Collection, in possession of Florence Knight Blaylock.

45. Grace Knight to Della Knight Bramwell [Barrett], May 21, 1948; T. B. Corley to Mrs. Ardella Bramwell [Barrett], July 15, 1948; copy of Oil, Gas, and Mineral Lease agreement between T. B. Corley and Della Bramwell, June 29, 1948, all in Ardella Knight Barrett Collection.

46. Knight, *Mississippi Girl*, preface.

"Down in Tupelo Everybody Seems to Be Feeling Grand"

Early Home Electrification Promotion in Northeast Mississippi

SARA E. MORRIS

At the beginning of the Great Depression, Mississippi offered few modern amenities to the women of its overwhelmingly rural population. Women lugged water from distant wells, washed laundry on washboards, cleaned the soot produced by stoves and lamps, and beat rugs to remove the endless dust found in country homes without electricity, running water, or labor-saving household appliances. Mail-order catalogs and magazines brought rural women news of modern household innovations, to which most of these women did not have access. No wonder so many young women sought to move off the farm and frequently outside the South.

At the beginning of the twentieth century, government agencies and progressives worried about the migration of rural residents to urban areas. Many of these individuals, seeking to slow the relocation to towns and cities, identified the farm's daily drudgery as the main reason young women chose to leave. Theodore Roosevelt's Commission on Country Life addressed the issue in its 1911 report, which concluded that without modern tools similar to those available to men for "outdoor work," a woman's life was generally "more monotonous and more isolated, no matter what the wealth or poverty of the family [might] be." According to the report, women benefited from general improvements to rural life, but they still lacked labor-saving household conveniences. Hoping to slow the migration from farm to city, the commission wanted to enhance local organizations working to improve rural standards of living.[1]

In 1915, the United States Department of Agriculture (USDA) published excerpts of letters from farm women explaining the realities of their lives. One Mississippi respondent suggested that large-power-plant technology be adapted for individual use. Understanding that housework for those with electrical power differed significantly from hers, she hypothesized that small streams could run power plants large enough "to do many of the innumerable small jobs that fall to the lot of most farm women—washing, milking, drawing water, churning, sweeping and with proper appliances heating rooms and cooking." She knew that modern conveniences were not manufactured with rural women in mind as potential consumers; after all, they did not have electric power. Electricity was becoming available to some rural households, but private utility companies were responsible for its production and delivery. As for-profit businesses, they refused to pay the two-thousand-dollar-per-mile cost to run wires to underpopulated areas. Rural families anticipated eventually having access to power, but they had little hope for immediate relief.[2]

Electrification had been on the minds of Mississippians for some time. Louis N. Goodman, an electrical engineering student at the Agricultural and Mechanical College of the State of Mississippi (Mississippi A&M), wrote in his 1923 master's thesis: "The statement that the day when rural distribution will be common practice in Mississippi is far off may sound discouraging, but it is safe to say that the day *is* coming." As the 1930 U.S. Census reported, Mississippi, with only a dismal 1.5 percent of farm dwellings lit by either electricity or gas, had the fewest electrified farm homes in the nation. When the economy crumbled in 1929, few rural Mississippians anticipated that an economic depression might be the catalyst for extending electric power to rural communities.[3]

Northeast Mississippi, historically plagued by poverty and minimal progress, surprisingly experienced federal electrification before any other area of the country. Lacking the rich soil of the Yazoo-Mississippi Delta or the lush pine forests of South Mississippi, life in the poor southernmost corner of Appalachia consisted mostly of subsistence farming. The absence of roads or other efficient transportation had stifled economic growth and ensured the region's isolation. The area's largest municipality, Tupelo, had become an industrial town because of rail-line recruitment and the abundance of natural and agricultural products in the surrounding countryside. Yet by the end of the Great Depression and the beginning of World War II, a persistent congressman and New Deal programs helped the town become a national model of technological advancement.[4]

Three key events that changed how rural citizens across the United States received electrical power originated in isolated Northeast Mississippi. Formed in the backroom of a Corinth furniture store in January 1934, the Alcorn

RURAL ELECTRIFICATION ADMINISTRATION (REA) PHOTO

Courtesy of Special Collections, Mitchell Memorial Library,
Mississippi State University, Starkville.

County Electric Power Association established the nation's first rural electric cooperative. In 1935, the Monroe County Electric Power Association became one of three cooperatives to receive the first Rural Electrification Administration (REA) loans; of the three it was the first to deliver power. Tupelo, the largest population center in the northeast quadrant of the state, became the first city to provide electrical power obtained from the Tennessee Valley Authority (TVA). Mississippi thus became a testing ground for the education and encouragement of the use of electricity on farms and in rural homes.

As women made the transition to electricity in their homes, they were encouraged by various groups to accept consumerism, home economics, and labor-saving tools. Such promotion, however, was premature since Mississippians in the early 1930s had little money to purchase more than necessities. They saw no reason to acquire anything that depended on electric power. Nevertheless, private and governmental organizations, including the Mississippi State College Cooperative Extension Service and the TVA, advocated that women make affordable changes to improve their living and working conditions. During these early years of electrification, both organizations focused their efforts on white middle-class women and their families. For this group of citizens, the suggestions of these government agencies became more relevant in the last half of the 1930s, when educational, financial, and technological resources became available to communities in Northeast Mississippi.

The Cooperative Extension Service advocated home improvement as an essential element to bettering rural life. The service geared its prewar electrification programs toward white landowning farmers and aspiring white tenant farmers. Overall the extension service approached home improvement realistically. Local agents who visited homes understood the harsh realities of women's lives. Recognizing the attainable, Mississippi's Home Demonstration division advocated and taught well-researched purchasing and stressed that while technology could improve rural life, an unplanned purchase could be worse than none at all.

The TVA and its subsidiary, the Electric Home and Farm Authority (EHFA), had more influence on the acquisition of electricity and electrical tools than any other institution in the South. Those two prongs of President Franklin D. Roosevelt's power program made electricity and electric appliances affordable. In an effort to ensure that the TVA succeeded, its leaders pushed consumption, leaving consumer education to others. Through the TVA's promotion of electrical technologies, families received messages encouraging purchasing but without concerns for wise consumer practices.

Since its founding, the Cooperative Extension Service worked to educate its constituents to be reluctant consumers. The "live-at-home" ideology of extension suggested that rural residents produce as much as possible at home and make do with what they already had; individuals should enter the marketplace only out of true necessity. Extension encouraged families to purchase appliances and wiring while also providing opportunities for learning about electrification through its established adult education network. The TVA's fears about the troubled economy and the potential failure of the nation's largest social experiment led to its advocacy of consumption and debt. The contradictory approaches of the two agencies toward consumption sent conflicting messages to their clients.

Before either the Mississippi Cooperative Extension Service or the TVA began promoting electrical appliances in rural homes, another national organization, Better Homes in America, set out to improve households. Secretary of Commerce Herbert Hoover recruited Marie Mattingly (Mrs. William Brown) Meloney, editor of the women's magazine the *Delineator*, to lead the effort. Meloney—who had been taught by her mother, Sarah Irwin Mattingly, a well-known Mississippi educator—used her editorship to support various social programs. Meloney and Hoover hoped that Better Homes would encourage women to improve their homes and create better lives for their families.[5]

Mississippi embraced the ideas and ideals of the organization, whose leaders' ability to localize programs yielded high levels of participation. Mississippi won a national Better Homes award in 1929, two in 1930, and three in 1931 (Jackson-Hinds County, second place, county-city; Winston County, third place, county; and Warren County, fourth place, county). Five other Mississippi communities won honorable mention in 1931. Mississippi's women had clearly taken an interest in Better Homes' programming and ideals.[6]

The winning record encouraged the state to increase its participation. Mississippi's 1931 Better Homes chair Ellen S. Woodward, assisted by Mississippi State College's Extension Service, organized six Better Homes schools for white women. Their geographic diversity—in Vicksburg, Tupelo, Meridian, Jackson, Gulfport, and Greenville—permitted wide participation. Better Homes field representative Blanche C. Lewton led small-house architecture and fences sessions. Attendees would share the new ideas they had learned at local programs in the coming year.[7]

County committees planned a Better Homes Week, with special activities each day showcasing the year's progress. Clergymen preached sermons on the importance of home in society. Most counties devoted one day to improving the home of a needy neighbor; such a spirit of cooperation showed that individuals worried about not only themselves but also other community members. They dedicated another day to public buildings such as schools or community centers. During the rest of the week, individuals worked on their own houses and attended lectures and demonstrations on home-improvement methods. Activities for the week usually concluded with a public announcement of contest winners. Through competitions, participants demonstrated their knowledge and application of Better Homes techniques in their neighborhoods.

Both white and African American Mississippi communities celebrated National Better Homes Week annually in the 1920s and 1930s, but the national office focused on urban life. State chair Woodward asked the national office for information to use in programs for rural homes. Her request must not have received much attention, as extension's state specialist in home management, Anne Jordan, wrote a memo to county agents indicating that some people in Mississippi believed the national program ignored farm homes. Jordan went on to announce that extension, along with other partners, would launch a Rural Homes Week.[8]

Rural Homes Week seemed almost identical to Better Homes Week. The activities were similar, and community, neighbors, and religion all played key roles. The difference was in the content. Rural Homes Week specifically focused on rural living and the methods advocated by the extension service.

Two years later the two homes programs merged. The state chairs of both committees agreed that more could be achieved if the two worked together; after the merger fifty-two counties (63 percent) participated in contrast to the year before, when only thirty-nine counties (48 percent) participated in either event. In the participating counties, 2,581 families improved lighting, and 657 installed running water in 1937. The Better Homes movement in the 1920s served as the centerpiece of Mississippi's grassroots efforts to help women change their home environments. Throughout the 1930s, Better Homes continued working with extension to carry out its programs.[9]

Mississippi's ties to demonstration work began even before the Smith-Lever Act of 1914 established the Cooperative Extension Service. In an effort to supplement the educational experiences of Holmes County, Mississippi, boys, Superintendent William "Corn Club" Smith established a corn club in 1907. The same year, after learning of the program's success, USDA agent Seaman Knapp asked Smith to become the first federally paid youth agent. Organized club work for Mississippi girls began in 1911 when Knapp asked Susie V. Powell, the state's school improvement supervisor, to attend a club work meeting in Washington. On her return, she established the state's first tomato clubs in Lincoln and Copiah counties. Powell then recruited rural schoolteachers, most without any training in home economics, to serve as the first agents. From such modest beginnings, the Mississippi Cooperative Extension Service grew into an organization with programs for all ages.[10]

Following the lead of the USDA's national extension office, Mississippi State College established its Home Management section in 1920. Home economist Victoria Hill, who served as the state's first household arts specialist, worked with rural women already involved in extension programs in two main areas— basic home improvement and household accounts—that had an important symbiotic relationship. Women who kept household accounts could evaluate their spending and then alter it to save money for home improvements.

Hill remained in the position for three years before Anne O. Jordan replaced her in 1923. Jordan, whose title changed in 1931 to home management specialist, guided Mississippi's program until 1935. Upon her resignation, Lorraine Ford, Lowndes County home demonstration agent and a recent master's graduate of the University of Tennessee, replaced Jordan. Jordan and Ford, both trained home economists, guided the state's women and girls throughout the 1930s, a time of significant change in the program's objectives and possibilities. The emergence of home economics transformed housekeeping from a chore into an occupation with methods and theories backed by science. Ford's 1938 annual report acknowledged that home management's ultimate goal was the "recognition of women and girls that homemaking is a profession."[11]

Belzoni native May Cresswell, a University of Mississippi graduate and a county and district agent since 1917, was named state home demonstration agent in September 1929. During World War I, she had begun a school lunch program in Greenville, and during the flood of 1927 she helped establish and administer refugee camps. By the 1930s, she possessed an extensive knowledge of the harsh realities facing rural Mississippi women.[12]

The passage of legislation bringing electricity to rural Mississippi forced the extension service to modify its teaching. To ensure that women made the best choices, in 1935 Mississippi's Home Management program abandoned the frugal ideology of "live at home" in favor of consumer education that emphasized smart choices in planning, purchasing, and using electrical appliances.

Anne Jordan's final report recognized the magnitude of the changes electrification would bring: "Home Management is just now getting into its stride." The USDA's Federal Extension Office increased the duties of home management specialists, whose responsibilities expanded to include home electric training. Concluding that a single individual would struggle to meet the growing demands electrification placed on Home Management, Jordan recommended that two individuals with advanced training in electricity be hired to replace her, one specializing in the home and the other in home furnishings. She observed, however, that no one in the state had the necessary skills to take Mississippi's Home Management program into the future.[13]

None of Jordan's requests would be easily met. The state's economic situation did not permit hiring two persons, and finding a replacement with advanced training in electricity would not be easy since only a few home economics programs had incorporated the study of electricity into their curricula. Iowa State University offered a program in household equipment, but its graduates usually found jobs in the federal government. Such a graduate would have been a perfect replacement for Jordan, but Mississippi probably could not obtain or afford such expertise.[14]

The state promoted Lorraine Ford to the Home Management position. To fill the need for electrical training, in 1936 Mississippi State College and the TVA signed the "Tennessee Valley Authority Contract for Cooperative Agricultural Research and Demonstration Work." They hired F. M. Hunter as rural electrification engineer; his contract stipulated that he promote the use of electricity in rural areas and provide instruction on wiring, lighting, appliances for farm and home, and community refrigeration. Extension editor Fred J. Hurst commented in his 1936 annual report, "The farmers are being informed how they can best avail themselves of electrical current and how they can use it in the home and on the farm in the operation of farm equipment and labor saving devices." Farms, not homes, became the main focus of the new program.[15]

Finally recognizing that needs of barn and home were significantly different, Mississippi's extension service hired Maude Smith in March 1939 to work with home electrification as assistant home management specialist in charge of rural electrification. She did not stay long in the position; on July 1, 1939, she joined the Agricultural Engineering Department as the rural electrification specialist. Upon her appointment, all responsibilities for home electrification were transferred away from Home Management. Such a move from the female-oriented home demonstration program to the male-dominated rural engineering aspect indicated a perceptual shift. When Smith had served with the Home Demonstration division, electrification was associated with women and the home; by moving her to engineering the administration signaled that electrical issues belonged to men. Ford and Smith continued to work together, however, because neither could achieve much working independently.[16]

After the creation of the TVA and the REA, extension altered its current projects. Kitchen improvement shifted from establishing correct work-space heights to water heaters, laundry space, and selecting electrical appliances. Lighting demonstrations that had focused on oil lamps, candles, or Aladdin Lamps changed to correct placement of light fixtures and electrical outlets. These new educational opportunities excited women and the agents who taught them. In 1938, twenty-seven counties selected home management as their yearly programming theme, but with only one specialist to assist with the programs, only nineteen counties got to keep this top choice. Women in the least electrified state in the nation wanted to learn about the life-altering technology, but their only local resource, the county home demonstration agent, often knew little more than her club members about electricity.[17]

The TVA administrators recognized that without education, families would remain ignorant about electricity's potential, and without citizens using electricity, the TVA might fail. Unable to provide its own local training, the TVA solicited help from the Cooperative Extension Service because of its proven record of rural education. The two groups quickly established training for their agents, at first primarily at the University of Tennessee. Knoxville, however, proved to be an unfeasible location for all seven states of the TVA, and the authority soon established training closer to the places where its agents worked and lived. Later in 1938, five Mississippi home demonstration agents attended a TVA-sponsored daylong program on electrical appliances in Tupelo. Attendees did not become experts, but the "quick fix" allowed them to remain one step ahead of their club members.[18]

Just two years later, the state's extension service implemented a more extensive training program. The REA's creation in 1935 had increased the need for trained personnel throughout the state. In 1937, home and farm rural electrification specialist F. M. Hunter hosted sessions in Tupelo, Greenwood, Jackson, and Meridian for county agents, who learned basic electrical concepts and terms, domestic wiring, the National Electric Code, causes and effects of voltage drops, meter reading, and kitchen planning. Each agent created a plan to wire a farm home, showing proper locations of outlets and light fixtures and necessary wiring for different appliances. Although the agents left prepared to help residents plan and wire their homes, the two groups still needed to create better training opportunities and facilities.[19]

In 1935, the TVA and Mississippi State College undertook building a training laboratory on the college's Starkville campus. The TVA would provide the latest model appliances, and the college would provide the space and utilities. The laboratory, located on the ground floor of Montgomery Hall, opened on July 20, 1937, the first day of Farm and Home Week. The lab fulfilled a need identified by Northeast Mississippi district agent Kate Lee in 1937: "Agents had not had technical training to actively participate with any degree of assurance as to accuracy of program and technical knowledge."[20]

The laboratory, consisting of two kitchens and one laundry area, each using a different type of wiring, provided facilities for teaching at all skill levels. The kitchens were built in the two configurations agents most frequently recommended—the L and the U. Because home demonstration agents practiced what they had preached, one kitchen had a homemade sheet-metal sink and homemade cabinets and floor covering. The other kitchen reflected the consumption model with its manufactured sink, commercially produced metal cabinets, and purchased flooring. The laundry area contained three types of washing machines, assorted irons, ironing boards, and mangles. With its mixture of homemade and industrial goods, the lab made it possible to understand various electrical methods and ways to integrate other home modifications advocated by the extension service.[21]

Each day the agents spent training in Starkville, they prepared their meals in the kitchens, which allowed them to use the new equipment themselves. When they left, they all had clean clothes, as they used their own garments to learn modern laundry techniques. By the end of 1939, eighty-two agents had completed the two-week training, and eventually club members could also attend programs held in the lab. The hands-on approach gave agents and clubwomen the skills to spread the extension service's gospel.[22]

In her last annual report, Anne Jordan remarked, "Electricity and lighting in this state will have to be introduced and induced by educational work. The 1930 census [indicating] only 1.5% of the farm homes wired is a mute testimony of our needs for education along this line." In her own report for 1935, May Cresswell wrote that the psychological time for educational programs on rural electrification had come.[23]

Even with an opportunity for training in Starkville, transportation barriers still existed. To ensure that no one missed out, an alternative was needed. When extension had begun, women often learned canning outdoors. They had raised funds to build efficient community canning centers, and when electricity came the facilities were adapted to community kitchens, also called demonstration kitchens. Here agents or visitors from outside agencies demonstrated how electrical appliances worked and offered hands-on experience.

Funding for demonstration kitchens usually came from local governments and community organizations. In Lincoln County, the chamber of commerce furnished a small demonstration house for a kitchen improvement program. In Clarke County in 1927, the Standard Oil Company donated an entire house to the Quitman Home Demonstration Club, and Mississippi Power donated a range. The club only had to contribute one hundred dollars for wiring.[24]

The demand for such learning centers peaked first in the TVA counties. In Alcorn County, agent Ruth Ethridge received ranges and refrigerators from the

TVA's appliance program, the EHFA, to be used in the local kitchen. When it was finally completed, the Alcorn County kitchen had a stove, refrigerator, water heater, space heater, iron, and washer. In Tishomingo County, the funds came jointly from the local county electric association and the TVA. The kitchen, located in the electric association's building, was filled with equipment donated by the TVA. The first of the TVA kitchens opened in Union County in 1936. The county supervisors gave home demonstration agent Bessie Hanks fifty dollars to replace a late-model electric stove and water heater in an existing building. With help from the TVA, she traded for replacements and purchased other new equipment. When the kitchen opened, Hanks and Ruth Frow and Clara Nale of the TVA welcomed 226 visitors at the grand opening.[25]

Without modern kitchens, women had no place to learn about features to look for when selecting electrical products or how to use them in their homes. Supporting such educational efforts benefited electric companies and appliance manufacturers because it provided a firsthand look at what the invisible helper could do. Local merchants selling appliances and other electrical equipment found education to be a different and effective kind of advertising.[26] Extension created other educational opportunities for rural women across the state, ranging from large community lectures to club-level demonstrations. Extension emphasized well-planned acquisition of electricity and new appliances and told stories of "hasty and ill considered" choices of equipment in homes.[27]

The TVA, the EHFA, and the REA began activity in Northeast Mississippi earlier than anywhere else in the United States. While all three agencies affected industry, these New Deal programs had the greatest impact for change in small towns, in rural single-family homes, and on farmsteads. For the farms of the area, electrification meant brightly lit chicken houses and automatic milking machines. White middle-class women living on farms, on backcountry roads, and in small rural towns gained the greatest emancipation. Recognizing the budding market's potential, the administrators of FDR's power programs specifically targeted women to excite them about the possibilities of electric homemaking. Although many New Deal programs intended to assist individuals first, TVA leaders, especially David Lilienthal, aimed to help businesses initially. His statements in a 1934 article explaining the purpose of the EHFA acknowledged the barriers to the consumer presented by high-cost appliances, and he hoped that government financing would increase demand. In making the technology affordable, the EHFA built a market not only for goods but also for TVA-generated power as well. Lilienthal, who personally avoided debt, encouraged Mississippians to purchase appliances with little regard for the debt they might be incurring, in order to ensure the success of the New Deal agency.[28]

Northeast Mississippi actually had some electric power before the TVA was established. Tupelo had agreed to pay fifteen thousand dollars to build a power plant in 1899, and Mississippi Power Company made electricity available to the city and some outlying areas. After completion of a larger plant ten years later, the *Tupelo Daily Journal* reported that power would be available beginning on February 2, 1912, but only after 1:00 p.m. Businesses could burn only one in four of their installed lights, while homes could burn only one light through the night. Rule violations resulted in doubling the already high rates.[29]

Mississippi's early involvement in rural electrification can be attributed to two factors. First, Northeast Mississippi was near the TVA dam at Muscle Shoals, Alabama, so adding new high wires to an already established infrastructure was relatively easy. Second, Congressman John E. Rankin, a resident of Tupelo and native of Itawamba County, had been the TVA's largest supporter in the House of Representatives. A graduate of the University of Mississippi School of Law, Rankin won election from Mississippi's first district in 1921, and from the beginning he recognized the potential of electrification in his own district as well as in other rural areas across the United States.

Rankin contributed significantly to improving the daily lives of rural residents whose incomes could make electrification a possibility, but these liberal ideas contradicted his endorsement of white supremacy. Many of his congressional activities confirm his racist ideologies. During his legislative career, he argued in favor of poll taxes, opposed passage of antilynching laws on the grounds that they would increase the number of rapes, and attributed battle defeats during World War II to the incompetence of African American soldiers. For him the benefits of the TVA and the REA would improve the lives of hardworking whites and increase the gap in living conditions between the two races.[30]

Rankin believed America's future lay in the countryside, not in urban industrial centers. In an NBC radio address on February 2, 1935, he stated, "There can be no permanent prosperity in this country so long as we have an impoverished agriculture." Later that night, he said, "Our young people are not going to remain on the farms under present conditions, to perform the drudgery and to bear the enormous burdens their fathers have borne if they can help themselves. They feel that they are entitled to enjoy some of the comforts and conveniences of life."[31]

Rankin joined Senator George Norris of Nebraska in planning for the great social experiment in the Tennessee Valley. Later called the "TVA's best friend in Congress" next to Norris, Rankin alleged that private power companies, with no social consciences, did not care if their services were available to all citizens. The government must step in to bring power to "every farm home in America at rates people [could] afford to pay." Electricity, he said, was the "greatest home builder ever known," and if it were extended to farmers and rural areas it would, "create the greatest back-to-the-farm movements of all time."[32]

Like many other politicians and reformers of the period, Rankin expressed concern for white women living in the countryside. While he often commented on the trials and difficulties rural men faced, he spoke most passionately about relieving women from household drudgery. On the floor of the House, he told his colleagues, "If the women in America realized what the TVA is doing for them, there would not be a candidate for public office from Maine to California who would dare to oppose it." The establishment of the TVA and its related programs, according to Rankin, had done more for women to "brighten their lives, lighten their burdens, and relieve their drudgery . . . than anything else ha[d] ever done in the entire history of this republic."[33]

During the TVA's inaugural years, female constituents lucky enough to have gotten electricity provided Rankin with many testimonials. One said that with the arrival of power, she and her peers had "now begun to live." Mrs. Dan E. Sullivan, who lived five miles from Tupelo, wrote that all the farm women in her community could now have almost any appliance they wanted. The most popular, Rankin reported, was the washing machine.[34]

Although Rankin could have told his fellow congressmen about electrical improvements in industry or in barnyards, he chose instead to speak of women who, before the arrival of electricity, spent hours of intense labor doing laundry. Their stories and their praise for the invisible servant provided a poignant and relevant reference point that everyone could understand.

When Congress passed the TVA legislation, Rankin acted quickly on behalf of his own district. In 1934, Alcorn County became the home of the first electric cooperative, which served as the model for subsequent REA utility providers. Mississippi's first connection with the REA, the Monroe County cooperative, was the first in the nation to provide power to its owner-members. Never forgetting his home city, Rankin arranged for meetings between Tupelo and TVA officials, including David Lilienthal.

An EHFA flyer noted, "Tupelo—first to take advantage of America's Cheapest electricity." It had made history by becoming the first TVA city. On October 27, 1933, Mayor J. P. Nanney signed the contract with the TVA ensuring twenty years of TVA power and cutting rates by 55 percent beginning February 7, 1934. At a celebratory parade of TVA officials, Rankin and Nanney spoke of the coming changes. Optimistic school children carried a sign declaring that in the future, "When the moon shines over the cowshed there will be a light inside."[35]

Shortly after the creation of the TVA, Lilienthal proposed to make prohibitively expensive appliances affordable through the EHFA, which aimed to foster "the increased use of electrical power through the reduction of the costs and price of electrical equipment appliances." Working with industry, the EHFA created high-quality appliances that sold for affordable prices. Customers who qualified for a credit line provided by the federal government purchased their new household and farm tools at local stores.[36]

The TVA chose Tupelo as the charter city for EHFA sales. During the first week of sales, the city hosted a celebration for people to visit the approved appliances display. With a population of only six thousand, Tupelo witnessed a surprising turnout of seven thousand. Consumers came to town and purchased, and by the seventeenth day sales for equipment reached an equivalent of thirty dollars per electric meter in the city.[37]

As anticipated, appliance sales rose quickly. In the summer of 1934, Federal Emergency Relief Administration reporter Lorena Hickok recounted from Tupelo that six companies were selling TVA and non-TVA model appliances. During the first seventeen days, residents in and around Tupelo purchased 137 refrigerators and 17 other appliances. EHFA pricing had dropped refrigerator and range prices from $137 to $80. The Tennessee River Valley had the highest appliance sales in the nation, and in Tupelo alone power consumption had risen 83 percent by July 1934. In a letter to administrator Henry Hopkins, Hickok noted, "Down in Tupelo everybody seems to be feeling grand."[38]

The success of appliance sales and electrical use in Northeast Mississippi became the subject of TVA literature. A flyer titled "Toward an Electrified America" noted, "The people of Tupelo [can] not only make fuller use of the appliances they now have but can buy any additional electrical equipment." The flyer stated that the citizens of "this progressive Mississippi Community" had embraced the New Deal program and, as Lilienthal had hoped, were "taking full advantage of the savings made possible by TVA rates."[39]

On April 5, 1936, a tornado ripped through the center of Tupelo. EHFA commercial representative Carter Chaney, describing the destruction to EHFA treasurer William Weaver, telegraphed, "NUMBER OF APPLIANCES DESTROYED." An estimated one hundred appliances had been completely ruined and many others damaged. The TVA office, still intact, was turned into a makeshift hospital. The loss of EHFA appliances worried local businessmen, six of whom wrote Rankin for help. With their stores completely devastated, they worried that an inability to fulfill EHFA contracts might cause their shops to go out of business. The businessmen reminded Rankin of their contributions to the TVA's success and asked him to intervene with the TVA for help. Rankin and the TVA would, in fact, play essential roles in rebuilding the city.[40]

Although the tornado slowed the TVA's progress, the area's people saw that they no longer lived in the land that progress left behind. The New Deal power programs had brought modernity to the hills and prairies of Mississippi. In June 1934, a man told Lorena Hickok about the water heater he had purchased before the lower TVA rates and before the help of EHFA. Although able to purchase the appliance, he could not afford the city's electric rates. He proudly reported, "Now with this new rate I can. I can run that, with all my other equipment—range, iron, mangle, vacuum cleaner, lights, and radio—all for the same cost as I went without it before." Early on TVA administrator George Rommel remarked, "Nothing in my long experience has so impressed me with confidence in the rank and file of the American People as the attitude of the folks of northeast Mississippi, toward the TVA program."[41]

The labor-saving devices from washing machines to water pumps all made possible by electricity lessened the demand for physical labor among women, but they did not generate the anticipated abundance of free time. Washing machines, for example, liberated women from the backaches and raw hands of hand washing in laundry tubs with washboards, but aided by their Maytags, they washed more laundry. Society now expected fresh clothing every day.

Such increased standards applied to housework in general, not just laundry. Home economics had emphasized the importance of women's work at home, and every day women worked to incorporate new scientific findings into their housekeeping methods. Research on germs, for example, called for keeping homes and children clean, and nutritional research encouraged balanced, well-planned meals. Home economists taught sewing methods, home improvement, and other skills that resulted in increased work to match expanded expectations. Technology helped to ease physical burdens, but women almost universally increased how much time they spent on housework. Time studies from 1920 to 1955 revealed few changes in farm women's schedules. They spent more time on chores that had previously been ignored or done differently, and their leisure time increased by only one-tenth of an hour per day. But for many in Mississippi, these new tools came many years later. For poor whites and the majority of African Americans in Mississippi, these tools arrived slowly throughout the rest of the century.[42]

Women played a key role in the acquisition of electrical power in Northeast Mississippi. Although their lobbying had not convinced the TVA's David Lilienthal that their sleepy area deserved to be first, their enthusiasm for electricity made the EHFA program a success. They attended training sessions, opened their homes to foreign visitors, and bought appliances. Today a city sign identifies Tupelo as the nation's first TVA city. There a movement began to bring electricity to those who previously had only dreamed of it. The area had not minded that Lilienthal had "pumped maximum drama out of Mississippi." Instead the citizens celebrated their lightened workloads and their new opportunities for urban life.⁴³ As May Cresswell observed, "There was a time when you could tell the city woman from the rural women, and the city man from the country man. But that time has passed, at least insofar as Mississippi is concerned."⁴⁴

NOTES

1. *Report of the Country Life Commission*, introduction by Theodore Roosevelt (1911, 1917; repr., Chapel Hill: University of North Carolina Press, 1944), 103–6; William L. Bowers, *The Country Life Movement in America, 1900–1920* (Port Washington, N.Y.: National University Publications, Kennikat Press, 1974), 62–66.

2. D. Clayton Brown, *Electricity for Rural America: The Fight for the REA* (Westport, Conn.: Greenwood, 1980), 3–9; United States Department of Agriculture, *Domestic Needs of Farm Women*, report no. 104 (Washington, D.C.: U.S. Government Printing Office, 1915), 32.

3. United States Census Bureau, *Fifteenth Census of the United States: 1930*, vol. 2: *Agriculture*, pt. 2: *The Southern States* (Washington, D.C.: U.S. Government Printing Office, 1932), 58; Louis N. Goodman, "Rural Distribution of Electric Energy in the State of Mississippi" (MS thesis, Agricultural and Mechanical College of the State of Mississippi, 1923), sec. 1, p. 1.

4. Vaughn L. Grisham Jr., *Tupelo: The Evolution of a Community* (Dayton, Ohio: Kettering Foundation Press, 1999), 38–43.

5. Herbert Hoover, *The Memoirs of Herbert Hoover: The Cabinet and the Presidency, 1920–1933* (New York: Macmillan, 1952), 92–93; Ishbel Ross, "Marie Mattingly Meloney," in *Notable American Women, 1607–1950: A Biographical Dictionary*, ed. Edward T. James, vol. 2 (Cambridge, Mass.: Belknap Press of Harvard University Press, 1971), 525–26.

6. "Three National Awards Captured by State in Better Homes Campaign," *Jackson Daily News*, July 26, 1931; "Better Homes State Honors Draw Praise," *Jackson Daily News*, August 9, 1931.

7. Martha H. Swain, *Ellen S. Woodward: New Deal Advocate for Women* (Jackson: University Press of Mississippi, 1995), 22–23; Claudia Mae Hopper, "Choctaw County Home Demonstration Annual Narrative Report, 1930," in *Narrative and Statistical Reports from State Officers and County Agents*, microfilm, National Archives and Records Administration, College Park, Maryland (henceforth cited as NSR); Anne O. Jordan, "Home Management Annual Narrative Report, 1931," NSR.

8. Janet Anne Hutchinson, "American Housing, Gender and the Better Homes Movement, 1922–1935" (PhD diss, University of Delaware, 1989), 257; Anne O. Jordan, "Home Management Specialist Annual Narrative Report, 1935," NSR.

9. Lorraine Ford, "Home Management Annual Narrative Report, 1936," NSR; Lorraine Ford, "Home Management Annual Narrative Report, 1937," NSR; Mississippi Cooperative Extension Service, *Annual Report Extension Service, 1939* (Starkville: Mississippi State College, 1939), 58–5.

10. Roy V. Scott, *The Reluctant Farmer: The Rise of Agricultural Extension to 1914* (Urbana: University of Illinois Press, 1971), 239–40; Danny Blair Moore, "'Window to the World': Educating Rural Women in Mississippi, 1911–1965" (PhD diss., Mississippi State University, 1991), 35–38; Ollie Dean McWhirter, "The Work of Susie V. Powell" (MA thesis, Mississippi State University, 1964), 24–29.

11. Moore, "Window to the World," 172; *Bulletin of the Mississippi Agricultural and Mechanical College, Forty-third Annual Catalog, 1922–1923* (Starkville: Mississippi Agricultural and Mechanical

College, 1924), 55–58; L. A. Olson, *Annual Report of Extension Work in Agriculture and Home Economics, 1931*, Mississippi Extension Bulletin 62 (Starkville: Mississippi Extension Service, 1931), 4; Kate Lee and Addie Kester, "Northeast Home Demonstration Annual Narrative Report, 1935," *NSR*; *Bulletin of the Mississippi State College, Fifty-sixth Annual Catalogue, 1936–1937* (Starkville: Mississippi State College, 1938), 162; Lorraine Ford, "Home Management Specialist Annual Narrative Report, 1938," *NSR*.

12. Sallie Hill, "Salute to Farm Women," *Progressive Farmer*, January 1953, 74; Obituary, Mississippi State University: Staff, Cresswell, May, vertical file, Special Collections Department, Mitchell Memorial Library, Mississippi State University, Starkville.

13. Jordan, "Home Management, 1935."

14. Amy Sue Bix, "Equipped for Life: Gendered Technical Training and Consumerism in Home Economics, 1920–1980," *Technology and Culture* 43 (October 2002): 729–30.

15. J. T. Copeland et al., "Agricultural Engineering Annual Narrative Report, 1937," *NSR*; J. T. Copeland et al., "Agricultural Engineering Annual Narrative Report, 1939," *NSR*; F. J. Hurst, *Annual Report of Cooperative Extension Work in Agriculture and Home Economics, Mississippi, 1936* (Starkville: Mississippi State College, 1937).

16. Copeland et al., "Agricultural Engineering, 1939"; Ford, "Home Management Specialist, 1938"; Lorraine Ford, "Home Management Specialist Annual Narrative Report, 1940," *NSR*.

17. Ford, "Home Management Specialist, 1938."

18. Kate Lee and May Cresswell, "Home Demonstration Annual Narrative Report, 1935," *NSR*.

19. Copeland et al., "Agricultural Engineering, 1937."

20. Lee and Cresswell, "Home Demonstration, 1935"; Kate Lee, "Northeast District Home Demonstration Annual Narrative Report, 1937," *NSR*; Copeland et al., "Agricultural Engineering, 1939"; Kate Lee and Sallie Spann Swann, "Northeast District Home Demonstration Annual Narrative Report, 1937," *NSR*.

21. Lee and Cresswell, "Home Demonstration, 1935"; Ford, "Home Management Specialist Annual Narrative Report, 1937"; Lorraine Ford, "Home Management Specialist Annual Narrative Report, 1939," *NSR*.

22. Ford, "Home Management Specialist, 1939"; Copeland et al., "Agricultural Engineering, 1939."

23. Jordan, "Home Management, 1935"; May Cresswell, "Home Demonstration Annual Narrative Report, 1935," *NSR*.

24. Sara Jane Craig, "Lincoln County Home Demonstration Annual Narrative Report, 1930," *NSR*; Julia Cook, "Clarke County Home Demonstration Annual Narrative Report, 1930," *NSR*.

25. Ruth Ethridge, "Alcorn County Home Demonstration Annual Narrative Report, 1935," *NSR*; Mary A. Stennis, "Tishomingo County Home Demonstration Annual Narrative Report, 1935," *NSR*; Lorraine Ford, "Home Management Specialist Annual Narrative Report, 1936"; Bessie A. Hanks, "Union County Home Demonstration Annual Narrative Statistical Reports, 1936," *NSR*.

26. May Cresswell, "Mississippi Home Demonstration Annual Narrative Report, 1939," *NSR*; Susie Parker, "Pontotoc County Annual Narrative Report, 1937," *NSR*; Lee, "Northeast Mississippi, 1937"; "Lauderdale County Home Demonstration Annual Narrative Report, 1939," *NSR*; Susie Parker, "Marshall County Home Demonstration Annual Narrative Report, 1939," *NSR*.

27. May Cresswell, "Mississippi Home Demonstration Annual Narrative Report, 1938," *NSR*.

28. David E. Lilienthal, "Business and Government in the Tennessee Valley," *American Academy of Political and Social Science* 172 (March 1934): 47–48; David Lilienthal, "February 25, 1939," in *The Journals of David E. Lilienthal*, vol. 1: *The TVA Years, 1939–1945* (New York: Harper & Row, 1964),

88; Thomas K. McCraw, *Morgan vs. Lilienthal: The Feud within the TVA* (Chicago: Loyola University Press, 1970), 44.

29. "Daytime Use of Electricity Voted," *Tupelo Daily Journal*, February 2, 1912; "Electricity Wins Wide Vote Approval," *Tupelo Daily Journal*, March 17, 1899; "Lights Cost Tupeloans 20 Cents per Month," *Tupelo Daily Journal*, February 24, 1902, all reprinted in *Tupelo Daily Journal Centennial Edition, 1870–1970* (Tupelo, Miss.: Tupelo Daily Journal, 1970), 7C, 16C, 14C; Karen Doyle, "TVA—Power to the People," *Tupelo Daily Journal*, Tennessee Valley Authority vertical file, Mitchell Memorial Library, Mississippi State University, Starkville.

30. Thomas N. Boschert, "John Elliott Rankin," in *American National Biography*, ed. John A. Garraty and Mark C. Carnes (New York: Oxford University Press, 1999), 18:144–45; "John Rankin Dies: Ex-Legislator, 78," *New York Times*, November 27, 1960; Joe Rutherford, "History of the First District," *Northeast Mississippi Daily Journal*, March 2, 2008.

31. Senator George Norris of Nebraska, Submission of Representative John E. Rankin on the Electrification of Farm Homes. 74th Cong., 1st sess., *Congressional Record* 79, pt. 2 (February 6, 1935): 1528–29.

32. McCraw, *Morgan vs. Lilienthal*, 64; Kenneth W. Vickers, "John Rankin: Democrat and Demagogue," (MA thesis, Mississippi State University, 1993), 54; Representative John E. Rankin of Mississippi, radio broadcast, 74th Cong., 2nd sess., *Congressional Record* 80, pt. 1 (January 3, 1936): 9.

33. Representative John E. Rankin of Mississippi, Statement: "What Cheap Electricity Means to The Farm Home," 74th Cong., 1st sess., *Congressional Record* 79, pt. 13 (August 26, 1935): 14774–75; Rankin, radio broadcast, *Congressional Record*, 10; Representative John E. Rankin of Mississippi, speech on the TVA and women, 74th Cong., 2nd sess., *Congressional Record* 80, pt. 10 (June 20, 1936): 10670–71.

34. Rankin, speech on the TVA and women, *Congressional Record*, 1067; Representative John E. Rankin of Mississippi, speech on Electric Home and Farm Authority, 74th Cong., 2nd sess., *Congressional Record* 80, pt. 4 (March 25, 1936): 4348; Rankin, radio broadcast, *Congressional Record*, 10.

35. EHFA, "Toward an Electrified America," Development of TVA, TVA Old Agricultural Relations file, Agricultural Industries Division Reports, Tennessee Valley Authority, RG 142, National Archives, Southeast Region, Atlanta, Georgia (henceforth cited as RG 142); "Tupelo Signs First TVA Contract in 1933," *Tupelo Daily Journal*, October 31, 1933, reprinted in *Centennial Edition*, 15D; TVA, *First Annual Report* (Knoxville: Tennessee Valley Authority), 27; Arthur E. Morgan, "Bench Marks in the Tennessee Valley," reprinted from *Survey Graphic*, January, March, May, 1934, Development of TVA, TVA Old Agricultural Relations file, RG 142.

36. Electric Home and Farm Authority, Inc., Minutes, vol. 1, Electric Home and Farm Authority, entry 298, Reconstruction Finance Corporation, RG 234, National Archives and Records Administration, College Park, Maryland.

37. Richard A. Colignon, *Power Plays: Critical Events in the Institutionalization of the Tennessee Valley Authority* (Albany: State University of New York Press, 1997), 144; Ruth Loden Johnson, "A History of Tupelo" (MA thesis, Mississippi State College, 1951), 52; William B. Phillips to David E. Lilienthal, "Meeting with Manufactures Advertising Managers held in New York, Wednesday, April 11," April 16, 1934, 040-EHFA-001-Publicitiy, Advertising, Etc., General Manager, RG 142; Steven M. Neuse, *David E. Lilienthal: The Journey of an American Liberal* (Knoxville: University of Tennessee Press, 1996) 87; V. D. L. Robinson to C. H. Garity, "EHFA Quarters in Tupelo," May 11, 1934, 040-EHFA-300-Officers, Quarters, Showrooms, General Manager, RG 142; George D. Munger to David E. Lilienthal, "Electric Home and Farm Authority Progress Report" June 7, 1934, 020.2 Power and Functions, General Manager, RG 142.

38. Lorena Hickok, *One Third of a Nation: Lorena Hickok Reports on the Great Depression*, ed. Richard Lowitt and Maurine Beasley (Urbana: University of Illinois Press, 1981), 276–80; Jordan Schwarz, *The New Deal: Power Politics in the Age of Roosevelt* (New York: Alfred A. Knopf, 1993), 240.

39. EHFA, "Toward an Electrified America."

40. Carter Chaney to William Weaver, April 6, 1936, 439.1 Losses (Tupelo) (Chattanooga), Electric Home and Farm Authority; Carter Chaney to William Weaver, April 7, 1936, 439.1 Losses (Tupelo) (Chattanooga), Electric Home and Farm Authority; John R. Barker, J. F. Hall, W. G. Wooley, W. H. Baker, W. B. Austin, E. R. Chisholm to John E. Rankin, April 8, 1936, 439.1 Losses (Tupelo) (Chattanooga), Electric Home and Farm Authority, entry 298, Reconstruction Finance Corporation, all in RG 234, National Archives and Records Administration, College Park, Maryland.

41. Hickok, *One Third of a Nation*, 270; George M. Rommel to John E. Rankin, January 27, 1934, Mississippi—Rankin, John E., Division of Agricultural Development Tennessee Valley Authority, RG 142.

42. Ruth Schwartz Cowan, *More Work for Mother: The Ironies of Household Technology from the Open Hearth to the Microwave* (New York: Basic Books, 1983); Joann Vanek, "Work, Leisure, and Family Roles: Farm Households in the United States, 1920–1955," *Journal of Family History* 5, no. 4 (1980): 424.

43. McCraw, *Morgan vs. Lilienthal*, 44.

44. May Cresswell, "Home Demonstration, 1937," NSR.

Gladys Presley, Dorothy Dickins, and the Limits of Female Agrarianism in Twentieth-Century Mississippi

TED OWNBY

Countless spokesmen for southern culture have claimed that the region derives its distinctiveness, and for some its superiority, from the continuing importance of farm life. The concept of agrarianism, a broad, vague, and sometimes debated term, suggests that the American South has benefited from the relative security of rural life, the independence of households that produced many of the goods they used, and the separation from the fads and ambitions of life off the farm. But what, if anything, did southern agrarian thinking offer women, and more importantly, how did women shape and interpret agrarian thinking? Contemporary scholars have rightly rejected the significance that male agrarian writers claimed for themselves as the self-appointed spokesmen for southern culture.[1] However, so many southerners asserted that rural life was superior to city life that it seems useful to ask how women saw themselves in those discussions. The array of male agrarian thinkers who considered the nature of southern life claimed the region offered independence, leisure, and community and family identity, which were becoming rare in the twentieth century. This essay examines how two women in Mississippi thought about those ideals of independence, leisure, and community or family identity. The agrarian ideal was largely masculine. Independence, sometimes called manly independence, rested on imperatives to take no orders and be subordinate to no one. The life of leisure, whether enjoyed on plantations or on pig farms, benefited men sitting on porches far more than women, who were busy with vegetables, chickens, guests, and many, many children.

Agrarianism often seems especially important to those who have lost or fear they are losing their places on the farm. The life stories of two white women in Mississippi bring to life the ways in which some women responded to farm life,

DOROTHY DICKENS
Courtesy of Agricultural Communications,
Mississippi State University, Starkville.

its changes, and life away from the farm. The two women spent much of their lives thinking about what rural life offered women and wondering if women were better off leaving the farm.[2] One was Dorothy Dickins, the leader of home demonstration efforts in Mississippi. First employed by the state in 1925, Dickins quickly became Mississippi's head of home economics research. She wrote her first publication in 1927 and continued to write about rural women until 1964. The other was Gladys Smith. She began her life on small tenant farms in northeastern Mississippi, moved to Tupelo to take a factory job, and then, as Gladys Presley, experienced surprising affluence in Memphis as the mother of a suddenly wealthy young son. Tracing the lives and opinions of Dickins and Smith illuminates the changing ways in which white women in twentieth-century Mississippi understood the traditions of farm life with its virtues and its limits for women.

In the 1920s and early 1930s, white southern writers and musicians were fascinated by the idea of a South with special agrarian virtues. Agrarianism had a range of meanings. The most self-consciously conservative agrarians, such as Mississippi's William Alexander Percy, lamented the passing of a clearly established rural hierarchy that had worked against urban disorder and social conflict. Other agrarians, especially the Vanderbilt University writers who contributed to *I'll Take My Stand*, upheld the rural South as a counterculture to a commercialized, industrial world in which facelessness, alienation, and secularism ruled over the southerners' sense of rural community, secure identities, and religious commitments. At about the same time, country musicians were idealizing the security of the old farm and home in contrast to the rootlessness of life on the road or in the city. Whether singing or writing or making government policy, southern agrarians in the early twentieth century tended to believe that women had a clear and cherished place in the agrarian ideal, sewing, cooking, giving birth, and holding together households through work and strength of character.

Some of the clearest statements about how farm life benefited Mississippi women are found in the early publications of the Mississippi State Extension Service.[3] Beginning around 1917, the extension service expanded its scope beyond the fields and tried to encourage women to learn new techniques to make homes healthier, cleaner, and more productive. Extension service director R. S. Wilson made clear that his goal was to oppose the movement of young farm people to the cities: "In our opinion, the only way we will ever materially check this tendency will be to bring about conditions on the farms and in the country home equally attractive with those in the town or city."[4] Home demonstration workers in the second and third decades of the century consistently said they hoped to help make farm life attractive enough that women would not want to leave. Mottoes adopted by the extension service—Stay at Home, Back to the Farm, Live at Home—celebrated the basic goodness of rural life, while the methods of the extension service brimmed with confidence that science could save the farm. A Starkville editorial in 1922 epitomized the condescending nature of the agrarianism that male home demonstration leaders proposed for women. "The women on the farm—God bless them—were shown how to make their numerous tasks easier, how to improve the social conditions of the community with their canning clubs, berry clubs and social clubs." The editorial insisted that only with such efforts would farm women "be more contented and there would be a check put on the city-ward movement."[5] Overcoming both taxing labor and falling cotton prices, new knowledge would supposedly bring on the best of both worlds: modern science on the old home place.

Dorothy Dickins started her home demonstration career as an agrarian, thinking farm life was superior to city life and designing policies to help keep people on the farm. She grew up in the Delta town of Greenwood, attended the Industrial Institute and College in Columbus, received her MA at Columbia University, and worked briefly in Jackson before taking a position in 1925 in Starkville, where she spent the rest of her professional life.[6] Her first publication appeared in 1927, examining the food habits of farming families and urging more-sophisticated planning and greater understanding of diet in order to retain the benefits of farm life. "Mississippi with its mild climate, abundant sunshine, and rich soil, offers superior advantages for physical health and well being," she observed. If people in the state were less than healthy, it was their mistake. Finding that rural people needed to eat more fruits, vegetables, and meat, she lectured, "Such deficiencies as these should not exist in dietaries from Mississippi, a state in which an all-year-round garden and any form of meat from beef to chicken is possible." The typical child growing up amid the potential abundance of the southern farm should be "much better than the average urban child."[7]

The agrarian imperative for women, as Dickins understood it, was to make things at home, and early in her career she supported that ideal with vigor. She insisted, "The rural housewife could provide her family with balanced meals furnished completely by the farm. As a general rule though, she uses little fore-sight in providing sufficient quantities of the different classes of food, and thus must supplement her menu by cash expenditure."[8] According to Dickins in her agrarian years, homemade was always better than store-bought. In her first publication, she made an agrarian assertion that she would investigate for years. People with more cash income, she stressed, did not necessarily live better than people who did not make as much cash. Instead, people who produced more goods at home were better off.

Unlike many agrarians such as Will Percy and the Vanderbilt writers, Dorothy Dickins was a professional social scientist and not a moralizer or a poet. To her, rigorous scientific study proved that farm life was superior to nonfarm life in productivity and good health. She began her numerous reports with questions she could test through empirical research and spent much of her efforts detailing her sources and methods. Her discussions of food habits, for example, analyzed calories, food quantities in pounds, energy per person, and amounts of vitamins, iron, calcium, minerals, and protein. She categorized the subjects of her research by income; race; family size; their status as owners, tenants, farmers, or nonfarmers; and the type of soil in their areas. As social scientists, Dickins and other extension service workers hoped they could join the agrarian ideal and scientific knowledge of nutrition.[9]

From the beginning of her career, Dickins used considerable subtlety in discussing the problems of tenant farmers. The health of poor people, especially poor African American tenants, disturbed her, and she saw improving rural health as an essential part of her mission. Dickins would have disagreed with fellow Mississippi Delta native Will Percy's description of sharecroppers on his plantation as "well-fed, decently clothed peasants."[10] Most agricultural workers, Dickins wrote in a 1928 study of African American tenants in the Delta, ate far too little and lacked variety in their diets. The greatest problems in the health of sharecroppers derived from two sources. First, their homes were not clean. Rather than resorting to racial stereotypes, Dickins stressed that sharecroppers' homes were unclean and unhealthy largely because the owners of those homes did not furnish them with running water and sewage connections. Second, they had limited opportunities to plant food crops and keep livestock for themselves. Dickins found that while 74 percent of the food that white farming people in Mississippi ate came from their own farms, black sharecroppers in the Delta grew only 44 percent of their own food.

Asking whom to blame and how to correct the problem, she began with the sharecroppers themselves. Some of them, she said, spent their money recklessly and did not work very hard. One can detect a note of paternalistic disapproval in her worried statement: "If a negro makes more than his expenses, it is generally spent by February. Therefore, February finds him without money or help from the landlord."[11] However, Dickins laid most of the blame for the poor health of tenants on the landowners, who worked against efforts by tenants to feed themselves. She quoted the reports of black sharecroppers who "claim[ed] that planters discourage[d] the planting of a garden, for they desire[d] this land for raising cotton."[12]

Compared to other extension service workers of her day, Dickins tended not to blame agricultural workers for their poverty. Other writers encouraged the state's poorest people to make clothing and household goods from feed sacks and other scrap materials and virtually turned cash-free clothing into a crusade. Dickins never joined them but never chose to write against them. During her agrarian years, she repeated the motto of the Negro Extension Service, "Take what you have and make what you can of it," but she always seemed troubled that sharecropping offered few of the rewards she thought farm people should enjoy.[13]

Along with emphasizing food and health, Dickins showed considerable interest in the possibilities of women making clothing. In her garment-by-garment examination, "Clothing and Houselinen Expenditures of 99 Rural Families of Mississippi during 1928–1929," Dickins again stressed the economic value of making things at home. She found that adult women sewed in all but one of the homes in the study. All but four owned foot-powered sewing machines. Sewing at home made good economic sense, but it also served the traditional agrarian function of giving people satisfaction in their own creativity. Sewing, she maintained, "cannot be viewed entirely from the economic standpoint. Many homemakers sew because they enjoy it—because they get personal satisfaction from creating a garment. Some are doubtless better pleased with garments they can make than with those they can buy."[14]

While Dorothy Dickins was writing about farm life in the 1920s, Gladys Smith was growing up on other people's farms. Movement dominated Gladys's life as it did the lives of most poor people in the twentieth century. Her father, Bob, was a sharecropper and day laborer who made occasional money digging ditches, sweeping cemeteries, making railroad ties, and selling whiskey. Gladys, born in Pontotoc County in April 1912, spent most of her childhood and early adult years moving around rural parts of Lee County outside Tupelo. The agrarian sense of fixing one's identity to a home place was not possible for such mobile people.[15]

Lee County in Gladys Smith's early years was extremely rural. Most of the land—86 percent—was in farms, a figure considerably higher than in most of the state.[16] The number of farms was decreasing, while the number of tenants like the Smith family was increasing. In the early 1930s, tenants ran 71 percent of the county's farms.[17] Like most farm families, the Smith family was large. Gladys's mother, Doll Smith, had nine children, eight of whom survived childbirth. The farm child's life was one of labor, and the Smith children probably worked more than most. Doll was sick and bedridden much of the time, so the oldest daughter, Lillian, did most of the work around the house. As a younger daughter, Gladys worked on farms, usually under someone else's supervision. Like many farm children, she went to school about four months a year but spent most of her time working either in the fields or as paid household help.

Gladys almost certainly heard the lessons commonly taught to farm children: work hard, respect parents, and avoid wasting money. As members of the Assembly of God Church, the Smiths heard warnings against pride and luxury. Ideals for farming women, both the traditional ideals of hard work and economizing and the newer ideals of scientific womanhood that Dorothy Dickins espoused, held that the good woman sewed as much clothing as possible. In fact, generations of women who had written in their diaries about doing their work or their duty were referring to sewing. The young Gladys Smith continued that tradition, making her own clothing during her school years.[18]

But Gladys Smith did not fit easily into the model farm woman that Dorothy Dickins imagined. According to biographer Elaine Dundy, Gladys impressed her friends and siblings from an early age with her excitement about dancing, movies, and shopping. Acquaintances said she was "crazy about buck dancing" (a rhythmic dance that predated tap dancing) and called her Clara Bow, the so-called It Girl of the late 1920s.[19] Clara Bow had risen to stardom in *It*, a movie about a fun-loving young working woman who attracted men with her good looks and dancing but also had to prove she was sexually pure.[20] "It" was sexiness without sex, sexiness for fun, enjoyed outside its traditional rural connotations of building a family large enough to work on a farm.

Even more surprising for a teenager from a poor Mississippi family was Gladys Smith's fascination with shopping. A neighbor recalled that the teenaged Gladys and her younger sister Clettes went in and out of the store "sixty times a day buying one item at a time, clearly enjoying purchasing almost as much as the purchase."[21] It is unsurprising to find a young woman in the 1920s fascinated by consumer goods and shopping. Historians generally associate the rise of shopping with the growth of an urbanizing population that was paid in cash, had disposable income, and lacked the farm family's traditional incentives to economize.[22] But Gladys was a poor member of a large, religious, agricultural family. Thus, she no doubt heard lessons about the virtues of thrift and hard work and the vices of luxury and selfish self-indulgence, but still she and Clettes went off to the store sixty times a day. This was far from the lesson Dorothy Dickins was suggesting when she told farm women to take over the shopping from their husbands and fathers. Instead, Gladys and Clettes seem to have been fascinated with the process of shopping and buying, that dreamy consumer state of imagining new possibilities and making some of them real.[23]

If we compare Dickins and Smith in the 1920s, it is clear that Gladys Smith was ready for much more change. Dorothy Dickins, optimistic that a few changes could help most farm women decide to stay on the farm, was moving only timidly beyond complete respect for agrarian traditions. For her, change during the 1920s meant only that women should improve their understandings of diet, household technology, and shopping so that they could become more efficient and productive mothers and contributors to rural households. Dickins also worried that increasing numbers of tenants—like the Smiths—were not enjoying the rewards of farm life. Her agrarian ideal had roots in farm owning, and she knew that the appeal of farm life was uncertain for poor people who did not own homes. But for Dickins, farm life was the good life, especially if it could change for the better. By contrast, the teenaged Gladys Smith, a shopper, pleasure seeker, and Lee County "It" girl from a poor family, showed signs of becoming a rebellious figure who did not envision a future based on agrarian assumptions. Perhaps for her the most appealing thing would have been to leave.

The Depression challenged agrarian society, and a growing group of southern writers and leaders began to question assumptions about the virtues of rural life. In the decade when Franklin Roosevelt declared the region America's greatest economic problem and when novelists, sociologists, and photographers produced countless works documenting poverty and debating its causes and consequences, Dorothy Dickins felt freer to write critically of forces that did not allow rural people to enjoy the traditional benefits of farm life. Also, Dickins earned a PhD in 1933 at the University of Chicago, and she began to use the critical tools of professional social science in studying and trying to improve life for rural women.[24]

During the 1930s, Gladys Smith rejected agrarian ideals faster than Dorothy Dickins, but both decided that many women were better off leaving the farm. In the late 1930s, Dickins's work lost most of its agrarian tone, and a bit like Smith before her, she began to show a side that was somewhat subversive, or at least critical. Although Dickins never abandoned the idea that people were better off growing some of their own food, she began to doubt that farming still held the key to the future of Mississippi.

In a 1937 report, *Occupations of Sons and Daughters of Mississippi Cotton Farmers*, Dickins showed her willingness to change. After studying farm people for a decade, and living in a period of economic depression, rural out-migration, and governmental experimentation, Dickins for the first time openly questioned the agrarian assumptions that farm life was always best and that her job was to teach the skills farm people needed to stay on the farm. She began her *Occupations* bulletin with a detailed study of a large group of nineteen- to thirty-four-year-old white Mississippians who had grown up on farms. Dickins asked if people who grew up on the farms did in fact benefit from farm life. Simply posing the question challenged agrarian assumptions about community and family identity.

The answer, she concluded, was no. Only 6 percent of the young Mississippians who had grown up on farms actually owned land, and most of the people working on farms were those who had no other choice.[25] Farm work, Dickins decided, lay mostly in the futures of people who grew up as tenants, especially people with poor educations and no other options. Agricultural change was producing a situation where cotton planting was lucrative for a few people but produced only poverty for the rest. Those who had left the farm were doing better than those who stayed.

This crucial point seems to have been a revelation to Dickins, who had spent her professional life working for an agency whose goal was to discourage farm people from leaving farms. At least for a few pages, she shunned the cautiously agrarian tone of most of her publications and addressed the future of Mississippi. She observed, "A desirable occupational situation for this group of cotton farmers' sons and daughters would be a situation in which each of them had the opportunity and training to engage in the occupation best suited to his ability." She called for more education, especially vocational training, more government supervision of health, and "an increase in the general level of incomes."[26] Rare for someone in the Agricultural Extension Service, she said young Mississippians needed more information about nonfarm opportunities outside the state, and she made a strident call for more and better industry.

Dickins's critique of 1930s farm life had a feminist side, and she gave voice to the grievances of rural women as she had never done before. Far beyond her earlier criticisms of men for doing too much of farm families' shopping, she now criticized economic, educational, and legal systems that limited the opportunities of rural women. First, she found that daughters in farming families worked much harder than sons: 88 percent of the daughters worked in the fields, and 95 percent worked in gardens and with chickens and cows. "The vast majority entered quite actively into farm and household tasks. This is as it should be, because if they are to live on the family farm and derive food and clothing from it, they in turn should give their services." Dickins wrote that most of the farm daughters "realized their responsibility," but not all. "A number chafed under it, 'but what else is there to do?' they asked. . . . Many were without outside interests and hobbies. Some were openly dissatisfied."[27] Sympathizing with that frustration, Dickins criticized circumstances that kept young women isolated and working too hard to notice better opportunities. Dickins said fathers kept money from daughters far longer than sons. "In these days of 'equal rights,' it is surprising how many out-of-school farm girls are found with a status similar to that of children of the family." Many teenaged sons worked crops, made and handled their own money, but daughters with "child status"

worked hard and still had to ask for goods or money.[28] Dickins seemed especially troubled that leaving the farm benefited men more than women. She concluded from her research that young men could find nonfarming jobs more
easily than young women. "In other words, . . . the girl is more dependent on
the economic resources of her family than is her brother. It would, therefore,
seem that there is a special need for vocational opportunities being provided for
girls of the poorer rural families." Many women who tried to balance jobs and
housework just worked harder than ever. Virtually all those women cleaned
their own homes. Dickins noted, "It is, of course, not customary for a gainfully
employed wife to take an easy seat by the fire when she returns from work and
to wait for her husband or children to serve the meal."[29]

In the last footnote of this long and important document, Dickins added
a final consideration: "There is in addition another possibility for improving
the financial status of the family; namely, a reduction in birth rate."[30] Here was
something no home demonstration worker in the state had said before. Calling for a decline in the birthrate showed the distance Dickins had come from
her agrarian beginning, but the fact that the statement appeared in a footnote
indicated her continued caution. Production and reproduction had long gone
hand in hand on the farm, but now Dickins was raising questions—if rather
quietly—about both large families and a future dominated by cotton.

Mississippi, Dickins urged with optimism, had a chance to develop forms of
industry without the accompanying social problems that southern leaders had
always feared. She wrote in the late 1930s, when Mississippians were debating
the nature of the industrial growth the state might develop.[31] Dickins recognized
that "pauper wages and poor working conditions cannot be labeled as progress,"
but she held out hope that "it is possible to develop an urban economy without low wages, child labor, crowded living conditions, and poor working conditions."[32] For the rest of her career, Dickins wondered if new types of industry
could avoid the poor health and low wages so common in southern factories.

In a 1941 report about women workers, Dickins asked "whether industrial
employment would provide a better living than the farm, even in poor agricultural areas."[33] Simply raising the question showed Dickins's willingness to challenge the agrarian assumptions of her agency and, more broadly, of many of
the leading voices in southern culture. More importantly, the study found that
some forms of industrial life had the potential to produce wealthier, healthier
people with a greater range of opportunities than the farm lives common to
most Mississippi women.

The study found, not surprisingly, that farming women made far more "non-
money income," specifically food and clothing, than factory working women.[34]

It found, also not surprisingly, that the families of factory women made more money than farm families, but they were also deeper in debt. To discover who benefited most from the trade-offs, Dickins analyzed the incomes and possessions but also the health, family, and social lives of white women on both farms and factories. She was impressed by the number of goods factory workers possessed that most women on farms did not. They owned far more silk and rayon dresses and hose, and far more of them had multiple pairs of shoes. More factory workers had cars, and most of them were better cars than the old models that farm families owned.[35]

Like most people with agrarian backgrounds, Dickins worried that industrial workers developed tastes for too many consumer products and bought things as soon as they had money or credit to afford them. Hinting at criticism of the kind of purchases that Gladys Presley and her son would make famous fifteen years later, she worried about the ways young industrial workers spent their money. "Some of the furniture and furnishings bought by these young wives was of the 'ginger bread and red plush' type. The majority had little training or experience in the use of the dollar for furnishing a home and were easy victims of persuasive salesmen."[36]

While investigating whether it was possible to have the benefits of industrialization without low wages, child labor, and excessive interest in cheap consumer goods, Dickins concluded that garment mill workers were far better off than textile mill workers. Dickins positioned herself as an aggressive opponent of textile factories, located in textile mill villages. Compared to garment factories, the textile factories she studied in Attala, Clarke, and Itawamba counties were older institutions, the sort of cloth and spinning establishments associated with the western Carolinas, where most commentators believed southern industry had failed southern people with labor that paid low wages and did not teach new skills.[37] Dickins said women working in the textile industry were sickly and impoverished, lived in unhealthy homes, and ate poorly. She was particularly distressed about textile mill women, because most of them married too early and to the wrong men—textile mill men. They could not grow vegetables and raise chickens to help out when times were bad, nor could they call on networks of rural family members.

Garment mill women were the real stars of the report and, for Dickins, the hope for the future. Their lives were somewhat similar to the lives of women in that dying breed of farm-owning household. They were fairly healthy, made enough money to afford the benefits of industrial life, but they also had access to the homemade food and helpful company of farm life. A major difference was that cars, trucks, and buses allowed twentieth-century industrial workers to have things both ways—living in the country while working in towns or cities. In that case, industrial women could supplement the household economy rather than relying entirely on industrial pay. Garment factories, she stressed, combined the benefits of farm life and factory life, with workers making cash wages but living in rural homes. A good many lived, as Dickins described them in agrarian language, "in the open country, many in homes of farm owner husbands and fathers."[38]

Gladys Smith was one of the young women Dickins was describing. Hers was the first generation in the Smith family to leave the farm and test the rewards of factory work. In the 1930s, Lee County was a leader in the growth of one industry in Mississippi. The state ranked high on few national indices of industrial production, but in 1940 it was second in the nation, behind only Tennessee, in making work shirts.[39] Lee County had the most factories in Mississippi (four) and the second highest number of employees (550) making work clothing.[40]

At several points in the 1930s, Gladys Smith was one of those 550. In 1932, the twenty-year-old Smith took a job at the Tupelo Garment Company, the largest factory in the area, where her twelve-hour shifts started at 6:00 a.m.[41] Later she worked at Reed's, also making work shirts. Smith was the kind of employee apparel manufacturers wanted: she was poor and female. Of those 550 workers, all but one was female. Since the origins of the American garment industry, employers had wanted women with sewing skills as their primary labor force.[42] At both of her jobs, Smith, who had known how to sew since childhood, spent most of her time sewing. Only a quarter of Lee County's women worked outside the home, but virtually all of those worked in shirt factories.[43] Like all 550 workers, Gladys Smith was white.[44] Many southern industries were rigidly segregated by both job, with blacks eligible only for the poorest paying work, and by physical location. Companies like the Tupelo Garment Company that employed white women were especially concerned not to employ white and black workers in the same jobs in the same location. Finally, Smith typified the Tupelo work force in that she had rural roots. Two-thirds of the women who made work shirts in Tupelo lived in rural areas outside the small city, and many, like Smith, took factory-owned buses to and from work.[45]

Moving off the farm did not satisfy the young Gladys's dreams of excitement. Life as the It Girl or a dancer or even a constant shopper was not waiting for her in Tupelo. In the late 1930s and 1940s, much as she had as a child, Gladys Smith moved numerous times. In 1933 at age twenty-one, she married a teenager named Vernon Presley. They lived in a shotgun house that Vernon put together next to his parents' home in East Tupelo. In 1935, Gladys gave birth in that home to their only surviving child, Elvis, whose twin, Jesse, died in childbirth. The Presleys could not make payments on the house in 1938, when Vernon went to prison for a few months for altering a check. The Presleys did not come close to owning another home until 1954. They rented houses and lived with family members around Tupelo, moved for a few months to the growing Mississippi port town of Pascagoula, then moved back to Tupelo, where they lived in several houses. As Elvis Presley biographer Peter Guralnick concludes, "People like the Presleys moved all the time."[46]

Had Gladys Smith Presley remained a garment worker employed in Tupelo but living outside it, she might have fulfilled Dorothy Dickins's ideal of a young woman who benefited from her own wages in town but also from the farm productivity of her family and the help of an extended network of rural family and friends. Dickins's ideal may have been too good to be true, but it clearly failed to materialize for Gladys and family. For the Presleys, neither work nor housing was ever stable. After Elvis was born, Gladys went back to work at the garment factory and later worked for a while in a Tupelo laundry. She occasionally worked at home cleaning or sewing other people's clothes, and sometimes she went back to the fields in cotton-picking season. But she gave most of her time and energy to her son and rarely had a full-time job. In the clearest tie to her rural past, Gladys continued to keep chickens in the backyards of some of their rental houses. Vernon Presley made most of the family income at a variety of unsteady jobs that included stints as a WPA worker, building a POW camp in Como, Mississippi, working in a Memphis defense plant, and, back in Tupelo, working at a lumberyard and as a truck driver.[47]

Paying the bills was almost always a problem. The Presleys left two homes because they could not make payments, and Vernon had a bad reputation among Tupelo bill collectors. Gladys often had to accept gifts—generally known as "help"—from relatives, which she tried to repay with sewing.[48] Years later, Gladys recalled both the depths of their financial worries and, perhaps too melodramatically, the comforting hopes of her son: "Elvis would hear us worrying about our debts, being out of work and sickness, and he'd say, 'Don't you worry none, Baby. When I grow up, I'm going to buy you a fine house and pay everything you owe at the grocery store and get two Cadillacs—one for you and Daddy, and one for me."[49] That Gladys's son fantasized about paying off the grocery bill at the same time he dreamed of buying two Cadillacs suggests that the Presleys had joined the agrarian ideal of debt-free independence with Gladys's youthful fascination with luxury goods. A Presley cousin recalled, also with considerable melodrama, that money problems led to family arguments. He described the young Elvis saying that his mother told him, "We'll starve to death if we can't find work. Daddy says we ain't goin' nowhere. That got mama all upset. . . . I hate it when they yell. I hate it when his yellin' makes her cry so hard."[50]

In the period when Dorothy Dickins was expanding her dreams for women beyond the farm, Gladys Presley was trying to get by. Every textbook on southern history describes the shift away from agricultural labor in the twentieth century as part of a dramatic change in the life of the region. If Gladys's life represents a larger story, the shift from the farm to a nonagricultural life was not a huge transition, even if Gladys hoped it would be. For her, both farm work and nonfarm labor meant working hard for other people, moving around frequently, and taking jobs that were far from permanent. Numerous historians see the rise in wages and the possibilities for government work as crucial changes in the traditionally low-wage South, but Vernon's work in construction in Pascagoula and Como did little to change the Presleys' situation.[51] What distinguished Gladys's life from generations of farming people before her was that in the 1920s she had become a "new woman," defined by interests in consumer goods, movies, and recorded music, but her family's financial struggles did not allow her to experience what a new woman was supposed to enjoy.[52] Except for her interest in chickens and the help she received from numerous relatives, the life Gladys Presley lived in the 1930s and 1940s conformed to few agrarian ideals.

Historians of many kinds have analyzed what happened to traditions of rural life after migration, urbanization, and industrial growth took so many southerners off the land. Too few have asked what happened to the traditions of farming women.[53] How did women like Presley and Dickins understand the shift toward nonagricultural work and the possibilities for prosperity in the Sunbelt South?

By the late 1940s, Dorothy Dickins recognized that the agricultural economy offered opportunities to fewer people than ever before.[54] Her most important standard for judging life became physical comfort and consumer possibilities. In a revealing report in 1948, she found that low-income cotton-farming families spent less of their incomes than wealthier farming families or other Americans, even those with similar incomes. To Dickins, low levels of spending had always made sense for people trying to make food and clothing at home. But as the number of farm owners and laborers dropped dramatically due to mechanization and migration, farming people needed not merely new jobs but a new perspective on how to spend money. Members of what Dickins for the first time called "low-consumption families" had a "tradition of poverty" that involved expecting and even accepting limited material lives. Now, in an economy based almost entirely on wages, "members of low-consumption families must have more direct contact with higher consumption levels. They must desire goods and services that only higher incomes can produce."⁵⁵ She urged home economists to emphasize consumption more than saving and production.

Dickins documented with satisfaction the rapid expansion of new technology, new products, and new stores. She was pleased that the numbers of rural Mississippians with running water and flush toilets, electric lights, refrigerators, and radios increased between the 1930s and 1948.⁵⁶ She also found that the old and troubling tendency for men to do most of the family shopping was declining, with more than three fourths of the rural women in a 1948 study shopping at grocery stores at least once a week.⁵⁷

In the post–World War II period, Dickins offered fewer challenges to the nature of Mississippi life than she had during the Depression. She seems to have decided to make her contributions by offering limited suggestions on limited topics. She no longer saw her work as either convincing farm people to stay on the farm, as she had argued in the late 1920s, or convincing Mississippi's government and people to explore possibilities outside agriculture, as she had done in the late 1930s. In most of her articles, she took on a flatter tone that offered friendly advice to the relatively few women who still lived on farms.

For example, a 1958 report, *Food Use and Gainful Employment of the Wife*, found that women with jobs outside the home spent almost an hour less every weekday in cooking than women without jobs. An earlier Dickins, believing women should contribute to household independence by cooking foods grown at home, would have been troubled by the decline of cooking. Now she simply urged that grocery stores make such food available. Four years later, Dickins cowrote a report on the clothing-buying "practices and preferences" of teenaged girls in Mississippi. She found that the great majority of teenagers bought their own clothing, and again she offered no criticism. She remarked, "The majority of teen-agers think of themselves as in a large group of other teen-agers, dressing the same as these other girls. This fact signifies the need for many garments in the market similar in style and appearance but different in price range."⁵⁸ Her main suggestion was that businesses direct more advertising at a teenaged market. Finally, Dickins wrote a report in 1963 that took a fairly positive tone toward the farm family's traditional enemy, debt. Credit was necessary, she said, both for farming people to keep up with technological advances in large-scale farming and for them simply to enjoy expensive goods like cars and washing machines. Debt-free independence was not an option, although she favorably reported, "Many are aware of the misuse of credit and often warn about carrying it too far." Dickins concluded, "Judicious use of credit . . . can bring about larger and more profitable farms as well as higher levels of living. The families themselves are realizing this fact."⁵⁹

In her earlier years, Dorothy Dickins would never have written favorably about women who used frozen foods in order to spend less time cooking, or teenaged girls who did most of their own shopping, or farm families who pursued better lives through credit. All those things violated agrarian traditions of making things at home and minimizing expenses.

Dickins's last two calls for change show that she had accepted major changes in rural life and was now hoping to help rural people cope with them. In the 1950s, she wrote a series of reports investigating whether industrializing towns might offer new markets for locally grown farm produce. She worried that they were not, concluding in a 1951 report that industrialization should help people who were losing jobs due to agricultural mechanization, but "it [might] not help those who continue[d] to devote their time to farming."[60] In the mid-1950s, she wrote about efforts and potential for communities such as Laurel, Columbia, and Natchez to make it easier for farm families to sell their produce locally through stores or farmers' markets or by storing their produce in community freezers, but she reached no conclusions about the success of such efforts.[61]

Dickins's last small crusade, lasting from 1956 to 1964, encouraged farm women to serve more dairy products.[62] The final report of her long career discussed ways that grocery stores could more effectively advertise cottage cheese.[63] It would be unfair to see these reports as representing a failure of nerve; for Dickins, they were an extension of her lifelong interest in the health of farming people. Still, considering Dickins's willingness to address fundamental social questions earlier in her career (and considering how many other people were challenging the nature of Mississippi life in this period), the reports seem limited in their scope.

In the 1950s and 1960s, Dickins confronted the limits of her profession. She began her career trying to reform farm life so that women would want to stay on the farm. In midcareer, she concluded that farming did not offer an ideal life for most Mississippi women, and she encouraged them to explore lives off the farm without agrarian assumptions about the need for big families and home production. Toward the end of her career, she set her sights lower, simply trying to make life a little more comfortable and a little healthier for Mississippians who remained in rural areas.

In 1948, Gladys, Vernon, and Elvis Presley left Tupelo for Memphis, Tennessee, according to some reports because Vernon had been accused of making illegal whiskey. Gladys Presley's ten years in Memphis began with no hints of the wealth they would have in just a few years. The Presleys moved into a government-sponsored apartment complex in which poor people had to fill out forms proving they were poor enough to need assistance. Vernon Presley went to work at a series of jobs but never settled into any of them. Gladys Presley continued to work hard for low pay. Three things changed between 1948 and 1954. Everything was more crowded, from their housing projects to the hospital where Gladys worked, to the schools that Elvis attended. Second, almost all the people in those crowds were strangers; the network of family connections that had sustained the Presleys in bad times was back in Mississippi. Finally, perhaps for the first time, the Presleys did not have chickens in the backyard.[64]

In 1954, the Presley family made more money than they ever expected from Elvis Presley's record sales and concerts. Gladys Presley had little trouble enjoying the money. This was no stretch for someone who had grown up enjoying shopping and identifying herself as the It Girl. Life in a debt-free, goods-poor farm household—what Dickins would have called a "low consumption household"—had never seemed particularly attractive to her. The Presleys moved quickly from living in an apartment complex for welfare families to having a new Cadillac and a maid (and even, before long, a maid with a new Cadillac). Gladys stopped scrubbing hospital floors and spent the last four years of her life wondering about the benefits or costs of wealth.

The Presleys moved twice in 1954, something not uncommon in their lives. But the second move took them to a comfortable and expensive ranch house on Audubon Drive in a Memphis suburb far from the downtown areas where they had lived since 1948. In this one-story house with neighbors who were not too pleased when an overnight sensation moved in and invited his fans to visit, Gladys and Elvis began the sort of frenzied, sometimes creative shopping they later enjoyed in furnishing Graceland. Elvis gave Gladys a pink Cadillac—something he had promised her as a child back in Tupelo. Gladys and Elvis enjoyed shopping together for furniture, taking obvious pleasure in buying things, sometimes in surprising quantities, that they had never been able to afford.[65]

Two years later, the Presleys moved again, into Gladys Presley's last home. The estate, already named Graceland, offered more room and created new opportunities for shopping. But for Gladys, these new opportunities for shopping and abundance created a new sense of nostalgia. Gladys Presley loved shopping, but like many rural southerners who moved into the suburbs, she looked for ways to retain or retrieve parts of her old life. Virtually everything one reads about Gladys Presley at Graceland indicates that she was uncomfortable and sometimes desperately unhappy there. A family friend quoted in Jerry Hopkins's biography of Elvis Presley said that Gladys "never got used to having money. Even when she was in Graceland, she bought twenty-five-cent bottles of shampoo and the smallest tubes of toothpaste available."[66] Brother-in-law

Vester Presley said Gladys was troubled by the size of Graceland: "She was used to a much smaller house like those she had lived in all her life."[67] Gladys's sister Lillian concurred: "She was never satisfied after she moved out there—I think the house was too big, and she didn't like it."[68]

In moving so quickly from small houses in Tupelo to an apartment in a Memphis housing project to a suburban ranch house to a gated estate, the Presleys were an overstated, perhaps too-obvious metaphor for the consumer possibilities of the postagricultural South. Gladys Presley was an extreme example of a newly wealthy southerner from a rural background who could choose which parts of her background to forget and which parts to retrieve in conscious acts of self-definition. Her son, with his tastes for Hollywood, Las Vegas, and bright colors, and who placed no value on caution and moderation, stood for those who wanted to retain very little from their past. Only a few people, Gladys most of all, and some forms of music, especially gospel, appealed to Elvis as parts of a meaningful southern identity. Gladys, on the other hand, made more choices rooted in the traditions of farm people.

One of the first changes Gladys made when the Presleys moved into Graceland in 1956 was to have a chicken coop built. This may seem an odd choice for the former It Girl (and the mother of the new It Boy), but it revealed Gladys Presley trying to reclaim a space, the chicken yard, and to remember a freedom, egg money, that had been so important to generations of southern farm women.[69]

In Memphis, when she could have adopted a life of luxury and idleness, Gladys Presley showed an unnecessary interest in home production as a female virtue. She grew some vegetables and worked with them in the kitchen. In a revealing reminiscence, June Juanico recalled that in 1956 at the house on Audubon Drive, Gladys Presley included her in some work in the kitchen, probably to check out the teenager's skills as a potential wife for Elvis. In their first meeting, Gladys asked June to join her and her new housekeeper, Alberta, at the table to shell field peas. The three women discussed June's interests in cooking and sewing, with Gladys obviously pleased to tell June, "Most girls your age don't know how to do all that."[70] Later that day, Gladys Presley cooked what Juanico remembered as a "traditional country-style meal" of fried chicken, the newly shelled field peas, mashed potatoes, and cornbread, perhaps as a further way to judge Juanico's domestic interests. The teenager got the point. When Gladys Presley fried chicken in a new deep-fryer, she told Juanico, "'It uses a lot of grease, June, but if you strain it real good afterwards and keep it in the icebox, you can use it over and over again.' Elvis was a millionaire, or close to being one, and bless her soul, she was still trying to be thrifty."[71] This was not a simple case of cultural continuity in a new setting, not Granny Clampett cooking up 'possum in her Beverly Hills kitchen. Instead, it represented Gladys's decision to keep alive farm women's traditions of thrift and productivity even when, with a housekeeper and plenty of kitchen technology, there was no need for them.

In what was fast becoming a postagricultural South, both Gladys Presley and Dorothy Dickins had to wonder if they were becoming irrelevant within the spheres where they had mattered most. Gladys Presley feared that her son no longer needed her company and advice, and she knew that her ability to find ways to put food on the table was no longer necessary. Dorothy Dickins, writing about better ways to advertise cottage cheese, probably wondered if her reports, once so important in questioning the nature of Mississippi's present and future, really meant much to anyone.

As a fully formed social ideal, agrarianism had belonged primarily to men. Neither Dickins nor Presley had ever had a particularly strong commitment to agrarian ideals. Dickins came closer in her earlier years, when she argued that women benefited from farm life in which their productive labor was both valuable and valued. But unlike most agrarian thinkers, she did not contrast moral and aesthetic virtues of agrarian life with social decay or breakdown off the farm. As soon as farm life seemed to offer more frustration than fulfillment, she was ready to recommend that women try other options, from birth control to migration to work in garment factories. Gladys Smith Presley spent most of her forty-six years imagining a better life than sharecropping and low-paying industrial work and frequent movement could provide. She came closest to upholding agrarian ideals only late in her life, when she could afford it, watching chickens in the backyard of a suburban mansion.

NOTES

1. See, for example, Michael Kreyling, *Inventing Southern Literature* (Jackson: University Press of Mississippi, 1998); Patricia Yaeger, *Dirt and Desire: Reconstructing Southern Women's Writing, 1930–1990* (Chicago: University of Chicago Press, 2000).

2. Parts of this essay are derived from material in Ted Ownby, *American Dreams in Mississippi: Consumers, Poverty, and Culture, 1830–1998* (Chapel Hill: University of North Carolina Press, 1999).

3. Lu Ann Jones, *Mama Learned Us to Work: Farm Women in the New South* (Chapel Hill: University of North Carolina Press, 2002); Melissa Walker, *All We Knew Was to Farm: Rural Women in the Upcountry South, 1919–1941* (Baltimore: Johns Hopkins University Press, 2000).

4. R. S. Wilson, *Annual Report of Extension Work in Agriculture and Home Economics in Mississippi for 1919*, Mississippi Agricultural and Mechanical College Extension Bulletin 16 (Starkville: Mississippi A&M College, July 1920), 16.

5. *Starkville News*, January 13, 1922, 2.

6. On Dickins's background, see Helen Sue Jolly, "Selected Leaders in Mississippi Home Economics: An Historical Inquiry" (PhD diss., Mississippi State University, 1995), 93–105.

7. Dorothy Dickins, *A Study of Food Habits of People in Two Contrasting Areas of Mississippi*, Mississippi Agricultural Experiment Station Bulletin 245 (November 1927), 3, 50, 37. This and all subsequently cited Mississippi Agricultural Experiment Station bulletins were published by that entity in Starkville.

8. Ibid., 13–14.

9. Dorothy Dickins, *Food and Health*, Mississippi Agricultural Experiment Station Bulletin 255 (July 1928); Dickins, *Market Basket Wisdom*, Mississippi Agricultural Experiment Station Bulletin 263 (January 1929); Dickins, *Food Consumption of Boys and Girls in Six Typical Agricultural High Schools of Mississippi*, Mississippi Agricultural Experiment Station Bulletin 292 (June 1931); Dickins, *Agricultural High School Dormitories of Mississippi*, Mississippi Agricultural Experiment Station Bulletin 293 (August 1931).

10. William Alexander Percy, *Lanterns on the Levee: Recollections of a Planter's Son* (1941; Baton Rouge: Louisiana State University Press, 1973), 280.

11. Dorothy Dickins, *A Nutrition Investigation of Negro Tenants in the Yazoo Mississippi Delta*, Mississippi Agricultural Experiment Station Bulletin 254 (August 1928), 11.

12. Ibid., 17.

13. Ibid., 47.

14. Dorothy Dickins, *Clothing and Houselinen Expenditures of 99 Rural Families of Mississippi during 1928–1929*, Mississippi Agricultural Experiment Station Bulletin 294 (September 1931), 12.

15. Material for this and following sections comes primarily from Elaine Dundy, *Elvis and Gladys* (New York: Macmillan, 1985), 30–63; Peter Guralnick, *Last Train to Memphis: The Rise of Elvis Presley* (Boston: Little, Brown), 11–29.

16. Mississippi Planning Commission, *Progress Report on State Planning in Mississippi, January 1, 1938* (Jackson: Tucker Printing, 1938), 43. The state average was 66 percent.

17. Ibid., 45, 56.

18. On Gladys Smith and sewing, see Dundy, *Elvis and Gladys*, 42; Earl Greenwood and Kathleen Tracy, *The Boy Who Would Be King: An Intimate Portrait of Elvis Presley by His cousin* (New York: Dutton, 1990), 14.

19. Dundy, *Elvis and Gladys*, 40.

20. On Clara Bow, see Lary May, *Screening Out the Past: The Birth of Mass Culture and the Motion Picture Industry* (Chicago: University of Chicago Press, 1980), 219.

21. Dundy, *Elvis and Gladys*, 114.

22. See Elaine S. Abelson, *When Ladies Go A-Thieving: Middle-Class Shoplifters in the Victorian Department Store* (New York: Oxford University Press, 1989); Ellen Gruber Garvey, *The Adman in the Parlor: Magazines and the Gendering of Consumer Culture* (New York: Oxford University Press, 1996); Jennifer Scanlon, *Inarticulate Longings: The Ladies' Home Journal, Gender, and the Promises of Consumer Culture* (New York: Routledge, 1995).

23. On consumer culture and dreaming about future possibilities, see Colin Campbell, *The Romantic Ethic and the Spirit of Modern Consumerism* (London: Basil Blackwell, 1987); T. J. Jackson Lears, *Fables of Abundance: A Cultural History of Advertising in America* (New York: Basic Books, 1994).

24. On the 1930s as a turning point for home extension workers, see Walker, *All We Knew*, 1928–137. On Dickins in the 1930s, see Jolly, "Selected Leaders."

25. Dorothy Dickins, *Occupations of Sons and Daughters of Mississippi Cotton Farmers*, Mississippi Agricultural Experiment Station Bulletin 318 (May 1937), 103.

26. Ibid., 104.

27. Ibid., 71. Dickins also emphasized the point that farm women did far more work than farm men in her *Family Living on Poorer and Better Soil*, Mississippi Agricultural Experiment Station Bulletin 320 (September 1937), 31.

28. Dorothy Dickins, "Greater Cash Income for Rural Girls a Community Problem," *Mississippi Farm Research* (March 15, 1939): 4.

29. Dickins, *Occupations*, 54–55, 71.

30. Ibid., 106.

31. See James C. Cobb, *The Selling of the South: The Southern Crusade for Industrial Development, 1936–1990*, 2nd ed. (Urbana: University of Illinois Press, 1993); Vaughn L. Grisham Jr., *Tupelo: The Evolution of a Community* (Dayton, Ohio: Kettering Foundation Press, 1999).

32. Dickins, *Occupations*, 106.

33. Dorothy Dickins, *Some Contrasts in the Levels of Living of Women Engaged in Farm, Textile Mill, and Garment Plant Work*, Mississippi Agricultural Experiment Station Bulletin 364 (November 1941), 8.

34. Ibid., 22.

35. Ibid., 28–30.

36. Ibid., 14.

37. Dickins found that one of the textile mills she studied began operation in 1868, the other two in 1903 and slightly later. For discussion of Carolina textile mills, see David L. Carlton, *Mill and Town in South Carolina, 1880–1920* (Baton Rouge: Louisiana State University Press, 1982); Jacquelyn Dowd Hall et al., *Like A Family: The Making of a Southern Cotton Mill World* (Chapel Hill: University of North Carolina Press, 1987).

38. Dickins, *Some Contrasts*, 50.

39. United States Department of the Census, *Sixteenth Census of the United States: 1940, Manufactures, 1930*, vol. 2, pt. 1: *Reports by Industries Groups 1 to 10* (Washington, D.C.: U.S. Government Printing Office, 1942), 416.

40. In 1940, the entire state had twenty-three factories making work clothes. With two factories, Washington County was the only other county with more than one. United States Department of the Census, *Sixteenth Census of the United States: 1940, Manufactures 1939*, vol. 3: *Reports* (Washington, D.C.: U.S. Government Printing Office, 1942), 538–40. Harrison County had the highest number of employees making clothing, with 685. United States Department of the Census, *Sixteenth Census of the United States: 1940, Population*, vol. 2: *Characteristics of the Population* (Washington, D.C.: U.S. Government Printing Office, 1942), 254–63. By the time the Presleys left Lee County, Lauderdale County had taken the state's lead with six garment factories, while Lee County and Union County each had four. Mississippi Agricultural and Industrial Board, *Index of Manufacturers in Mississippi* (1946), 44. On Tupelo's garment industry, see Grisham, *Tupelo*; Joseph S. Bonica, "Stick By the Home Folks: Labor Unrest and Social Formation in Tupelo, 1937–1938" (MA thesis, University of Mississippi, 1996).

41. Jerry Hopkins, *Elvis: A Biography* (New York: Simon & Schuster, 1971), 19. See also on Gladys Smith's factory work, Guralnick, *Last Train to Memphis*, 11–16; Dundy, *Elvis and Gladys*, 53–57.

42. See John F. Kasson, *Civilizing the Machine: Technology and Republican Values in America, 1776–1900* (New York: Penguin Books, 1976); Thomas Dublin, *Women at Work: The Transformation of Work and Community in Lowell, Massachusetts, 1820–1860* (New York: Columbia University Press, 1979).

43. *Sixteenth Census: 1940, Population*, 2:259.

44. Statewide, 1 percent of apparel workers were African American. None lived in Lee County. United States Department of the Census, *Sixteenth Census of the United States: 1940, Population*,

vol. 3: *The Labor Force*, pt. 3: *Iowa–Montana* (Washington, D.C.: U.S. Government Printing Office, 1942), 809.

45. *Sixteenth Census: 1940, Population*, 2:277, 298. On Gladys Smith taking a bus to work, see Dundy, *Gladys and Elvis*, 60.

46. Guralnick, *Last Train to Memphis*, 28.

47. Ibid.; Dundy, *Elvis and Gladys*.

48. Greenwood and Tracy, *Boy Who Would Be King*, 14; 34–35. See also Guralnick, *Last Train to Memphis*, 12–16.

49. Quoted in Guralnick, *Last Train to Memphis*, 16.

50. Greenwood and Tracy, *Boy Who Would Be King*, 25.

51. See Bruce J. Schulman, *From Cotton Belt to Sunbelt: Federal Policy, Economic Development, and the Transformation of the South, 1938–1980* (1991; Durham, N.C.: Duke University Press, 1994); Gavin Wright, *Old South, New South: Revolutions in the Southern Economy since the Civil War* (New York: Basic Books, 1986).

52. On young women in industrial jobs and the "new woman," see Jacquelyn Dowd Hall et al., *Like a Family*, 253–54; Jacquelyn Dowd Hall, "Disorderly Women: Gender and Labor Militancy in the Appalachian South," *Journal of American History* 73 (September 1986): 354–82; Kathy Peiss, *Cheap Amusements: Working Women and Leisure in Turn-of-the-Century New York* (Philadelphia: Temple University Press). On Gladys Smith as "new woman" while she worked in Tupelo, see Dundy, *Elvis and Gladys*, 54.

53. An exception is Jack Temple Kirby's *Rural Worlds Lost: The American South, 1920–1960* (Baton Rouge: Louisiana State University Press, 1987).

54. Dorothy Dickins, *The Labor Supply and Mechanized Cotton Production*, Mississippi State Agriculture Experiment Station Bulletin 463 (June 1949).

55. Dorothy Dickins, "Consumption Patterns of Cotton-Farm Families and an Agricultural Program for the South," *Rural Sociology* 13, no. 1 (March 1948): 27, 28.

56. Dorothy Dickins, "The Farm Home Improves Its Equipment," *Journal of Home Economics* 40, no. 10 (December 1948): 567–70; Dickins, "The Southern Family in an Era of Change," *Rural Sociology* 15, no. 3 (September 1950): 232–33.

57. Dorothy Dickins, "Needs for Storage of Farm-Owner-Families," typescript, Special Collections, Mississippi State University Library, Starkville, Mississippi; Dickins, "Southern Family," 233.

58. Dorothy Dickins, *Food Use and Gainful Employment of the Wife*, Mississippi State Agricultural Experiment Station Bulletin 558 (1958); Dorothy Dickins and Virginia Ferguson, *Practices and Preferences of Teen-Age Girls in the Selection of Blouses, Skirts, Dresses and Sweaters*, Mississippi State Agricultural Experiment Station Bulletin 636 (February 1962), 23.

59. Dorothy Dickins, *Factors Related to the Use of Credit Resources by Farm Families*, Mississippi State Agricultural Experiment Station Bulletin 658 (March 1963), 11, 25.

60. Dorothy Dickins, *The Rural Family and Its Source of Income*, Mississippi State Agricultural Experiment Station Bulletin 481 (March 1951), 20.

61. Dorothy Dickins, L. D. Welch, and W. E. Christian, *Industrialization and a Market for Food Products in the Columbia Trade Area*, Mississippi Agricultural Experiment Station Bulletin 537 (October 1955); Dorothy Dickins et al., *Industrialization and a Market for Food Products in the Laurel Trade Area*, Mississippi Agricultural Experiment Station Bulletin 540 (March 1956); Dorothy Dickins et al., *Industrialization and a Market for Food Products in the Natchez Trade Area*, Mississippi Agricultural Experiment Station Bulletin 543 (April 1956); Dorothy Dickins and Virginia Ferguson, *The Market for Locally-Produced Foods for Freezing*, Mississippi Agricultural Experiment Station Bulletin 567 (October 1958).

62. Dorothy Dickins and Virginia Ferguson, *Dairy Products Consumption and the Market: Four Mississippi Towns*, Mississippi Agricultural Experiment Station Bulletin 542 (April 1956); Dickins and Ferguson, *Educational Programs for Increasing Milk-Drinking among Women: A Pilot Study*, Mississippi Agricultural Experiment Station Bulletin 587 (January 1960); Dickins, *Use, Knowledge, and Attitudes concerning Milk Production by Homemakers*, Mississippi Agricultural Experiment Station Bulletin 642 (April 1962); Dickins, *Milk, Ice Cream, and Competing Beverages and Desserts*, Mississippi Agricultural Experiment Station Bulletin 646 (May 1962).

63. Dorothy Dickins and Alvirda F. Johnston, *Consumer Response to Selected In-Store Promotion of Cottage Cheese*, Mississippi Agricultural Experiment Station Bulletin 691 (July 1964).

64. Guralnick, *Last Train to Memphis*, 31–56; Dundy, *Elvis and Gladys*, 134–54; Greenwood and Tracy, *Boy Who Would Be King*, 85–87; Hopkins, *Elvis*, 35–43.

65. Dundy, *Elvis and Gladys*, 231, 260–76; Greenwood and Tracy, *Boy Who Would Be King*, 193; Guralnick, *Last Train to Memphis*, 396–98; Vester Presley, as told to Deda Bonura, *A Presley Speaks* (Memphis: Wimmer Brothers Books, 1978), 52. On the house on Audubon Drive, see Karal Ann Marling, *Graceland: Going Home with Elvis* (Cambridge, Mass.: Harvard University Press, 1996), 110–16.

66. Hopkins, *Elvis*, 215.

67. V. Presley, *Presley Speaks*, 57.

68. Guralnick, *Last Train to Memphis*, 427.

69. On the chicken coop, see Guralnick, *Last Train to Memphis*, 420. On women and egg money on southern farms, see Jones, *Mama Learned Us to Work*, 110–47; Walker, *All We Knew*, 75–82.

70. June Juanico, *Elvis: In the Twilight of Memory* (New York: Arcade, 1997), 44–46, quote on 46.

71. Juanico, *Elvis*, 52–53.

"The Lady Folk Is a Doer"

Women and the Civil Rights Movement in Claiborne County, Mississippi

EMILYE CROSBY

In 1996, while discussing why she had decided to run for justice of the peace in 1971 only after it was clear that no men were willing to do so, Mrs. Marjorie Brandon explained, "I guess we just think, thought, a man should step forward. A man should be the man. A man should lead. But in some cases, you know, that's not always true."[1] Because of her successful run for political office and her years of service as local NAACP secretary, Brandon is usually mentioned as one of the "women leaders" in the Claiborne County civil rights movement. Yet much of her movement leadership is obscured today, just as it was limited in the 1960s, by hierarchical, status-oriented, and gendered perceptions of leadership. As more scholars and activists address questions of gender and leadership, our understanding of women's work in the civil rights movement is growing and becoming more complex. We can more clearly see when and how women provided important leadership and the ways in which their leadership potential remained untapped or even circumscribed.

Virtually everyone agrees that throughout the South women participated in the movement in disproportionate numbers. They canvassed door-to-door, attempted to register to vote, attended meetings, participated in demonstrations, and housed and fed civil rights workers more often than men did. Yet, despite this consistent and overwhelming participation, most well-known civil rights leaders are men, and there are few in-depth examinations of women's work. This is, in part, because most scholars and activists initially equated movement leadership almost exclusively with public spokespeople and organizational heads, most of whom were men. Through an increased focus on women, however, scholars have begun to suggest that leadership needs to be more broadly defined and that less-visible forms of leadership (which women were likely to perform) were essential to a successful movement.[2] Women's roles within the Claiborne County, Mississippi, civil rights movement reflect those of many women throughout the movement and illustrate some of the important questions with which scholars and activists are grappling.

Emerging as a mass movement in early 1966, the Claiborne County movement was led by the NAACP, and on the surface, it appeared to be overwhelmingly male. In 1952, when the county's first NAACP branch was organized, fifty-five of the fifty-nine members listed on the charter were men. With no complete listing available, it is difficult to know with certainty how many women joined, but they were clearly outnumbered by men and only men attended the sporadic, secret meetings.[3] Similarly, when the branch was rejuvenated in 1965, forty-three of the sixty charter members were men.[4] Women quickly joined in a ratio similar to men, but all of the organization's officers were men, and when local civil rights leaders sent a demand letter to the white community, it was signed by seven men and no women.[5]

The predominance of visible male leadership is closely tied to the movement's association with the national NAACP and Charles Evers, who succeeded his assassinated brother, Medgar Evers, as the state field secretary for the organization. The NAACP was bureaucratic, hierarchical, and practiced individual, top-down leadership. Its style and structure were very much tied to traditional conceptions of leadership, and this approach was embraced by Evers as he identified local people for day-to-day leadership. Because the movement was consciously built on the NAACP tradition and reinforced by Evers's preferences, older, elite men dominated the visible leadership roles.

Most of the NAACP officers and the movement "leaders" were better educated and from a more secure economic class than their constituents. They were vocal in meetings, led marches, negotiated with whites, and ran for public office. There were no women among the members of the inner circle, who were known throughout the community as the "leading mens." During marches, Evers implied that women needed protection and typically asked men to march in front and back with women and children in the middle. During a court-protected march that limited the number of participants, Evers called for ministers and businessmen to demonstrate, asking everyone else to wait on the sidelines.[6] Reports about NAACP mass meetings are filled with the names of male speakers and officers. Even at a special meeting sponsored by the "Ladies Auxiliary," most of the speakers were men who, according to the report, "commended the ladies for their efforts."[7]

JULIA JONES, CLAIBORNE COUNTY'S FIRST BLACK
CHANCERY CLERK, WITH BROWNIE GIRL SCOUTS
Courtesy of Patricia Crosby.

Despite the seeming male dominance, many participants from Claiborne County, as in movements throughout the South, note the importance of women who were responsible for much of the daily work that sustained the movement. One younger activist claims, "Women carried the movement. There's no doubt about it. I mean, there were some men who stood up, but it was a minority. Women were the backbone of the movement. I'll stand on that."[8] An older minister agrees with that interpretation, explaining: "We do a lot of talk, we men, but the lady folk is a doer. They don't do much talk, but they doing. We'll do a lot [of talking about] what we gon' do . . . and the ladies gon' on getting the job done."[9] Another activist makes a similar assessment: "Women . . . they quicker to do the work than the fellows. Lot of fellows don't want to be standing out there."[10] Other details support this depiction of women's overwhelming participation and critical importance. For example, despite the visibility of the all-male leadership, 80 percent of the first fifteen hundred blacks who registered to vote were women.[11]

Similarly, when the NAACP initiated a boycott against white merchants in April 1966, women did the shopping and took on the extra work and planning necessary to shop almost exclusively—with limited transportation and income—more than forty-five minutes from home. In addition to their crucial role as consumers, women worked closely with Rudy Shields, an organizer who came from Chicago to work in the movement and who had an informal association with the NAACP and Charles Evers. Together, they coordinated and supervised the young people. A woman sponsored the youth chapter of the NAACP. She and several other women took care of the details associated with picketing and store watching. They bought poster board, made signs, and made sure there were picketers most afternoons and every Saturday. Based on instruction from civil rights attorneys and guidelines from the national NAACP, they taught store watchers and picketers what was legal and what was not. They made sure picketers kept a tight formation and did not block the sidewalk or go onto private property.[12]

Mrs. Thelma Crowder was one of the most visible and prominent of these women. By the time she was born in 1908, her grandparents, who had been enslaved, were fairly prosperous, owning farmland and a cotton gin. Living on their farm with her parents, she attended school full-time and was able to graduate from the tenth grade in 1924. Unable to attend college and not interested in teaching, she supported herself as a seamstress and was married with grown children when the movement began. She, like her family, was actively engaged in community work. Her grandparents donated land to their church, and both her father and a cousin served as superintendent of her one-room elementary school. She continued this tradition, serving on committees and doing fundraising for charitable causes. Well read and knowledgeable about the NAACP, she quickly applied her sense of civic responsibility to the movement when it took hold in Claiborne County. She attended meetings and marched, led singing, raised money, solicited NAACP memberships, and helped bring federal registrars into the community by describing the white registrar's rejection of her voter application. Her commitment never wavered, even when white women cancelled their dressmaking orders and her husband grew ill and asked that she stay home with him.[13]

Like Mrs. Crowder, many of the most active movement women were well known and had spent years doing social welfare work for the community. Some were fairly elite, with the resources to spend considerable time on movement work. In addition to their being important workers, their presence provided instant legitimacy to the movement, to Rudy Shields, who did not have roots in the community, and to the teenagers, who were the most consistent picketers and canvassers.

Mrs. Leesco Guster was another woman who played a major role in the movement, especially the voter registration campaign. For several months in 1966, she drove Rudy Shields from house to house throughout Claiborne County. Together they encouraged African Americans to register to vote. Canvassing all over the county was tedious work, and it could also be dangerous. When some prospective registrants asked them to return the next day, they did and were met by a white man with a gun prominently displayed in his truck. The people who had asked them to return were frightened and refused to go with them to register. Guster remembers their return trip as harrowing. "This [white] man . . . parked on the other side of this little one-way bridge and, talk about scared, I was. Cause I was driving. Mr. Shields had got, he was in the back with my old .45. When I got along near the bridge, I said, 'Mr. Shields, there he is parked. What should I do?' . . . He said, 'You just drive.' I say, 'But if . . . he get to shooting, don't I have to duck?' And I was so scared. But we had to go across the bridge."[14] Though they were not attacked that day, Guster did face repercussions for her work. She was fired almost immediately, and her husband, a prominent contractor, also lost all of his work. They were able to live on his veteran's pension and Social Security. Instead of slowing her down, being fired made Guster more determined and gave her more time for movement work. She became even more of a target for antimovement harassment when she began to house Shields and white civil rights attorneys. One night a telephone caller, who identified himself as a member of the Klan, called her abusive names and asked if she was tired of living. Guster was not intimidated and told him that "he would be a dead one if he came down here." She spent that and many other nights standing guard with her gun. And she continued her movement work.[15]

Guster's experience also reflects the complexity of prevailing assumptions about gender. She and others explicitly identify the car she used to drive Shields around as belonging to her husband. Moreover, in describing her premovement job, she says that her husband "allowed" her to work cleaning house for one of his biggest customers. These comments suggest that she, her husband, and the surrounding community assumed a gendered hierarchy within her marriage that reflected prevailing norms. And although her movement work was extensive, it was largely work typically done by women: canvassing, housing workers, selling NAACP memberships, singing in the choir, working with the youth chapter, raising money, and picketing and store watching.[16]

Yet some aspects of the Gusters' experience seem more ambiguous in terms of prevailing gender norms. Although she and her husband were both activists, Mrs. Guster took the lead. She participated in marches but says she would not "allow" her husband to do so. She worried that, with high blood pressure, he could not handle being jailed if he were arrested. Moreover, although most of her work was associated with repetition and tedium, it also exposed her to danger. In addition to facing armed whites while canvassing with Rudy Shields, she joined the armed guard protecting her house.[17]

One historian, writing about several relatively well-known black women civil rights leaders, notes a pattern that Claiborne County women appear to follow. She argues that many women's behavior "showed contradictions—on the one hand a boldness in initiating protests and applying pressure on whites in power, while at the same time a submissiveness in their acceptance of the authority of the Black male clergy."[18] In Claiborne County, Guster and other women stepped up to do the work that needed doing—whether it was canvassing, challenging whites through public marching, or defending their homes with weapons—and simultaneously accepted prevailing gender hierarchies without question. Perhaps their experience and perspective are similar to that described by another Mississippi civil rights activist, Joyce Ladner. According to Ladner, racism and poverty were so pervasive for her female relatives and other black women in Mississippi that considering gender discrimination was a luxury they could not afford. She observes, "They had grown up in a culture where they had had the opportunity to use all of their skills and all of their talents to fight racial and class oppression. . . . And perhaps they didn't know they were oppressed because of their gender, they were so busy trying to survive and fight day to day. It would have been a luxury for my mother to focus on gender concerns. It would never have occurred to her."[19]

Mrs. Marjorie Brandon, whose quote opens this essay, demonstrates many of these contradictions and the complexity of defining leadership. As a woman in her sixties, Brandon has vivid memories of her outrage at white children who spat on her as they rode to school on buses while she and other African American children walked to school. At the time, she talked to her father about it and remembers not being fully satisfied with his response. "[He told me,] 'Well, that's just the way the whites treat the blacks.' He say, 'I read my Bible, and I really do believe that the rail that's on the bottom is not going to always be on the bottom.' He would always tell me that cause I could just not understand it. I just feel like it was so cruel."[20] Married and a mother at a young age, Brandon consciously taught her six children a more aggressive attitude of protest and was determined that they have better opportunities than she had. Her oldest son, Ken Brandon, remembers that on trips to town, he and his siblings would want to buy hamburgers, but the café that sold them only served blacks from a window in the back. He says, "Mom couldn't stand that. And we got hungry. [But she'd say,] 'You can wait until you get home.' She would never allow us—'If I can't have it out of the front door, my money is not good as yours.'—But that was part of her, [that] 'I will not stoop to that.'"[21]

Before the movement, Mrs. Brandon defied white supremacy by flatly refusing to use courtesy titles for whites her age and younger. Ken Brandon remembers that one of his parents' few arguments was over his mother's refusal to say "sir" to a younger member of the white family that employed his father. Brandon and her husband also disagreed about joining the NAACP in the 1950s. There was considerable secrecy and fear surrounding the NAACP during that early membership period. Marjorie Brandon recalls, "I was always told that the white people would threaten you or maybe they might kill you and so once you got your card, you didn't make them visible. . . . I believe I burned [mine]." Despite this danger and her husband's opposition, Mrs. Brandon insisted on joining. She remembers talking to her husband and says, "I just kept convincing him that, you know, that [joining the NAACP] was the only way that we were going to be free or only way we were going to have any rights."[22] Years later, Ken Brandon discusses his parents' conflict about challenging the racial status quo. "I can understand it more as I become an adult. She was trying to work a line. She respected my dad as head of the house. She wanted to support him, but, at the same time, she wanted us to be free thinkers. She wanted us to know what was happening, and she wanted to do what she could to be a part of the movement and express her opinion and she did."[23] Reflecting on her willingness to risk retaliation, Brandon says, "I just felt like someone had to take a stand. Life itself is just a chance. Who knows what's going to happen tomorrow?"[24]

With this vivid sense of racial inequities and a determination to combat them, Mrs. Brandon spent her life trying to find the movement. Yet despite this and her longstanding NAACP membership, Brandon's early movement contributions were even less visible than Guster's, though like hers, they combined typically female tasks with a willingness to take stands. She registered to vote right away, participated in protest marches, and attended mass meetings, taking her older children with her and leaving the younger ones home with her husband. She encouraged friends and relatives to register and join the NAACP. Over the years, she served on a number of traditionally female NAACP committees, canvassed for NAACP members, participated in the volunteer work necessary to initiate a Head Start program, and in the late 1960s became the NAACP branch secretary.

Brandon's role as a parent also provides important insight into her leadership potential. When the local public schools began their first year of token school integration, forty-nine African American students were assigned to the "white" school, five in the high school and forty-four in grades one through eight. Given Brandon's insistence that her children have greater opportunities and resist white supremacy, it is not surprising that all six of them attended the formerly white-only schools. Ken, twelfth grade; Vivian, eleventh grade; Carl, eighth grade; Maxine, sixth; Dennis, fifth; and John, second, faced an onslaught of verbal harassment and isolation throughout the year. And the entire family received threatening phone calls and considerable harassment.[25]

Throughout the year, Marjorie Brandon stood up for her children when they had difficulty with teachers or with classmates who physically assaulted them. And like Guster, Brandon was prepared to defend herself and her family. She carried a gun in the car and had permission from the sheriff to shoot back if her house was attacked. Ken Brandon had learned his mother's lessons well and saw his year of harassment as a necessary part of achieving a community goal and furthering the struggle for racial equality. He says, "It meant so much to older people who had been told all of their lives, 'You're dumb. You can't compete.' And to go over there and to make the honor roll and be right out there with everybody else, taking the same courses. For some older people, that was just—.... So things like that were really inspiring.... That gave you encouragement, cause I'm doing this for all of these people."[26] The willingness of Brandon's children to participate and their ability to excel in the face of considerable abuse are a testament not only to them but to her. It reflects her ability to inspire and support her children as well as her courage and determination.

Brandon's ability to take on additional leadership is evident in the 1971 election (the second countywide election held after blacks became a majority of registered voters). Racially biased redistricting had moved a black incumbent out of the district, and Brandon was one of the people searching for a replacement candidate. She describes how, as the deadline approached, one of the movement's male leaders suggested she run. "[He said,] 'We can't get a man, so I think you'll be the good woman to go for that position.' I said, 'All right, if a man don't come forward between now and the deadline, I'll run.'"[27] Her experience was not unusual. Mrs. Unita Blackwell, who subsequently served as mayor of Mayersville, traveled the world, and won a MacArthur Genius award, had a similar experience in nearby Mayersville. She recalls, "Women wasn't supposed to be running. . . . I'm the organizer, but I'm organizing men cause that's the way they did it. And this one man stood up and said, . . . 'Why don't you be justice of the peace?' . . . We had one slot left and nobody would do it and then they pointed to me and I was honored."[28] She marvels at that attitude and says, "I hadn't even [gotten] near my own potential of what I was supposed to do."[29]

The active involvement of women as movement workers and the gender-based limitations they encountered are also evident in two long-term Claiborne County movement-related projects: the founding of Our Mart, a cooperative grocery store, and the local Head Start program. The idea for a cooperative grocery store originated with a schoolteacher whose husband was an NAACP officer. She and two other women, also formally educated and prominent in the community, took charge of the project. They promoted the store at mass meetings, sold shares, and met with a lawyer to get the organization incorporated. When the lawyer drew up the papers, he objected to the all-female list of officers. On the spot, one of the women replaced herself with her husband. Before the lawyer's comments, the women had not questioned their abilities or the correctness of having all female officers. Yet they instantly implemented the lawyer's suggestion for change. In part they accepted that type of gendered hierarchy, and in part they believed the project was far more important than the particular officers.[30]

Similarly, the workers, almost exclusively women, who did the advance volunteer work necessary to bring Head Start into the community were many of the same people who canvassed and worked with the community's youth during the height of the activist phase of the movement. They used the same methods that worked for building NAACP membership and recruiting new registered voters, going door-to-door to explain the benefits of Head Start and gathering financial information. Many of these women later worked with Head Start as teachers, aides, trainees, cooks, and social workers.[31] While women did these traditionally female jobs—cooking, cleaning, and interacting with children—movement men participated on advisory boards, worked as consultants and supervisors, and occasionally contracted to provide goods and services to the Head Start centers.

The gender-based division of labor related to Head Start, the lawyer's perception that men should be officers of Our Mart, and the preference for male political candidates reflected a widespread pattern and inclination that permeated the Claiborne County movement. According to a black woman who came into the community in the late 1960s, "Although women played key roles in Claiborne County in doing things . . . there was still this deference to men. There was an incredible deference to men. And, I recall . . . there were women who were honorary men in that they could, they were acknowledged and listened to, but I think . . . it was because they were honorary men."[32] A young black man, who was a teenaged activist during the movement's earliest years and an organizer later, also comments on the strict hierarchy within the movement. He says, "The leadership, which was all black males, saw young leadership, and they saw women, as footstools for the movement, not as people who could bring some innovative and creative ideas and strategies to the movement. Because they were the total repositories of all the knowledge. Often anything that you could bring or women could bring would be something as defined by them to support the agenda that they got going on."[33]

In addition to Brandon, several other women ran for and won political offices in Claiborne County. Two of the earliest successful candidates for countywide offices (in 1967 and 1971) illustrate the critical role that traditional ideas about status, not just gender, played in what was widely perceived as necessary for leadership, including elective office. Although both women were movement participants, they were less involved in its daily work than other women, like Brandon and Guster. They were almost certainly selected to run for office because they were teachers with relatively high standing in the community. Moreover, both were married to "leading mens." Here their elite class and connection to important men were more important than the fact that they were women. Their community status, not their leadership potential or past movement work, was probably the most significant factor in their candidacies.

Given the public prominence of male leaders and the gendered division of labor that tended to obscure and devalue women's work, it is important to make visible women's individual and collective contributions. Women, including Mrs. Brandon, Mrs. Guster, Mrs. Crowder, and others involved in Our Mart, Head Start, and voter registration campaigns were crucial to the success of the Claiborne County movement. This understanding fits with what scholars have found more generally: in the civil rights and other social movements, women and men often performed different tasks, and men's tasks were typically more visible and more highly valued. Nonetheless, women obviously made essential contributions, and some forms of women's activism, much of it invisible and behind the scenes, should be seen as leadership. The extent and exact nature of women's contributions become clearer if we look more closely at the broad range of movement participation and expand our definition of leadership.[34]

By looking beyond organization officers and public speakers, we can begin to see where and how women's work was crucial in Claiborne County, despite the appearance of male dominance. For example, Leesco Guster was involved in at least six different movement tasks that could be considered leadership— raising money, initiating action, mobilizing and persuading followers, serving as an example, organizing and coordinating action, and teaching followers.[35] Because of her class, she also had access to resources—her time, a vehicle, and her house—which she contributed to the movement. Despite this retrospective analysis, few in the community point to her as a leader. One former NAACP leader, who is somewhat an exception, recalls, "She did so much. And, look like to me she got less credit than anybody. Hardly ever anybody mention her . . . [but] she was a real civil rights worker."[36] Most people probably overlook Guster because she did not fit the common conception of leadership, which equates it with public speaking. Guster describes herself as a "doer" and says, "I'm not a great talker; I'll sing and I'll work."[37] Although these traits meant that Guster had little visible prominence in a movement best known for its speakers, according to an expanded model of multidimensional leadership, she was clearly a leader. Similarly, Marjorie Brandon's and Thelma Crowder's ability to mobilize networks of family and friends and their day-in, day-out work of canvassing, fundraising, and nurturing provided the almost invisible base for the successes of more visible leaders.

However, while it is important to recognize and acknowledge the ways that women made significant contributions and provided leadership, we also must recognize the ways in which their potential was circumscribed. Despite Guster's contributions, she had little or no say in strategy or tactics. She had no authority to negotiate with white leaders. And she probably had little opportunity to influence movement priorities. Similarly, despite Brandon's long history of defiance, NAACP membership, and a willingness to make stands and take risks, there was little or no room for her in the NAACP's inner circle.

The contributions and experiences of women in Claiborne County are probably typical of women throughout the civil rights movement. Nevertheless, they were also influenced by the NAACP's central role in the community. As a hierarchical and bureaucratic organization, it reinforced gendered divisions of labor and the inequalities of the society and permitted few possibilities for women's involvement in decision-making roles. In contrast, the Student Nonviolent Coordinating Committee (SNCC) and the Mississippi Freedom Democratic Party (MFDP) were much more open to leadership from women and others who lacked formal education or middle-class status. sncc's "distaste for bureaucracy and hierarchy" and its commitment to finding and developing local leadership made the organization particularly receptive to women's leadership.[38] A former sncc activist describes the organization as an open and supportive place for her. She remembers, "sncc gave us the first structured opportunity to use our skills in an egalitarian way without any kind of subjugation because of our race or our class or our gender."[39] Thus, while women who worked for and with sncc and the mfdp had the common female experience of doing much of the organizing and day-to-day nitty-gritty work, they also actively participated in developing strategy and making decisions. We can see the important implications inherent in that through the critical intellectual, tactical, and strategic contributions of women such as Ella Baker, Fannie Lou Hamer, Diane Nash, and Ruby Doris Smith Robinson. Their work with sncc and the mfdp gives us a sense of how women respond in an environment open to a broader range of their leadership abilities.[40]

Looking more closely at women's and men's movement work and being open to broader definitions of leadership allow us to question the hierarchy that privileges public, usually male, forms of leadership. Moreover, with sncc and the mfdp as a point of contrast, we can go beyond reclaiming women's contributions and rethinking the relative values placed on different types of work. We can also begin to explore the differences in movements that more fully embraced women's participation, not solely or primarily as workers but also as strategists and decision makers. Some historians and activists believe that hierarchical, limited conceptions of leadership during the movement left it too dependent on charismatic individuals and may have also contributed to competition for resources and rewards or status. Descriptions of Marjorie Brandon and Leesco Guster highlight their courage, determination, and strong sense of community. They were hard workers who acted on their beliefs despite threats and uncertainty. While searching for and emphasizing the multiple ways they contributed to the successes of the Claiborne County movement, we can also speculate about how they might have strengthened the movement if their creativity, clarity, and compassion had been included in strategy and decision making.

NOTES

A version of this essay was originally published in *Stepping Forward: Black Women in Africa and the Americas*, ed. Catherine Higgs, Barbara A. Moss, and Earline Rae Ferguson (Athens: Ohio University Press, 2002), 189–202 (http://ohioswallow.com/book/stepping+forward). I am grateful to the Carter G. Woodson Institute, University of Virginia; State University of New York–Geneseo; and

the State of New York/United University Professions Drescher Affirmative Action Leave program
for their financial support for my work on the Claiborne County civil rights movement.

1. Marjorie Brandon interview, July 23, 1996. All interviews by author unless noted. In subsequent citations, I include dates only when necessary to distinguish multiple interviews with the
same person. Interviews are in author's possession.

2. See, for example, Bernice McNair Barnett, "Invisible Southern Black Women Leaders in the
Civil Rights Movement: The Triple Constraints of Gender, Race, and Class," in *Gender & Society* 7
(June 1993): 162–82; Vicki L. Crawford, Jacqueline Anne Rouse, and Barbara Woods, eds., *Women
in the Civil Rights Movement: Trailblazers and Torchbearers, 1941–1965* (Brooklyn, N.Y.: Carlson,
1990); Charles Payne, *I've Got the Light of Freedom: The Organizing Tradition and the Mississippi
Freedom Struggle* (Berkeley: University of California Press, 1995); Karen Brodkin Sacks, *Caring by
the Hour: Women, Work, and Organizing at Duke Medical Center* (Urbana: University of Illinois
Press, 1988); Belinda Robnett, *How Long? How Long? African-American Women in the Struggle for
Civil Rights* (New York: Oxford, 1997); Christina Greene, "'Our Separate Ways': Women and the
Black Freedom Movement in Durham, North Carolina, 1940s–1970s" (PhD diss., Duke University,
1996); Rhoda Lois Blumberg, "Women in the Civil Rights Movement: Reform or Revolution?" *Dialectical Anthropology* 15 (1990): 133–39.

3. Membership list, Claiborne County, November 22, 1951, NAACP Papers, Library of Congress,
Washington, D.C.; Marjorie Brandon interview, May 4, 1992.

4. Charles Evers to Gloster Current, January 14, 1966, NAACP Papers.

5. Nathaniel H. Jones, Walter L. Griffin Sr., James N. Dorsey, Calvin C. Williams, Alexander Collins, Floyd D. Rollins, Charles Evers, to Mayor and Board of Aldermen, Claiborne County Board
of Supervisors and of Education, Sheriff Dan S. McCay, Port Gibson, Mississippi, March 14, 1966,
NAACP Papers.

6. Memo from Charles E. Snodgrass, April 1, 1966, box 147, folder 2; Snodgrass report, March
14, 1966, box 147, folder 1, both in Paul B. Johnson Papers, University of Southern Mississippi, Hattiesburg.

7. *Vicksburg Citizens' Appeal*, September 21 and October 19, 1966, Ed King Papers, Tougaloo College, Tougaloo, Mississippi.

8. James Miller interview, February 11, 1994.

9. J. L. Sayles interview, May 20, 1992.

10. Charles Bunton interview, August 5, 1996.

11. Smith, Bill B., MS v. file, microfilm edition, reel 109, in *Southern Civil Rights Litigation
Records*, ed. Clement E. Vose, Yale University Photographic Sources (New Haven, Conn.: Yale University, 1977) (henceforth cited as *SCRLR*).

12. James Devoual interview, July 23, 1992; testimony of Lawrence Rice, September 20, 1966,
p. 71, in *Shields v. Mississippi* file, reel 110, *SCRLR*.

13. Thelma [Crowder] Wells, *I Ain't Lying* 4 (Fall 1989): 61–70; Thelma Crowder Wells interview,
April 7, 1992; *Port Gibson Reveille*, January 14, 1960; January 31, 1963.

14. Leesco Guster interview, July 3, 1996.

15. Ibid.

16. Nate Jones interview, June 30, 1996; Guster interview.

17. Guster interview.

18. Anne Standley, "The Role of Black Women in the Civil Rights Movement," in Crawford,
Rouse, and Woods, *Women in the Civil Rights Movement*, 187.

19. Joyce Ladner, quoted in *A Circle of Trust: Remembering SNCC*, ed. Cheryl Lynn Greenberg
(New Brunswick, N.J.: Rutgers University Press, 1998), 142–43.

20. Marjorie Brandon interview, 1992.

21. Ken Brandon interview, October 11, 1994.

22. Marjorie Brandon interview, 1992.

23. Ken Brandon interview.

24. Marjorie Brandon interview, 1996.

25. Port Gibson High Yearbook, 1966–67, in author's possession; Marjorie Brandon interview, 1992.

26. Ken Brandon interview.

27. Marjorie Brandon interview, 1996.

28. Unita Blackwell interview, July 17, 1996.

29. Ibid.

30. Nate Jones interview; Julia Jones interviews, June 29, 1992; June 30, 1996; Marguerite Thompson interview, May 12, 1992.

31. *Port Gibson Reveille*, October 20 and 27, 1966; March 16, 1967; James Miller interviews, February 1994; December 21, 1994; Celia Anderson interview, April 14, 1992; Wells interview.

32. Barbara Sullivan interview, September 8, 1998.

33. James Miller interview, July 26, 1996.

34. This pattern of women's participation was repeated throughout the South and is becoming visible through the work of scholars explicitly exploring leadership and gender. They have offered new interpretations and analyses that are useful for seeing and understanding women's movement work and for exploring broad questions of leadership, gender, and successful social movement dynamics.

Bernice McNair Barnett, for example, used interviews and surveys with activists to identify and rank fifteen different types of work that women and men did in the civil rights movement. In this broad range of activities, she found, not surprisingly, that women and men often performed different tasks, and those done by women were typically less visible, rarely considered leadership, and generally undervalued. She concludes that women's invisibility involves a limited conception of leadership and argues for an expanded "multi-dimensional" definition of leadership. See Barnett, "Invisible Southern Black Women Leaders," 166, 172. Barnett's list of leadership roles in ranked order (of importance) is articulate/express concern and needs of followers; define/set goals; provide an ideology justifying action; formulate tactics and strategies; initiate action; mobilize/persuade followers; raise money; serve as an example to followers and leaders; organize/coordinate action; control group interactions (e.g., conflict); teach/educate/train followers and leaders; avoid alienating colleagues and followers; lead or direct action; generate publicity; obtain public sympathy and support.

Karen Sacks, in her study of a hospital-based union-organizing drive, makes similar arguments about the gendered basis of leadership. She found that men held the leadership positions of "public and solo speaker," while women were "centerpersons" who nurtured and politicized existing networks of friendship and kinship. Women "created the detail," "made people feel part" of the movement, and "did the menial work upon which things depended, while men made public pronouncements, confronted, and negotiated with management." She concludes that interpretations of successful grassroots movements that stress the relationship between a public orator and individuals fail to recognize the movement's complexity. She argues that social movements are "profoundly collective" and depend on an "interactive process among network members, centers, and spokespeople." See Sacks, *Caring by the Hour*, 120–21, 216.

In his groundbreaking study of civil rights organizing in Greenwood, Mississippi, Charles Payne builds on Sacks's work, making similar arguments about the gendered nature of women's leadership in the civil rights movement. He says women were particularly effective at organizing preexisting networks of family and friends and at performing the "everyday maintenance of the Movement." He also suggests that women's participation may have helped to "establish and maintain trust" and to make movement relationships "less competitive [and] more nurturing." He notes that at times "race women" (African American activists) have been more trusted than "race men" because "of the perception that women could not as easily capitalize off of their activism." See Payne, *I've Got the Light*, 275. See also Blumberg, "Women in the Civil Rights Movement," 135, 138.

Noting how, as Payne says, women's contributions have been "effectively devalued, sinking beneath the level of our sight," Payne, Barnett, and others show us how peeling back the layers or bringing an alternative perspective can expand and shift our understanding. See Payne, *I've Got the Light*, 276.

35. Barnett, "Invisible Southern Black Women Leaders," 172.

36. Nate Jones interview.

37. Guster interview.

38. Payne, *I've Got the Light*, 268.

39. Ladner, quoted in Greenberg, *Circle of Trust*, 143.

40. For more on women in SNCC and the MFDP, see, for example, Payne, *I've Got the Light*; Greenberg, *Circle of Trust*; Cynthia Griggs Fleming, *Soon We Will Not Cry: The Liberation of Ruby Doris Smith Robinson* (Lanham, Md.: Rowman & Littlefield, 1998); Joanne Grant, *Ella Baker: Freedom Bound* (New York: John Wiley & Sons, 1998); Chana Kai Lee, *For Freedom's Sake: The Life of Fannie Lou Hamer* (Urbana: University of Illinois press); Kay Mills, *This Little Light of Mine: The Life of Fannie Lou Hamer* (New York: Dutton, 1993); Barbara Ransby, "Ella J. Baker and the Black Radical Tradition (Civil Rights)" (PhD diss., University of Michigan, 1996).

Discovering What's Already There

Mississippi Women and Civil Rights Movements

J. TODD MOYE

In Mississippi, as in other states, women participated in civil rights movements in disproportionate numbers. To a greater degree than elsewhere, Mississippi women involved themselves in every facet of movement organizing,
from mimeographing broadsides to canvassing communities to directing community relief organizations and voter registration programs. As historian and
Port Gibson native Emilye Crosby makes clear in the preceding essay, early
scholars of civil rights history wrote almost exclusively about male leaders.[1] In
contrast, a new generation of scholarship on the Mississippi movement defines
leadership more broadly. These scholars find that women provided extensive
forms of leadership, sometimes just below the visible surface that was chron-
icled by contemporary journalists and many of the civil rights activists themselves. This scholarship also extends the chronological boundaries of the movement past the 1960s and finds that women shouldered an even heavier burden
of civil rights leadership in the Magnolia State movements of later years. In fact,
the portrait of civil rights organizing in Mississippi that has recently begun to
emerge places women at the center of the picture.[2]

New histories of the civil rights era also find that besides these female activists, other Mississippi women opposed, accommodated, or attempted to blunt
the effects of the movement. A few white Mississippi women were instrumental
in efforts to create truly interracial institutions, such as the struggle to build the
new Mississippi Democratic Party, and others were active in the fight to save
the state's public schools. The majority of white Mississippians, both female

CAMPAIGN HEADQUARTERS OF VICTORIA GRAY (ADAMS),
THE 1964 U.S. SENATE CANDIDATE FOR THE
MISSISSIPPI FREEDOM DEMOCRATIC PARTY
Courtesy of McCain Library and Archives, the University
of Southern Mississippi, Hattiesburg.

and male, however, resisted the black freedom struggle. They did so in part on grounds of sex and gender. They also used massive violence and daily coercion in an attempt to dissuade black women from asserting their citizenship rights. Many of the battles Mississippians fought under the banner of "civil rights" were as much about gender roles as they were about race.[3]

This essay, which draws heavily on the new literature on women and Mississippi civil rights movements, is not exhaustive. It focuses on a few areas in which women's leadership was obvious and crucial; it also suggests subjects for further research. The essay highlights two initiatives that emerged as part of Freedom Summer, the turning point of the Mississippi movement. These initiatives, the biracial Wednesdays in Mississippi program and the organization of the Mississippi Freedom Democratic Party (MFDP), attacked white supremacy in Mississippi from different directions and to varying degrees found ways to bring women together across racial lines. The essay also examines developments in the black freedom struggle after the national legislative successes of the mid-1960s. Because it focuses only on specific features of movement organizing and white resistance to the movement, the essay highlights only a few individual women whose experiences illustrate those particular aspects.

Mississippi became the proving ground for the young activists of the Student Nonviolent Coordinating Committee (SNCC) after that group's founding in 1960. Partly due to the primacy of SNCC among civil rights organizations in the state between 1962 and 1968, the era of greatest social change in Mississippi in the twentieth century, women participated more fully in civil rights activities in Mississippi than in any other state. SNCC fostered a radically egalitarian atmosphere in which staffers, volunteers, and "local people" all were allowed and even expected to question and debate the goals and strategies of the movement. Moreover, it created a movement culture in Mississippi in which the work of making people feel part of the civil rights struggle was as important to its success as the work of organizing campaigns or leading marches.

African American churchwomen in Mississippi had been doing the work of making people feel welcome in their churches and organizations for decades before SNCC arrived in Mississippi. Much of SNCC's success in the state can therefore be traced to its ability to tap into the southern black church's time-tested organizing strategies. Among other things, SNCC's organizing strategy moved traditional "women's work" into the public sphere.[4] SNCC's organizational "distaste for bureaucracy and hierarchy" opened doors to women that traditionally had been closed in other civil rights organizations. The organization's motto was "Let the People Decide." The young SNCC staffers who traveled to Mississippi were to identify potential leaders, help them develop organizing

skills, and then step back and let them lead. One such SNCC organizer, Ivan-
hoe Donaldson, likened his experience in uncovering nascent leaders like Mayersville's Unita Blackwell to that of Christopher Columbus when he "found"
America: "You're discovering what's already there."[5]

At the same time, SNCC activists tended to ignore or reject the labels that
stigmatized some individuals in society, essentially believing that anyone was
capable of redeeming himself or herself and the world at large. As a result, the
women who joined civil rights movements in Mississippi ran the gamut from
professionals to sharecroppers, from "mothers of the church" to self-described
"misfits." One of the "misfits," Ida Mae "Cat" Holland of Greenwood, was turning tricks as a prostitute the year she met Bob Moses of SNCC. He enlisted her
as a typist for his voter registration project, and Holland later looked upon
their serendipitous meeting as the turning point in her very successful life.
"Being treated with respect was something wholly new for me," she wrote. Jessie Divens of McComb recalled, "I always knew I was equal to everybody else,"
but it was only after SNCC activists entered her community that she began to act
on that knowledge. "To me, it was a revolution that had started . . . something I
had to be a part of or [else I would] just burst wide open."[6]

Because of its radically egalitarian culture, in which blacks and whites, men
and women lived in what one activist called "this new way" as equals, SNCC
included more women as workers on equal terms and as recognized leaders
than any of the other major civil rights organizations (even if it never operated
as democratically and gender neutrally as its proponents claimed). SNCC attracted a disproportionate number of headstrong men and women, "the most
independent-minded people you'll ever meet," in the words of another activist. Moreover, the women who debated responses to the oppression of African
Americans in time naturally raised questions about the oppression of women
in American society. Indeed, some historians have traced the roots of the modern feminist movement to a November 1964 SNCC retreat at Waveland, Mississippi, where white SNCC veterans Mary King and Sandra "Casey" Hayden provoked a discussion on gender roles in the organization. King and Hayden had
been inspired by black women leaders in the movement and recognized that
both black and white women faced discrimination from their male comrades
in the struggle.[7]

The multigenerational group of willful women who were attracted to SNCC
in Mississippi included Joyce Ladner of Palmer's Crossing. She identified herself as having descended from "a long line of . . . strong black women who historically never had allowed anyone to place limitations on them." Many of the

women in Ladner's generation who fought against the effects of racial discrimination and poverty in the 1950s and 1960s, however, did not see themselves
as members of a feminist vanguard. But in fighting racial concerns, African
American women *did* topple traditional expectations concerning how women
should behave. Some did so openly. As another SNCC organizer remembered,
when a pastor balked at opening his Mississippi Delta church to the movement,
the women of his church "threatened his fried chicken." The preacher knew
where the authority lay in that church, and he relented.[8]

Local women served as guides to the young civil rights organizers who canvassed Mississippi in the early 1960s. When Matt Suarez began organizing in
Canton, he found Annie Devine, a divorcée, an agent for the Security Life Insur-
ance Company, and a pillar of her community. "She directed us to blacks who
were trustworthy in the community, told us what blacks would do and what
they wouldn't," he remembered in a 1978 oral history interview. "In many ways,
she acted like a go-between with black, male leaders and young folks." When
Charles McLaurin moved into Ruleville, located in the center of the Delta, to
register voters, he needed a crash course on community dynamics to determine
whom he could and could not trust. He spent hours on the porch of a local
woman's convenience store learning the lay of the land. Because she could not
afford to be seen with McLaurin in broad daylight, the woman, whom McLaurin knew only as "Mrs. Anderson," sat just inside the doorway and lectured the
young man on the community's power relationships. McLaurin remembered
the experience as invaluable.[9]

When McLaurin did finally convince a small number of Ruleville residents
to travel to Indianola, the Sunflower County seat, to attempt to register to vote,
he made arrangements to meet the group in Ruleville and drive them to the
courthouse. The only three who showed up were elderly women. "They got out
of the car and went up the walk to the courthouse as if this was the long walk
that [led] to the Golden Gates of Heaven, their heads held high," he recalled. "I
stepped outside the door and waited, thinking how it was that these ladies who
have been victimized by white faces all of their lives would suddenly walk up
to the man and say, *I want to vote.* This did something to me." In reflecting on
what he had learned from the three women, McLaurin remembered the experience as "the day that I became a man."[10]

Donaldson, Suarez, McLaurin, and dozens of their counterparts "discovered"
literally hundreds of African American women in Mississippi. For all practical
purposes, women quietly wielded the balance of power in most of Mississippi's
African American congregations and other community institutions. Between

1962 and 1968, black churchwomen used the organizing skills and the power
they had consolidated in the course of doing "women's work" to transform their
communities. In several cases, as in that of Fannie Lou Hamer, they did so in
open defiance of male church "leaders." Historian Vicki Crawford has observed
that "male leadership dominated at the national and regional levels of the . . .
black freedom struggle," but "women's activism was strongest on the local level
where black women extended their roles within church communities and secu-
lar organizations to organize for political change." As Crawford implies, the
sea change in scholars' view of the roles that women played in the civil rights
movement has come about as historians have dug down to the grassroots level
of civil rights organizing during the movement's heyday.[11]

Changes swept through Mississippi remarkably quickly. In the early years
of civil rights organizing in Mississippi, roughly until 1962, women performed
what had traditionally been defined as "women's work" in their communities:
they fed volunteers, sold NAACP memberships, and sang at mass meetings. By
1968, Fannie Lou Hamer was running for office, leading a political faction in
the state Democratic Party, creating a cooperative farm, and giving speeches
around the country.

Hamer was by far the most prominent woman for whom SNCC provided a
platform. She was easily the most famous poor person in the country at the
time, but she was not alone. When local movements organized boycotts against
white merchants, as in Port Gibson, Natchez, Jackson, and Hattiesburg in the late
1960s, Indianola in 1986, and several other communities in the years in between,
men made the speeches, but women organized picket lines and transportation
to alternate shopping sites for the overwhelmingly female shoppers. Despite the
common popular understanding of the civil rights movement as nonviolent,
plenty of women in Mississippi also defended their homes with guns.[12]

The women who put their lives at risk to change Mississippi society had
counterparts who worked with equal vigor to maintain the status quo. White
Mississippians who fought to preserve segregation in the arena of public education did so ostensibly to "save" their daughters from young African American
men, and women were active in the effort. The men and women who represented themselves as the protectors of southern womanhood threatened sexually by African American males succeeded in convincing others to join them,
and their negative depiction of blacks struck chords outside Mississippi. Even
President Dwight Eisenhower defended the segregationists, saying, "These are
not bad people." He told Chief Justice Earl Warren, "All they are concerned
about is to see that their sweet little girls are not required to sit in school alongside some big overgrown Negroes."[13]

In 1953, State Representative Wilma Sledge warned a group of parents that the Supreme Court was going to desegregate their schools, and there was precious little that they could do about it. In response, Robert Patterson, a white Delta plantation manager, began organizing to save Mississippi's segregated school system. He created the Citizens' Council, which in time became the country's preeminent prosegregation operation. Wilma Sledge, who was regarded as being too passive in the face of interracial doom to suit men like Patterson, tried to play catch-up by championing the Citizens' Councils on the floor of the Mississippi House of Representatives. "The Citizens' Councils are a widespread group of local organizations composed of reliable white male citizens who believe that segregation is not discrimination and are organized for the sole purpose of maintaining segregation of the races," she said. "I am sure you will agree with me that such motives and methods are laudable, timely and impressive." Sledge's efforts went for naught, however, as she was soon replaced in the legislature by John Hough, a notoriously tough Sunflower County planter and leader in the councils movement.[14]

The councils spread rapidly throughout the state and most of the South. Membership in many of the councils from their inception was restricted to adult white men; the constitution of the Lowndes County Citizens' Council, for instance, reads: "The membership of the council shall consist of adult white male citizens." Even so, women's auxiliaries were active in communities throughout Mississippi.[15] After 1956, as the uproar over the U.S. Supreme Court's *Brown v. Board of Education* decision died down and men willing to become dues-paying members grew increasingly difficult to find, the statewide Citizens' Councils movement made a special effort to cultivate women activists. State Citizens' Councils director William Simmons encouraged local councils "to [bring] ladies into active, working membership" and advised, "Determined ladies will put backbone in some of your timid men." Still, women were not tapped for leadership positions in the councils. Citizens' Council women did not challenge traditional hierarchies or traditional gender roles but emphasized them and saw passing along racially orthodox values and behavior to the next generation as their role in the movement. "We women have an opportunity to do a job that is particularly ours: [teach] the children," wrote council member Janice Neill.[16]

Women segregationists like Neill and Florence Sillers Ogden, a sister of Mississippi's powerful speaker of the house Walter Sillers and an influential newspaper columnist whose articles appeared in Jackson and Greenville newspapers, worked to preserve Jim Crow by influencing what children read, a continuation of a tradition begun by the United Daughters of the Confederacy. In

1960, under Ogden's direction and with the support of the newly elected governor and staunch segregationist Ross Barnett, the state chapter of the Daughters of the American Revolution monitored the content of school textbooks in an effort to deny white students the chance to read that African Americans had ever done anything to advance themselves. Ogden cheered Barnett for "his leadership in helping keep our schools American."[17]

As director of the Citizens' Councils' youth activities division, Sarah McCorkle led that organization's efforts to remove from the state's textbooks any hint of racial equalitarianism. By the Citizens' Councils' estimate, she spoke over a span of eighteen months in 1958 and 1959 to students at every white high school in the state about "the dangers of integration." With money funneled by Barnett and the legislature from the state treasury to the Citizens' Councils, McCorkle and her volunteers scanned textbooks, encyclopedias, and documentary films to ensure that public-school students were not being exposed to integrationist themes. She made a minor media splash when she exposed "Playtime Farm," a mass-produced plastic play set used in some Mississippi schools, for featuring "a dark-skinned father and a white mother . . . [which represented] a subtle effort to promote integration." As active as they were, however, McCorkle and other women in the councils movement operated largely within traditional women's roles, speaking to PTAs and organizing essay contests.[18]

Other white women in the state worked to undermine Jim Crow. White churchwomen had organized the Association of Southern Women for the Prevention of Lynching in the early 1930s; at the organization's peak the Mississippi state council had more members than any other state. Mississippi churchwomen participated in various other racially liberal groups such as the Commission on Interracial Cooperation and Dorothy Rogers Tilly's Fellowship of the Concerned in the 1940s and 1950s. Several had their first interracial experiences at church functions outside the state and returned to Mississippi determined to break down the barriers of segregation.[19]

Not a Mississippian but a native of Athens, Georgia, Anne Firor Scott, the distinguished historian of American women, attended Lake Junaluska Methodist Assembly, a retreat facility in the western North Carolina mountains, in the late 1930s. There she first heard a black person deliver a speech to a white audience. Scott would later write about the work of southern Methodist women's groups to help African Americans and also to challenge Jim Crow segregation as early as 1901, efforts that she attributed to their commitment to the social gospel. Scott also learned and wrote about how the women's division of the Board of Missions and Church Extension of the Methodist Church commissioned attorney Pauli Murray to make the first full-scale study of segregation laws in all the states so that their members could know how best to challenge Jim Crow. What was originally designed as a pamphlet grew to a seven-hundred-plus-page manuscript published by the women's division that became a source for scholars and attorneys who planned the *Brown v. Board* suit.[20]

Such experiences inspired some white Mississippi women to work for change. Like thousands of other southern Methodist women, Betty Rogers Inis of New Albany remembered interacting with African Americans as equals for the first time in 1947 while traveling on a Methodist caravan in Texas. Inis would later work to create interracial opportunities for Mississippi college students. Historian Elizabeth Anne Payne of Nettleton attended a Lake Junaluska conference and had a similar experience as a teenager in 1959. Payne worked one summer while she was a student at Mississippi State College for Women as a lobbyist for the National Council of the Methodist Youth Fellowship in support of the 1964 Civil Rights Act.[21]

At the same time, other white women organized to discuss problems across racial lines in an effort to manage the changes they now knew were inevitable. A significant number of African American and white women made efforts at genuine cross-racial dialogue, if not actual integration, in Mississippi during Freedom Summer, a time when it was courageous for them to have done so. By 1964, Claire Collins Harvey of Jackson had distinguished herself as an especially capable organizer, and she capitalized on the presence of dozens of northern college students during Freedom Summer to build bridges to women outside the state. Harvey had founded Womanpower Unlimited, a Jackson-based grassroots movement, to meet the personal needs of the Freedom Riders who were arrested in Jackson in 1962 and sentenced to Parchman Penitentiary. Womanpower Unlimited would go on to organize a network of "freedom houses," safe places for civil rights workers who descended on the state, around the capital, and collaborated with other local civil rights organizations to register voters as early as 1962. By 1964, Harvey had devised the Chain of Friendship, an informal network of white women outside Mississippi who were interested in supporting women integrationists inside the state. Dorothy Height, president of the National Council of Negro Women (NCNW), and Polly Cowan, a white political activist and NCNW volunteer, built on Harvey's concept when they cofounded an organization called Wednesdays in Mississippi (WIMS) and targeted what Cowan called the "Cadillac crowd."[22]

WIMS sought the participation of upper-class women of both races whose participation would open doors in Mississippi and occasion great notice in their own communities. Cowan recruited renowned volunteers in the North under the assumption that "private citizens of stature and influences [would] make it known that they support[ed] the aspirations of the citizens of Mississippi for full citizenship, that they deplore[d] violence and that they [would] place themselves in tension-filled situations as a point of contact and communication to try to initiate both understanding and reconciliation." Many of Cowan's recruits had distinguished themselves as professional women; she chose others because they were married to powerful men. (Cowan's husband, Lou, had been a Columbia Broadcasting System executive.) At least one was a delegate to the Democratic National Committee. When the Council of Federated Organizations (COFO) planned to bring hundreds of white college students into Mississippi for the Freedom Summer project in 1964, Cowan arranged for her prominent northern volunteers to visit local Freedom Summer projects throughout the state and add to the storm of media coverage that focused national attention on inequities in Mississippi society. Several of the women, including Cowan, had children planning to join the Freedom Summer volunteers.[23]

Cowan and Height conceived of WIMS after attending a meeting in Atlanta of representatives of the NCNW, the YWCA, the National Council of Catholic Women, the National Council of Jewish Women, and United Church Women. Dorothy Rogers Tilly, a white native Georgian and longtime committed civil rights activist, spoke passionately at the meeting about the need for white southern women to look into the treatment of their black neighbors and "to see for themselves how the laws [were] being administered." So inspired, Claire Collins Harvey encouraged Height and Cowan to explore the possibility of creating a program whereby Mississippi women might host northern women who could come to the state to provide a "ministry of presence" during Freedom Summer. After traveling to Jackson to gauge the feasibility of such a program, Cowan wrote, "Not one woman" with whom she had met said, "'Don't come.' Many said, 'Try it. Try anything.'"[24]

WIMS brought biracial groups of women from northern cities together with women in Mississippi to discuss their "common ground and mutual concerns" and to visit with northern students who were in Mississippi as Freedom Summer volunteers. The visitors traveled as integrated teams but self-segregated once their airplanes landed in Mississippi. Cowan and Height arrived at this seemingly self-contradictory but ultimately practical strategy only after a great deal of discussion and soul searching. "We were careful not to offend the mores of the community by flaunting our own integration," Cowan wrote, but it was important to demonstrate that "women of both races" could travel and work "together as much of the time as was feasible." The elite women of WIMS sought incremental progress, not revolution. African American visitors stayed with black Mississippi families. Whites slept in hotels during their visits through most of the summer, but Cowan considered it "a sign of definite progress" when a few white Mississippi families volunteered to host visitors later in the course of the project. WIMS paired individual northern volunteers with southern women who shared a professional affiliation or membership in a sorority or volunteer interests.[25]

Mass-media outlets in Mississippi provided the state's citizens with drastically distorted reports of the civil rights movement within the state and outside it. If nothing else, the face-to-face meetings allowed a few Mississippi women a perspective on events that their newspapers and television stations had denied them. The WIMS volunteers met with about 150 Jackson white women, who "represented every shade of conviction from wholehearted segregationist to the most liberal integrationist," through the course of the summer. The northerners were astonished at how little knowledge their white hostesses had of the African Americans who lived in such close proximity. They found white Mississippians all too willing to believe the worst innuendo then in circulation about civil rights workers. These included rumors that the Freedom Summer volunteers were all Communists and sex-crazed miscegenists; that Michael Schwerner, James Chaney, and Andrew Goodman had staged their own disappearance in Neshoba County as a publicity stunt; and that all blacks carried venereal diseases. That they were able to counter those stories calmly and sensibly led at least to some of the incremental advances that WIMS had in mind. In the course of these conversations, the women explored topics that concerned all of them as citizens and as women. In some ways, the WIMS modus operandi amounted to "consciousness raising" before American feminists began using the term.[26]

It is difficult to assess the program's effect on the women involved, but Jessie Bryant Mosley, a black Jacksonian, remembered the WIMS experience as the first time in her community that "people were treating each other as people." Few if any white southerners appeared to have had a change of heart on racial matters based on the encounters, however, leading one northern participant to conclude: "The average Mississippi white person does not want change." The northerners also came away from the experience disappointed that middle-class black women were not doing more to further the civil rights movement in the state, though they certainly understood why. Still, the WIMS experience itself did at least force some white Mississippi women to confront their beliefs regarding race, and WIMS did identify at least a few women in the state who wanted to transform the "Closed Society," as University of Mississippi historian James W. Silver famously described the Magnolia State. When one white Jackson woman was forced at the last moment to retract an invitation to house a volunteer, she admitted to a WIMS staffer, "It's a crazy way to live. We're not free." She recognized that whites, too, lived drastically constrained lives behind the cotton curtain.[27]

The forty-eight northern women who participated in the project returned to their communities with eyewitness accounts of the situation in Mississippi and renewed commitments to work for social justice. They worked through their churches, college and university alumnae groups, social and professional clubs, and circles of friends to keep a national spotlight on Mississippi after the Freedom Summer project ended. They brought several Mississippi women into dialogue with the rest of the nation. A few of the Mississippi women who participated in the project worked afterward to liberalize their churches and community organizations, and some joined the fight to keep white families in the public schools. One participant, Kate Wilkinson, led two workshops for public-school teachers to prepare them for desegregation on the campus of the University of Mississippi in the summers of 1964 and 1965. "They could not have done this without meeting—through our teams—women who were already hard at work on these efforts" in other communities, Cowan reported.[28]

At the behest of WIMS Mississippi women, the NCNW again sponsored Wednesdays in Mississippi in the summer of 1965. Like other civil rights organizations active in the state, the NCNW altered its goals and strategies after Lyndon Johnson signed into law the Voting Rights Act of 1965. The goals of the WIMS program shifted again in 1966, when it changed its name to Workshops in Mississippi and began working to assist poor women of both races in their families' struggles against poverty. In contrast to many of the other "national" civil rights organizations, the NCNW remained active in the state, sponsoring Head Start and antipoverty programs well into the 1970s.

The initiative most noted for gender egalitarianism among Mississippi civil rights movements was also an offshoot of Freedom Summer and SNCC. Women participated in disproportionate numbers in the creation of the Mississippi Freedom Democratic Party (MFDP) and its challenge to the so-called Regular party delegates at the 1964 Democratic National Convention.[29]

In an effort to build upon the momentum of Freedom Summer and to expose the injustices of a political system that allowed Mississippi whites to exclude African Americans from the Democratic Party within their state with impunity, the COFO called for the organization of an alternative political party. Through the spring and summer, the "Freedom Democrats" shadowed the Democrats, holding their own precinct, district, and state conventions to select delegates to the Democratic National Convention in Atlantic City, which would convene that August. They did everything just as the Regular Mississippi Democrats did, with one important difference: the MFDP was open to everyone who supported the goals of the national Democratic Party. Largely because

SNCC built the MFDP from scratch and from the grassroots up, it too was more accessible to women. Historian Vicki Crawford found that the MFDP "created more expansive opportunities for female leadership and participation." As Emilye Crosby observes, the leadership women provided to the two organizations "gives us a sense of how women can respond in an open and receptive environment."[30]

The minutes of an MFDP meeting in Indianola, the seat of Sunflower County, document the significant role of women in the party's operations. The county's MFDP members, all of whom had been restricted from voting in Regular elections on account of their race but who nonetheless showed a remarkable understanding of the political party process, chose four women and four men to represent Sunflower County at upcoming district and state party conventions. They also elected twelve women to a sixteen-member executive committee. Women held a comparable number of statewide offices in the MFDP, and no other institution in Mississippi came close to matching its gender balance.[31]

The MFDP failed to achieve its immediate goal to win recognition as Mississippi's rightful delegation at the Atlantic City convention. Fearing that a televised walkout of Mississippi's all-white Regulars would doom the party for a generation in the previously solid Democratic South, Lyndon Johnson arranged a "compromise" by which the Democrats would seat the Regulars along with two hand-picked members of the MFDP. "Compromise" normally connotes an agreement arrived at through negotiation between two parties, but the MFDP was shut out of negotiations and had the solution chosen *for* them by national Democratic Party functionaries. (Characteristically, the party men determined that two males would represent the MFDP.) The rank and file of the party, with Fannie Lou Hamer as their spokesperson, rejected it. "We didn't come all this way for no two seats," Hamer famously declared. But MFDP members continued to engage the political process. They campaigned aggressively for the national party's ticket in Mississippi that fall, which was physically courageous in itself. Three members of the party, all women, kept it in the national spotlight with a challenge to the seating of Mississippi's delegation to the House of Representatives.[32]

Fannie Lou Hamer, Annie Devine, and Victoria Gray challenged the seating of the state's one Republican and four Democratic congressmen on the grounds that blatant discrimination against black would-be voters had made the 1964 election in the state unfair on its face. The Freedom Democrats surely would have lost even a fair vote, but the State of Mississippi had refused to place their names on the ballot. William Fitts Ryan (D-N.Y.), perhaps the most liberal member of the House, filed two motions to deny the seating of the Mississippi delegation, keeping Mississippi in the national spotlight for several months in

1965. The resulting public hearings provided a setting for Hamer, Devine, and Gray to expose Mississippi's overt voter discrimination once again. Gray captured the trio's feelings when she said, "We feel the time is ripe to begin to let people know that we're serious about this whole thing of becoming first-class citizens." The three ultimately failed in their bid to win seats in the House, but they did succeed in keeping the "Closed Society" in the minds of Americans at a time when the national news media would have been happy to move on from Mississippi.[33]

The MFDP would continue to press the national party to recognize the Freedom Democrats, and not the Regulars, as the true representatives of the party in Mississippi. A new coalition (the "loyalists") composed mostly of white moderates and liberals would eventually claim that mantle and win recognition from the party, but the MFDP's continued pressure did result in systemic changes in the way the national Democratic Party recognized state delegations, literally forcing southern delegations to integrate. In joining forces with the loyalists in time for the next national party convention, however, the MFDP also compromised its gender egalitarianism. Whereas a majority of MFDP delegates had been women in 1964, the "loyalists" sent an overwhelmingly male delegation to the 1968 Democratic National Convention in Chicago. Only four of the forty-two delegates were women, one of whom was the indomitable Hamer.[34]

The MFDP's "challenge concept," which had resulted in the Atlantic City demonstration and the contest for Mississippi's seats in the U.S. House, continued in the federal courts. Peggy Jean Connor of Hattiesburg, one of the cofounders of the MFDP and later its executive secretary, lent her name to the party's suit against Governor Paul Johnson Jr. *Connor v. Johnson*, initially filed in 1965, wound its way through the federal courts (including nine hearings before the U.S. Supreme Court) until 1979, when the Supreme Court ruled that Mississippi had malapportioned the state's population to dilute black voting strength and implemented a new plan that more closely met the ideal of one-person, one-vote. The *Connor* verdict had the practical effect of opening the statehouse to African American representatives for the first time.[35]

Mississippians who had been radicalized by the experience of Freedom Summer did not give up the fight when the college-student volunteers returned to the North and the national news media followed them. The civil rights movements they built in Mississippi after 1964 allowed women to assume leadership roles in even greater numbers. Women staffed, organized, and led the efforts in part because the issues they confronted had commonly been defined as women's issues and in part because they were now accustomed to and accepted in such roles.

Voter registration and political organizing continued to be major goals of civil rights activists in Mississippi, but for several years after Freedom Summer—arguably, to the present—public education became the preeminent civil rights issue. Members of Womanpower Unlimited publicized Jackson's school desegregation plan after federal U.S. District Court judge Sidney Mize decreed that the school system had to integrate in the fall of 1964. When forty-three African American children entered previously all-white Jackson schools, Womanpower members "adopted" several of the children and their families, providing everything from school supplies and food to a wheelchair in an effort to make the families' transitions smoother.[36]

The organization of Head Start centers throughout the state proceeded almost seamlessly from Freedom Summer's community organizing efforts. Women who had learned organizing skills from SNCC workshops and church activities now wrote grant applications and set up Head Start facilities in the buildings that had recently housed COFO Freedom Schools. They were advocates for the families whose children desegregated previously all-white schools fifteen and twenty years after the Supreme Court's *Brown* rulings. Winson Hudson, of the Harmony community in Leake County, was emblematic of the women who continued the civil rights struggle after 1964.[37]

As she recalled, Hudson got organized when the Leake County board of education attempted to close Harmony School, which she described as "our pride and the center of the community," in a consolidation plan. She became active in voter-registration efforts in the early 1960s and with her husband, Leroy Cleo Hudson, joined the Freedom Democratic Party. James Chaney lived in her home for three weeks in 1964; Hudson's sister Dovie hosted Michael Schwerner. The murders of Chaney, Schwerner, and Andrew Goodman shocked the people of Harmony and focused national attention on Mississippi during Freedom Summer.[38]

Hudson added to her agenda the issue of racial disparities in access to health care. By 1971, she had turned access to health care into a civil rights issue. She testified at the annual meeting of the American Hospital Association in Chicago: "There's not a single doctor in my county who will accept black Medicare or Medicaid patients, except the few they need to treat to get government money. We have more than 300 Head Start children in our county that we have to transport to other counties for treatment." Hudson became a national voice on behalf of the rural poor, testifying before presidential commissions during the Carter and Clinton administrations. Leake County children now receive care at the Winson G. Hudson Head Start Center in Carthage.[39]

As scholars have diverted their attention from "national" personalities to locally prominent figures like Winson Hudson, they have found that, rather than ending in the 1960s, civil rights struggles in Mississippi continued for decades. The Mississippi women who have received the most attention from the national media in the civil rights context in recent years, however, have been widows fighting for long-delayed justice for the killers of their husbands. In the 1990s, Myrlie Evers-Williams and Ellie Dahmer bore witness at the two most prominent of these spectacles, the trials of Byron de la Beckwith and Sam Bowers for the murders of Medgar Evers and Vernon Dahmer Sr., respectively.[40]

In 1998, Ellie Dahmer looked on as Sam Bowers, the former imperial wizard of the Ku Klux Klan in Mississippi, was tried for the fourth time for the 1966 murder of her husband, Vernon Dahmer Sr. Vernon and Ellie Dahmer had opened their Hattiesburg home to civil rights workers and made their business a headquarters for efforts to register black voters in Forrest County. It was the latter transgression that incensed Bowers. At the 1998 trial, former Klansmen testified that Bowers had assembled members of the Klan and demanded to know why "something hadn't been done" to terrorize the Dahmers. On January 10, 1966, they said, Bowers organized two carloads full of Klansmen, gasoline, and shotguns. The mob firebombed the Dahmer home and shot through the windows. Vernon Dahmer was able to return fire with his shotgun long enough to allow his wife and children to escape through the back door, but he was burned severely before he, too, escaped. He died from his injuries the next day.

Ellie Dahmer was determined to see Bowers convicted in 1998. He had previously been tried three times by the State of Mississippi and once in federal court for his involvement in Dahmer's murder. The 1968 and 1969 trials had resulted in hung juries; in 1998 newly released documents from the Mississippi State Sovereignty Commission indicated that Bowers and the Klan had tampered with the jurors, all of whom were white. (Bowers did serve six years for a federal conspiracy conviction resulting from his role in the 1964 murders of Chaney, Schwerner, and Goodman.) "This is a terrible thing we have to remember," Ellie Dahmer told a reporter at the 1998 trial. "But we've been preparing ourselves for 37 years, trying to get here." This time, the jury voted to convict.[41]

As the recent prosecutions of the murderers of Dahmer, Evers, Schwerner, Chaney, and Goodman indicate, the civil rights movement continues in Mississippi, even as Mississippians persist in contesting its meanings. Many Mississippians now boast that thousands of African Americans have won elected office since the passage of the 1965 Voting Rights Act, and as of 2001, Mississippi had more black elected officials than any other state in the union. Less noticed, but just as significant, many of these elected officials are women. Indeed, one of the most substantive changes in southern politics in the last generation has been the dramatic increase in the number of black women in office.[42]

Like Unita Blackwell, the Mayersville woman whom civil rights workers "discovered," and who was later elected to several terms as the town's mayor, Ellie Dahmer participated in the revolution.[43] Those who followed news accounts of the 1998 Bowers trial might have thought Ellie Dahmer was a tenacious widow but that this was the extent of her public role. In reality, after the murder of her husband, Dahmer had continued her family's decades-long work to register African American voters. After retiring from her career as a teacher in the public schools, she was twice elected to the Forrest County election commission in the 1990s. Her work to register new voters helped to diversify the county's voter rolls by 1998. As a result, the jury drawn from these rolls that decided the fate of Sam Bowers was much more representative of the community than were those that had allowed him to walk free. The 1998 panel was composed of five whites, one Asian American, and six blacks.

Mississippi women like Blackwell, Dahmer, and thousands of others can point to concrete examples of such successes in their communities, the results of difficult and in many cases decades-long civil rights work. Born into a society that expected less than full civic participation of them because they were black and because they were female, they have instead contributed fully to the revolutionary reform of Mississippi society that has taken place over the last half century.

NOTES

1. Emilye Crosby, "'The Lady Folk Is a Doer': Women and the Civil Rights Movement in Claiborne County, Mississippi," in *Stepping Forward: Black Women in Africa and the Americas*, ed. Catherine Higgs, Barbara A. Moss, and Earline Rae Ferguson (Athens: Ohio University Press, 2002), 190.

2. The new generation of scholarship touching on issues of gender in the Mississippi movement is best represented by Charles Payne, *I've Got the Light of Freedom: The Organizing Tradition and the Mississippi Freedom Struggle* (Berkeley: University of California Press, 1995), and includes, among others, John Dittmer, *Local People: The Struggle for Civil Rights in Mississippi* (Urbana: University of Illinois Press, 1994); Emilye Crosby, *A Little Taste of Freedom: The Black Freedom Struggle in Claiborne County, Mississippi* (Chapel Hill: University of North Carolina Press, 2005); Steve Estes, *I Am a Man!: Race, Manhood, and the Civil Rights Movement* (Chapel Hill: University of North Carolina Press, 2005); and Tiyi Morris, "Local Women and the Civil Rights Movement in Mississippi: Re-visioning Womanpower United," in *Groundwork: Local Black Freedom Movements in America*, ed. Jeanne Theoharris and Komozi Woodward (New York: New York University Press, 2005), 193–214.

3. For women in the white resistance movement, see Estes, *I Am a Man!* 46–50, and Elizabeth Gillespie McRae, "White Womanhood, White Supremacy, and the Rise of Massive Resistance," in *Massive Resistance: Southern Opposition to the Second Reconstruction*, ed. Clive Webb (New York:

Oxford University Press, 2005), 181–202. For highly personal accounts of what happened to white women who empathized with the black freedom struggle, see, for example, Florence Mars with Lynn Eden, *Witness in Philadelphia* (Baton Rouge: Louisiana State University Press, 1977); Hodding Carter, *So the Heffners Left McComb* (New York: Doubleday, 1965). For the importance of violence used against women activists and the effects it had on them, see Chana Kai Lee, *For Freedom's Sake: The Life of Fannie Lou Hamer* (Urbana: University of Illinois Press, 1999).

4. For the importance of SNCC's "movement culture," see Payne, *I've Got the Light*, 265–83; and J. Todd Moye, *Let the People Decide: Black Freedom and White Resistance Movements in Sunflower County, Mississippi, 1945–1986* (Chapel Hill: University of North Carolina Press, 2004), 33–36.

5. Payne, *I've Got the Light*, 268; Donaldson quoted in Lynne Olson, *Freedom's Daughters: The Unsung Heroines of the Civil Rights Movement from 1830 to 1970* (New York: Scribner, 2001), 251.

6. Endesha Ida Mae Holland, *From the Mississippi Delta: A Memoir* (New York: Simon & Schuster, 1997), 204–10; Divens quoted in Olson, *Freedom's Daughters*, 203.

7. SNCC organizer Casey Hayden repeatedly used the term "new way" of living when describing SNCC culture. "The most independent-minded" description is Joyce Ladner's. See Cheryl Lynn Greenberg, ed., *A Circle of Trust: Remembering SNCC* (New Brunswick, N.J.: Rutgers University Press, 1998), 132–36, 143. See also Dittmer, *Local People*, 331–32; Sara Evans, *Personal Politics: The Roots of Women's Liberation in the Civil Rights Movement and the New Left* (New York: Random House, 1979); Mary King, *Freedom Song: A Personal Story of the 1960s Civil Rights Movement* (New York: William Morrow, 1988).

8. Joyce Ladner quoted in Greenberg, *Circle of Trust*, 142–43. The "fried chicken" memory is recorded in Charles Cobb, oral history interview with John Rachal, October 21, 1996, University of Southern Mississippi Center for Oral History and Cultural Heritage, Hattiesburg.

9. Suarez quoted in Vicki Crawford, "African American Women in the Mississippi Freedom Democratic Party," in *Sisters in the Struggle: African-American Women in the Civil Rights–Black Power Movement*, ed. Bettye Collier-Thomas and V. P. Franklin (New York: New York University Press, 2001), 127; McLaurin quoted in Moye, *Let the People Decide*, 103.

10. Charles McLaurin, "To Overcome Fear" [report to SNCC headquarters], ca. 1964, SNCC Papers, box 104, Martin Luther King, Jr. Center for Nonviolent Social Change Library and Archives, Atlanta, Georgia (henceforth cited as MLKL).

11. Crawford, "African American Women," 121–38, quotes on 121. For Hamer's defiance of black ministers, see Tracy Sugarman, *Stranger at the Gates: A Summer in Mississippi* (New York: Hill & Wang, 1966), 120–21.

12. Crosby, "Lady Folk Is a Doer," 194. There is now an overwhelming amount of anecdotal evidence from oral histories with movement participants suggesting that the majority of participants did not adhere to the philosophy of nonviolence, as has previously been supposed. See especially Akinyele K. Umoja, "1964: The Beginning of the End of Nonviolence in the Mississippi Freedom Movement," *Radical History Review* 85 (Winter 2003): 201–26.

13. Earl Warren, *The Memoirs of Earl Warren* (New York: Doubleday, 1977), 291.

14. Sledge quoted in *Southern School News*, October 1, 1954, 9. See also Moye, *Let the People Decide*, 64–73, 85.

15. Citizens Councils/Civil Rights Collection, box 1, McCain Library and Archives, University of Southern Mississippi, Hattiesburg.

16. Simmons and Neill quoted in the *Citizens Council* [newspaper], November 1956 and February 1957.

17. For Ogden, see McRae, "White Womanhood," 181–202. For the efforts of the United Daughters of the Confederacy, see Karen Cox, *Dixie's Daughters: The United Daughters of the Confederacy and the Preservation of Confederate Culture* (Gainesville: University Press of Florida, 2003).

18. Neil McMillen, *The Citizens Councils: Organized Resistance to the Second Reconstruction, 1954–64* (Urbana: University of Illinois Press, 1971, 1994), 241–42.

19. For Mississippi churchwomen and the Association of Southern Women for the Prevention of Lynching, see Caroline Herring, "The Mississippi Council of the Association of Southern Women for the Prevention of Lynching" (MA thesis, University of Mississippi, 1999); Jacquelyn Dowd Hall, *Revolt against Chivalry: Jessie Daniel Ames and the Women's Campaign against Lynching* (New York: Columbia University Press, 1993). For Tilly, see Edith Holbrook Riehm, "Dorothy Rogers Tilly and the Fellowship of the Concerned," in *Throwing Off the Cloak of Privilege*, ed. Gail S. Murray (Gainesville: University Press of Florida, 2004).

20. See Anne Firor Scott, *The Southern Lady: From Pedestal to Politics, 1830–1930* (Chicago: University of Chicago Press, 1970), 143–45; Scott, ed., *Pauli Murray and Caroline Ware: Forty Years of Letters in Black and White* (Chapel Hill: University of North Carolina Press, 2006), 44; letter from Anne Firor Scott to the author, October 26, 2008. See also Pauli Murray, *States' Laws on Race and Color, and Appendices: Containing International Documents, Federal Laws and Regulations, Local Ordinances and Charts* (Cincinnati: Women's Division of Christian Service, Board of Missions and Church Extension, Methodist Church, 1950).

21. Betty Rogers Inis, interviewed by Elizabeth Anne Payne, September 8, 2005, in *Makin' Do: The North Mississippi Women's History Project*, Department of History, University of Mississippi, Oxford, http//www.outreach.olemiss.edu/media/documentary/women_history/main.html (accessed November 13, 2006); letter from Elizabeth Anne Payne to Todd Moye, November 13, 2006.

22. For Harvey and Womanpower Unlimited, see "Her Dream Has Moved Back to Home Town," *Jackson Daily News*, April 30, 1975, Claire Collins Harvey Papers, Mississippi Department of Archives and History, Jackson (henceforth cited as MDAH); and Morris, "Local Women," 193–97. For the creation of WIMS, see Polly Cowan to Lee White, November 24, 1964, including "Preliminary Report: Wednesdays in Mississippi," General Human Rights files, box 39, Lyndon B. Johnson Library, Austin, Texas. See also Kate Wilkinson, "A Sociological Analysis of an Action Group: Wednesdays in Mississippi" (MA thesis, University of Mississippi, 1966); Dorothy Height, *Open Wide the Freedom Gates: A Memoir* (New York: Public Affairs, 2003), 167–99.

23. Cowan, "Preliminary Report."

24. Ibid.

25. Ibid.; Polly Cowan, "Wednesdays in Mississippi," *Church Woman* (Fall 1964).

26. Cowan, "Preliminary Report." For the importance of the media blackout of civil rights news in Mississippi, see Charles Cobb, "Some Notes on Education" (ca. 1963), SNCC Papers, box 104, MLKL; Kay Mills, *Changing Channels: The Civil Rights Case That Transformed Television* (Jackson: University Press of Mississippi, 2004); Steven D. Classen, *Watching Jim Crow: The Struggles over Mississippi TV, 1955–1969* (Durham, N.C.: Duke University Press, 2004).

27. "Personal Style: Jessie Mosley," *Jackson Clarion-Ledger*, June 30, 1991, Jessie Mosley Papers, MDAH; James W. Silver, *Mississippi: The Closed Society* (New York: Harcourt Brace, 1964); Cowan, "Preliminary Report."

28. "Proposal to Establish Program in Social Work," Records of Department of Sociology and Anthropology, 1970, University of Mississippi, Oxford (the author thanks Freda Knight for providing this document); Cowan, "Preliminary Report."

29. Strangely, the history of the Mississippi Freedom Democratic Party has not yet received a book-length treatment. See, however, Vanessa Lynn Davis, "'Sisters and Brothers All': The Mississippi Freedom Democratic Party and the Struggle for Equality" (PhD diss., Vanderbilt University, 1996); Michael Paul Sistrom, "'Authors of the Liberation': The Mississippi Freedom Democrats and the Redefinition of Politics" (PhD diss., University of North Carolina–Chapel Hill, 2002); Rachel Reinhard, "Politics of Change: The Emergence of a Black Political Voice in Mississippi" (PhD diss., University of California–Berkeley, 2005).

30. Crawford, "African American Women," 135; Crosby, "Lady Folk Is a Doer," 201.

31. "Sunflower County [MFDP] Meeting, August 1, 1964," MFDP Papers, box 20, MLKL.

32. See John Dittmer, "The Transformation of the Mississippi Movement, 1964–1968: The Rise and Fall of the Freedom Democratic Party," in *Essays on the American Civil Rights Movement*, ed. W. Marvin Dulaney and Kathleen Underwood, Walter Prescott Webb Memorial Lectures 26 (College Station: Texas A&M University Press, 1993), 9–43; Kay Mills, *This Little Light of Mine: The Life of Fannie Lou Hamer* (New York: Plume, 1993); Leslie McLemore, "The Mississippi Freedom Democratic Party" (PhD diss., University of Massachusetts, Amherst, 1971); William Simpson, "The Birth of the Mississippi 'Loyalist' Democrats," *Journal of Mississippi History* 44, no. 1 (February 1982): 27–45.

33. See Mills, *This Little Light of Mine*, chap. 8, pp. 145–71; Chana Kai Lee, *For Freedom's Sake: The Life of Fannie Lou Hamer* (Urbana: University of Illinois Press, 1999), 69–84; Gray quoted in Mills, *This Little Light of Mine*, 94.

34. For a list of the 1968 delegates, see *Jackson Clarion-Ledger*, August 12, 1968.

35. See Frank R. Parker, *Black Votes Count: Political Empowerment in Mississippi after 1965* (Chapel Hill: University of North Carolina Press, 1990), 85–91.

36. Morris, "Local Women," 206.

37. For the battles that Mississippi women fought to make the Brown decision a reality, see Constance Curry, *Silver Rights* (Chapel Hill: Algonquin Books, 1995); Winson Hudson and Constance Curry, *Mississippi Harmony: Memoirs of a Freedom Fighter* (New York: Palgrave Macmillan, 2002); Charles Bolton, *The Hardest Deal of All: The Battle over School Integration in Mississippi, 1870–1980* (Jackson: University Press of Mississippi, 2005).

38. Hudson and Curry, *Mississippi Harmony*, 33.

39. Ibid., 96–97.

40. See, for example, "Hard Memories in Mississippi: Families of Klan Victims Share Bond of Grief at Murder Trial," *Atlanta Journal-Constitution*, June 17, 2005; Myrlie Evers-Williams with William Peters, *For Us, the Living* (New York: Doubleday, 1967); Willie Morris, *The Ghosts of Medgar Evers: A Tale of Race, Murder, Mississippi and Hollywood* (New York: Random House, 1998).

41. See "Racial Slaying: New Trial Reopens Bitter Era," *Atlanta Journal-Constitution*, August 17, 1998; "Jurors Convict Former Wizard in Klan Murder," *New York Times*, August 22, 1968. See also Ellie Dahmer, oral history interview with Orley B. Caudill, July 2, 1974, University of Southern Mississippi Center for Oral History and Cultural Heritage, Hattiesburg.

42. See, for example, David A. Bositis, "Black Elected Officials: A Statistical Summary, 2001," Joint Center for Political and Economic Studies, http://www.jointcenter.org/publications1/publication-PDFs/BEO-pdfs/2001-BEO.pdf (accessed April 14, 2006).

43. See Unita Blackwell with Joanne Prichard Morris, *Barefootin': Lessons from the Road to Freedom* (New York: Crown, 2006).

In the Mainstream

Mississippi White Women's Clubs in the Quest for Women's Rights in the Twentieth Century

MARTHA H. SWAIN

According to conventional wisdom, Mississippi women's clubs and associations lagged far behind women's organizations nationwide in the struggle for women's rights. To the contrary, organized women in the state have been no more progressive or regressive than women in most states, if seen in the light of national trends. Like many women elsewhere, for almost three-quarters of a century Mississippians did not identify women's rights as dependent upon passage of an equal rights amendment. Rather, they have defined women's rights as equal access to education, safeguards for mothers and infants, improved sanitation and health care, and fair workplace treatment.

Such were the goals of the Mississippi Federation of Women's Clubs (MFWC), the American Association of University Women (AAUW), and the Business and Professional Women (BPW), whose members could be considered "mainstream." However, any account of the fate of the Equal Rights Amendment (ERA) in Mississippi requires attention to its early championship by the National Woman's Party in Mississippi in the 1920s and the later opposition of the Women for Constitutional Government after 1972.

The impetus for cohesiveness among early women's literary and culture clubs in some states was the planning for the Women's Pavilion at the Chicago World's Fair (Columbian Exposition) in 1893. In Mississippi, however, the state legislature, constrained by economic depression, denied appropriations for the state's representation in Chicago. Thus members of the nascent club movement in Mississippi had no opportunity to witness the initiatives of the Chicago Women's Club and similar groups outside the South that had already

STARKVILLE BUSINESS AND PROFESSIONAL WOMEN'S
(BPW) CLUB AT FORUM ON EQUAL RIGHTS AMENDMENT,
MISSISSIPPI STATE UNIVERSITY, 1978

From BPW Scrapbook, 1978–79, Starkville BPW Records.

Courtesy of Special Collections, Mitchell Memorial Library,

Mississippi State University, Starkville.

undertaken progressive reforms to protect women's and children's health and welfare.[1]

Reference to federated clubs in Mississippi is absent in standard histories, but the histories of the clubs themselves briefly tell the story.[2] In 1898, representatives from six clubs convened in Kosciusko to form the MFWC. In 1904, the group, which then included more than twenty clubs, affiliated with the fifteen-year-old national General Federation.[3]

"Clubwomen" have often been portrayed as portly matrons given to vacuous causes. One Mississippi woman wrote, "No group has been more ridiculed and caricatured than the clubwomen, yet no group has contributed more vitality and variety to the cultural scene in this country. . . . They have prodded and pushed men into action for civic community." Federated clubs have contributed womanpower and dollars to establishing local libraries, sanitation systems, and playgrounds; clubwomen have promoted art, kindergartens, forest conservation and state parks, and more humane treatment of juvenile offenders.[4] In times of crisis, the Mississippi federation has assisted women and their families, cooperated with the Red Cross during the great flood of 1927, and sponsored local work-relief projects for women during the Great Depression.[5]

Historians of the General Federation of Women's Clubs (GFWC) have determined that in the decades before ratification of the woman suffrage amendment in 1920, women's clubs were more feminist minded than in the years that followed.[6] Like the GFWC, the Mississippi federation in its early years gave considerable attention to expanding women's opportunities. In 1910, Ellen Sullivan Woodward explored the question, "Is Woman's Invasion a Fad," at the Fortnightly Club in Louisville. In view of the subsequent experience of many clubwomen in public life, the question was not merely rhetorical. In New Albany, Daisy Rogers, a future officer of the Mississippi Suffrage Association, was a charter member of the Twentieth Century Club, which in December 1913 discussed *Hagar*, Mary Johnston's suffrage novel, and held discussions on "Votes for Women."[7]

The MFWC early focused on expanding women's educational opportunities. When graduate programs were not offered or open to women faculty in Mississippi colleges and universities, the MFWC scholarships sent them out of state. Martha Eckford, who studied biology in New York, and Mable Ward, who studied home economics in Massachusetts, held long tenures at the Industrial Institute and College in Columbus. The MFWC also improved educational opportunities within the state, for example, the establishment of the State Normal College in Hattiesburg.[8] From its beginning, the MFWC insisted that quality education was a woman's right. In subsequent years, it also lobbied for faculty salary parity at the Industrial Institute and College, later Mississippi State College for Women (MSCW). Similarly the federation fought for equal pay for women public-school teachers, though it never completely succeeded. The federation did, however, manage to prevent legislative appropriations cuts to MSCW in the 1920s.[9]

At the end of World War I, MFWC members returned to the promotion of woman suffrage under its last wartime president, Mrs. B. I. (Janie) Saunders, who presided over the "Peace Convention" in 1919 and remained president until 1920. In those years, many clubwomen worked to persuade the Mississippi legislature to ratify the Nineteenth Amendment. In November 1919, a remnant of the Mississippi Suffrage Association joined the MFWC in convention, where delegates voted to ratify with only one dissenting ballot, and in January 1920 members lobbied the legislature for twelve days.[10]

Frustrated suffrage advocates witnessed a resounding defeat by the House of Representatives. Saunders described the scene to her club: "I saw the maneuvering," she said. "Even women can learn a great deal about practical politics if they sit in the legislative galleries a few days and keep their eyes open." She spoke of the foundation of the state League of Women Voters "laid during [their] stay in Jackson" and noted the invaluable experience women had gained in their legislative campaign, "knowledge [they must] pass on and to bear fruit."[11] She could not anticipate the irony of her remarks: in the next biennial legislative session, it would be her new League of Women Voters that would stand in the way of an advanced call for women's rights.

The first major clash among women's organizations in Mississippi arose after the 1920 suffrage victory. The National Woman's Party (NWP) and the League of Women Voters (LWV) were most visibly adversarial, and to a lesser extent the federated women's clubs entered the fray. Unlike the MFWC, however, neither the NWP nor the LWV was easily organized in the state because suffrage leaders such as Nellie Nugent Somerville expressed open hostility. Somerville, like other former leaders of the National American Woman Suffrage Association (NAWSA), resented the NWP's claim that it had played a more crucial part than the NAWSA in obtaining suffrage. To Somerville, the nonpartisan stance of the LWV was detrimental to the Democratic Party's continued success and diverted women's activism from partisan politics, which she viewed as the avenue to real power.[12]

Janie Saunders emerged as first president of the Mississippi LWV soon after the NAWSA became the League of Women Voters in 1919. Although Saunders assumed the presidency of the Mississippi league, the organization existed only in skeletal form until national organizers created local leagues in larger towns.

It was slow going for LWV national organizer Liba Peshakova as she met with groups around the state. She found a "prevalent feeling among women as well as men that the League was militant, aggressive and a political party." Matters changed as she continued to meet with women's groups, thanks to Jackson president Mrs. Henry Yerger, "a brilliant woman and enthusiastic worker" whose position as women's editor of the *Jackson Clarion-Ledger* and as Jackson correspondent for the *Memphis Commercial Appeal* assured favorable reports.[13] The Jackson league began to grow, and by the first state convention in November 1921, the leagues counted 250 Mississippi members in Greenwood, Columbus, and Brookhaven.[14] Ironically, Peshakova could not organize Clarksdale, where Minnie Brewer published the *Woman Voter*, considered to be the official organ of the Mississippi league.[15]

The NWP had less success in Mississippi. An early clash between clubwomen and the NWP centered on the latter's attempt to pass its so-called blanket bill. The NWP had evolved between 1913 and 1916, led by Alice Paul and others displeased by the NAWSA's leadership. Influenced by English suffragettes, whose tactics were more militant than the NAWSA's, the NWP soon alienated mainstream women's groups. Tensions continued in the years following the suffrage victory, when NWP leaders turned immediately to drafting an equal rights amendment to the Constitution, which the LWV and the GFWC opposed as a threat to the hard-won protective legislation women had achieved during the Progressive Movement era.[16] The NWP sought to have its "blanket bill" adopted state by state before passage of a federal amendment. As an interim panacea, the bill would free states to remove all remaining legislative restrictions on women: provisions that denied jury service, dictated domicile, forbade use of maiden names, denied freedom of contract, and discriminated in child custody and postdivorce earnings.[17]

Only Wisconsin adopted the blanket bill at the state level, but the controversy significantly affected the Mississippi LWV and MFWC. The NWP had first recruited in Mississippi in 1917 with little success.[18] Recruiter Anita Pollitzer reported from Jackson to Alice Paul, "This is the most tightly sot town we've yet struck and you have to speak and speak before anyone makes any motion of joining or approving." Appalled by the character and politics of powerful men whom the clubwomen were compelled to support, she reported, "The men they fall at the feet of are *such* terrible specimens."[19]

The MFWC presented to the legislature a limited agenda that avoided the issue of an equal rights amendment. The LWV managed to have national president Maud Wood Park deliver an anti–blanket bill address to the legislature. She asked only that the lawmakers endorse a bill that most former suffragists, excluding the NWP, had made their national legislative agenda centerpiece. The federal Sheppard-Towner Maternal and Infancy Act of 1921 would allow the state to share in federal funds—initially ten thousand dollars—for maternal and infant care.[20]

The ineffectiveness and extreme deafness of Ellen Crump, the only woman whom NWP national leaders could draft to be nominal head of the Mississippi party, led the national headquarters to dispatch Isabelle Kindig Gill to lobby in Jackson. She confided to Alice Paul that the LWV was "an effective political machine [with] a constructive moderate program," while the NWP was viewed as "a vague, invisible, unpopular" organization.[21] As expected, the blanket bill went down in resounding defeat.[22]

Additional animosity in Mississippi between the NWP and the LWV surfaced in 1922 over credit for legislation that both had supported, an equal guardianship law extending equal parental rights to mothers regarding the custody, services, and earnings of their children. Although the NWP claimed credit for passage, the bill had been drafted by the national LWV, introduced through Yerger, and passed unopposed. Mississippi was the second southern state to enact such a law, and the federated clubs attributed the accomplishment—as well as the victory in securing legislative appropriation for the Sheppard-Towner program—to the league. The LWV also won in 1922 an appropriation for MSCW larger than that for the University of Mississippi.[23] Mississippi native Burnita Shelton Matthews, legal counsel for the NWP in Washington, drafted a bill to open jury service to women. She periodically sent the proposal to the legislature throughout the 1920s, but it was given short shrift. Mississippi was not unusual; even by the mid-1930s, women were denied jury service in half of the then forty-eight states.[24]

In reality, the NWP never gained a Mississippi following of more than a dozen members. Only an occasional notice—the last in 1944—from Ellen Crump appeared in the NWP's publication *Equal Rights*. Crump had not underestimated herself when she demurred in 1921, "I do not feel very confident of my abilities."[25] Writing in 1926, a LWV leader surmised, "If the Woman's Party is here it is certainly keeping undercover."[26]

The LWV also experienced many early challenges. In 1922, Jeffries Heinrich, the LWV's southern regional secretary, wrote that past state president Janie Saunders had confessed, "Mississippi is hopeless," with Jackson the only place where "the League has kept together at all." Mississippi, she reported, "is going to be a hard nut to crack."[27] Heinrich further lamented that the head of the league in Greenwood was also the state women's organizer for the Ku Klux Klan. At the national Democratic convention in 1924 she had pinned camellias—symbolic of KKK women—on convention delegates. Heinrich also feared that Mississippi women would not follow an organization based on nonpartisanship in a state where all meaningful political action took place within the Democratic Party. The LWV also had to compete with the citizenship department of the MFWC, whose members confronted the LWV with "a great deal of hostility." Even more discouraging, Heinrich noted, "Some of the women still feel it is degrading to vote."[28]

For unknown reasons, the Mississippi LWV revived and in April 1927 reaffiliated with the national league, which claimed branches in five towns.[29] The Mississippi league prioritized continuation of the Sheppard-Towner Act. In the area of maternal health, the Mississippi LWV focused on registration and instruction of midwives, who delivered half of Mississippi's babies.[30]

Within a year, the Mississippi LWV faced another leadership crisis when the chair of its Legal Status of Women department, state representative Pauline Alston Clark, was too busy to promote the league program. Furthermore, she wrote, "Our state is not organized and the women as a rule are afraid of politics. . . . They do not seem inclined to join the League." From her lawmaker's perspective, she observed, "The legislators do not like women lobbyists."[31]

Women's organizations that focused on social reform, including the GFWC and the LWV, were victims of the "Spider Web" conspiracy that targeted them as "socialistic or even worse as communistic." Whether or not red-baiting caused Mississippi women's organizations to retreat from reform, by 1930 membership nationally had declined in both the LWV and the GFWC. Also, the movement of national offices of both organizations toward decentralized decision making left state affiliates without effective leadership.[32]

In 1929, a regional LWV director reported that the Mississippi league was "very small" but contained "the germ of something very good." Her prediction seemed fulfilled when the state league convened in May 1931, but by that time it focused principally on preventing war, a topic that consumed the interests of most women's organizations of the day. Nonetheless, the skeletal Mississippi LWV ambitiously listed child-labor reform, maternity and infancy hygiene, jury service for women, women's representation on the state textbook committee, and public employment for women as topics for the legislature's continuing study and action.[33]

By 1935, national LWV membership had fallen to a new low. Studies of the LWV point to recruiting difficulties in most states, and in Mississippi, as a member reported to the national office, "It is hard to find people whose interest does not wane when the newness is worn off."[34] One scholar suggests that the small Mississippi league continued to hold together, but "whatever the reason, the

League in Mississippi did not participate in shaping national issues from 1930 to 1950."[35]

Inexplicably, no Mississippi records for 1930–46 exist in the national LWV papers except for scattered correspondence. Perhaps demands for partisan political activity by the state's predominantly Democratic women in presidential elections from 1928 through 1952 depleted membership, or maybe the Great Depression took its toll. The experience of the LWV in the 1920s described by Nancy Cott of "competing with women's partisan activity as much as preparing women for it" undoubtedly continued until midcentury. The evolving thought of Lucy Somerville Howorth, an appointee of President Franklin D. Roosevelt, provides a clue. In the early 1920s, she chaired the Mississippi league's Committee on Industry. Later she left the LWV when she became a vibrant Democratic partisan and described it as too much a "studious, lady-like group that wouldn't really tangle."[36]

Still, there was reason for optimism. When national LWV field workers came South to reorganize after World War II, they found a new cadre of women eager to reinstate the league in Mississippi. "I was impressed by the group that gathered last night—a cross-section as to age and highly intelligent," wrote national LWV organizer Jeanne Blythe after a 1946 visit to Jackson. A year later, she lamented that the Jackson league was "adamant that they [would] not accept a negro applying for membership." She was told it would be "foolish" to attempt to organize in the state "unless [they were] willing to accept the situation down here." Evidently the national league was willing.[37]

Orell Pitard, recent state president of the federated clubs, and Mrs. Hubert Lipscomb spearheaded the new LWV in Jackson, while a Greenville league was organized by women Blythe described as "intellectuals, liberal and possessing a deep social consciousness." "Everyone knows everyone in Mississippi," national organizer Rae Horner reported, which may have accounted for the development of strong leagues outside Jackson. In the early 1950s, local leagues developed in Bay St. Louis, Pass Christian, Gulfport, and Natchez. Under the competent leadership of state presidents Laurie Ratcliffe (1952–53) and Aline Powers Fisher (1953–57), a revitalized and influential Mississippi LWV, despite membership that peaked at only 510, concentrated on voting reform and jury service.[38]

By 1960, however, the Mississippi LWV had devolved in disarray over civil rights and segregation controversies. "I feel that it is pretty wonderful for Leagues to exist in Mississippi at all now," Mathilde Dreyfuss wrote in 1959. Two years later, national LWV visitor Caroline Toms described the Mississippi leagues as a "very courageous band of women" in view of the fact that the

White Citizens Council "ran the state." Still, under state president Pat Eichols seven local leagues functioned in 1959–61, and in 1961–1963 the state LWV took up abolishing the poll tax, a reform that offered a boost to low-income, disfranchised women. The effort may have earned the LWV the suspicion of conservatives, who resented any attempt to democratize the political process.[39]

By the time the NWP had disappeared in Mississippi and activities of the LWV had lessened in the late 1930s and early 1940s, the National Federation of Business and Professional Women's Clubs (NFBPW) and the AAUW had attracted many public-minded women. Even before the national Business and Professional Women's Club formed in 1919 from working-girls' clubs within the national Young Women's Christian Association (YWCA), there were Business Girls Clubs in several larger Mississippi towns. These groups banded together in 1924 to form the Mississippi Federation of Business and Professional Women.[40] By 1940, there were over nine hundred members in twenty-six clubs, and by midcentury the clubs counted more than two thousand members, more than in any other state.[41]

As had the MFWC and the LWV, the BPW advocated women's jury service, ratification of the child-labor amendment, and the appointment of women to county and state offices. Unlike other state women's organizations, the Jackson BPW members had achieved national prominence by 1940: Ellen Woodward was a member of the Social Security Board, and Lucy Somerville Howorth served on the Board of Appeals of the Veterans Administration. Earlene White, postmistress of the U.S. Senate, had represented Mississippi Business Girls Clubs in St. Louis in July 1919, when the National Federation was formed, and she would soon be national president of the NFBPW.[42] Mississippi's unusually capable women chose the BPW rather than the LWV as the organization more likely to advance their professional interests.

During White's presidency in 1937, the national BPW, first among women's organizations, endorsed the ERA. As career women in a constricted job market exacerbated by state employment strictures penalizing married women, BPW members had a vital stake in equal job rights.[43]

With strong leadership at the national level from women such as Lucy Howorth, who continued her close association with the Mississippi BPW from Washington, the state BPW also took an advanced stand for the appointment of women to policy-making positions in state government.[44] In 1943, the state president called for submitting a roster of qualified women to Governor-Elect Thomas L. Bailey, which achieved modest gains.[45]

In 1944, a year after the ERA resurfaced in Congress, the GFWC endorsed ratification, but the Mississippi federation remained silent, as did the national and the Mississippi LWV. Thus campaigning fell to the Mississippi BPW, which in 1939 went on record supporting the ERA and in 1943 included ERA adoption in its legislative program.[46] Even so, some local BPW clubs, aware of public opinion against the ERA in Mississippi, cautiously advocated the amendment. One scholar has surmised that BPW women were reluctant to bring up any matter that would ruffle state lawmakers, upon whom they were dependent for legislation favorable to their employers.[47] Nevertheless, as many local clubs studied the amendment, an increasing number more boldly supported ratification, particularly after 1953, when the ERA was passed by the U.S. Senate.[48]

Smaller than the BPW, the Mississippi Division of the AAUW soon joined other organizations in advocating the advancement of women. The Association of Collegiate Alumnae, formed in 1884, merged in 1921 with the Southern Association of College Women (SACW) to form the AAUW. Mississippi women graduates were early members of the SACW at branches in Oxford (1906), Columbus (1907), Meridian (1910), and Jackson (1916). The Mississippi Division of the AAUW (1927) sought, like the national AAUW, to promote opportunities for women students and faculty in higher education and to enhance the status of women.[49] More immediately, the state division sought AAUW accreditation for the University of Mississippi and MSCW so that their graduates could join AAUW. Such accreditation assured that the colleges would provide equal services and programs for women. As did the MFWC, the AAUW considered a myriad of civic improvements, particularly those relating to education, to be women's issues. The Jackson branch in the late 1920s gained an appointment for its member Martha Catching Enochs as the first woman member of the Board of Institutions of Higher Learning, the governing agency of the state's public colleges and universities. Allied with the MFWC and the BPW, the AAUW advocated equal salaries for women faculty in higher education. In the early 1920s, AAUW branches in Mississippi worked to remove politics from the state's public colleges and universities after Governor Theodore Bilbo's interference cost them regional accreditation.[50] AAUW membership only began to grow after more Mississippi colleges and universities met AAUW criteria for adequate programs and student life for women. In the Mississippi organization's earliest years, leadership came from women educated outside the state, including state (1938–40) and national (1941–45) AAUW president Dr. Dera Parkinson, wife of the president of MSCW.

World War II and the cold war led women's organizations into unprecedented cooperative endeavors. During World War II, Mississippi clubs led by Susie V. Powell, former MFWC president (1926–28), aligned under the Coordinating Council of Women's Organizations for War Services to promote home-front efforts.[51] During the cold war, organized women who concerned themselves more with international affairs and world peace than with women's issues garnered considerable criticism.[52] In 1954, a *Saturday Evening Post* writer referred to the LWV as "the League of Frightened Women" because of its interest in the debate over internationalism and its internal conflict over President Harry Truman's cold war initiatives. Even more than the LWV, the AAUW was shaken by criticism from anti-Communist witch-hunters, who considered discussion of international affairs and support of the United Nations to be anti-American.[53]

One positive outcome of the cold war collaboration among women's organizations was a movement early in the 1960s to create the governor's Commission on the Status of Women. Heeding the recommendation of the 1963 report of President John F. Kennedy's President's Commission on the Status of Women (PCSW) that each state form its own commission, Mississippi governor Paul B. Johnson Jr. appointed one in 1964. If progressive women expected results from the report issued by the sixteen women and four men, all white, who comprised the commission, they were sorely disappointed. Chaired by Hattiesburg city judge Mildred W. Norris and including political wives and several conservative legislators, the commission in June 1967 released its report with ambivalent recommendations about substantial improvements in the status of women.[54]

The report bore the distinct imprint of Mary Dawson Cain, editor of the *Summit Sun* and state BPW president (1964–66). Its findings and recommendations, covering employment, legal status, education, citizenship volunteers, and the family and working mothers, assessed shortcomings but limited its mandate for reform. The state legislature should open jury service to women, revise inheritance laws to increase the rights of surviving spouses and children, and enact equal pay for equal work (with stipulations to protect employers). The report's significant recommendations were tempered by several ingratiating statements, such as, "Mississippi has always been kind to her women." The report concluded, "Our study has shown that in most respects it is not the laws of Mississippi that hamper the progress of women in our state but rather that the majority of women are not aware of their rights under our law." Although it seemingly applauded the growing number of women in the workplace, the report nevertheless stated, "Yet we feel that the care of the home and children is still primarily the mother's responsibility."[55]

AAUW, LWV, and BPW members pressured the legislature to grant jury service to women. The BPW had begun to work on this issue in 1941, but the groups' combined efforts failed to get the measure out of legislative committees. Finally in 1968, the state legislature granted jury service to women after Jean Muirhead, a freshman state senator from Jackson, in a deft, little-noticed parliamentary move, amended a juror qualification bill to delete the word "male." Despite a barrage of opposition calls to members of the House, the momentum for women jurors, led particularly by the LWV, was so strong that the House acquiesced.[56]

The growing ideological rift between the political establishment in Mississippi and the federal government spawned a new organization of Mississippi women after federal marshals and troops converged upon the University of Mississippi in September 1962, to support James Meredith, the first black student admitted to the university. On October 1, Florence Sillers Ogden of Rosedale, "Dis 'n Dat" reporter in the *Jackson Clarion-Ledger*; Margaret Peaster; and several other women met in Jackson to form the Women for Constitutional Government (WCG), which would be the state's only indigenous women's group. Charter member Mary Cain edited its monthly organ, the *Woman Constitutionalist*, until her death in 1984. Cain, state president of the BPW again in 1972–74 and national president of the WCG in 1966–68, was a popular speaker among right-wing groups.[57]

Described by Ogden as a forum for "just conservative women who believe in standing up for their constitutional rights," the first meeting, held in Jackson on October 30, 1962, reportedly drew fifteen hundred women from eight states, who heard Cain read a "Bill of Grievances" against the federal government and commend Mississippi governor Ross Barnett for his actions at Ole Miss to "preserve constitutional government" and to attempt to thwart Meredith's admission. The organization grew rapidly with chapters in Tupelo, Vicksburg, Biloxi, Jackson, Gulfport, Pascagoula, Pontotoc, Leland, Moss Point, Indianola, Clarksdale, Grenada, and western Bolivar County.[58] At annual national conventions, the WCG assailed the "new math" taught in schools, the demise of silver coins, urban renewal, and fluoridated water. At the state meeting in 1968, the Mississippi WCG resolved to oppose a bill to grant the state welfare department the authority to license nursery schools and day-care centers.[59]

After almost a decade, the WCG appeared to be losing ground, especially after its futile battle against integration and civil rights. Cain called for funds to sustain the *Woman Constitutionalist* when it was only intermittently published in the late 1960s. The WCG found new life in the 1970s as it opposed the feminist movement and particularly the ERA.[60] At its state meeting in 1970, the WCG gave its Patriot's Award to anti-ERA legislators.[61]

The influential Mary Cain favored equal pay for equal work and voluntary jury service for women and had encouraged women to vote and stand for office. "Equal pay for equal work? Yes—but making us equal to men—God forbid," Cain wrote in her "Jottings" column in the *Constitutionalist* in 1972.[62] The June

1972 issue carried an article titled "The Fraud Called the Equal Rights Amendment." Cain insisted that it would negate a man's obligation to support his wife and children, abolish laws protecting women from sex crimes, subject women to the draft and combat, override protective legislation for women in dangerous jobs, and eliminate women's right to privacy. To this, Cain added, "The ERA would not promote women to jobs, will not elect more women to public office, and will not convince men they should help with the housework."[63]

Other Mississippi women's groups, however, continued to push for the ERA. The NFBPW had supported the amendment since 1937. Some local clubs hesitated, but by March 1972, when the amendment had finally been proposed by both houses of Congress, most BPW clubs had declared their support. Even so, some members opposed the amendment and probably agreed with Cain's editorials that "it would destroy the American home."[64]

The LWV, according to one historian, had traditionally avoided being identified with women's rights per se and did not endorse the amendment until 1971.[65] More precisely, as one student of the Mississippi League of the 1950s concluded, "It never identified itself as a feminist organization," and "women's rights were simply not part of the state League's agenda."[66] When the national league did endorse the ERA, however, it also endorsed reproductive rights, a stand that put it in the forefront of women's organizations.[67] As for the BPW, at least in the early years of pro-choice, most Mississippi members did not consider the issue a business or professional concern.[68]

By the mid 1970s, the Jackson league, in the vanguard of the state LWV's push for ERA ratification, shared the annual Legislative Day lobbying effort with the AAUW.[69] After the Mississippi league's board adopted a pro-choice position in 1990, only three of seven chapters concurred, and the league lost chapters and members. As one local league president remarked, "It was something I didn't want to touch."[70]

The MFWC may never have discussed the ERA, but the state convention in 1958 passed a resolution pointing to inequities in Social Security benefits for wage-earning women, a move that may indicate that more members were working outside the home or were concerned about survivor's benefits.[71]

At its national convention in 1971, the AAUW endorsed the ERA as well as reproductive rights.[72] If national leaders believed that such stands would mobilize women and enhance membership, they had the opposite effect in Mississippi. Seventeen local branches in 1957 and sixteen in 1986 had fallen to twelve in 1992, and the number continued to decline.[73] But, as was true for other women's organizations, remaining members and new recruits were far more liberal minded than older members. Their voices continued to be heard. In

1979, a writer for the *Jackson Clarion-Ledger* wrote of the Jackson LWV, then under President Fran Leber: "Mississippi legislators are beginning to realize their lives are marked by three 'inevitables,' death, taxes, and the Mississippi League of Women Voters."[74]

Even though a *Clarion-Ledger* survey in 1973 indicated that a majority of Mississippi voters supported the ERA, neither house of the legislature heeded demands for approval. The amendment was never reported to the floor from committee at any time, even after committee hearings.[75] In 1980, the Senate Constitution Committee would not take up the subject of ratification; its inaction consistently blocked any floor consideration of the amendment, which in all likelihood would have met defeat.[76] In 1982, the final year in which states could ratify the extended ERA, the refusal of the Senate Constitution Committee to vote on ratification sounded the death knell for Mississippi's approval of the ERA. Thus the Mississippi legislature was the only state legislature that never voted on the amendment. Even prominent women legislators opposed the measure.[77] Neither were state senate leaders inclined to consider a proposal for a state ERA.[78]

By the time the ERA was reintroduced in both houses of Congress in 1983, its traditional backers—the AAUW, the LWV, and the BPW—were joined by other advocates of women's rights, including state affiliates of the National Organization for Women (NOW), the National Women's Political Caucus (NWPC), and the National Council of Negro Women (NCNW). Despite the groups' probably unwarranted optimism that the Mississippi legislature would reconsider the amendment, their opponents carried the day. One powerful House leader, Charles Capps Jr., expressed the common view: "The ERA is a dead issue. . . . All the ladies I know are perfectly happy the way they are."[79] Indeed, action on the federal ERA in Mississippi appeared to be a moot issue when the amendment failed by six votes in the U.S. House of Representatives.

Though diminished in membership in the final decades of the twentieth century, Mississippi's organized women's groups continued to lobby politicians, to influence public opinion, to promote women's rights, and to improve their lives. Revitalized groups have pursued additional women's issues that earlier local branches and clubs had not approached: family planning, child and spousal abuse, child care, women in prisons, career counseling, mental health, and self-protection.

As more women have gained access to once exclusively male professions, as formerly all-male civic organizations have been opened to women, and as women have turned from volunteer and club work to paid jobs, membership in mainstream women's organizations has declined. Despite those developments, many organizations remain active. The LWV, the AAUW, the BPW, the NCNW,

NOW, and other women's organizations are members of the modern-day professionally directed Mississippi Coalition of Women. They beat the drums for remedial state and local laws despite the Mississippi electorate's skepticism that some problems are the proper concerns of government.

NOTES

1. Paul R. Beazley, "Exhibiting Visions of a New South: Mississippi and the World's Fairs, 1884–1904" (PhD diss., University of Mississippi, 1999), 130, 134; Anne Firor Scott, *Natural Allies: Women's Associations in American History* (Urbana: University of Illinois Press, 1991), 142–43.

2. Hattie B. Stuckey, comp., "History of the Mississippi Federation of Women's Clubs," Historical Records Survey, Works Progress Administration, series 447, Mississippi Department of Archives and History, Jackson (henceforth cited as MDAH); Tommy Hogue Rosenbaum, *A History of the Mississippi Federation of Women's Clubs, 1898–1948* (Jackson: Mississippi Federation of Women's Clubs, 1998).

3. Rosenbaum, *History*, 8,11.

4. Evelyn Oppenheimer, quoted in *Jackson Clarion-Ledger*, April 26, 1958; "Women's Clubs Deserve Bouquet for Good Works," *Jackson Clarion-Ledger*, April 22, 1990.

5. *Yazoo Tri-Weekly Sentinel*, May 20, 1927; *Jackson Clarion-Ledger*, May 26, 1927.

6. William H. Chafe, *The American Woman: Her Changing Social, Economic, and Political Roles, 1920–1970* (New York: Oxford University Press, 1972), 36; Scott, *Natural Allies*, 173.

7. *Winston County Journal*, February 18, 1910; *New Albany Gazette*, commemorative edition, July 26, 2004.

8. Stuckey, "History," 25–27.

9. Ibid.

10. A. Elizabeth Taylor, "The Woman Suffrage Movement in Mississippi," *Journal of Mississippi History* 30 (February 1968): 25–26; Rosenbaum, *History*, 64.

11. Saunders, quoted in *Mississippi Federation of Women's Clubs Yearbook, 1919–1920*, unpaginated, MDAH.

12. Marjorie Spruill Wheeler, *New Women of the New South: The Leaders of the Suffrage Movement in the Southern States* (New York: Oxford University Press, 1993), 194.

13. Liba Peshakova to Mrs. B. F. Saunders, May 12, 1921; Peshakova reports, September 24–29, 1921, in LWV Papers, series II, box 1, Library of Congress (henceforth cited as LC).

14. Peshakova report, September 19–October 7, 1921, Membership Pyramid, 1921, LWV Papers, series II, box 4, LC.

15. *Woman Voter*, August 10, 17, and 21, 1922, microfilm, Mitchell Memorial Library, Mississippi State University, Starkville.

16. Nancy F. Cott, "The National Woman's Party," in *Major Problems in American Women's History*, ed. Nancy F. Cott (Lexington, Mass.: D. C. Heath, 1989), 332–40.

17. "Proposed Blanket Bill for Introduction in the State Legislature," copy in Pat Harrison Papers, Special Collections, Williams Library, University of Mississippi, Oxford; "How Mississippi Laws Discriminate against Women," 1922, copy in Somerville-Howorth Collection (henceforth cited as SHC), carton 5, folder 195, Arthur and Elizabeth Schlesinger Library (henceforth cited as AES), Radcliffe Institute for Advanced Study, Cambridge, Massachusetts.

18. *Suffragist*, June 9, 1917 (NWP weekly bulletin).

19. Anita Pollitzer to Alice Paul, November 29, December 4, 1921, NWP Papers, reel 11, microfilm in Women's Collection, Texas Woman's University, Denton (henceforth cited as WC-TWU).

20. *Jackson Clarion Ledger*, January 12, 1922.

21. Isabelle Gill to Alice Paul, February 19, 1922, NWP Papers, reel 13, WC-TWU.

22. *Jackson Clarion-Ledger*, March 22, 1922.

23. *Woman Voter*, November 2, 1922; *Equal Rights*, July 21, 1923. The MSCW was given $342,000 and the university $308,056. *Jackson Daily News*, April 10, 1922.

24. J. Stanley Lemons, *The Woman Citizen: Social Feminism in the 1920s* (Urbana: University of Illinois Press, 1973), 69–73. On Matthews's lobbying, see Kate Greene, "Burnita Shelton Matthews (1884–1988): The Struggle for Women' Rights," in *Mississippi Women: Their History, Their Lives*, ed. Martha H. Swain, Elizabeth Anne Payne, and Marjorie Julian Spruill, vol. 1 (Athens: University of Georgia Press, 2003), 148–52.

25. Ellen Crump to Maud Younger, August 2, 1921, NWP Papers, reel 9, WC-TWU.

26. Pauline Alston Clark to Miss Hicks, April 8, 1929, LWV Papers, series III, box 658, LC.

27. Jeffries Heinrich to Adele Clark, November 6, 1024. LWV Papers, series II, box 18, LC.

28. Ibid. On the Camellias, see Jeffries Heinrich to Misses Clark and Hart, November 17, 1924, LWV Papers, series II, box 18, LC.

29. "Mississippi League of Women Voters News," November 1927, LWV Papers, series II, box 653, LC.

30. Lemons, *Woman Citizen*, 155, 172–73; "Program of Study and Work" (November 1927), LWV Papers, series II, box 650, LC; Dorothy Kerchway Brown to Mary O. Osborne, RN, March 15, April 4, 1919, Brown Papers, AES.

31. Pauline Alston Clark to Miss Hicks, April 5, 1928, LWV Papers, series II, box 653, LC.

32. Molly Ladd-Taylor, *Mother's Work: Women, Child Welfare, and the State, 1890–1920* (Urbana: University of Illinois Press, 1994), 97; Lemons, *Woman Citizen*, 221–22; Nancy F. Cott, *The Grounding of Modern Feminism* (New Haven, Conn.: Yale University Press, 1987), 249, 259.

33. Mrs. B. L. Turman, "Report of Third Regional Director," May 10, 1929, LWV Papers, series II, box 190, LC; *Clarksdale Daily Register*, May 4, 1931.

34. Constance Roach to Daisy Sandidge, September 12, 1936, LWV Papers, series II, box 265, LC.

35. Debra Lynn Northcart, "The League of Women Voters in Mississippi: The Civil Rights Years, 1954–1964" (PhD diss., University of Mississippi, 1997), 3.

36. Nancy F. Cott, "Across the Great Divide: Women in Politics and Reform after 1920," in *One Woman, One Vote: Rediscovering the Woman Suffrage Movement*, ed. Marjorie Spruill Wheeler (Trousdale, Ore.: New Sage Press, 1995) 361; Lucy Somerville Howorth, interviewed by Constance Myers, June 20, 1975, p. 44, Southern Oral History Collection, University of North Carolina, Chapel Hill.

37. Jeanne Blythe to Olive McKay, March 26, 1946; Jean Blythe to Anna Lord Strauss, January 27, 1947, both in LWV Papers, series II, box 845, LC.

38. Jeanne Blythe to Anna Lord Strauss, February 16, 1947, LWV Papers, series II, box 845, LC; Rae Horner to Anna Lord Strauss, September 28, 1948, LWV Papers, series II, box 805, LC.

39. Mathilde Dreyfuss to Mrs. Phillips, February 3, 1959; Caroline Toms to Christine Urban, December 11, 1961, both in LWV Papers, series II, box 1277, LC; *Mississippi Voter*, June 1961, copy in LWV, series II, box 805, LC. The Citizens Council, a statewide organization, sought to maintain all forms of social segregation through threats and intimidation of its supposed enemies.

40. Salli Vargis, "History of the Mississippi Federation of Business and Professional Women's Clubs, 1924–1995" (PhD diss., Mississippi State University, 2004), 13–28.

41. Ibid., 46.

42. *Memphis Commercial Appeal*, September 1, 1940.

43. Geline Bowman, *History of the National Federation of the Business and Professional Women's Clubs, 1919–1944* (New York: NFBPWC, 1944), 122–23; "Earlene White—Career Woman," *Democratic Digest* 15 (September 1938): 34.

44. Bowman, *History of the National Federation*, 74.

45. Vargis, "History," 94, 275.

46. *Mississippi Business Woman*, June 9, 1939; Vargis, "History," 114.

47. Jane J. Mansbridge, *Why We Lost the ERA* (Chicago: University of Chicago Press, 1986), 121.

48. Vargis, "History," 114–16.

49. Helene Daniel, "History of the American Association of University Women in Mississippi" (MA thesis, Mississippi College, 1954), 23, 50–51, 58–59, 64–65, 75. Minutes of the Oxford SACW (1906) are in box 11, Mississippi Division, AAUW Papers, Williams Library, University of Mississippi, Oxford.

50. Ada N. Barker, "A History of the Jackson Branch of the American Association of University Women" (1964), unpaginated, box 6, Mississippi Division, AAUW Papers, Williams Library, University of Mississippi, Oxford.

51. See "Mississippi Federation of Women's Clubs, National Defense Department," Susie V. Powell Papers, unprocessed, MDAH.

52. Laura McElnaney, *Civil Defense Begins at Home: Mobilization Meets Everyday Life in the Fifties* (Princeton, N.J.: Princeton University Press, 2000), 93.

53. Warner Olivier, "The League of Frightened Women," *Saturday Evening Post*, October 23, 1954, 33–34. See the chapter "From International Activists to Cold War Warriors," in Helen Laville, *Cold War Women: The International Activities of American Women's Organizations* (Manchester: Manchester University Press, 2002), 106–10.

54. Report, "Status of Women in Mississippi, 1967," copy in University Libraries, University of Southern Mississippi, Hattiesburg.

55. Ibid., 9, 12, 29.

56. Bill Minor, "Only 30 Years Ago, Women Fell Off 'Pedestal,'" *Jackson Clarion-Ledger*, November 29, 1998; Mary Libby Pane, notes on speech, "Women on the Jury in Mississippi" (November 17, 1998), in possession of the author.

57. *Hattiesburg American*, October 2, 1962; Lisa K. Speer, "Contrary Mary: The Life of Mary Dawson Cain" (PhD diss., University of Mississippi, 1998), 261.

58. *Jackson Daily News*, October 31, 1962; Speer, "Contrary Mary," 268.

59. *Woman Constitutionalist*, January 1, 1966; June 1, 1966; November 9, 1968; February 8, 1969; Florence Sillers Ogden, "Women for Constitutional Government" (October 30, 1962), box 12, Ogden Papers, Capps Archives, Delta State University Library, Cleveland, Mississippi. Microfilm of the *WC* is in the Blagg-Huey Library, Texas Woman's University, Denton.

60. Speer, "Contrary Mary," 275.

61. *Woman Constitutionalist*, September 2, 1970.

62. Ibid., August 12, 1972; Speer, "Contrary Mary," 276–77.

63. *Woman Constitutionalist*, June 10, 1972.

64. Vargis, "History," 130; Cain quoted in *Memphis Commercial Appeal*, August 3, 1979; "Let's Upgrade ERA," *Mississippi Business Woman* 48 (October 1977).

65. Janet K. Boles, *The Politics of the Equal Rights Amendment: Conflict and the Decision Process* (New York: Longmans, 1979), quotation on 41. See also Leila J. Rupp and Verta Taylor, *Survival in*

the Doldrums: The American Women's Rights Movement, 1945 to the 1960s (New York: Oxford University Press, 1987), 49.

66. Northcart, "League of Women Voters," 125.

67. Boles, *Politics of the ERA*, 50.

68. Vargis, "History," 185.

69. *Jackson Clarion-Ledger*, February 1, 1976.

70. Ibid., January 10, 1983.

71. Rosenbaum, *History*, 81, 205.

72. Susan Levine, *Degrees of Equality: The American Association of University Women and the Challenge of Twentieth-Century Feminism* (Philadelphia: Temple University Press, 1995), 164.

73. "AAUW Majors in Service through Education," *Starkville Daily News*, March 3, 1968; *Mississippi State Bulletin*, Mississippi Division, AAUW (1995).

74. *Jackson Clarion-Ledger*, February 18, 1979.

75. Boles, *Politics of the ERA*, 177, survey by *Jackson Clarion-Ledger* cited on 101–2; letter from Jean Muirhead to the author, October 31, 1980.

76. *Memphis Commercial Appeal*, August 14, 1980; letter from Theodore Smith to the author, May 12, 1982.

77. Marjorie Julian Spruill and Jesse Spruill, "The Equal Rights Amendment and Mississippi," *Mississippi History NOW*, March 2003.

78. State ERA Proposal Introduced in Senate," *Starkville Daily News*, January 24, 1983.

79. "Backers Prepare Battle Plans for Passage of ERA," *Jackson Clarion-Ledger*, March 30, 1983.

The Mississippi "Takeover"

Feminists, Antifeminists, and the International Women's Year Conference of 1977

MARJORIE JULIAN SPRUILL

In 1977, the eyes of the nation, which had focused on Mississippi during the civil rights movement, were again focused on the state. Advocates for change and defenders of tradition were again embattled, but this time the conflict was over women's rights. A series of federally funded conferences in observance of International Women's Year (IWY) set the stage for the conflict, which polarized and politicized Mississippi women.

The IWY conferences, convened in each state and territory and culminating in the National Women's Conference in Houston, Texas, were mandated by Congress in 1975 at the behest of the United Nations and leading feminists, including Congresswoman Bella Abzug of New York. The goal was to involve a broad spectrum of American women in formulating the National Plan of Action to guide the federal government on policy regarding women: the congressional guidelines stipulated that the delegates elected to participate in the national IWY conference reflect the full diversity of the state's population. The National Commission on the Observance of International Women's Year, appointed by President Gerald Ford (and subsequently, President Jimmy Carter), was a predominantly feminist group that hoped the conferences would unite and expand the women's movement and move it beyond its white, middle-class base. In this, the IWY was highly successful. However, the conferences also mobilized social conservatives across the United States, who organized to challenge feminists for the right to speak for American women. And nowhere was the conservatives' challenge to feminists as dramatic as in Mississippi. At the July 8–9, 1977, IWY conference in Jackson, conservatives managed to achieve a complete

CORA NORMAN AND JESSIE MOSLEY DELIVERING
THE REPORT OF MISSISSIPPI'S COORDINATING
COMMITTEE ON OBSERVANCE OF INTERNATIONAL
WOMEN'S YEAR TO PRESIDENT JIMMY CARTER

Courtesy of Cora Norman.

"takeover" that would have enduring consequences for Mississippi women and for state politics.[1]

The modern women's rights movement, inspired and informed by the civil rights movement, was strongest outside the South, but it had considerable support in the region. In Mississippi, support was strongest in larger cities and university towns. It came from women's organizations, the press, and several prominent politicians, including Lieutenant Governor Evelyn Gandy of Hattiesburg, elected in 1975, and William Winter of Grenada, who would be elected governor in 1979. Since 1972, when the Equal Rights Amendment (ERA)—a proposed amendment to the U.S. Constitution and a key feminist goal—was approved in Congress and sent to the states for ratification, it had been introduced repeatedly in the Mississippi legislature. Yet there was little chance it would be ratified in this conservative state. As a result, women's rights advocates were far more vocal and visible in Mississippi than social conservatives who opposed their ideas generally and the ERA in particular. Until 1977, the conservatives saw little need to organize. This situation changed as a strong antifeminist movement emerged in the state in response to the IWY conferences.[2]

At the national level, the conflict between feminists and social conservatives developed gradually. In the late 1960s and early 1970s, the modern women's rights movement experienced phenomenal success. While internal divisions and militant participants played disproportionately and negatively in the media, the movement enjoyed widespread support. National politicians responded positively to many demands of the feminists and seemed to accept them (at least, the more moderate feminists) as speaking for American women. For the most part, socially conservative women focused on other causes or were apolitical. As President Richard Nixon developed his "southern strategy," he focused on race rather than gender as he wooed white conservatives in the region.[3]

To a limited degree, social conservatives, especially Catholics, began to mobilize as several states legalized abortion in the late 1960s. The major backlash against the women's rights movement came later, however, as a growing number of conservatives came to believe that the women's movement had moved beyond the pursuit of equality and was offering too drastic a challenge to traditional gender roles. In 1972, feminists proposed the ERA as a means of guaranteeing women's constitutional equality that would render unconstitutional all laws that discriminated against women, and precluded future passage of such laws. The ERA was approved overwhelmingly by Congress and sent to the states, and many rushed to ratify. But conservative women—fearing that the vaguely worded amendment would usher in unwanted changes—found their

voices, and their leader, Phyllis Schlafly, and began an organized challenge to
the ERA and feminism. Their ranks swelled further after the Supreme Court in
1973 announced its decision in *Roe v. Wade*, which made abortion legal nationwide. Opinion polls continued to show strong support for the ERA throughout
the decade, but as its opponents raised doubts about its impact, the ERA lost its
forward momentum. By 1975, the year the IWY program was established, thirty-
four of the necessary thirty-eight states had ratified, but only one more state
would ratify, and several others would try to rescind ratification.[4]

Conservatives, elated by their success, were therefore appalled when Congress established the IWY program with a $5 million appropriation and the
feminists appointed to lead it declared their intent to promote the ERA as well
as many other feminist goals.[5] Many of these goals were anathema to social
conservatives, who believed in social hierarchy and "traditional family values."
While agreeing that legal obstacles to women's equality should be removed, they
opposed government action that they viewed as promoting social change. They
believed that any problems facing women or families should be addressed by
strengthening the traditional family rather than by enacting federal programs.
If government action proved to be necessary, they favored reliance on local or
state governments, which they found to be more responsive. More fundamentally, critics of feminism objected to the movement's underlying assumption
that most behavioral differences between the sexes were the result of nurture
as opposed to nature, and they opposed most of the policies that followed from
that assumption. Unlike the ERA supporters, who believed laws that discriminated between men and women were the product of outmoded traditions and
should be made unconstitutional, the conservatives were convinced that innate
differences between the sexes justified such discrimination.[6]

Thus while feminist leaders looked to the IWY to involve greater numbers of
women in establishing an agenda to improve their lives, conservatives saw it as
a U.N.-conceived, federally funded effort to force unwanted changes on those
Americans just starting to rise up against the ERA and the legalization of abortion. They insisted that the federal government had given $5 million to fund
one side of a national debate. Between 1975 and 1977, they sought to halt the
IWY program through Congress and the courts. When it was clear that the conferences were going forward, they resolved to challenge the feminists for control of them. In 1975, Schlafly created an organization called the Eagle Forum,
"an alternative to women's lib," whose ranks would expand dramatically during
the IWY controversy.[7]

As the state IWY conferences got under way in February 1977, conservatives
were alarmed when participants at the first one, held in Vermont, approved

staunchly feminist resolutions and delegations to the national conference. The resolutions supported the ERA, "choice" on abortion, and what conservatives called "an additional anti-family goal—gay rights." Then, in March, the newly elected president Carter appointed Bella Abzug, regarded by conservatives as radical, as chair of the National IWY Commission. The last straw was the commission's sending to state IWY organizers a list of feminist-inspired "core recommendations" for consideration at the state conferences. At that point, conservatives created a formal organization, the IWY Citizen's Review Committee, to coordinate their challenge. Its head, Rosemary Thomson, a close associate of Phyllis Schlafly and also from Illinois, said that the feminist recommendations shocked her fellow conservatives and confirmed their worst fears about the intentions of feminists. They were horrified that the recommendations would be approved and presented to Congress as an official wish list of American women.[8]

In May 1977, Schlafly urged readers of her newsletter, the *Phyllis Schlafly Report*, to turn out en masse for the state IWY conferences. A devout Catholic, she was remarkably successful at uniting varied religious groups that had in the past been hostile to one another, including Catholics, Mormons, and previously apolitical evangelical and fundamentalist Protestants. Led by ministers, including the Reverend Jerry Falwell, who had criticized African American ministers for mixing politics and religion during the civil rights movement, conservative Protestants proved surprisingly responsive to a northern Catholic woman's appeal for "Christian soldiers" to defend traditional values. Members of Congress were soon deluged with letters protesting IWY, and coalitions of social conservatives varying in composition from state to state made their presence felt at the state conferences.[9]

In a few states, including Oklahoma, Missouri, Ohio, Nebraska, Utah, Alabama, and Mississippi, conservatives "took over" the IWY conferences, voted down the "core recommendations" (at times substituting their own recommendations), and elected solidly conservative delegations to send to the culminating IWY Conference in Houston. The first of these takeovers took place on June 16–18 in Oklahoma, where, according to conservative leader Diane Edmondson, they "relied heavily on the fundamentalist church groups here to tell their members to attend and vote against the feminist slate." Later that month in Utah, fourteen thousand women and men—many of them Mormons—elected a solidly antifeminist group of delegates and "reversed the intent of all of the workshops designed by the pro-IWY State coordinating committee." Across the nation, conservatives celebrated that "the radicals [were] being challenged and defeated where[ever] concerned Americans [saw] the dangers."[10]

The National IWY Commission notified state IWY organizers about the unexpectedly large conservative turnout but did little more. They *wanted* women of all points of view to participate in the IWY state conferences and the workshops where women's issues would be debated, hoping they would respond positively to feminist ideas.[11] Mississippi IWY leaders, busy planning the state IWY conference to be held in July, remained unaware of the systematic challenge conservatives were organizing nationally and in Mississippi. IWY committee members later noted that information about the surprise tactics employed elsewhere would have been quite welcome as they planned the conference they ironically chose to call "Mississippi Women: Awake and Aware."[12]

The IWY Coordinating Committee for Mississippi began its work on February 26, 1977, at a meeting hosted in Oxford by Dr. Katherine Rea of the University of Mississippi. This was a racially diverse group of women, moderate to liberal in political leanings and active in a variety of organizations including churches. Few had known one another previously. As in other states, the members were selected by the national IWY organizers (who had decided not to rely on state governors to appoint progressive and diverse commissions) on the basis of years of leadership in women's advocacy organizations including the American Association of University Women (AAUW), the League of Women Voters (LWV), the National Council of Negro Women (NCNW), the Mississippi State Federation of Colored Women's Clubs, the National Organization for Women (NOW), and the Business and Professional Women's Federation (BPW).[13] There were committee members active in the American Civil Liberties Union (ACLU), the Democratic Party, arts commissions, chambers of commerce, the American Cancer Society, the Afro-American Historical Society, and the Mississippi Humanities Council. Many were involved in religious organizations including the Young Women's Christian Association (YWCA), Church Women United, the National Council of Jewish Women, and other religious groups, and some were wives of clergymen. The group included university professors, a dean, a hairdresser, lawyers and law students, homemakers, bankers, mental health and social workers, and the head of a displaced homemakers aid organization.[14] There were advisors to the U.S. Civil Rights Commission, members of the National Association for the Advancement of Colored People (NAACP), and officeholders whose elections had been made possible by the Voting Rights Act of 1965 (Mayor Unita Blackwell of Mayersville and city councilwoman Sarah Johnson of Greenville). Natalie Mason's husband had led the "wade-ins" that desegregated Gulf Coast beaches, and Dr. Jessie B. Mosley had been active in Wednesdays in Mississippi, an interracial women's group that quietly promoted interracial understanding.[15]

At the opening meeting, the group heard from a representative of the National Commission on the Observance of IWY and elected Dr. Mosley as their chair. Mosley, a leader among African Americans in Jackson, had held national and state offices in the NCNW, chaired the Committee on Property Development of the Mississippi State Federation of Colored Women's Clubs, and served as secretary of the ministers' wives organization of the National Convocation of the Christian Church. Her equanimity and flexibility allowed her to handle the unexpected developments that would follow in a manner that would win respect from all factions. The other principal officers were Dr. Kathie Gilbert, vice-chair; Barbara Pittman, fiscal officer; Bobbye Henley, for arrangements; Sarah Johnson, publicity chair (later replaced by Willie Mae Latham Taylor); Thelma Zinner, for finance; Natalie Mason, for outreach; and Dr. Cora Norman, for the program.[16]

Particularly because so few of these women had worked together previously, it was an enormous challenge to organize the state conference in such a short time. Looking back on their work, Janice Moor, the author of the committee's final report, speculated that it was "a wonder the conference ever got off the ground." As she later recalled, given the "diversity of the 32 women who were appointed," the "wide-spread distances over which they were scattered," and the "initial shock of having to work with virtual strangers in such close contact," plus the fact that many of the members were employed full time and gave their time "at a great financial sacrifice," only their great commitment to the goals of the conference enabled them to accomplish their task.[17]

Through the spring and into the summer, the coordinating committee continued its work. Barbara Pittman and Jessie Mosley were soon bonded, and Pittman traveled to Washington for instruction in managing Mississippi's $36,000 share of the federal funds. They opened a headquarters at 1018 Pecan Circle in Jackson and compiled a list of women's organizations to receive IWY announcements. As in all states, some IWY funds were used for research; Mississippi lawyer Constance Harvey Slaughter was commissioned to produce a report on the status of homemakers in Mississippi, "which showed many problems and less protection than many women in the state assumed they had."[18]

The organizers planned a full agenda for the conference, which, according to newspaper accounts was intended "to highlight the achievements of women, assess their status in social, political, and economic institutions and project the roles they will play in the future" as well as to vote on resolutions and elect delegates. "We intend to examine women's lives and their experiences," said volunteer Nancy Ruhl. "This is an effort, hopefully, to build an appreciation of contributions women have made to the country in roles other than that of the traditional homemaker." They planned a book exhibit, an art display, a history exhibit—all highlighting Mississippi women—as well as entertainment by the Mississippi Opera Company. But the main agenda, in Mosley's words, was "to help women realize their potential and help them realize that they do have some clout."[19]

The committee's choices coincided often but not always with the national commission's suggestions. With years of experience operating in a conservative social climate, they knew that some of the national commission's ideas "did not have enough Mississippi in them" to be palatable to people in the state. They designated fourteen workshops and conveners: Displaced Homemakers, Dr. Kathie Gilbert; ERA, Bobbye Henley; Women and the Law, Jean D. Muirhead; Consumer Power and Protection, Louise Spears; International Relations, Dr. Cleopatra Thompson; Rural Women, Edna Williamson and Marie Shields; Rape, Dr. Sarah Banks; Careers, Dr. Katherine Rea; Alternate Life Styles, Josie Brooks; Parenting and Child Care, Eva Bishop; Agents of Change, Dr. Cora Norman; Women in Politics, Sarah Johnson; Aging, Melerson Dunham; and Education, Dr. Katherine Rea," but significantly, there was no workshop on "reproductive rights." Keynote speakers included Mississippi native Velma McEwen Strode, director of Equal Employment Opportunity with the U.S. Department of Labor and formerly employed by the Urban League; and Dorothy R. Steffens, director of the U.S. section of the Women's International League for Peace and Freedom. Steffens was one of two Americans invited by the Vietnamese Women's Union to represent the American peace movement at the time of the signing of the Paris Peace Accords and had recently returned from Cuba, where she had studied the education and status of women.[20]

That the organizers were bent on planning a program palatable to Mississippians and yet selected such a slate of speakers suggests that, despite strenuous efforts to publicize a conference open to all, they expected only progressive-minded Mississippians to participate. Alison Steiner, a young lawyer who attended the conference as one of the "rank and file," said that she and other Mississippi women who regarded themselves as "more progressive" attended the conference expecting it to be "an excellent place to join with other women doing similar types of things." Perhaps they were living in "a fool's paradise," Steiner observed years later, adding, "It never occurred to us that there would be an organized right-wing." Women's political activism seemed contradictory to the ideas Mississippi conservatives espoused. Thus supporters of women's rights believed, she said, "that we had fertile ground for organizing women who had not previously been involved" in public discussion of women's issues.[21]

There is no record of which women's organizations received IWY announcements, but it is clear that the coordinating committee went to great lengths to reach the public through the media. IWY speakers appeared on Judy Denson's *Coffee with Judy* on WLBT-TV each morning from June 27 through July 8. WABC-TV in Greenwood-Greenville and Mississippi ETV aired programs about IWY, and stations WJTV and WAPT were also "especially helpful." The committee sent spot announcements to all Mississippi television and radio stations; particularly on the Gulf Coast, in Starkville, and in Tupelo they were able to get the message across through numerous radio interviews. The committee commended the *Greenwood Commonwealth*, the *Greenville Delta Democrat-Times*, and the *Tylertown Times*, and *Mississippi Today*, a Catholic Church publication, for advance coverage of conference preparations, but cited them as "notable exceptions" and complained that it was difficult to get the press to pay much attention to the IWY before the conference. The committee tried to compensate for the neglect by purchasing newspaper advertisements. Significantly, Mississippi conservatives later insisted that they had heard little about the upcoming Mississippi IWY conference and accused the organizers of following a national strategy to prevent conservatives from hearing about it. Later, after conservatives turned out in dramatic numbers, publicity chair Willie Mae Latham Taylor observed that, had the publicity been as good as the conservatives said was needed, she did not know where they would have put everybody.[22]

Mississippi conservative leaders, including Eddie Myrtle Moore, a self-described "farmwife" from Pelahatchie who would emerge as a leader of the group, said they had learned of the upcoming IWY from conservatives outside Mississippi. Moore was active in the Mississippi Farm Bureau; she said she "accidentally" became involved in the state conference after she began hearing about the IWY in a speech by Phyllis Schlafly and discussion at Farm Bureau Federation meetings. In June, she began receiving phone calls about the feminists' "radical" proposals and the oppositional stands taken by conservatives at other state conferences. Then, she said, "We just got on the telephone and called friends." The minister of Jackson's First Presbyterian Church was also among the first to hear about the conference and promptly spread the word to Jackson's First Baptist Church. Jackson anesthesiologist Dr. Curtis Caine and his wife, Lynn, recalled that they heard about the IWY through their church and from word of mouth among Christian friends.[23]

According to press reports, Dr. Caine was also a member of the John Birch Society. So was Carolyn Morgan of Hattiesburg, state chairman of STOP ERA and another leader of the conservative takeover. Morgan called their group a "loose coalition" representing, among others, Women for Constitutional Government, the American Party of Mississippi, STOP ERA, the John Birch Society, Right to Life, and many churches. "It's a mass effort by Christian people," she said. There were Eagle Forum members involved in planning, including Patricia Fawcett of Oxford, a Catholic who "distribut[ed] Schlafly material" at the conference. Other conference attendees were involved in the Southern Conservative Lobby, the Mississippi Farm Bureau Federation, and the Ku Klux Klan. However, insisted Eddie Myrtle Moore, "The ones [conservatives] who came didn't represent any groups. The question wasn't even asked. We were just all concerned about the basic assault on the American principle of the family."[24]

Word circulated among the conservatives that a group of feminist radicals planned to hold a meeting in Jackson and promote resolutions supporting the ERA, gay rights, federally controlled day care, and other issues abhorrent to social conservatives. They would also elect delegates to a national conference that would then advise Congress on what American women wanted. Conservatives, they said, must turn out to challenge the feminists' "pre-packaged" slates and resolutions. According to the Caines and Eddie Myrtle Moore, the group did not expect to take over the conference but wanted to be sure their voices were heard.[25] Whatever their goal, they pursued a stealth strategy: feminists later concluded that they carefully planned a takeover and believed their success depended on keeping IWY organizers ignorant of their plans. Dr. Shelton Hand, a specialist in constitutional and family law at the Baptist-affiliated Mississippi College School of Law, was invited to take part in the conference but declined. He then emerged at the conference as one of its most influential conservative leaders.[26]

On the day of the conference, the organizers were astounded; though only 350 people had preregistered, another 1,119 persons turned up, including 145 men. Many arrived on church buses. Attendees stood in long registration lines and organizers scrambled to print additional programs and handouts. Quite a few women, perhaps averse to using the day-care services provided, carried children throughout the two-day conference. Workshops, particularly those on controversial subjects of particular interest to conservatives, overflowed, and people pushed and shoved in the hallways.[27] L. C. Dorsey recalled that music was used to relieve—and sometimes create—tension: "Finally everyone was out in the hall, packed together like sardines in a can, waiting to get back in," she wrote. "After two women almost got into a fight, someone started to sing an old spiritual ('Amazing Grace') and then the patriotic songs: 'My Country 'Tis of Thee,' 'Oh Beautiful,' etc. When a group of us tried to sing 'We Shall

Overcome,' it was drowned out by a battle song, while a peace advocate shouted 'Peace, not War.' "[28]

According to both sides, an atmosphere of hostility between feminists and conservatives prevailed. Conservatives claimed that feminist organizers treated them like interlopers or spoilers. Eddie Myrtle Moore said they had to fight to be heard and to oversee ballot counting by the distrusted feminists. The organizers--most of them married women with children; from strong religious backgrounds; and with extensive service to their state, nation, and churches— were shocked and dismayed to be called "godless communists" as well as "anti-family," "immoral," and advocates of promiscuity and perversion by members of the conservative coalition calling itself "Mississippians for God, Country, and Family." Such accusations from people who had known them for years— and who certainly knew better—flabbergasted Cora Norman and others on the coordinating committee.[29]

Mississippians for God, Country, and Family, making good use of the pre-rogatives of a majority, passed substitute recommendations and selected a slate of delegates that reflected their own values and ideas about women and public policy. The well-organized conservatives, including a group of male "control-lers" using the handheld radios then called "walkie-talkies," often instructed the conservative women on how to vote. Linda Williams, a reporter for the *South Mississippi Sun*, observed that the "group that wielded the most power . . . was a group of Pentecostal ministers who bused in entire congregations and controlled their every move."[30]

The adopted resolutions underscored the fundamental differences between the conservatives and the feminists. Beyond "equal pay for equal work," they agreed on very little. Though most in each group were religious, their religion spoke to them quite differently on women's issues. To the conservatives, denying gender differences and roles was not only socially destructive but sacrilegious. Many believed that God had created woman to be honored by but obedient to man; that her highest calling was wife and mother; that feminists disdained that role; and that feminism held forth false promises about the benefits and satisfactions of work outside the home.

Some opposed the very idea of equality between the sexes. Mrs. M. P. Wheling, who attended the conference with her husband, told a reporter, "The only way for women to be equal with men is to step down from the pedestal where men have us. I wouldn't want to be thrown away from what 2,000 years of Christianity has done for us." Elizabeth Mitchell, of Jackson, later stated, "I believe as a Christian we have a responsibility to stand up for God's word," and

"You are to submit yourself to the husband just as the husband submits himself to God." Others said they were there to act against "sinful" resolutions. "I'm a Christian and I'm totally opposed to what they're for," said Martina Hicks. "They're going against God's wishes," she said, insisting that hundreds of other attendees agreed that the feminist-sponsored resolutions must be stopped. Carolyn Morgan, a member of a Missionary Baptist church, said the group opposed resolutions concerning day care for children, abortion, equality in sports, and the ERA. "The women of Mississippi don't want laws passed like they're recommending," she said, noting that ERA-ratification bills had been introduced twice unsuccessfully in the Mississippi legislature.[31]

The conservatives' resolutions reflected their convictions that families suffered, children were poorly reared, and the nation was weakened when women left traditional roles. They approved only one plank suggested by the organizers—one supporting improvements in public education—but only after omitting endorsement of public kindergarten. Conservatives saw federal programs to assist women and children as wasteful, indeed "communistic," and their own resolutions called for major spending cutbacks. Many were convinced that programs favored by the feminists, including Social Security benefits for homemakers, would lead to higher taxes and would drive even more women into the paid labor force. Their resolutions opposed all affirmative action (which they called "reverse discrimination") and programs, including Title IX, that required equal opportunities for women in educational institutions. They opposed proposals for gender equality in the military and international cooperation to promote women's rights and world peace. These ideas were anathema to many conservatives who were ardent nationalists and isolationists, opposed to the United Nations and taxes to support foreign aid, and advocates of a strong military—with no women in combat—that was able to withstand the threat of communism. Dorothy Gunter, declaring herself to be "very much a patriot," saw feminism as part of the "communist menace" and said she was there to speak out against the threat. Eddie Myrtle Moore insisted that the whole IWY program was "a plan started back in 1972 in the United Nations to bring about the destruction of the American family and home as we have known it."[32]

The conservatives opposed the ERA as unnecessary for women's freedom. In their eyes, it threatened women's special protections, including the requirement that husbands support their families after divorce, and could be a "Pandora's Box" that would open the door to federal trampling of valued traditions. Shelton Hand believed that the ERA and the women's movement would weaken "the moral fiber and spiritual base of this nation"; it would also have serious legal consequences harmful to women, including the drafting of women for combat duty, the elimination of fathers' legal obligations to support their children, and the removal of all gender-based legal protections for women. Hand also insisted that the women's movement had caused the breakup of families by planting doubt and confusion in women's minds.[33]

A sweeping resolution proposed and adopted by the conservatives summed up their position: "BE IT RESOLVED that the IWY conference declare itself opposed to sin and injustice in all their forms." It was then amended to read: "BE IT RESOLVED that sin and injustice be defined as that which is condemned in the Holy Bible." They were adamant that homosexuality and abortion were heinous sins and that sex education must be removed from the schools as a matter to be handled solely within families. Laura Huff and Patricia Maddox of Pelahatchie told a reporter from Memphis, "We were told in our church that ERA meant the end of marriage," that schoolbooks would depict bestiality, and that "we've got to protect our children."[34]

With the civil rights movement in Mississippi still fresh in their minds, many conservatives remained angry over what they viewed as ill-advised and unwanted federal intervention in the form of court decisions and federal legislation. To white Mississippians who had opposed civil rights for African Americans, further expansion of federal power—especially in the sensitive arena of gender relations—must be opposed to the last ditch, just as many white southerners had opposed the woman suffrage amendment earlier in the century. Perhaps, with white supremacy legally overturned, preserving traditional gender hierarchies and the protection of women seemed to them more important than ever.[35]

One of the conservatives at the conference, Dallas Higgins, wife of George Higgins, the Mississippi grand dragon of the United Klans of America, told the press that communists had tried to take over the country through "the blacks," and having failed, they now hoped to gain control of the nation by appealing to blacks and women. In an interview with a reporter from the *Clarion-Ledger*, she said, "My husband's been telling me about socialism and communism for years. But I didn't really know until I saw it for myself in Jackson during the IWY state conference." Richard Barrett, a Jackson lawyer well known as a white rights advocate and one of the most vocal conservatives, introduced several successful resolutions, including one stating, "The IWY extends our moral support to our anti-communist allies and friends of the Free World" including not only the Republic of China (Taiwan) but Rhodesia (Zimbabwe) and South Africa, which were then fighting to preserve white supremacy.[36]

Mississippians for God, Country, and Family elected a solidly conservative group of delegates to the National Women's Conference: Eddie Myrtle Moore, of Pelahatchie, chair; Patricia Fawcett, of Oxford; Mark Godbold and Dr. Shelton Hand, of Clinton; Mary Kerlee, of Columbus; Carolyn and Homer Morgan and Vanera Morris, of Hattiesburg; Pat Revell, of Grenada; Dr. Curtis and Lynn Caine, Helen Campbell, Pauline Earles, Dorothy Gunter, Elizabeth Mitchell, Lillian Temple, Norma and William Temple, and Helen Boone, of Jackson; and Reid Smith and Dallas Higgins, of Liberty. The men in the group would be the only men elected from any state as delegates to the Houston conference. Two of them, Curtis Caine and Homer Morgan, were elected in absentia. "I didn't seek to go. I was asked and elected to go," said Caine. "I'm flattered the ladies thought I would have their best interests at heart." Hand said he "absolutely object[ed]" to spending federal money for the conference but agreed to go because "untold numbers of women" had asked him to. The delegates elected included three married couples and only one African American, Willie Mae Latham Taylor, who promptly declined and was replaced by a white alternate.[37]

The election of Dallas Higgins, a Klan leader's wife, shocked the nation and embarrassed most of the conservatives. Eddie Myrtle Moore denied adamantly that there were any Klan members in the delegation, insisting, "There's been a smear on the Mississippi delegates.... As chairman I can assure you that not one member is a Klansman." She had the delegates sign affidavits to that effect, but Dallas Higgins revealed that, though not an official member, she had attended Klan rallies "as a concerned citizen." She said that attending the IWY conference was something she did on her own, but that upon seeing the "communistic" ideas being promoted by the feminists, she got in touch with her husband, George, and said, "You've got to get to Jackson." At the conference, according to Dallas Higgins, the Klan was but one of several organizations that united to elect delegates. Her husband however, later boasted to reporters that the KKK had run the Mississippi conference.[38]

Both Eddie Myrtle Moore and Dallas Higgins denied that their group had chosen an all-white delegation, insisting that they had elected Willie Mae Latham Taylor but that she had been pressured to resign by other blacks. Evidently, Latham wanted to attend the Houston conference and had allowed her name to be put in nomination by the conservative group, and for this she was strongly criticized by white and black feminists.[39] Nonetheless, the fact that a state with a 36 percent black population was sending an all-white delegation to Houston was the news that stuck, and it was roundly condemned by IWY leaders nationwide. Unita Blackwell said, "Even if they say they are for God, country, and family, they're the same group of people that have always oppressed black people" in the state.[40]

After the Mississippi conference, Richard Barrett boasted of the conservatives' triumph and denounced the defeated feminists' "core recommendations" for seeking "to set men against women and to increase federal power," adding, "Women don't want quotas, men don't want quotas." He bragged about the passage of resolutions against gay-rights legislation, saying, "When you talk about legalizing homosexuality, when you talk about legalizing perversion, you're touching the soul of America." The conservative takeover in Mississippi, he proclaimed, was of utmost importance: "It's undisputed and undoubted that we have sent a mandate to the nation. That the ERA is dead, and that the moral womanly woman is alive and well in Mississippi, and that she will win this battle."[41]

The organizers regrouped at the home of Dr. Kathie Gilbert in Starkville to console one another and complete their obligations by preparing their final report to the national commission. "It was not at all as we had envisioned, a chance for Mississippi women to come together to discuss their problems, their dreams, and plans," they wrote. "Perhaps it was naive of us, but we never dreamed for a moment that such an innocent goal could be construed by observers as a meeting meant to tear down those institutions that all of us on the Committee hold dear: our families, our churches, and our country."[42]

A sympathetic columnist, Paul Pittman of the *Tylertown Times*, called the Mississippi IWY conference a "disaster." He predicted that "the sweeping defeat of even the most innocuous of the resolutions at the weekend Jackson conference almost certainly [would] stiffen sentiment against women's rights in the state legislature" and adversely affect feminists' plans to push for relatively noncontroversial proposals including aid to displaced homemakers and help for the aging. Legislators "already uneasy about bills tainted by the outcry over the ERA and a relaxed view toward unorthodox lifestyles" would now "have something tangible" with which "to rationalize their votes against legislative relief sought by the women's movement." The members of the coordinating committee, he said, "were so pessimistic now that one suggested the conference slogan 'Mississippi Women—Awake and Aware' be changed to 'Mississippi Women—Barefoot and Pregnant.'" Whatever the future holds for the women's movement in the state, he concluded, "the recent conference underscores the fact that the whole question evokes emotions not seen in this state since the civil rights movement died a peaceful death several years ago. Moreover, the victory of the 'antis' leaves a tantalizing residue of arch conservative troops now seeking new causes."[43]

Columnist Bill Minor, a leading analyst of Mississippi politics, also predicted a lasting influence. The state, he wrote, had just gotten "a look-see" at "a new form of militant conservatism" that had "emerged to replace the old-time antiblack militancy of the White Citizens' Councils and the Ku Klux Klan." Though "ostensibly not racist," it "comes out of a strong reactionary backlash led by religious fundamentalism, self-acclaimed patriotic organizations and some old-time staunchly conservative political groups. Their overall enemy now is not the black man but 'liberalism' in any form, as they see it." In place of opposition to civil rights and voting rights bills, wrote Minor, they are now focusing on "such issues as ERA, gay rights, and abortion." Stating that "once state legislators were afraid to move without getting approval from the Citizens' Council hierarchy," he asked, "Is it possible a new fear of the right may emerge in the halls of the legislature?"[44]

When viewed in a national context, Mississippi's takeover was as unusual as it was thorough. When the last of the state conferences ended, it was clear that feminists prevailed at most IWY conferences; 80 percent of the delegates elected to participate in the Houston IWY conference supported the feminist movement. In thirty states, participants adopted all the "core recommendations" and in eleven states approved most of them. But a new a round of controversy over the IWY followed the state conferences and lasted until the national conference in November.[45] Conservatives nationwide filed challenges with the national commission, accusing IWY state coordinators of trying to exclude or silence them. The charges received national attention when Senator Jesse Helms (R-N.C.), working with the IWY Citizens Review Committee, organized congressional hearings at which conservative women from many states testified. Letters protesting the conferences poured in, and many politicians began to wonder which group of women they should appease. Schlafly denounced the conferences for "rigging, ruthlessness, and railroading" and "lesbian aggressiveness" and urged conservatives to save American society from "the libs," who would "replace it with a society that does not respect gender differences, moral values, church, or family."[46]

Feminists fought back, alarmed by the attention the conservatives commanded from politicians and from the press, which developed a strong interest in the IWY conferences only after the battles among women began. Feminists accused Schlafly of "seeking a resurgence of the far right by exploiting the women's movement," and led by the AAUW, forty women's organizations formed "Truth Squads" to "rebut the false or exaggerated charges anti-change groups had been making to the press and even in Congress."[47]

As conservatives elsewhere challenged the legitimacy of the delegates elected to attend the Houston conference, in Mississippi it was the feminists who challenged the legitimacy of their state's delegation. Calling themselves the Minority Caucus, they protested the methods used by conservatives in taking over the state IWY conference, denounced the conservative resolutions as racist as well as antifeminist, and charged that the election of an all-white delegation violated the letter as well as the spirit of the IWY's congressional mandate.[48]

National IWY leaders, while "shocked" by the all-white delegation, nonetheless denied the Mississippi feminists' challenge along with the conservative challenges from other states. Instead, they decided to appoint "at-large delegates" in states where the elected delegation did not meet the diversity requirement. They appointed nine at-large delegates from Mississippi including eight black women: Greenville city councilwoman Sarah Johnson; Mayersville mayor Unita Blackwell Wright; Joan Brown, of Greenville; Natalie Mason, of Biloxi; Edna Williamson, of Grenada; and Valerie Jackson, Merlene Walker, and Jessie B. Mosley, of Jackson. There was, however, one white at-large delegate, Karen Kester of Gulfport, the leader of the Minority Caucus and perhaps the state's best known NOW leader.[49]

Eddie Myrtle Moore, returning from the Helms Senate hearings, held a press conference at the Mississippi Farm Bureau to protest the at-large appointments and to accuse IWY leaders of stacking the deck in Houston even more surely in favor of the ERA. As the Mississippi press, now totally into the story, ran feature stories and newspaper and television interviews galore, both groups of Mississippi delegates prepared for Houston. In October, Dorothy Gunter, Pat Revell, and Ellen Campbell attended Phyllis Schlafly's annual leadership training conference, that year dedicated to planning for Houston. And they joined national conservative leaders in planning a massive rally to be held in Houston's Astro Arena coinciding with the national IWY conference.[50]

Dianne Edmondson, leader of the Oklahoma takeover and one of the rally organizers, came to Jackson to urge Mississippians to take part in the Houston protest. The *Clarion-Ledger* wrote of her speech: "Feminism took it on the chin Saturday as conservative women and men held a pep rally of sorts in Jackson in preparation for next week's International Women's Year (IWY) national conference in Houston, Texas. About 150 people, mostly women, turned out for the rally which was billed as a meeting for the Committee for God, Family, and Country. A majority of Mississippi's 20 delegates to the IWY conference attended." Insisting that "feminism is a fraud," Edmondson told her audience that the movement may have started out to attain equal opportunity but had moved away. "It has nothing to do with equal pay and equal opportunities anymore. It has become more radical. . . . The new goal of the feminist movement is the destruction of the family as an institution and the denial of God." She urged her listeners, if unable to come to the Houston gathering, to attend a protest rally at Riverside Methodist Church in Jackson on the same day. The antifeminist rallies, she said, are "all toward one goal—discrediting the IWY conference," which would be dominated by "radical leftwing feminists who don't represent the mainstream of thought held by most American women."[51]

When the long-awaited National Women's Conference got under way, television audiences around the world watched as the celebrities arrived in Houston, including feminist leaders Bella Abzug, Gloria Steinem, and Betty Freidan; actress Jean Stapleton, then famous as Edith Bunker on the hit television sitcom *All in the Family*; civil rights leader Coretta Scott King; poet Maya Angelou; scholar Margaret Meade; former First Ladies Lady Bird Johnson and Betty Ford, and the current First Lady, Rosalynn Carter.[52] But the press also swarmed the elected delegates from Mississippi, especially Dallas Higgins, who expressed concerns that IWY organizers were going to harass conservatives by assigning them black lesbians as roommates. She was accompanied by her husband, George; KKK imperial wizard Robert Shelton of Alabama had announced that Klansmen would be going to Houston "to protect our women from all the militant lesbians."[53]

Other Mississippi delegates were also in the spotlight. A special edition of the *Houston Breakthrough* included the article "Meet the Delegates: Mississippi Style," with a photo of a man with a banner reading: "Woman's Lib Follow Jesus Christ and Your Husband and Your Pastor . . . Repent." The article featured arriving delegates William and Norma Temple and Mark Godbold. Asked why she came, Norma Temple replied, "Because I believe they [feminists] are asking for rights which will hinder, not help, women" and "cause reverse discrimination against men." Also, she said, feminists "want marriage licenses for homosexuals and at the same time they're tearing down the family." Billy Temple added, "I don't know who they're trying to fool. They're not having any effect on middle-class women, but they're promising the poor and underprivileged a gravy train."[54]

When asked about the all-white delegation with a Klan leader's wife, Billy Temple "hastened to deny that the women's rights movement had anything to do with civil rights or that the antis were segregationists. He insisted that very few of the participants knew each other beforehand and in fact had not found out until the voting was over that they had elected someone with Klan connections"—or "a black." Apparently unaware that the African American delegate elected, Willie Mae Taylor Latham, had been publicity chair of the Mississippi IWY coordinating committee, Norma Temple said the black delegate they elected "was a conservative, professing Christian like the rest of us. We heard there would be trouble for her afterwards from the pro-ERA people so we stuck around. We were in fear for her safety. Sure enough they cornered her. She has admitted she was threatened by them. Then she resigned. We didn't hear from her again." Norma Temple also noted that the conservative coalition was organized through churches and that most of the blacks at the conference were invited by the pro-ERA people.[55]

In Houston, Mississippi's elected delegates were surprised to find that a second effort to unseat them was under way. A group called Women for Racial and Economic Equality circulated a flyer stating: "The IWY has been, among other things, about the representation and political power for those who have been denied it" and was inspired by the example of Fannie Lou Hamer and other black Mississippians who challenged the seating of the state's all-white delegation to the Democratic National Convention in 1964. Yet, thirteen years later, it read, "An all-white delegation, including several men, claim to speak for Mississippi women," and, "worse yet, outspoken advocates of the Ku Klux Klan are among them." Proclaiming that it was impossible "to win equality for women without eliminating the scourge of racism," the petitioners declared, "Women, Black, white and brown, must join hands to forge a new unity and strength of sisterhood" and, in the spirit of Fannie Lou Hamer, "demand that the delegation from Mississippi be unseated and that a truly representative delegation of Mississippi women be seated in its place."[56]

Both groups of Mississippi delegates, elected and at-large, participated in the conference. The 20 percent conservatives were outvoted as the 80 percent feminist majority adopted all but one plank—that calling for a cabinet-level women's department—of the proposed National Plan of Action. When planks they deemed sinful were adopted, the conservatives stood and turned their backs to the podium. Curtis Caine recalled, however, that the Mississippi delegates surprised observers by agreeing with parts of the Plan of Action that were "reasonable" and "proper." Lynn Caine insisted that the conservatives were primarily upset that so much power was being placed in the hands of the federal government.[57]

As the conference ended, the Mississippi delegation issued a flyer protesting the massive extension of federal power that the Plan of Action called for: "To all those here assembled be it known and remembered, as the federal chain forged at this time and place in the history of our great republic binds more tightly in the years to come, that the great, sovereign state of Mississippi did not forge its links."[58]

After the Houston conference, feminists celebrated their victory. But they were soon in conflict with President Carter, who in their eyes did not do enough to implement the National Plan of Action and fired Abzug as head of the IWY continuing committee when she criticized him to the press.[59] Over the next decade, the women's movement continued to pursue the Houston objectives but with little federal support and considerable opposition as the nation turned politically and culturally to the right. It appeared that the rest of the nation was catching up with Mississippi in defense of tradition against change. When in 1979 Congress extended the deadline for ERA ratification over the bitter protests of opponents, Mississippi senator John Stennis—one of the few senators who had voted against the ERA back in 1972—was one of those protesting most forcefully. Jimmy Carter continued to work hard for the amendment, but it had little effect. Meanwhile, Ronald Reagan—who launched his postconvention campaign at the Neshoba County Fair near Philadelphia, Mississippi, to a mostly white throng of around ten thousand—led the Republican Party to reverse its forty-year history of support for the ERA. As the controversy over women's rights polarized the nation's major political parties, there were new challenges for Mississippi's Democratic leaders. Some politicians, including ones on record as supporting the ERA, were distressed when the national Democratic Party's platform withheld funds from candidates who opposed ERA ratification and when the NOW-sponsored boycott of unratified states began to hurt the Gulf Coast tourist industry.[60]

The IWY experience solidified coalitions and networks for both conservatives and feminists in Mississippi, and after the 1977 conference both sides remained politically active. After Houston, Mississippi conservatives celebrated their victory and vowed to continue their work. A March 1978 article in the *Jackson Clarion-Ledger* described Eddie Myrtle Moore as "blessed with a bottomless pool of confidence" as she recounted tales of "facing off a mass of feminists" and having her views sought after by reporters from all across the country. Though her housework had suffered, she said, "[The whole experience] made me realize that as concerned Christian people we need to stand up for what we believe in.... There was a lot at stake and there still is."[61] In January 1979, over two hundred conservative women—including members of the Pro-Family Forum, Citizens for Decency through Law, Eagle Forum, STOP ERA, and the Conservative Caucus—visited the capitol to tell legislators that "all kinds of ladies oppose the ERA," that they should oppose federal initiatives connected with the United Nations' "Year of the Child," and promote laws against pornography and obscenity. Charles Pickering Sr., a leading Republican senator from Laurel, interrupted discussion of a bill to introduce the women.[62] That spring the Eagle Forum brought Rosemary Thomson, former head of the IWY Citizen's Review Committee and author of the newly published *The Price of Liberty* (about the victory of the conservative "Davids" versus the feminist "Goliaths in 1977") to Jackson as a speaker. She insisted that despite being a travesty of justice and display of "wicked intentions," the federally financed IWY may have been "the best spent $5 million ever, because women came out of their kitchens and said 'Stop!' to register displeasure at what they saw coming from the convention." As a result, said Thomson, "We now know who we are, where we are. We were a silent majority, now we are in the mainstream of politics." For over thirty years thereafter, Moore continued to be active in the Eagle Forum, serving as its leader for Mississippi.[63]

Mississippi feminists also learned from their IWY experiences and continued their political activity. Despite all that had happened, they believed it to be a good thing that the IWY had led to far more discussion of women's issues, including more coverage on local and national radio and television. Some later regretted not having created some sort of enduring feminist organization just after the state conference but said they had been too demoralized at first. They had nevertheless kept their network intact, lobbying continuously afterward through existing women's organizations and confederations.[64] For example, even as the conservative coalition was lobbying the legislature in January 1979, the Jackson chapter of NOW, leading a group including the LWV, the NCNW, and the ACLU, held a candlelight vigil on behalf of the ERA at the state capitol building.[65]

For women's rights supporters, the most important legacy of the IWY in Mississippi was the additional strength they drew from newly created alliances across racial and class lines. Black and white feminists who had been gathered together on the coordinating committee and others who had experienced the Mississippi takeover of July 1977 would never forget the experience or the sense of being connected in a common cause against a common foe. Jessie Mosley told a reporter, "We sincerely feel that something has been started here. Just working together as a committee, we have discovered a feeling of oneness that one would not expect to find between black and white women of all strata in Mississippi."[66] In its final report, the Mississippi IWY Committee wrote: "The Houston Meeting helped us to realize that we are not alone; it showed us that the movement for Equal Rights includes representatives from all segments of society—old, young, black, white, Chicano and Indian." As for the state meeting, it "made clear to us that sexism and racism are the same. Those who are against equal rights for women are also opposed to equal rights for blacks. Therefore both black and white women have to fight both sexism and racism or whichever one they may choose, it really means the same thing."[67]

Reflecting on the future, the committee members observed, "As Mississippi moves into the third century of America . . . the future is brighter for women in the sciences, business, and technical fields. It is brighter for the educational opportunities and educational involvement of women." Yet, they said, there were many challenges, not the least of them that too many women were in "dead-end jobs" and needed help to prepare for "emerging job opportunities." For there to be a better future for Mississippi women, they stated, there was clearly a need for new ways of thinking in regard to gender roles in the state:

"The full equality between men and women will necessitate changes in deep-rooted assumptions and attitudes about women's and men's roles in social and economic arrangements." They were eager that, despite the conservative take-over, Mississippi women still have a voice in the national and international discussions ongoing during the United Nations' 1975–1985 International Decade for Women. "There is a need," they wrote, "not only to work for women's rights, but to work for human rights around the world. There must be mutual respect for multinational cultural diversity which is essential to lasting peace."[68]

Recognizing that the recent events were too close to be fully understood, they surmised that "the full impact of the IWY upon the women's movement will be fully appraised by historians in years to come." In their eyes, the IWY conferences across the nation had provided an "opportunity for women to sit down to face the problems which affect their daily lives," something "never before accomplished on such a large scale." The process left women with "a history and an awareness that was not present before." They concluded: "In the years ahead we must busy ourselves with the implementing of the plan of action. We must bear in mind 'those who protest also contribute to progress,' . . . Mississippi women are on the move."[69]

The Mississippi IWY conference of 1977 was deeply disturbing to everyone involved, but it was also an awakening. The IWY conferences brought the state's women—many of whom had little previous awareness of current debates on women's issues taking place elsewhere in the United States and abroad—into the discussion and into politics. The experience also made Mississippi women, feminist and conservative alike, more aware of one another and of their profound differences. If, as it seems, Mississippi women had not been "Awake and Aware" before July 1977, after the state's IWY conference they surely were. And both sides would remain awake, aware, deeply polarized, and very active in the years ahead.

NOTES

The author wishes to thank the National Endowment for the Humanities; the Schlesinger Library on the History of Women in America, Harvard; and the Radcliffe Institute for Advanced Study, Harvard, for grants that supported this research.

1. National Commission on the Observance of International Women's Year Papers (henceforth cited as National Commission Papers), Schlesinger Library, Harvard University, Cambridge, Massachusetts; see Mississippi Commission on the Observance of International Woman's Year Papers, and subject file "International Women's Conference," Mississippi Department of Archives and History, Jackson (henceforth cited as MDAH); Janice Moor, ed., "Mississippi IWY Conference Final Report, July 8–9, 1977" (henceforth cited as "Final Report"), and "Mississippi Report to the

National Commission on the Observance of IWY," carton 2, Mississippi folder, National Women's Conference file, Mississippiana vertical files, Mississippi State University Library, Starkville; AAUW Collection, Archives and Special Collections, John Davis Williams Library, University of Mississippi, Oxford; Equal Rights Amendment (ERA) file, McCain Library, University of Southern Mississippi, Hattiesburg; Dr. Cora Norman, interviewed by the author and Sara Farnsworth, March 2001, Jackson, Mississippi; Dr. Jessie Mosley, interviewed by the author, March 9, 2001, Jackson, Mississippi; interviews by Sheryl Hansen, Mississippi Oral History Program of the University of Southern Mississippi: Dr. Cora Norman, April 7, 1992 (vol. 432); Alison Steiner, September 28, 1992 (vol. 416); Dr. Katharine Rea, October 15, 1992 (vol. 429); Natalie Mason, November 17, 1992; Thelma Zinner, November 17, 1992 (vol. 427); Dr. Kathie Gilbert, November 20, 1992 (vol. 428); William T. Temple and Norma Temple, February 16, 1993; Dr. and Mrs. Curtis Caine, February 28, 1993 (vol. 438).

2. Marjorie J. Spruill and Jesse Spruill Wheeler, "The Equal Rights Amendment and Mississippi," *Mississippi History Now*, March 2003, http://mshistory.k12.ms.us.

3. Marjorie J. Spruill, "Gender and America's Right Turn," in *Rightward Bound: Making America Conservative in the 1970s*, ed. Bruce J. Schulman and Julian E. Zelizer (Cambridge, Mass.: Harvard University Press, 2008), 71–89.

4. Proponents secured an extension of the ERA's original deadline of 1979 but were unable to secure the remaining three states needed for ratification by 1982, when the second deadline passed; Spruill, "Gender and America's Right Turn"; Jane J. Mansbridge, *Why We Lost the ERA* (Chicago: University of Chicago Press, 1986); Carol Felsenthal, *The Sweetheart of the Silent Majority: The Biography of Phyllis Schlafly* (Garden City, N.Y.: Doubleday, 1981); Donald T. Critchlow, *Phyllis Schlafly and Grassroots Conservatism: A Woman's Crusade* (Princeton, N.J.: Princeton University Press, 2005); Susan M. Hartmann, *From Margin to Mainstream: American Women and Politics since 1960* (New York: Knopf, 1989), 137–39.

5. National Commission on the Observance of International Women's Year, *The Spirit of Houston: The First National Women's Conference; An Official Report to the President, the Congress and the People of the United States* (Washington, D.C.: U.S. Government Printing Office, 1978), 9–12, 99–102; National Commission on the Observance of International Women's Year, *"To Form a More Perfect Union" . . . Justice for American Women* (Washington, D.C.: U.S. Government Printing Office, 1976); Phyllis Schlafly, "The Commission on International Women's Year, or, Bella Abzug's Boondoggle," *Phyllis Schlafly Report* (henceforth cited as *PSR*), January 1976.

6. Angela Howard and Sasha Ranaé Adams, *Antifeminism in America: A Reader; A Collection of Readings from the Literature of the Opponents to U.S. Feminism, 1848 to the Present* (New York: Garland, 2000); Phyllis Schlafly, *The Power of the Positive Woman* (New York: Harcourt Brace Jovanovich, 1977); Rosemary Thomson, *The Price of LIBerty* (Carol Stream, Ill.: Creation House, 1978).

7. *Spirit of Houston*, 274, 275; *PSR*, January 1976; *Eagle Forum Newsletter* (henceforth cited as *EFN*), May, July, August 1977; Thomson, *Price of LIBerty*; Felsenthal, *Sweetheart of the Silent Majority*.

8. *Spirit of Houston*, 9–11, 99–103; *EFN*, March 31, 1977; Thomson, *Price of LIBerty*, 92–94.

9. Thomson, *Price of LIBerty*; Felsenthal, *Sweetheart of the Silent Majority*, 261–64, 276–81; *PSR*, May 1977; Jerry Falwell, *Falwell: An Autobiography* (Lynchburg, Va.: Liberty House, 1997), 360, 361; *Greenville (Miss.) Delta Democrat-Times* (henceforth cited as *DDT*), July 14, 1977; "Women's Year: Peril on the Right," *Philadelphia (Pa.) Inquirer*, August 23, 1977; clippings, Official Briefing Book, National Women's Conference, National Commission Papers; *Spirit of Houston*, 109, 113, 121, 122, 142.

10. *Spirit of Houston*, 104–17; *Wichita (Kans.) Eagle & Beacon*, August 3, 1977; *Detroit News*, September 1, 1977; clippings in Briefing Book, National Commission Papers, September 11, 1977; "Feminists, Conservatives Face Houston Standoff," *Memphis Commercial Appeal*, September 11, 1977, 2E; Ellen Cohn, "Mama Said There'd be Days like This," *Village Voice*, July 11, 1977; *Mindszenty Report* 19, no. 7 (July 1977).

11. Bella Abzug Memo to State Chairs, May 2, 1977, with Phyllis Schlafly's letter to "Dear Eagles" of March 31, 1977 and instructions attached, National Commission Papers; National Commission on the Observance of International Women's Year, "Update on the State Women's Meeting and the National IWY Conference," May 31, 1977, AAUW Collection, J. D. Williams Library, University of Mississippi, Oxford.

12. Hansen interview with Cora Norman; Moor, "Final Report," 6.

13. "Abstract of Minutes of Miss. IWY Coordinating Committee," in "Accomplishments of Mississippi Women: Movements, Groups and Individuals" (1978), 47, MDAH.

14. Announcement of Mississippi IWY Coordinating Committee Members, in Cora Norman Papers on loan to the author.

15. Ibid.; "Klansman's Wife Equates Women's Rights With Communism," and "Nine At-Large Members Must Carry Rights Banner," both in *CL*, November 17, 1977; Gilbert R. Mason and James Patterson Smith, *Beaches, Blood, and Ballots: A Black Doctor's Civil Rights Struggle* (Jackson: University Press of Mississippi, 2000).

16. "Abstract of Minutes of Mississippi IWY Coordinating Committee", MDAH; List of Mississippi IWY leaders and their affiliations; Cora Norman to Mary Grefe, AAUW Educational Foundation President, "Nomination of AAUW Achievement Award," September 7, 1988, Cora Norman Papers; Hansen interview with Cora Norman; author and Farnsworth interview with Cora Norman.

17. Moor, "Final Report."

18. Ibid.; Constance Iona Slaughter, "The Legal Status of Homemakers in Mississippi," commissioned and distributed by the National Commission on the Observance of International Women's Year, Homemakers Committee, June 1977, MDAH.

19. "Planners Hope for 1,000 At Weekend IWY Meet," *Jackson (Miss.) Clarion-Ledger-Daily News*, July 3, 1977.

20. Moor, Final Report; "Planners Hope for 1,000."

21. Hansen interview with Alison Steiner.

22. Moor, "Final Report."

23. Hansen interviews with Lynn and Curtis Caine, William and Norma Temple; "2 Groups To Attend IWY Confab," *JDN*, November 15, 1977; "Delegates Brace for IWY Storm," *CL*, November 17, 1977.

24. *DDT*, July 14, 1977; "Delegates Brace for IWY Storm"; "Klansman's Wife."

25. Hansen interview with Curtis and Lynne Caine.

26. Hansen interviews with Curtis and Lynn Caine, Alison Steiner, and Cora Norman; "Women's Year: Walthall Group Are State Participants," *Tylertown (Miss.) Times*, July 14, 1977.

27. Moor, "Final Report"; "Outlook" column, *Tylertown (Miss.) Times*, July 21, 1977.

28. L. C. Dorsey, "International Women's Year Meeting," n.d., in unidentified newsletter, Martha Swain clippings collection, in possession of the author.

29. "State Women's Year Group Not Going 'Liberal,'" *CL*, September 28, 1977; Hansen interview with Cora Norman.

30. Memo to Bella Abzug, Chair, National Commission on Women, from Kathie Gilbert, a Citizen of the State of Mississippi and Vice-chair Mississippi IWY Coordinating Committee, July ?,

1977, in Cora Norman Papers; "Feminists, Antifeminists See IWY Meeting as Grassroots Test," *Biloxi-Gulfport (Miss.) South Mississippi Sun* (henceforth cited as *SMS*), November 15, 1977.

31. "Get Mixed Reaction," *CL*, July 9, 1977; Mitchell quotation from *CL*, November 17, 1977.

32. "Delegates Brace for IWY Storm"; "IWY 'Alerted' About Voting," *JDN*, September 28, 1977,.

33. "IWY 'Alerted' about Voting."

34. Moor, Final Report; "Get Mixed Reaction."

35. Marjorie Spruill Wheeler, *New Women of the New South: The Leaders of the Woman Suffrage Movement in the Southern States* (New York: Oxford University Press, 1993).

36. "Klansman's Wife."

37. "Feminists, Antifeminists"; "Delegates Brace for IWY Storm"; "Women's Group Shocked at Delegation," *CL*, September 9, 1977.

38. Thomson, *Price of LIBerty*, 131; "2 Groups To Attend IWY Confab," *JDN*, November 15, 1977; "Feminists, Antifeminists"; "Klansman's Wife."

39. "Klansman's Wife"; Hansen interview with Cora Norman; "Anti-ERA Force Sees Return to Moral Values," (Biloxi) *Daily Herald*, July 12, 1977, A-8.

40. "Nine At-Large Members."

41. "Conservative Lawyer Helped Engineer Anti-ERA Victories," *Columbus (Miss.) Commercial Dispatch*, July 12, 1977; unidentified clipping in Mississippi Report to the National Commission on the Observance of IWY, National Commission Papers.

42. Moor, "Final Report."

43. Outlook, *Tylertown (Miss.) Times*, July 21, 1977.

44. "Militant Conservatives Form New Coalition," *DDT*, July 14, 1977.

45. *Spirit of Houston*, 99–117.

46. Summaries of executive committee meetings, August 10–12, 1977; press release from National Commission Executive Committee; and Abzug to Fellow Commissioners, September 2, 1977, carton 1, folders September 15, 16, 1977, Shelah Leader Papers, Schlesinger Library, Harvard University, Cambridge, Massachusetts; "Conservative Movement among Women Grows: Two Groups Oppose ERA," *Alabama Journal*, July 18, 1977; *EFN*, July 1977.

47. Press release from National Commission, September 2, 1977; *Spirit of Houston*, 112, 113.

48. Moor, "Final Report"; "Report from the Minority Caucus of the *Mississippi* IWY State Meeting, submitted and prepared by Karen M. Kester, Chair, July 16, 1977," and Kathie Gilbert to Bella Abzug, "Challenge of the Mississippi Delegation to the National Conference on Women to Be Held in Houston, Texas during November 18–21, 1977," July ?, 1977, both in Cora Norman Papers.

49. "Women's Group Shocked at Delegation"; "IWY Selects Nine Delegates from State," *SMS*, September 29, 1977; "Coast's IWY Delegate Hopes Houston Won't Be Another Jackson," *SMS*, n.d.; National Women's Conference file, Mississippi State University Archives, Starkville.

50. "State Women's Year Group Not Going 'Liberal,'" *CL*, September 28, 1977; untitled article, *SMS*, September 28, 1977; "IWY 'Alerted' about Voting," *JDN*, September 28, 1977; "Delegates Brace for IWY Storm"; "Feminists, Antifeminists."

51. "Anti-ERA Group Holds Rally Critical of IWY Conference," *CL*, November 13, 1977.

52. *Spirit of Houston*, 122–29.

53. "Klansman's Wife"; "Klan's 'Spies' Plan to Disrupt Feminist Parley," *Detroit News*, September 1, 1977; clipping, Official Briefing Book, National Women's Conference, Houston, in National Commission Papers; "New Coalition Braces for Attacks against IWY," *Women Today* 7, no. 19 (September 19, 1977).

54. "Meet the Delegates: Mississippi Style," *Houston Daily Breakthrough* November 19, 1977, 27.

55. Ibid.

56. "Women for Racial and Economic Equality," flyer, copy in possession of the author.

57. *Spirit of Houston*, 166; Hansen interview with Curtis and Lynne Caine.

58. Flyer in possession of the author.

59. Spruill, "Gender and America's Right Turn"; Suzanne Braun Levine and Mary Thom, *Bella Abzug: How One Tough Broad from the Bronx Fought Jim Crow and Joe McCarthy, Pissed Off Jimmy Carter, Battled for the Rights of Women and Workers, Rallied against War and for the Planet, and Shook Up Politics along the Way* (New York: Farrar, Straus & Giroux, 2007), 218–28.

60. Susan M. Hartmann, "Feminism, Public Policy, and the Carter Administration," in *The Carter Presidency: Policy Choices in the Post–New Deal Era*, ed. Gary M. Fink and Hugh Davis Graham (Lawrence: University Press of Kansas, 1998), 224–43; Emily Walker Cook, "Women White House Advisors in the Carter Administration: Presidential Stalwarts or Feminist Advocates?" (PhD diss., Vanderbilt University, 1995); "'No' On ERA Hits Business for Coliseum," Jackson, Miss. (UPI), Martha Swain clipping collection; Earl Black and Merle Black, *The Rise of Southern Republicans* (Cambridge, Mass.: Harvard University Press, 2002), 216–17.

61. "Moore: Says She'll Still Serve," *CL*, March 10, 1978.

62. Ibid.; article in *CL*, June 16, 1979, Equal Rights Amendment subject file, MDAH.

63. Thomson, *Price of LIBerty*, 47, 48; "Warning Is Sounded over 'Far-Reaching' ERA," *JDN*, May 23, 1979, 12A; Eagle Forum Web site, http://www.eagleforum.org/misc/states/states.html.

64. Cora Norman, speech to AAUW regional meeting, Jackson, Mississippi, April 15, 1984.

65. "NOW Applies Pressure for ERA Ratification," *JDN*, January 25, 1979; "ACLU Seeks Ban on Law Banning Capitol Protests," *CL*, February 3, 1979, 3A.

66. Spruill and Hansen interviews with Cora Norman; "Planners Hope for 1,000 at Weekend IWY Meet," *Jackson (Miss.) Clarion-Ledger-Daily News*, July 3, 1977.

67. Accomplishments of Mississippi Women: Movements, Groups, and Individuals (all) by IWY Special Projects Committee, Mississippi Commission on the Observance of International Women's Year, 55, National Women's Conference file, Mississippi State University Library, Starkville.

68. Ibid.

69. Ibid.

The Unknown Grandmother, African American Memory, and Lives of Service in Northern Mississippi

ELIZABETH ANNE PAYNE, HATTYE RASPBERRY-HALL,

MICHAEL DE L. LANDON, AND JENNIFER NARDONE

Every three years, descendants of an "unknown grandmother" reunite in Okolona in northeastern Mississippi, to remember their ancestor's experiences on a slave march around 1850. The "unknown grandmother" and her small son left Bowling Green, Kentucky, for the Columbus, Mississippi, slave market. Only the son survived the grueling trip. The "unknown grandmother," pregnant and weak, collapsed along the way and was beaten and abandoned because she could not continue.

Her son, Simon, watched his mother dying on the roadside as he was forced to keep pace. As an older freedman, Simon Tilghman Tucker would tell his descendants about his mother's final moments, always adding that he had prayed she would die quickly. According to the family, these "slave stories" were repeated from generation to generation, told on front porches, at after-church gatherings, at Sunday dinner, and at bedtime. Through years of storytelling, Simon transformed his memories of his mother into a tale about the pain and sacrifice of the family's ancestors. Family members later realized that the stories they knew by heart were tools for teaching their history to succeeding generations. The family came to understand itself through the story of the "unknown grandmother" and the small boy who was determined to honor his mother. Simon's children and grandchildren heard often that the best way to honor her memory and sacrifice would be to follow lives of service and commitment.[1]

Simon's granddaughter, Willa Tucker Raspberry, called "Grande Dame" by the family, was born in 1906, the daughter of Simon's son Winford and his wife, Ophallon Dilworth Tucker. The dramatic storytelling at the Tucker-Raspberry-Dilworth reunions cannot begin without her nod of permission. At the age of 103, Willa Raspberry connects the enslaved woman who died nameless and neglected on the slave march to her own children and their descendants. Her life offers a particular angle of vision on the possibilities for black women in northern Mississippi in the twentieth century and of the space that African Americans shaped for themselves under oppressive conditions. Having grown up in the Jim Crow era, she is nevertheless well educated and has frequently traveled. She served as a leader in the Episcopal Church, a teacher in public schools, a home extension agent, and a librarian at Okolona College. After the Episcopal school closed in 1964, she created and ran the Okolona Child Development Center. And although she never took part in a civil rights march, Willa Raspberry became in 1965 the first African American woman in Chickasaw County to register to vote.[2]

Willa Tucker Raspberry's memories of Okolona and those of her family help to clarify the regional context of race, class, and gender in the Jim Crow South.[3] The gradations between middle-class and lower-class African Americans proved to be more permeable in the rural South than the model of class relations often furnished by historical analysis.[4] The population of the northern Mississippi hill country in the twentieth century was more eclectic than that of suburban America. And that difference, coupled with the power of the family's understanding of itself as descendants of the "unknown grandmother," indicate that local history and family self-understanding often take precedence over monolithic models and theories.[5]

The shaping narrative that dominated her family's understanding of itself ensured that Willa Raspberry would embrace the entire African American community. Unlike many black women portrayed in studies of other parts of the country, her role as matriarch in a small northern Mississippi community engaged her as a partner with the men in that community. Her story rebuts the theory that the authority of African American men diminished when black women gained power. At the same time, she is always eager to deflect attention from herself to the legacy of her husband.

To be sure, her family held a distinct place among northern Mississippi African Americans even during slavery. "Miss Willa"—as she is called by many in the Okolona community—recalls her grandfather Simon saying that other slaves envied his status as a slave to Tilghman Tucker, Mississippi's governor from 1842 to 1844 and later a congressman. "He [Simon] was well fed and treated like a human being. Mrs. Tucker, his mistress, treated them [slaves] like human beings." But while Governor Tucker may have felt that his status did not allow him personally to mistreat his slaves, he nevertheless on at least one occasion allowed a visitor to beat Simon severely.[6]

After slavery, Simon Tucker bought his own land in Monroe County near Smithville and later divided it among his three children, Zachary, Winford, and Talena. Willa Tucker spent part of her childhood helping to farm that land and living with her grandparents and parents in a spacious dogtrot house, a residence typical of the rural South with front and back porches and with the middle of the house open. She adored her grandfather, Simon, a Methodist preacher who later converted to the Campbellite Church of Christ after attending a local three-week revival. Formed in the early nineteenth century under Thomas Campbell and later led by his son Alexander, the Campbellites often traveled around the South for revivals, preaching the significance of biblical worship and baptism, as opposed to church hierarchy and dogma. They believed that "Christian union can result from nothing short of the destruction of creeds and confessions of faith, inasmuch as human creeds and confession have destroyed Christian union."[7] The Campbellites believed in full-body adult immersion baptism upon a person's joining the church. Willa Raspberry remembers seeing Simon Tucker participate in such a ceremony in the nearby Tombigbee River when she was a child. The Reverend Tucker, who followed the sect's code of rigorous self-discipline, later helped to build a black Church of Christ in Smithville, Mississippi.[8]

Willa Tucker grew up knowing that both blacks and whites in Monroe County held her grandfather in high regard. "He had a long beard," she remembers, "and I thought he was next to Santa Claus."[9] But despite Simon Tucker's enviable status both during and after slavery, he made sure that his family always understood the humiliation and pain of slavery. For the rest of his life, he avoided returning to Columbus, Mississippi, where he had been auctioned as a child.[10]

Simon's sale to Tilghman Tucker had occurred shortly before the Civil War, around 1857. In both the 1900 and 1920 censuses, he gave 1845 as his date of birth. After Governor Tucker's death in 1859, young Simon continued in the service of the governor's wife, Martha Tucker. Around 1880, he married Martha Ann Dean, who was born in 1858 and was a former slave who lived on a neighboring plantation. The slave stories that Willa Raspberry heard on the front porch after Sunday dinner encompassed the experiences of both of her grandparents. "It was very important for Martha to be a lady," she recalls. "She would don her riding habit and ride sidesaddle over to the Tucker plantation on Saturdays."[11]

Martha Ann Dean's presumed biological grandmother, Jerusha Dean, treated her son's slave in the same respectful manner as the Tuckers had dealt with

Simon. Martha Ann, for example, remembered jumping up and down on a feather-mattressed tall bed to the delight of Jerusha.[12] The 1860 census reports Jerusha as living with her son, twenty-four-year-old J. H. Dean. Slave schedules from that year indicate that J. H. Dean owned a twenty-four-year-old black slave and five mulatto females, aged ten, seven, six, two, and one. As the census listed only the age and sex of slaves, we do not know the names of the twenty-four-year-old woman and her children. In 1870, however, Martha Ann Dean emerges in the census as Ann Dean in the household of Abby Dean and one of six children between the ages of four to seventeen. Abby Dean's family lived next door to Jerusha Dean, J. H. Dean, and Martha Dean, the twenty-one-year-old wife of J. H.[13]

Simon and Martha's son, Winford Tucker, worked on the family farm until 1919, when he bought a piece of land near Smithville.[14] There he farmed cotton and logged pine trees. In 1905, Winford married Ophallon Dilworth, whose family, the census shows, were neighbors.[15] Willa, the oldest of their seven children, excelled in school even as a young child. In 1918, the future Mrs. Raspberry met the Reverend Marshal Kable, a visiting minister from Nashville, Tennessee, at the Church of Christ built by her grandfather.[16] Kable, who recognized the academic potential of twelve-year-old Willa Tucker, convinced her father to let her move to Nashville, live with Kable and his wife, Minnie, and attend the Ashcroft School.[17] Years later, Willa Raspberry recognized the importance of the year spent there. "It made me want more schooling," she said. "I have lived a better and more profitable life because of Minister Kable."[18]

When Willa Raspberry returned to Smithville in 1919, she found her family in a state of upheaval that ended in her parents' bitter separation and divorce. Thus, she became, at the age of thirteen, a surrogate mother to her six younger siblings. For a time, her life was in turmoil. During the week, she lived with her father's sister, Aunt Talena, in nearby Amory. Having just returned from attending school in a big city, she enjoyed an elevated status among her fellow students at Jonesboro High School. "I was a queen of my school in Amory," she would later recall. But at the same time, she felt intense pain over her mother's absence and feared that she might "die of a broken heart."[19]

Still, the dutiful Willa obeyed her father's command not to speak to her mother and indeed had no contact with Ophallon again until after her marriage to James Raspberry in 1925. Meanwhile, her father remained her primary authority figure, a strong and disciplined man, extremely protective of his family and a leading citizen in Smithville's black community. Although never obsequious to whites, he also showed little tolerance for aberrant behavior within the black community. Willa Raspberry's sister Dona Tucker Floyd remembers a young girl who became pregnant out of wedlock during their 1920 high school year. Winford Tucker, a member of the school board, had the girl expelled. The girl's mother was so shamed by her daughter's action and her consequent expulsion that she eventually committed suicide by drinking poison. The girl's father would frequently burst into tears during church services, but Floyd recalled, "Papa said that he had to expel that girl." Just the year before, he had insisted on the expulsion of a girl of lower social status for the same reason, and the community had strongly supported that decision.[20] Some may interpret Winford Tucker's actions as harsh and judgmental. From his perspective, however, it was a matter of racial solidarity. His Church of Christ commitment to social equality demanded that he support expulsion of the middle-class girl because he had previously called for the same action for the poor student.

Indeed, Winford Tucker exemplified a strong male presence not only for his own family but for the entire black community at a time when black men were often portrayed as politically impotent and socially uninvolved. Mississippi had adopted a new, oppressive constitution in 1890 that reversed the achievements of Reconstruction for blacks.[21] He suffered the humiliations of segregation, as he later revealed to his children on the day in 1965 when he finally was allowed to register to vote after the passage of the Voting Rights Act: "Today I finally feel like a man."[22]

His experience differed from that of his daughter. When asked about her response to registering to vote, Willa Raspberry sanguinely reflected that although she was gratified to register, she did not consider it an emotional or spiritual high point. Voting did not signify a confirmation of her womanhood, but for her father, who had witnessed the narrowing of political participation for black men during his youth, registering to vote was deeply tied to his sense of manhood and masculinity.

Willa Tucker found another man much like her father when, after graduating from Jonesboro High School in 1924, she moved to Friendship in neighboring Itawamba County and met James Raspberry. A teacher at Jonesboro High School had told her that the new Rosenwald School needed teachers and urged her to apply. She was accepted, but before reporting she returned to Nashville to take a teacher's training class at Fisk University, an educational beacon for African Americans in the mid-South.

The Rosenwald School Fund operated out of Tuskegee University in Alabama. It had been founded in 1912, when Booker T. Washington solicited from Sears Roebuck president Julius Rosenwald a matching grant to build schools for African American children in the countryside surrounding the university. By 1918, Washington and Rosenwald's rural school program had expanded throughout the South, and in the prime years of its program—1920–28—between four and five hundred schools were built annually with funds totaling from $356,000 to $414,000.[23]

In the peak period, Rosenwald funded 556 schools in Mississippi. In fact, more Rosenwald schools were built in Mississippi than in any other state except North Carolina.[24] James Raspberry had helped to build the Rosenwald school at Dorsey in Itawamba County before moving to Friendship to serve as principal of Mississippi's eighth Rosenwald school. Building the school had cost a total of $2,235, only $800 of which had come from the Rosenwald Fund. None of the remainder had come from the local white community, but the African American community had contributed both money and labor. Willa Tucker enjoyed teaching English there. "We weren't bound by anything at that school," she said. "We had perfect freedom to teach anything we wanted."[25]

By all accounts, James Raspberry and Willa Tucker fell in love immediately. "As soon as I saw him, I knew," Willa Raspberry remembers. "I loved him through and through, from the top of his head to the tip of his toes." In fact, she immediately called off her engagement to a young man who lived next door to her parents. In 1925, James and Willa married and moved to his hometown of Okolona. They remained there, happily married, until James Raspberry's death in 1991.[26]

James Raspberry's grandfather Abram had survived slavery just as had Willa Raspberry's grandparents. Abram Raspberry spoke with Winford Tucker's formality, and both fathers emphasized education and proper behavior. In fact, Willa Raspberry always insists that any respect she gained from the white community in Okolona resulted as much from her role as James Raspberry's spouse as from her own position.

The newlywed couple lived in faculty housing at the Okolona Industrial School, a black high school where James Raspberry taught carpentry and woodworking and Willa Raspberry worked as librarian; later she also taught in several public schools around Okolona. She and her husband reared five children, all of whom received their high school educations at the industrial school. She always remembers their life there as one of warm relationships with both friends and students.

The school offered a stimulating setting for the Raspberry family. It had been founded in 1904 by Dr. Wallace Battle, a black man who had graduated from Berea College in Kentucky in 1902, when Berea was still an integrated college. Born in Alabama, Battle came to Mississippi looking for a way to "improve the race problem." He believed in Booker T. Washington's philosophy of industrial education, and as James Raspberry later reported, at the school "the course work was based on the idea that no one is truly educated unless one is trained to earn a living with his hands as well as [with] his head."²⁷ Beginning with Battle, the school's administration enjoyed a good relationship with both blacks and whites in Okolona. Battle had raised the foundational four thousand dollars from both communities as well as from northeastern states, and the school always had an interracial board of directors.

James Raspberry remembered that "several local white families—the Stovalls, Chandlers, Edens, Morrisons and Abbotts—became interested in the school. Many served on the Board of Trustees during the life of the institution. They also served as good will ambassadors to the community, thereby easing some latent animosity concerning education for blacks."²⁸ Generous grants from Episcopal Church communities in New York, New Jersey, and Massachusetts encouraged Dr. Battle in 1920 to approach the Right Reverend Theodore DuBose Bratton, bishop of the Episcopal Diocese of Mississippi, who pledged at least one thousand dollars annually from the diocese. In 1926, St. Bernard's Episcopal Chapel was built on the campus. Its presence helped to garner continued attention and financial support from the local white community.²⁹

Racial tensions, however, occasionally flared in Okolona and Chickasaw County. What brought the Raspberrys there in 1925, in fact, involved the worst racial incident in the town's history. James Raspberry had been hired to replace previous superintendent of industrial training Ulysses S. Baskin, who had been murdered by a white man. Baskin, a Tuskegee alumnus and World War I veteran, killed several dogs belonging to Hob Anderson after they had attacked school livestock. In retaliation, the dogs' owner shot and killed Baskin. When a local jury acquitted Anderson of manslaughter, Dr. Battle suffered a nervous breakdown and resigned the school presidency. His wife, Effie, however, took over the position and remained in office until 1932.³⁰ During their early years at the school, therefore, the Raspberrys actually served under the administration of a black woman.

Baskin's murder for a time blew the lid off the seeming racial harmony of Okolona and fractured the black community. Battle had claimed that the killing was part of a "concerted plot on the part of bad white men in the community" to ruin his school. To be sure, the Ku Klux Klan had reigned unchecked in parts of northern Mississippi from 1919 to 1925, and lynchings were common. In nearby Union County, for example, a mob lynched seventeen-year-old L. Q. Ivy only a few weeks after the Baskin murder.³¹ Ruth Hawkins Payne, who was born in 1924 and grew up in nearby Itawamba County, recalled childhood memories of talk about the lynching of an African American man whose body had been hung from a tree by the Frisco Railroad track to frighten passengers.³²

After his resignation, Dr. Battle told a colleague that "there was no use in his returning to the school . . . as the morale of the faculty and of the Negroes in the community was so shattered that the school's usefulness was permanently crippled."[33] Willa Raspberry, however, claims, "We did not live in fear. We knew that sort of thing did not [regularly] happen here [in Okolona]." In fact, the mayor of Okolona called a mass meeting at which a unanimous resolution was passed to support and protect the school's future, and the city pledged an additional six thousand dollars in aid.[34]

Throughout the 1920s, the Episcopal Church's American Church Institute for Negroes (ACIN) continued to provide both financial and moral support for the school. Although neither of the Raspberrys had been reared as Episcopalians, both became members of St. Bernard's Chapel. Mrs. Raspberry recalls that for her a feeling of genuine religious dedication began only after she found the Episcopal Church and became familiar with the Book of Common Prayer. "It spoke to me," she recalls. "The Church of Christ seemed a little narrow after the [reading of it]."[35] Her son William later explained that when asked by a friend how a black Mississippian could be an Episcopalian, he responded to the questioner that his own attraction to the Episcopal Church concerned esthetics and well-crafted sermons. He reflected, "The thing I think about above all when I think of the [Episcopal] church is its service and its commitment to uplift. Maybe it's because St. Bernard's Church . . . was joined at the hip to Okolona College." Considering the black Episcopalians of his youth, he remarked, "I think of people who routinely made a life-altering difference for so many hundreds of mostly poor black folks during the darkest days of segregation."[36]

James Raspberry, who had been reared a Baptist, came to feel the same affinity for the church as did his wife. They both immediately became involved in the life and further development of both the school and its chapel. In an unpublished history of St. Bernard's, Willa Raspberry wrote that "there was a real marriage between church and school. The two were so closely intermeshed that one could hardly tell where one's activity began and the other's ended."[37]

Okolona had a small business district located on and around Main Street. Most black businesses were relegated to side streets, but blacks shopped in the same stores as whites. Charlie Gilliam, a black business owner, supported the industrial college with both time and money and served on its board of directors during the 1920s. His mercantile store anchored the black business district, which also included a café, a shoe-repair shop, Dr. Charles Wheeler's medical practice, and a Masonic lodge. James Raspberry belonged to the lodge, and he and his family counted Gilliam and Wheeler among their close friends.[38]

By the mid-1930s, a junior college had been added to the high school at what then became Okolona College, and it included a diverse community. William

Raspberry remembers that many black speakers, musicians, artists, and writers would often visit, and that gave the student body, as well as him and his siblings, a good sense of the larger world. "We came to think of ourselves as fairly sophisticated," he recalls.[39] Hattye Raspberry-Hall remembers that, although blacks were not normally allowed inside Okolona's Carnegie Public Library, her mother came and went there regularly. Willa Raspberry recalls: "I got to be friends with the white women who worked there because I was the librarian at the college. They would let me borrow books we didn't have."[40]

Willa Raspberry always insists, "Any respect I had in the town came from him [James Raspberry]." In addition to his status as a teacher, a Mason, and a leader of the local African American Episcopal Church, James Raspberry was a respected craftsman and builder. Their son describes his father as "very smart in a folksy sort of way because he could fix anything and make anything." In fact, James Raspberry helped to build the interior of Grace Episcopal Church—later renamed St. Bernard's/Grace Episcopal Church—as well as many of the buildings on campus. His talent and good nature afforded him high standing among both whites and blacks.[41]

Outside Okolona, however, few whites knew anything about the town's black college and its mission or anything about the Raspberry family. Whites from surrounding communities who came to the Fourth of July parade and to use the public whites-only swimming pool seldom knew that the college down the road sponsored an interracial summer institute promoting both education and integration. White Methodists knew about Rust College in Holly Springs, but only Episcopalians knew about Okolona College.

The Right Reverend Bishop Duncan Gray Jr. recalls visiting the summer training institute several times in the mid-1950s, when he was in charge of two mission churches in Bolivar County. He found his visits to the school a welcome respite from the rigid segregation of the Delta. In the summer of 1954, when the U.S. Supreme Court's decision in *Brown v. Board of Education* was expected daily, he felt he "needed the camaraderie, the interracial comfort and openness of Okolona." And when the *Brown* decision was handed down, the Reverend Gray, James Raspberry, and two other northern Mississippi Episcopalians—including Elizabeth Nobles, wife of Mississippi State University's baseball coach—composed a letter titled "The Church Considers the Supreme Court Decision," a copy of which was mailed to every Episcopal congregation in the state. Addressing the connection between Christian doctrine and *Brown*, it "fully supported school desegregation" as being "in accord with the principles of Christian democracy."[42]

James Raspberry did not feel optimistic. In regard to the letter's title, he reportedly commented, "The Church will consider it all right. And then table it." Willa Raspberry had similar doubts. "I couldn't believe it would really happen at the time," she later recalled. But the letter's text ended with a challenge: "If we find ourselves resenting this, then we should examine our attitude toward democracy itself." The wording was eventually adopted by the national leadership of the Episcopal Church and also by several other mainstream Protestant churches in official response to *Brown*. The statement from Okolona, therefore, ultimately provided the sense of urgency and the eloquent language of theological affirmation that defined the National Council of Churches' stance on desegregation.[43]

The success of Okolona College demonstrates the distinction between northern Mississippi and the Delta. Okolona did not have the sharp class distinctions that often encouraged racial oppression in other small towns. William Raspberry remembers that "there were no rich people in Okolona, not even rich white people."[44] Class and race relations were different from those in Mississippi towns where "antebellum work patterns reappeared in but slightly altered form after Reconstruction."[45]

Most historically black colleges were founded during Reconstruction by northern whites interested in the progressive ideal of industrial education. Whites maintained control of many black schools well into the 1960s. In his novel *Invisible Man*, Ralph Ellison describes tensions within the black communities that typically surrounded historically black schools. Blacks who worked at the school were often seen as tools of the white president and board of directors by the rest of the black community. The presence of a black college often exacerbated class divisions between educated and uneducated blacks.[46]

Okolona College defied the stereotypes. Founded by a black man with funds from both blacks and whites in the local community, Okolona College offered an alternative blueprint for race and class in Mississippi. William Raspberry maintains, "The presence of that little black school helped to transform our town into what these days we would call a learning community, at least for the black half of the town and we had some effect on the other . . . but I'm principally talking about what happened to black kids and black families in that town in those days." He emphasizes, "It was really quite extraordinary what a few committed people can do to lift the sights of people who didn't have much previous reason for lifting their eyes."[47]

Meanwhile, although neither of the Raspberrys ever personally participated in protest movements or civil rights activity, either in Okolona or elsewhere in Chickasaw County, they devoted their lives to community service. Willa Raspberry insists she always "tried to keep color out of it" as a teacher and librarian and did not talk to her students directly about racial issues. She remembers being "scared to death" when James Meredith integrated the University of Mississippi in 1962. National Guard units throughout northern Mississippi were federalized, and a resident of nearby Nettleton remembered the fear she saw in the eyes of her former classmates as their truck pulled away from the armory on its way to Oxford, Mississippi.[48] "That was not my way," Willa Raspberry states, regarding Meredith's entry into the University of Mississippi. "I didn't fight, but I didn't work with them [whites] either. And I always got what I wanted in the end."[49]

James Raspberry had a similar approach to segregation. He never protested or marched but expressed his feelings about the system in various and very subtle ways. Bishop Gray remembers that James Raspberry would joke about going to dinner with the white faculty members assisting at the summer institutes. "He would laugh and say, 'Well, we could all go to such-and-such restaurant, but I'll have to wait in the car.' But he continued to love all the people around him. He was never hostile to anyone."[50] William Raspberry explained to Julian Bond: "They [his parents] were able to make us believe that no matter what happened around us and to us, we were to behave like Raspberry kids. I mean that meant something in those days, that other people's mistreatment of us did not relieve us of the responsibility of behaving decently in the world."[51]

Willa Raspberry avoided outright controversy, but the realities of racism and segregation strongly influenced both how she raised her own children and what she taught the hundreds of black students who came through her schools and the college. William Raspberry remembers, "After we were grown up, my mother said to us once that she had tried, when we were kids, to build us up in our own heads, because she knew the world was going to knock us down some. She anticipated what society would do to us."[52] The Raspberry children's own estimation of themselves was also enhanced by the fact that Willa and James Raspberry each thought of the other as the smartest person in the world.[53]

Willa Raspberry's attentiveness to both family and community refutes the historical notion of "racial uplift" as the means by which "through uplift ideology, elite blacks devised a moral economy of class privilege, distinction, and even domination within the race, often drawing on patriarchal gender conventions as a sign of elite status and race progress."[54] Willa Raspberry describes herself differently and in the simplest terms: "When I saw a need, I tried to help."[55] While she held a typical "uplift" position within the community as a teacher, she was never removed from the larger black community by a self-imposed sense of middle-class stature.

Although she lived on campus and worked as the unofficial college librarian, Willa Raspberry engaged the extended Okolona community. In the early 1940s, when her husband had to spend several months in a sanatorium in southern Mississippi, Willa Raspberry began teaching full-time again, first in Prairie Mount and later in Mount Union, both located just outside Okolona and inhabited mostly by African American sharecroppers who bartered for services and goods. Willa Raspberry taught all the subjects in one-room schoolhouses and encouraged many students to continue their education up the road at Okolona College. Often her former students would take care of her own children while she worked. "Everyone took care of my children," she recalls. She emphasizes: "People were good to teachers."[56]

She herself often provided her students' basic necessities, including books, food, and clothes. Hattye Raspberry-Hall recalls: "We were forbidden to seem to recognize certain clothing items that we had outgrown when they appeared on the back of Mom's students." She brought to the schoolhouse each day a huge jar of clean water and jelly jars from which the children could drink, rather than use the school's communal tin dipper. In return, her students' families often shared their harvests. In the fall, students brought her daily gifts of hickory nuts and meat during hog-killing time. At Christmas she would receive country hams, sweet potatoes, and homemade cakes.[57]

Willa Raspberry's efforts at community building were focused on the classroom. Generations of black children in Chickasaw County and at the college remember her as a tireless facilitator of black education. Neither of her schools had any supplies or books, but through her connections at Okolona College and in the town library, she procured enough copies of older textbooks to teach the children basic lessons. The Chickasaw County superintendent of education told her that black children had no need for civics lessons, but she taught the subject anyway. Every day she picked up children who lived too far from the school to walk and took them home again. She managed to collect leftover farm commodities to provide lunches for children who could not bring their own. She convinced both black and white Okolonans to contribute surplus cheese, powdered milk, and peanut butter for her students. At one point, she found an advertisement for a book-donation program funneled through the Free Public Library in Newark, New Jersey, and she immediately took advantage of it. Her daughter describes her mother's reaction when the books arrived as "ecstatic."[58]

Every day that Willa Raspberry taught in the rural schools, she left the Okolona College campus to offer poverty-stricken children the same educational opportunities her own children received in town. During World War II, she briefly left teaching to become a home demonstration agent, but she suffered resentment from the white community, which did not have an agent of its own. Hattye Raspberry-Hall remembers that her mother taught sharecroppers how to grow their own crops instead of relying on the community gardens often provided by white landowners, brought books to the families, and helped the rural families learn canning and preserving techniques. Several white landowners felt that Willa Raspberry's position undermined the dependence that whites expected from their black sharecroppers. Threats against Raspberry and her work ultimately led her to return to teaching, where her efforts seemed less menacing to the white community.[59]

Other than her experience as a home demonstration agent, Raspberry remembers her relationship with the white community of Okolona and Chickasaw as relatively stable. "I didn't have problems with folks," she remembers. "People were good to us."[60] Much of Raspberry's acceptance came from the fluidity of class in Okolona. Even though her family worked and taught at the college, they lived much like the rest of the black and white communities. Willa Raspberry depended on her garden and spent the fall canning and preserving to make it through the winter, just as she had instructed other families to do. Dona Tucker Floyd, her sister, also lived in Okolona and sold homemade pound cakes during the Christmas season to pay for presents. One Christmas season, Floyd sold one thousand dollars worth of cakes. James Raspberry often worked as a carpenter to earn extra money.

Willa Raspberry's strongest association with the traditional image of black middle-class uplift came from her role as an educator. Although she insists, "I tried to keep color out of it [her teaching]," Raspberry spent her entire career helping black Chickasaw County citizens to gain access to education. One of the saddest times of her life came in 1964—the year before she registered to vote—when Okolona College closed for lack of funds. "It was like a death," she remembers. James and Willa Raspberry left the faculty house in which they had lived for over thirty-five years to move across the street from campus. Duncan Gray II, who was bishop when Okolona College closed, recalls the irony of the circumstances. "Really, integration closed it [Okolona College]," he remembers. "They [private schools] offered better-than-average education for African Americans when they had nowhere else to go, but after integration took hold, those private colleges were no longer needed."[61] Despite the seeming support the college received from the white community through the years, Calvin Buchanan, who grew up in Okolona, remembers that no effort was made to help the college stay open. "Everyone agreed the school was a good asset to Okolona, but the city didn't do anything to help the school when it ran out of money."[62]

In response to the closing of Okolona College and her own retirement from teaching, Willa Raspberry found a new way to serve the community. In 1969, she opened the Okolona Child Development Center with state grant money. Located in an empty classroom building at Okolona College, the center helped unwed mothers and low-income families learn parenting skills and home economics. In many ways, she picked up where her job as home demonstration agent had left off twenty-five years earlier. The center offered low-cost day care. Raspberry and her staff, consisting mostly of family members she convinced to volunteer, traveled to homes to assist in any way they could. Raspberry continued to collect donated books, clothes, food, baby supplies, and anything else she could for the low-income families.

When the grant money ran out, Willa Raspberry canvassed the community for donations to keep the center open. As they did for Okolona College, both whites and blacks donated, and the center stayed open until 1989, when Willa Raspberry retired for the second time. Raspberry's three careers—as teacher, home demonstration agent, and community-center director—reflected her larger need to serve the Okolona community. Even today, many Okolonans remember the Okolona Child Development Center as simply "the Raspberry Center."[63]

At age 103, Willa Raspberry clearly knows what drove her work. The image of the "unknown grandmother" that takes shape at the family reunions remains central to her self-understanding. She recalls holding her first great-grandchild and remembering her own unknown great-grandmother, who never knew what became of her own son, Simon, and his descendants.[64] Willa Raspberry dedicated her life to ensuring that her family and other African American families in Chickasaw County could honor their ancestors, who were gone but would not be forgotten.

Current family members report each generation's progress to the "unknown grandmother" at family reunions as they follow the African tradition of communicating with dead ancestors. They assure her that the family remains strong and connected. In call-and-response format, the "unknown grandmother" and her descendants discuss their family's fate since coming to northern Mississippi.

First, the family tells the "unknown grandmother" Simon's story, assuring his mother that her son lived a long, fulfilling life that included many years of freedom. Then they tell the stories of Simon's children, revisiting important details, as when Winford Tucker voted for the first time. Next come the stories of Simon's grandchildren, including "Miss Willa" Tucker Raspberry and her sister, "Miss Dona" Tucker Floyd, the two oldest living sisters in Chickasaw County. Then come Miss Willa's children, including Hattye Raspberry-Hall,

Jamesetta Ferguson, and William and David Raspberry—Winifred Eunice Coleman has died—and their cousins who tell the "unknown grandmother" about their lives. They go down the family line and even include the "buds," those conceived but not yet born. A rose is placed in a vase for each generation, which makes a floral offering for the next morning's altar at St. Bernard's/Grace Episcopal Church, where the family worships together.[65]

The family's triennial reports to their "unknown grandmother" reflect the vitality and sense of accountability of the family. While the family celebrates its teachers, writers, community activists, social workers, and musicians, it also honors struggles and hard times. At one reunion, the family applauded an alcoholic's forty-two years of sobriety as well as the longevity of Willa and Dona and a fifty-second wedding anniversary. Such personal milestones represent the most significant offerings the family makes to the "unknown grandmother." Survival and countenance offer as much evidence of family success as the big events. At a reunion in the 1990s, family members announced new births, graduations, and weddings. Later it occurred to someone that they had forgotten to tell the "unknown grandmother" that William had won the Pulitzer Prize, and the family laughingly fixed the oversight.[66]

For the Tucker-Raspberry-Dilworth family, narrative and story mute class and hierarchy. The enduring story of a beloved ancestor has transformed stereotype and convention. The family's story crafted over eight generations exemplifies that narrative and place can be even more compelling than the power of social forces and national politics.[67]

When Lee Pryor Caldwell, a white woman in Tupelo, Mississippi, read an account of the Raspberry-Tucker-Dilworth reunion in the *Northeast Mississippi Daily Journal* in 2004, she was inspired to write a script for a similar pageant for her husband's (Irish) family. She wanted, she said, "to make our family reunions more meaningful." The Caldwell pageant dramatized the distant ancestor's leaving Ireland for the new world. Family members representing each generation reported back to the family left behind and explained how their son and his descendants had fared in the New World.[68]

The legacy of Okolona College and St. Bernard's Chapel continues to inspire William Raspberry and Hattye Raspberry-Hall and their siblings and cousins. At a church service at St. Bernard's/Grace Episcopal Church, William preached on March 9, 2003, from the pulpit that his father had crafted. During the sermon, he announced that his children's inheritance would be significantly diminished by the family's decision to create Baby Steps, an effort to assist parents in Okolona who were not successful in school to help their own children succeed as students.[69] Later he invited the community to help him launch the program: "Join me in ... the transforming task of making Okolona a community that is devoted to the wellbeing of all its children, to giving them the best possible start in life." Then he added, "Okolona is small enough, compact enough, and smart enough to understand that we are in this together. We need to get serious about saving *Okolona's* children."[70] At the March service at St. Bernard's/ Grace Episcopal when William first mentioned Baby Steps, James and Willa's son chose for the processional a hymn that speaks to the spirit of eight generations who dedicated themselves to honoring the memory of their "unknown grandmother" through service.

> Come, labor on.
> Who dares stand idle on the harvest plain
> While all around us waves the golden grain?
> And to each servant does the Master say,
> "Go work today."
>
> Come, labor on,
> The enemy is watching night and day,
> to sow the tares, to snatch the seed away,
> while we in sleep our duty have forgot,
> he slumbered not.
>
> Come, labor on,
> Away with gloomy doubts and faithless fear!
> No arm so weak but may do service here:
> by feeblest agents may our God fulfill
> his righteous will.
>
> Come, labor on,
> Claim the high calling angels cannot share—
> to young and old the Gospel gladness bear:
> redeem the time; its hours swiftly fly.
> The night draws night.
>
> Come, labor on,
> No time for rest, till glows the western sky,
> Till the long shadows o'er our pathway lie,
> And a glad sound comes with the setting sun,
> "Servants, well done."[71]

NOTES

The authors thank Linda Denning, Wendy Smith, and Carol Stewart for their assistance. We also appreciate the comments and suggestions of Alfred A. Moss Jr., Daina Berry, William Raspberry, and Louise Floyd Cole.

1. Elizabeth Anne Payne, "Family Rivers Nourish the Unknown Future," *Northeast Mississippi Daily Journal*, August 14, 2004; Hattye Raspberry-Hall, unpublished family history (2004), copy in authors' possession.

2. Raspberry-Hall, unpublished family history

3. For a study of North Carolina in the context of these issues but for a generation of African American women who came of age a generation ahead of Willa Raspberry, see Glenda Gilmore, *Gender and Jim Crow: Women and the Politics of White Supremacy in North Carolina, 1896–1920* (Chapel Hill: University of North Carolina Press, 1996).

4. See Mark Schultz, *The Rural Face of White Supremacy: Beyond Jim Crow* (Urbana: University of Illinois Press, 2005), for a study of Hancock County, Georgia, an area similar to Chickasaw County.

5. Willa Tucker Raspberry, interviewed by Elizabeth Anne Payne, July 7, 2005, North Mississippi Women's History Project, copy in Elizabeth Anne Payne's possession.

6. Willa Tucker Raspberry interview, July 7, 2005.

7. For an introduction to the Campbellite religion, consult *A Religious Encyclopedia*, ed. Philip Schaff, 3rd ed., vol. 1 (New York: Funk & Wagnalls, 1894), s.v. "Alexander Campbell." For a background on the Campbellite churches, see David Edwin Harrell Jr., *Quest for a Christian America: The Disciples of Christ and American Society to 1866* (Nashville: Disciples of Christ Historical Society, 1966); Harrell, *The Social Sources of Division in the Disciples of Christ, 1865–1900* (Atlanta: Georgia Publishing Systems, 1973). It is noteworthy that the new Church of Christ proselytized among African Americans in the rural South during the Jim Crow era.

8. Raspberry-Hall, unpublished family history.

9. Willa Tucker Raspberry and Dona Tucker Floyd, interviewed by Elizabeth Anne Payne, June 14, 2005, North Mississippi Women's History Project, in Elizabeth Anne Payne's possession.

10. Raspberry-Hall, unpublished family history

11. See Department of Commerce, Bureau of the Census, *Tenth Census of the United States: 1880 — Population*, Monroe County, Mississippi, Smithville Township, Enumeration District no. 124, sheet 25B. Also see Department of Commerce, Bureau of the Census, *Twelfth Census of the United States: 1900 — Population*, Monroe County, Mississippi, Smithville Township, Enumeration District no. 69, sheet 12A; Department of Commerce, Bureau of the Census, *Fourteenth Census of the United States: 1920 — Population*, Monroe County, Mississippi, Hatley Township, Enumeration District no. 56, sheet 16A. The 1880 census lists Simon and Martha as thirty-three and twenty-two years old, respectively. In 1900, they are listed at the same address. Simon gave his year of birth as 1845; Martha reported hers as 1858. The quote is from Willa Tucker Raspberry, interview, June 14, 2005.

12. Raspberry-Hall, unpublished family history.

13. Department of Commerce, Bureau of the Census, *Twelfth Census of the United States: 1900 — Population*, Monroe County, Mississippi, Smithville Township, Enumeration District no. 69, sheet 12A; Department of Commerce, Bureau of the Census, *Eighth Census of the United States: 1860 — Population*, Monroe County, Mississippi, Eastern Division, Enumeration District no. 44, sheet 46; Department of Commerce, Bureau of the Census, *Eighth Census of the United States:*

Slaves Schedule, Monroe County, Eastern Division, Enumeration District no. 42, sheet 8; Bureau of the Census, *Ninth Census of the United States: 1870—Population*, Monroe County, Township 13, Enumeration District no. 49, sheet 25.

14. A Monroe County land deed shows that Winford Tucker purchased fifty acres from Charlie and Flora Perkins on November 26, 1919, for one thousand dollars, paid in full upon purchase. Land Deed Record Book 1919, N–Z, Monroe County, Mississippi Courthouse, Aberdeen, Mississippi.

15. Department of Commerce, Bureau of the Census, *Thirteenth Census of the United States: 1910—Population*, Monroe County, Mississippi, Beat 1, Enumeration District no. 54, sheet 13A. The 1910 census shows Winford (Winfred) and Ophallon (Ophelan) as having been married for five years.

16. See Department of Commerce, Bureau of the Census, *Fourteenth Census of the United States: 1920—Population*, Davidson County, Tennessee, Nashville Ward 4, Enumeration District 21, sheet 12A. Kable (Ruble) is listed as "gospel preacher."

17. Raspberry-Hall, unpublished family history.

18. Willa Tucker Raspberry, interviewed by Jennifer Nardone, November 2, 2005, copy in Jennifer Nardone's possession.

19. Ibid.; *The Handbook of the Amory Public Schools, 1919–1920* does not mention Jonesboro High School, a presumably African American private school. At the time, few Mississippi towns provided public education for white students beyond the eighth grade or for blacks beyond the fifth.

20. Dona Tucker Floyd, interviewed by Elizabeth Anne Payne, June 14, 2005, copy in Elizabeth Anne Payne's possession.

21. See Stephen Cresswell, *Multiparty Politics in Mississippi, 1877–1902* (Jackson: University Press of Mississippi, 1995), 100–125.

22. Quoted in Willa Tucker Raspberry, interview, June 14, 2005.

23. For a background on Rosenwald schools, see Thomas W. Hanchett, "The Rosenwald Schools and Black Education in North Carolina," *North Carolina Historical Review* (October 1988): 387–444. Also consult Mary S. Hoffschwelle, *The Rosenwald Schools of the American South* (Gainesville: University of Florida Press, 2006).

24. See Hoffschwelle, *Rosenwald Schools*, 283.

25. Rosenwald Schools in Mississippi, County Index (Miss.: S.N. 19999), Mississippi Department of Archives and History, Jackson (henceforth cited as MDAH); the Julius Rosenwald Fund Account Book for the State of Mississippi, July 1, 1920–June 30, 1921, MDAH; Willa Tucker Raspberry, interviewed by Jennifer Nardone, July 28, 2005, notes in Jennifer Nardone's possession.

26. Willa Tucker Raspberry, interviewed by Elizabeth Anne Payne, July 5, 2003, notes in Elizabeth Anne Payne's possession; Raspberry-Hall, unpublished family history.

27. James Raspberry, "History of the Okolona College" (1965), written for the Okolona Library's History of Okolona Collection, Okolona Public Library, Okolona, Mississippi.

28. Ibid.

29. Ibid. See also Willa Tucker Raspberry, "History of St. Bernard's Church" (1982), Okolona Public Library, Okolona, Mississippi; and *The Episcopal Church in Mississippi, 1763–1992* (Jackson, Miss.: Episcopal Diocese of Mississippi, 1992), 86; Willa Tucker Raspberry, interviewed by Jennifer Nardone, November 2, 2005, notes in Jennifer Nardone's possession; Eric Anderson and Alfred Moss, *Dangerous Donations: Northern Philanthropy and Southern Black Education, 1902–1930* (Columbia: University of Missouri Press, 1999), 168–69.

30. See James Raspberry, "History of Okolona College."

31. Macy Visor Ferrell, interviewed by Elizabeth Anne Payne, December 21, 2005, copy in Elizabeth Anne Payne's possession.

32. Ruth Hawkins Payne, quoted in personal journal of Elizabeth Anne Payne, July 6, 1967.

33. Willa Tucker Raspberry, "History of St. Bernard Church," 3.

34. Willa Tucker Raspberry, interview, July 7, 2005; Willa Tucker Raspberry, "History of St. Bernard Church," 3.

35. Willa Tucker Raspberry, interview, November 2, 2005.

36. William Raspberry, speech given at the celebration of Mississippi's four historically black Episcopal churches, Jackson, Mississippi, May 2, 2003, copy in Elizabeth Anne Payne's possession.

37. Willa Tucker Raspberry, "History of St. Bernard's Church," 3.

38. William Raspberry, interviewed by Chester Morgan, December 6, 1983, Civil Rights Documentation Project, Center for Oral History and Cultural Heritage, University of Southern Mississippi, Hattiesburg, http://anna.lib.usm.edu/%7Espcol/crda/oh/ohraspberrywp.html (accessed March 6, 2006).

39. Ibid.

40. Willa Tucker Raspberry, interview, July 28, 2005.

41. William Raspberry, interview, December 6, 1983; Willa Tucker Raspberry, interview, July 28, 2005.

42. Will Campbell, *And Also with You: Duncan Gray and the American Dilemma* (Franklin, Tenn.: Providence House, 1997), 54, 124, 125; Bishop Duncan M. Gray Jr., interviewed by Jennifer Nardone, October 7, 2005, notes in Jennifer Nardone's possession.

43. Campbell, *And Also with You*, 125; Willa Tucker Raspberry, interview, July 28, 2005.

44. William Raspberry, interview, December 6, 1983.

45. Neil McMillian, *Dark Journey: Black Mississippians in the Age of Jim Crow* (Urbana: University of Illinois Press, 1990), 141.

46. Ralph Ellison, *Invisible Man* (New York: Random House, 1952), 55–115.

47. William Raspberry, interviewed by Julian Bond, "Explorations in Black Leadership," University of Virginia, Charlottesville, Virginia, November 1, 2006, http://www.virginia.edu/publichistory/bl/index.php (accessed November 16, 2008).

48. Elizabeth Anne Payne, personal journal, September 29, 1962.

49. Willa Tucker Raspberry, interview, July 28, 2005.

50. Bishop Duncan Gray Jr., interview.

51. William Raspberry, interview, November 1, 2006.

52. William Raspberry, interview, December 6, 1983.

53. Raspberry-Hall, unpublished family history.

54. Kevin Gaines, *Uplifting the Race: Black Leadership, Politics, and Culture in the Twentieth Century* (Chapel Hill: University of North Carolina Press, 1966), 17.

55. Willa Tucker Raspberry, interview, July 7, 2005.

56. Ibid.

57. Raspberry-Hall, unpublished family history.

58. Ibid.

59. Ibid.

60. Willa Tucker Raspberry, interview, July 28, 2005.

61. Bishop Duncan Gray Jr., interview.

62. Calvin "Buck" Buchanan, interviewed by Jennifer Nardone, December 21, 2005, notes in Jennifer Nardone's possession.

63. Raspberry-Hall, unpublished family history.

64. Willa Tucker Raspberry, interview, June 14, 2005.

65. Payne, "Family Rivers."

66. Raspberry-Hall, unpublished family history.

67. Payne, "Family Rivers."

68. Lee Pryor Caldwell, interviewed by Elizabeth Anne Payne, July 28, 2006, notes in Elizabeth Anne Payne's possession.

69. Elizabeth Anne Payne, notes from William Raspberry's sermon, March 9, 2003.

70. William Raspberry, "Our Long Journey Begins with Baby Steps," speech given at open community meeting in Okolona, Mississippi, August 23, 2003, copy in Elizabeth Anne Payne's possession.

71. "Come, Labor On," lyrics by Jane Laurie Borthwick, sung to the tune of *Ora Labora*, by Thomas Tertius Noble, in *The Hymnal 1982 according to the Use of the Episcopal Church* (New York: Church Hymnal Corporation, 1982), 541.

Selected Bibliography

Aldridge, Martha Jean. "The Founding of Blue Mountain College." PhD diss., University of Iowa, 1994.

Adams, Inez Berryhill. *The Class of 1912*. Lafayette, Cal.: Thomas-Berryhill, 1995.

Anderson, Nancy Scott. "Varina Howell Davis: At Home in Natchez." *Journal of Mississippi History* 54, no. 4 (November 1992): 349–64.

Appleton, Thomas, and Angela Boswell, eds. *Searching for Their Pasts: Women in the South across Four Centuries*. Columbia: University of Missouri Press, 2003.

Asch, Christopher Myers. "No Compromise: The Freedom Struggles of James O. Eastland and Fannie Lou Hamer." PhD diss., University of North Carolina at Chapel Hill, 2005.

————. *The Senator and the Sharecropper: The Freedom Struggles of James O. Eastland and Fannie Lou Hamer*. New York: New Press, 2008.

Bailey, Ben E. "Music in Slave Era Mississippi." *Journal of Mississippi History* 54, no. 1 (February 1992): 29–58.

Bardaglio, Peter W. *Reconstructing the Household: Families, Sex, and the Law in the Nineteenth-Century South*. Chapel Hill: University of North Carolina Press, 1995.

Bedwell, Randall J. "A History of the Fraternities and Sororities at Ole Miss: 1848–1930." MA thesis, University of Mississippi, 1991.

Behel, Sandra. "The Mississippi Homefront in World War II: Tradition and Change." PhD diss., Mississippi State University, 1989.

Bercaw, Nancy D. *Gendered Freedoms: Race, Rights, and the Politics of Household in the Delta, 1861–1875*. Gainesville: University Press of Florida, 2003.

Berg Burin, Nikki. "A Regency of Women: Female Plantation Management in the Old South." PhD diss., University of Minnesota, 2007.

Berry, Trey. "A History of Women's Education in Mississippi, 1819–1882." *Journal of Mississippi History* 53, no. 4 (November 1991): 303–19.

Black, Patti Carr. *Of Home and Family: Art in Nineteenth-Century Mississippi*. Jackson: Mississippi Museum of Art, 1999.

Blackwell, Unita, with Joanne Prichard Morris. *Barefootin': Lessons from the Road to Freedom*. New York: Crown, 2006.

Bleser, Carol, ed. *In Joy and Sorrow: Women, Family, and Marriage in the Victorian South*. New York: Oxford University Press, 1991.

344

4444444

Bondurant, Alexander L. "Sherwood Bonner—Her Life and Place in the Literature of the South." *Publications of the Mississippi Historical Society* 2 (1899): 43–68.

Boyd, Elizabeth. "Sister Act: Sorority Rush as Feminine Performance." *Southern Cultures* 5, no. 3 (Fall 1999): 54–73.

Breen, William J. "Black Women and the Great War: Mobilization and Reform in the South." *Journal of Southern History* 44, no. 3 (August 1978): 421–40.

Broussard, Joyce L. "Female Solitaires: Women Alone in the Lifeworld of Mid-Century Natchez, Mississippi, 1850–1880." PhD diss., University of Southern California, 1998.

———. "Occupied Natchez, Elite Women, and the Feminization of the Civil War." *Journal of Mississippi History* 70, no. 2 (Summer 2008): 179–208.

Burchfield, Edna F. "Women in the Mississippi Legislature: The Impact of Gender on Policy and the Political Process." MA thesis, University of Southern Mississippi, 1997.

Bynum, Victoria E. *The Free State of Jones: Mississippi's Longest Civil War*. Chapel Hill: University of North Carolina Press, 2001.

Cashin, Joan. *First Lady of the Confederacy: Varina Davis's Civil War*. Cambridge, Mass.: Belknap Press of Harvard University Press, 2006.

———, ed. *Our Common Affairs: Texts from Women in the Old South*. Baltimore: Johns Hopkins University Press, 1996.

Cherry, Gwendolyn, Ruby Thomas, and Pauline Willis. *Portraits in Color: The Lives of Colorful Negro Women*. New York: Pageant, 1962.

Childress, Jill C. "'Rugged Individual': Mary Dawson Cain and Her Fight for States' Rights, 1936–1984." MA thesis, University of Southern Mississippi, 2002.

Collier-Thomas, Bettye, and V. P. Franklin, eds. *Sisters in the Struggle: African American Women in the Civil Rights–Black Power Movement*. New York: New York University Press, 2001.

Cook, Cita. "The Modernized Elitism of Young Southern Ladies at Early Twentieth-Century Stanton College." *Journal of Mississippi History* 62, no. 3 (Fall 2000): 199–223.

Cook, Florence Elliot. "Growing Up White, Genteel, and Female in a Changing South, 1865 to 1915." PhD diss., University of California, Berkeley, 1992.

Cotton, Gordon A., ed. *From the Pen of a She-Rebel: The Civil War Diary of Emilie Riley McKinley*. Columbia: University of South Carolina Press, 2001.

Cox, Karen L. *Dixie's Daughters: The United Daughters of the Confederacy and the Preservation of Confederate Culture*. Gainesville: University Press of Florida, 2003.

Crawford, Vicki Lynn. "Grassroots Activists in the Mississippi Civil Rights Movement." *SAGE* 5, no. 2 (Fall 1988): 24–29.

———. "Race, Class, Gender, and Culture: Black Women's Activism in the Mississippi Civil Rights Movement." *Journal of Mississippi History* 58, no. 1 (Spring 1996): 1–21.

———. "'We Shall Not Be Moved': Black Female Activists in the Mississippi Civil Rights Movement, 1960–1965." PhD diss., Emory University, 1987.

Crawford, Vicki L., Jacqueline Anne Rouse, and Barbara Woods, eds. *Women in the*

Civil Rights Movement: Trailblazers and Torchbearers, 1941–1965. Bloomington: Indiana University Press, 1993.

Crosby, Emilye. *A Little Taste of Freedom: The Black Freedom Struggle in Claiborne County, Mississippi*. Chapel Hill: University of North Carolina Press, 2005.

Cunnigen, Donald. "Men and Women of Goodwill: Mississippi's White Liberals." PhD diss., Harvard University, 1988.

Curry, Constance. *Silver Rights*. Chapel Hill, N.C.: Algonquin, 1995.

Curry, Constance, et al. *Deep in Our Hearts: Nine White Women in the Freedom Movement*. Athens: University of Georgia Press, 2000.

Daniel, Helen Thurstensen. "The History of the American Association of University Women in Mississippi." MEd thesis, Mississippi College, 1954.

Davis, Vanessa Lynn. "'Sisters and Brothers All': The Mississippi Freedom Democratic Party and the Struggle for Equality." PhD diss., Vanderbilt University, 1996.

Deen, Jeannie Marie, ed. *Annie Harper's Journal: A Southern Mother's Legacy*. Denton, Tex.: Flower Mound Writing, 1983.

Dittmer, John. *Local People: The Struggle for Civil Rights in Mississippi*. Champaign: University of Illinois Press, 1995.

Ditto, Susan. "Hearth and Home: Constructing Domesticity in Mississippi, 1830s–1910s." PhD diss., University of Mississippi, 1998.

Drake, Claribel. "Mississippi's Elizabeth Academy: Its Claim to Be the Mother of Women's Colleges in America." *Daughters of the American Revolution Magazine* 96, no. 5 (May 1962): 487–88, 514.

Dresser, Rebecca M. "Kate and John Minor: Confederate Unionists of Natchez." *Journal of Mississippi History* 64, no. 3 (Fall 2002): 189–216.

Dunn, Cherry Watkins. "Women and Music in the Victorian South: The Music Department of Mississippi University for Women under Weenona Poindexter." DMA thesis, University of Alabama, 2001.

Early, Frances H. *A World without Wars: How U.S. Feminists and Pacifists Resisted World War I*. Syracuse, N.Y.: Syracuse University Press, 1997.

Elias, Louis, Jr. "James Chappel Hardy: Founder of Gulf Park College for Women." *Journal of Mississippi History* 46, no. 3 (August 1984): 213–26.

Evers-Williams, Myrlie, and Melinda Blau. *Watch Me Fly: What I Learned on Becoming the Woman I Was Meant to Be*. Boston: Little, Brown, 1999.

Evers-Williams, Myrlie, with William Peters. *For Us, the Living*. New York: Doubleday, 1967.

Farnham, Christie Anne, ed. *Women of the American South: A Multicultural Reader*. New York: New York University Press, 1998.

Faust, Drew Gilpin. *Mothers of Invention: Women of the Slaveholding South in the American Civil War*. Chapel Hill: University of North Carolina Press, 1996.

Feimster, Crystal Nicole. "Ladies and Lynching: The Gendered Discourse of Mob Violence in the New South, 1880–1930." PhD diss., Princeton University, 2000.

Ferrell, Chiles Clifton. "The Daughter of the Confederacy—Her Life, Character, and Writings." *Publications of the Mississippi Historical Society* 2 (1899): 69–84.

Frank, William L. *Sherwood Bonner.* Boston: Twayne, 1976.

Frankel, Noralee. *Freedom's Women: Black Women and Families in Civil War Era Mississippi.* Bloomington: Indiana University Press, 1999.

———. "Workers, Wives, and Mothers: Black Women in Mississippi, 1860–1870." PhD diss., George Washington University, 1983.

Galbraith, William, and Loretta Galbraith, eds. *A Lost Heroine of the Confederacy: The Diaries and Letters of Belle Edmondson.* Jackson: University Press of Mississippi, 1990.

Galloway, Charles Betts. "Elizabeth Female Academy—the Mother of Female Colleges." *Publications of the Mississippi Historical Society* 2 (1899): 169–78.

Gardner, Sarah E. *Blood and Irony: Southern White Women's Narratives, 1861–1937.* Chapel Hill: University of North Carolina Press, 2004.

Giddings, Paula J. *Ida: A Sword among Lions; Ida B. Wells and the Campaign against Lynching.* New York: Amistad/Harper Collins, 2008.

———. *When and Where I Enter: The Impact of Black Women on Race and Sex in America.* New York: William Morrow, 1984.

Gilmer, Robert. "Chickasaws, Tribal Laws, and the Mississippi Married Women's Property Act of 1839." *Journal of Mississippi History* 68, no. 2 (Summer 2006): 131–48.

Goree, Cathryn T. "Steps toward Redefinition: Coeducation at Mississippi State College, 1930–1945." PhD diss., Mississippi State University, 1993.

Gowdy, Anne Razey, ed. *A Sherwood Bonner Sampler, 1869–1884: What a Bright, Educated, Witty, Lively, Snappy Young Woman Can Say on a Variety of Topics.* Knoxville: University of Tennessee Press, 2000.

Greene, Kate. "Torts over Tempo: The Life and Career of Judge Burnita Shelton Matthews." *Journal of Mississippi History* 61, no. 3 (August 1994): 181–210.

Greene, Kathanne W. "Fear and Loathing in Mississippi: The Attack on Camp Sister Spirit." *Women and Politics* 17, no. 3 (1997): 17–37.

Gullette, Charles A. "The Career of Belle Kearney: A Study in Reform." MA thesis, Mississippi College, 1967.

Guyton, David E. *Mother Berry of Blue Mountain.* Nashville, Tenn.: Broadman, 1942.

Hamlet, Janice D. "Fannie Lou Hamer: The Unquenchable Spirit of the Civil Rights Movement." *Journal of Black Studies* 26, no. 5 (May 1996): 560–76.

Harding, Lee Emling. "'A Strategy for Living': Selected Autobiographical Writing by Nineteenth-Century Mississippi Women, with Representative Transcriptions and Checklist of Sources." PhD diss., University of Southern Mississippi, 1983.

Hardy, Gayle J. *American Women Civil Rights Activists: Biobibliographies of 68 Leaders, 1825–1992.* Jefferson, N.C.: McFarland, 1993.

Hawks, Joanne V. "Like Mother, Like Daughter: Nellie Nugent Somerville and Lucy Somerville Howorth." *Journal of Mississippi History* 45, no. 2 (May 1983): 116–23.

———. *Mississippi's Historical Heritage: A Guide to Women's Sources in Mississippi Repositories.* Jackson: Society of Mississippi Archivists, 1993.

————. "Nancy McDougall Robinson (1808–1873): A Personal Story, a Shared Experience." *Journal of Mississippi History* 55, no. 1 (February 1993): 19–30.

Hawks, Joanne V., M. Carolyn Ellis, and J. Byron Morris. "Women in the Mississippi Legislature (1924–1981)." *Journal of Mississippi History* 43, no. 4 (November 1981): 266–93.

Herring, Caroline. "The Mississippi Council of the Association of Southern Women for the Prevention of Lynching." MA thesis, University of Mississippi, 1999.

Higgs, Catherine, Barbara A. Moss, and Earline Rae Ferguson, eds. *Stepping Forward: Black Women in Africa and the Americas*. Athens: Ohio University Press, 2002.

Hinds, Katherine Powell. "The Life and Works of Eudora Welty." MA thesis, Duke University, 1954.

Hobbs, Richard Stanley. "The Cayton Legacy: Two Generations of a Black Family, 1859–1976." PhD diss., University of Washington, 1989.

Holland, Endesha Ida Mae. *From the Mississippi Delta: A Memoir*. New York: Simon & Schuster, 1997.

Hudson, Janet Maria. "The Hub City Home Front: Women of Hattiesburg, Mississippi, during World War II." MA thesis, University of Southern Mississippi, 2002.

Hudson, Winson, and Constance Curry. *Mississippi Harmony: Memoirs of a Freedom Fighter*. New York: Palgrave Macmillan, 2002.

Ingram, Anthony Bruce. "Surviving in Tippah County: Farm, Faith, and Family Connections, Tippah County, Mississippi, 1840–1880." PhD diss., University of Mississippi, 2001.

Johnson, Michael P. "Smothered Slave Infants: Were Slave Mothers at Fault?" *Journal of Southern History* 47, no. 4 (November 1981): 493–520.

Jones, Jacqueline. *Labor of Love, Labor of Sorrow: Black Women, Work, and the Family from Slavery to the Present*. New York: Basic, 1985.

Kearney, Belle. *A Slaveholder's Daughter*. New York: Abbey, 1900.

Kinchen, Oscar A. *Women Who Spied for the Blue and the Gray*. Philadelphia: Dorrance, 1972.

King, Mary. *Freedom Song: A Personal Story of the 1960s Civil Rights Movement*. New York: William Morrow, 1988.

Kling, Susan. *Fannie Lou Hamer: A Biography*. Chicago: Women for Racial and Economic Equality, 1979.

Kondert, Nancy T. "The Romance and Reality of Defeat: Southern Women in 1865." *Journal of Mississippi History* 35, no. 2 (May 1973): 141–52.

Lee, Chana Kai. *For Freedom's Sake: The Life of Fannie Lou Hamer*. Urbana: University of Illinois Press, 2000.

————. "A Passionate Pursuit of Justice: The Life and Leadership of Fannie Lou Hamer." PhD diss., University of California, Los Angeles, 1993.

Lemons, J. Stanley. *The Woman Citizen: Social Feminism in the 1920s*. Urbana: University of Illinois Press, 1973.

Locke, Mamie E. "The Role of African-American Women in the Civil Rights and

Women's Movements in Hinds County and Sunflower County, Mississippi." *Journal of Mississippi History* 53, no. 3 (August 1991): 229–39.

MacInerney, Dorothy McLeod. "Elizabeth Whitfield Croom Bellamy: The Life and Works of a Southern Belle." PhD diss., University of Texas, 1996.

MacInerney, Dorothy McLeod, and William Warren Rogers. "Elizabeth Croom Bellamy, the Delta, and the Enduring Importance of Family." *Journal of Mississippi History* 65, no. 1 (Spring 2003): 73–86.

Mangum, Bethany Case. "The History of Nurse Midwifery in Mississippi." MA thesis, University of Southern Mississippi, 1999.

Marrs, Suzanne. *Eudora Welty: A Biography*. Orlando, Fla.: Harcourt, 2005.

———. *One Writer's Imagination: The Fiction of Eudora Welty*. Baton Rouge: Louisiana State University Press, 2002.

Mars, Florence, with Lynn Eden. *Witness in Philadelphia*. Baton Rouge: Louisiana State University Press, 1977.

Massey, Mary Elizabeth. *Bonnet Brigades: American Women and the Civil War*. New York: Knopf, 1966.

May, Robert E. "Southern Elite Women, Sectional Extremism, and the Male Political Sphere: The Case of John A. Quitman's Wife and Female Descendants, 1847–1931." *Journal of Mississippi History* 50, no. 4 (November 1988): 251–85.

McAlexander, Hubert Horton. *The Prodigal Daughter: A Biography of Sherwood Bonner*. Baton Rouge: Louisiana State University Press, 1981.

McMurry, Linda O. *To Keep the Waters Troubled: The Life of Ida B. Wells*. New York: Oxford University Press, 1998.

McWhirter, Ollie Dean. "The Work of Miss Susie V. Powell." MA thesis, Mississippi State University, 1964.

Meredith, Mary Louise. "The Mississippi Women's Rights Movement, 1889–1923: The Leadership of Nelllie Nugent Somerville and Greenville in Suffrage Reform." MA thesis, Delta State University, 1974.

Miles, Alice Loyce Braswell. "Forgotten Scholars: Female Secondary Education in Three Antebellum Deep South States." PhD diss., Mississippi State University, 2003.

Miller, Margaret E. "Mississippi Women of the Confederacy." MA thesis, Mississippi State University, 1963.

Mills, Kay. *This Little Light of Mine: The Life of Fannie Lou Hamer*. Lexington: University Press of Kentucky, 1993.

Mitchell, Beverly E. "The Vocation of Fannie Lou Hamer, Civil Rights Activist." *American Baptist Quarterly* 23, no. 2 (2004): 179–93.

Moncrief, Sandra. "The Mississippi Married Women's Property Act of 1839." *Journal of Mississippi History* 47, no. 2 (May 1985): 110–25.

Moody, Anne. *Coming of Age in Mississippi*. New York: Dial, 1968.

Moore, Danny. "To Make the Best Better": The Establishment of Girls' Tomato Clubs in Mississippi, 1911–1915." *Journal of Mississippi History* 63, no. 2 (Summer 2001): 101–18.

Morgan, Madel Jacobs. "Sarah Truly, a Mississippi Tory." *Journal of Mississippi History* 37, no. 1 (February 1975): 87–95.

Morris, Sara Elizabeth. "'Good Equipment Makes a Good Homemaker Better': Promoters of Domestic Technology in Mississippi, 1930–1940." MA thesis, Mississippi State University, 2004.

Morris, Tiyi Makeda. "Black Women's Civil Rights Activism in Mississippi: The Story of Womanpower Unlimited." PhD diss., Purdue University, 2002.

Moye, J. Todd. *Let the People Decide: Black Freedom and White Resistance Movements in Sunflower County, Mississippi, 1945–1986*. Chapel Hill: University of North Carolina Press, 2004.

Murray, Gail S., ed. *Throwing Off the Cloak of Privilege: White Southern Women Activists in the Civil Rights Era*. Gainesville: University Press of Florida, 2004.

Nguyen, Julia Huston. "Laying the Foundations: Domestic Service in Natchez, 1862–1877." *Journal of Mississippi History* 63, no.1 (Spring 2001): 35–60.

———. "Useful and Ornamental: Female Education in Antebellum Natchez." *Journal of Mississippi History* 67, no. 4 (Winter 2005): 291–309.

Northart, Debra Lynne. "The League of Women Voters in Mississippi: The Civil Rights Years, 1954–1964." PhD diss., University of Mississippi, 1997.

Olsen, Christopher J. "'Molly Pitcher' of the Mississippi Whigs: The Editorial Career of Mrs. Harriet N. Prewett." *Journal of Mississippi History* 58, no. 3 (Fall 1996): 237–54.

———. "'Respecting the wise allotment of our sphere': White Women and Politics in Mississippi, 1840–1860." *Journal of Women's History* 11, no. 3 (Autumn 1999): 104–25.

Olson, Lynne. *Freedom's Daughters: The Unsung Heroines of the Civil Rights Movement from 1830 to 1970*. New York: Scribner's, 2001.

Ott, Victoria. *Confederate Daughters: Coming of Age during the Civil War*. Carbondale: Southern Illinois University Press, 2008.

Pace, John Mac. "The Arts in Jackson, Mississippi: A History of Theatre, Painting, Sculpture, and Music in the Mississippi Capital since 1900." PhD diss., University of Mississippi, 1976.

Patton, W. H. "History of the Prohibition Movement in Mississippi." *Publications of the Mississippi Historical Society* 10 (1909): 181–201.

Payne, Charles M. *I've Got the Light of Freedom: The Organizing Tradition and the Mississippi Freedom Struggle*. Berkeley: University of California Press, 1995.

Pearman, Eric Gerard. "Ida B. Wells: Familial and Religious Influences in Holly Springs, Mississippi." *Journal of Mississippi History* 68, no. 3 (Fall 2006): 213–39.

Pieschel, Bridget Smith, and Stephen Robert Pieschel. *Loyal Daughters: One Hundred Years at Mississippi University for Women, 1884–1984*. Jackson: University Press of Mississippi, 1984.

Pollack, Harriet, and Suzanne Marrs, eds. *Eudora Welty and Politics: Did the Writer Crusade?* Baton Rouge: Louisiana State University Press, 2001.

Prenshaw, Peggy Whitman, ed. *Conversations with Eudora Welty*. Jackson: University Press of Mississippi, 1984.

Selected Bibliography

———. *More Conversations with Eudora Welty.* Jackson: University Press of Mississippi, 1996.

Price, Beulah M. D'Olive. "Dr. Hallie Garrett: Corinth Physician." *Journal of the Mississippi State Medical Association* 21, no. 8 (August 1980): 171.

Prince, Vinton M., Jr. "Will Women Turn the Tide?: Mississippi Women and the 1922 United States Senate Race." *Journal of Mississippi History* 42, no. 3 (August 1980): 212–20.

———. "The *Woman Voter* and Mississippi Elections in the Early Twenties." *Journal of Mississippi History* 49, no. 2 (May 1987): 105–14.

———. "Women, Politics, and the Press: The Mississippi *Woman Voter.*" *Southern Studies* 19, no. 4 (Winter 1980): 365–72.

Randall, Herbert, and Bobs M. Tusa. *Faces of Freedom Summer.* Tuscaloosa: University of Alabama Press, 2001.

Ribianszky, Nik. "'She Appeared to Be Mistress of Her Own Actions, Free from the Control of Anyone': Property-Holding Free Women of Color in Natchez, Mississippi, 1779–1865." *Journal of Mississippi History* 67, no. 3 (Fall 2005): 217–45.

Rice, Kathleen George. "A History of Whitworth College for Women." PhD diss., University of Mississippi, 1985.

Roberts, Giselle. *The Confederate Belle.* Columbia: University of Missouri Press, 2003.

———. "The Confederate Belle: The Belle Ideal, Patriotic Womanhood, and Wartime Reality in Louisiana and Mississippi, 1861–1865." *Louisiana History* 43, no. 2 (2002): 189–214.

———. "'Our Cause': Southern Women and Confederate Nationalism in Mississippi and Louisiana." *Journal of Mississippi History* 62, no. 2 (Summer 2000): 97– 121.

Rosenbaum, Tommy Hogue. *A History of the Mississippi Federation of Women's Clubs, 1898–1948.* Jackson: Mississippi Federation of Women's Clubs, 1998.

Rothschild, Mary Aicken. "White Women Volunteers in the Freedom Summers: Their Life and Work in a Movement for Social Change." *Feminist Studies* 5, no. 3 (Fall 1979): 466–95.

Royster, Jacqueline Jones, ed. *Southern Horrors and Other Writings: The Anti-Lynching Campaign of Ida B. Wells, 1892–1900.* New York: Bedford/St. Martin's, 1997.

Sabin, Linda Emerson. "From the Home to the Community: A History of Nursing in Mississippi, 1870–1940." PhD diss., University of Mississippi, 1994.

———. *Struggles and Triumphs: The Story of Mississippi Nurses, 1880–1950.* Jackson: Mississippi Hospital Association, 1998.

Schechter, Patricia A. "'All the Intensity of My Nature': Ida B. Wells, Anger, and Politics." *Radical History Review* 70 (Winter 1998): 48–77.

———. *Ida B. Wells Barnett and American Reform, 1880–1930.* Chapel Hill: University of North Carolina Press, 2000.

Scott, Anne Firor. "After Suffrage: Southern Women in the Twenties." *Journal of Southern History* 30 (1964): 298–318.

———. *Natural Allies: Women's Associations in American History.* Urbana: University of Illinois Press, 1991.

———. *The Southern Lady: From Pedestal to Politics, 1830–1930.* Chicago: University of Chicago Press, 1970.

Sedevie, Donna Elizabeth. "The Prospect of Happiness: Women, Divorce and Property." *Journal of Mississippi History* 57, no. 3 (Fall 1995): 189–206.

———. "Women and the Law of Property in the Old Southwest: The Antecedents of the Mississippi Married Women's Law, 1798–1839." MA thesis, University of Southern Mississippi, 1996.

Shakoor, Jordana Y. *Civil Rights Childhood.* Jackson: University Press of Mississippi, 1999.

Shawhan, Dorothy. "Women Behind the *Woman Voter*." *Journal of Mississippi History* 49, no. 2 (May 1987): 115–28.

Shawhan, Dorothy S., and Martha H. Swain. *Lucy Somerville Howorth: New Deal Lawyer, Politician, and Feminist from the South.* Baton Rouge: Louisiana State University Press, 2006.

Smith, Chesley Thorne. *Childhood in Holly Springs: A Memoir.* Lafayette, Cal.: Thomas-Berryhill, 1996.

Smith, Jessie Carney. *Epic Lives: One Hundred Black Women Who Made a Difference.* Detroit: Visible Ink, 1993.

Smith, Judy Teresa. "Magnolia Matriarchs: Six Women's Contributions to the Community Press in Mississippi." PhD diss., University of Southern Mississippi, 2005.

Speer, Lisa K. "Contrary Mary: The Life of Mary Dawson Cain." PhD diss., University of Mississippi, 1998.

Stamper, Anita Miller, and Mary Edna Lohrenz. "Manuscript Sources for 'Mississippi Homespun: Nineteenth-Century Textiles and the Women Who Made Them.'" *Journal of Mississippi History* 53, no. 3 (August 1991): 185–217.

———. *Mississippi Homespun: Nineteenth-Century Textiles and the Women Who Made Them.* Jackson: Mississippi Department of Archives and History, 1989.

Sumrall, Robbie Neal. *A Light on a Hill: A History of Blue Mountain College.* Nashville, Tenn.: Benson Printing, 1947.

Swain, Martha H. *Ellen S. Woodward: New Deal Advocate for Women.* Jackson: University Press of Mississippi, 1995.

———. "A New Deal for Mississippi Women, 1933–1943." *Journal of Mississippi History* 46, no. 3 (August 1984): 191–212.

———. "Organized Women in Mississippi: The Clash over Legal Disabilities in the 1920s." *Southern Studies* 23, no. 1 (Spring 1984): 91–102.

———. "Politics and Public Affairs: Twentieth Century Mississippi Women Activists." *Journal of Mississippi History* 53, no. 3 (August 1991): 175–83.

Swain, Martha H., Elizabeth Anne Payne, Marjorie Julian Spruill, and Susan Ditto, eds. *Mississippi Women: Their Histories, Their Lives.* Vol. 1. Athens: University of Georgia Press, 2003.

Taylor, A. Elizabeth. "The Woman Suffrage Movement in Mississippi." *Journal of Mississippi History* 30 (February 1968): 1–34.

Theoharris, Jeanne, and Komozi Woodward, eds. *Groundwork: Local Black Freedom Movements in America.* New York: New York University Press, 2005.

Thompson, Elizabeth Lee. "Southern Women, Gender Roles, and the Unconventional Alice Jenkins." *Journal of Mississippi History* 62, no. 1 (Spring 2000): 21– 56.

Tipton, Nancy Carol. "'It Is My Duty': The Public Career of Belle Kearney." MA thesis, University of Mississippi, 1975.

Uffleman, Minoa Dawn. "'Rite Thorny Places to Go Thro': Narratives of Identities, Southern Farm Women of the Late Nineteenth and Early Twentieth Century." PhD diss., University of Mississippi, 2003.

Vargis, Salli. "History of the Mississippi Federation of Business and Professional Women's Clubs, 1924–1995" PhD diss., Mississippi State University, 2004.

Viera, Michelle Margaret. "A Summary of the Contributions of Four Key African American Female Figures of the Civil Rights Movement." MA thesis, Western Michigan University, 1994.

Waldrep, Christopher. "Women, the Civil War, and Legal Culture in Vicksburg, Mississippi." *Journal of Mississippi History* 61, no. 2 (Summer 1999): 137–47.

Walker, Melissa, Jeannette R. Dunn, and Joe P. Dunn, eds. *Southern Women at the Millennium: A Historical Perspective*. Columbia: University of Missouri Press, 2003.

Weaver, David E. *Black Diva of the Thirties: The Life of Ruby Elzy*. Jackson: University Press of Mississippi, 2004.

Webb, Clive, ed. *Massive Resistance: Southern Opposition to the Second Reconstruction*. New York: Oxford University Press, 2005.

Wells, Ida B. *Crusade for Justice: The Autobiography of Ida B. Wells*. Edited by Alfreda M. Duster. Chicago: University of Chicago Press, 1970.

Wheat, Edward M., and Kate Green. "Camp Sister Spirit vs. Ovett: Culture Wars in Mississippi." *Southeastern Political Review* 23. no. 2 (June 1995): 315–32.

Wheeler, Marjorie Spruill. *New Women of the New South: The Leaders of the Woman Suffrage Movement in the Southern States*. New York: Oxford University Press, 1993.

———, ed. *One Woman, One Vote: Rediscovering the Woman Suffrage Movement*. Trousdale, Ore.: New Sage Press, 1995.

———. *Votes for Women!: The Woman Suffrage Movement in Tennessee, the South, and the Nation*. Knoxville: University of Tennessee Press, 1995.

White, Calvin, Jr. "They Danced and Shouted into Obscurity: The Church of God in Christ and Its Impact upon the Politics of Respectability." PhD diss., University of Mississippi, 2007.

White, Deborah Gray. *Too Heavy a Load: Black Women in Defense of Themselves, 1894– 1994*. New York: Norton, 1999.

White, Geneva Brown Blalock, and Eva Hunter Bishop, eds. and comps. *Mississippi's Black Women: A Pictorial Story of Their Contributions to the State and Nation*. [Corinth, Miss.]: Mississippi State Federation of Colored Women's Clubs, 1976.

Wiencek, Henry. *The Hairstons: An American Family in Black and White*. New York: St. Martin's, 1999.

Wiley, Bell Irvin. *Confederate Women*. Contributions in American History 38. Westport, Conn.: Greenwood, 1975.

Wilkinson, Kate. "A Sociological Analysis of an Action Group: Wednesdays in Mississippi." MA thesis, University of Mississippi, 1966.

Willis, Angela Renee. "'God Is a Black Woman from Mississippi': Biography of the Reverend Dr. Johnnie Coleman, Spiritual Leader/Adult Educator." EdD diss., Northern Illinois University, 2001.

Winner, Lauren F. "'Cooking, Tending the Garden, and Being Good Hostesses': A Domestic History of White Women's Opposition to the Freedom Movement in Mississippi." *Mississippi Folklife* 31, no. 1 (Fall 1998): 28–35.

Winter, Robert Milton, ed. *Civil War Women: The Diaries of Belle Strickland and Cora Harris Watson—Holly Springs, Mississippi, July 24, 1864–June 22, 1868*. Lafayette, Cal.: Thomas-Berryhill Press, 2001.

———. "Many Daughters Have Done Excellently: Women's Leadership in Mississippi Churches." *Presbyterian Voice* 11 (May 2000): 10–11.

———, ed. *Our Pen Is Time: The Diary of Emma Finley*. Lafayette, Cal.: Thomas-Berryhill, 1999.

Wood, Kirsten. *Masterful Women: Slaveholding Widows from the American Revolution through the Civil War*. Chapel Hill: University of North Carolina Press, 2004.

Woods, Troy, III. *A Delta Diary: Amanda Worthington's Civil War Diary*. N.p.: Olivewoods, 2008.

Wyatt-Brown, Bertram. *The House of Percy: Honor, Melancholy, and Imagination in a Southern Family*. New York: Oxford University Press, 1994.

———. *The Literary Percys: Family History, Gender, and the Southern Imagination*. Mercer University Lamar Memorial Lecture series 37. Athens: University of Georgia Press, 1994.

Contributors

MICHAEL B. BALLARD is university archivist at Mississippi State University and coordinator at the Congressional and Political Research Center. A civil war and reconstruction historian, he is associate editor of the U.S. Grant Papers Project.

NANCY BERCAW, a historian of the American South, is an associate professor of history and southern studies at the University of Mississippi. She writes on the relationships among gender, race, and the meanings of freedom in the wake of the Civil War.

JOYCE L. BROUSSARD, an assistant professor of history at California State University, Northridge, received her PhD at the University of Southern California. Her research centers on gender and southern history.

VICTORIA E. BYNUM researches gender, race, and class in the nineteenth-century South and southern Unionists during the Civil War. She is a professor of history at Texas State University, San Marcos.

JAMES TAYLOR CARSON, a professor of history and associate dean in the Faculty of Arts and Science at Queen's University, Kingston, Ontario, Canada, writes about the South's native past, ethnogeography, and cultural contacts in the colonial America.

KAREN L. COX, an associate professor of history and director of public history at the University of North Carolina at Charlotte, writes on southern history and culture and the South in mass culture.

EMILYE CROSBY, an associate professor of history at the State University of New York at Geneseo, writes about the civil rights movement and is interested in self-defense, gender, and local-national interactions.

SUSAN DITTO, a senior communications analyst for the United States Government Accountability Office in Washington. D.C., received a PhD in history from the University of Mississippi and wrote her dissertation on Mississippi's yeoman farming families.

BRENDA M. EAGLES, a former research bibliographer at the Center for the Study of Southern Culture at the University of Mississippi and bibliographical editor of the *Journal of Mississippi History*, is the author of the *Bibliography of Mississippi History* (available online).

MICHAEL DE L. LANDON, professor emeritus of history at the University of Mississippi, writes on the legal history of England and the United States and is particularly interested in legal training.

KEVIN D. MCCARTHY, associate vice president for instruction at Blue Mountain Community College in Pendleton, Oregon, writes about the intersection of law and society using trial court documents and explores how southerners have contested the meaning of social relationships.

SARA E. MORRIS is the librarian for American history at the University of Kansas and a PhD candidate in history at Purdue University. Her research interests include rural women, technology, and changes in twentieth-century rural life.

J. TODD MOYE, a historian of the civil rights movement, is an associate professor of history and director of the Oral History Program at the University of North Texas.

JENNIFER NARDONE completed her PhD in history at the University of Mississippi. Her dissertation, "The Rosenwald School Building Program in Mississippi, 1919–1929," was inspired by Willa Tucker Raspberry.

TED OWNBY, director for the Center for the Study of Southern Culture at the University of Mississippi, teaches history and southern studies and has written two books and edited or coedited four books on southern social and cultural history.

ELIZABETH ANNE PAYNE is a professor of history at the University of Mississippi. She writes on reform, labor, and feminism in late nineteenth- and twentieth-century America.

HATTYE RASPBERRY-HALL, a native of Okolona, Mississippi, lives in Indianapolis, where she is a community leader and active in the Episcopal Church.

RANDY J. SPARKS is a professor and chair of the history department at Tulane University. He is a scholar of southern religion and the Atlantic world.

MARJORIE JULIAN SPRUILL is a professor of history at the University of South Carolina.

She is currently writing about the role of gender issues in shaping modern American political culture.

MARTHA H. SWAIN is Cornaro Professor emerita at Texas Woman's University and has taught at Mississippi State University. She writes about southern women's history as well as Mississippians in Washington during the Roosevelt-Truman era.

Index

Aberdeen, Miss., 51
abortion, 290, 299, 302
Abzug, Bella, 287, 291, 304, 305
Adams, John Quincy, 16
Adams County, 23, 24, 26, 28, 62, 78
Adams County Circuit Court, 30
adultery, 66, 67, 68, 78, 82
African American Episcopal Church, 321
African Americans, 206; Afro-American
    Historical Society, 292; agency, 116;
    blackness, 23, 121; children, 88, 116;
    Civil War, 115, 117; custody issues, 80,
    87–94; education, 153, 255, 257, 263,
    317–18, 321–22; men, 116; resistance
    strategies, 141; segregation, 139;
    sexuality, 80, 175; stereotypes, 165;
    tenant farming, 215, 219; voting rights,
    119, 159, 238, 241–42, 314, 317; women, 4,
    116. *See also* civil rights movement; race
Afro-American Historical Society, 292
agrarian ideal, 211, 218, 229
agrarianism, 153, 211–29
Agricultural and Mechanical College of
    the State of Mississippi, 193
Alcorn County, 129, 201, 204
Alcorn County Electric Power
    Association, 195
Alexander, Sally, 121
Allen, Betsy Love, 1, 18
Alston, James, 77
American Association of University
    Women (AAUW), 269, 277–79, 281,
    282–83, 292

American Cancer Society, 292
American Church Institute for Negroes,
    320
American Civil Liberties Union (ACLU),
    292, 307
American Hospital Association, 263
American Medical Missionary College,
    186
American Party of Mississippi, 296
American Revolution, 12, 46, 109
Amite County Unity Church, 41
Anderson, Hob, 319
Anderson, Mrs., 253
Anderson, William, 29
Angelou, Maya, 304
Anglicans, 45
Arendt, Hannah, 52
Assembly of God Church, 217
Association of Southern Women for the
    Prevention of Lynching, 256
Attala County, 129, 221
Atwood, Julia Luccock, 187
Atwood, Parker, 187

Baby Steps, 327, 328
Bachelor's Bend, Miss., 40
Bailey, Thomas L., 277
Baker, Ella, 245
Balance, Emily, 29
Baldwin, Rosetta, 184
Baldwyn, Miss., 155
Balfour, Emma, 106, 108
Ballard, Michael, 4

Norris, Mildred W., 279
Noxubee County, 17
nurses, 24, 108, 149

Oakwood College, 184, 188
Ogden, Florence Sillers, 255–56, 280
Okolona Child Development Center, 326
Okolona, Miss., 154, 313, 328
Okolona College, 318–27
Old Capitol, 164, 165, 170
Old Natchez District, 70–71n2
one-drop rule, 24, 36n6, 174, 179
oral history, 163, 266n12
Ordinance of Secession, 164, 167
Orphans Court, 25
Osteen, Elizabeth, 42
Our Heritage, 166
Our Mart, 242, 243
Overaker, Margaret, 27, 28
Owen, Sherra, 151
Ownby, Ted, 153
Oxford, Miss., 102

Page, Thomas Nelson, 166
Pallie, William, 133
Pardo, Juan, 10
Park, Maud Wood, 273
Parker, George, 116
Parker, Marla, 116, 117
Parkinson, Dera, 278
Pascagoula, Miss., 223, 224
paternalism, 61–62, 115, 215
patriarchy, 40, 43, 45, 52, 70, 78–79
Patterson, Robert, 255
Paul, Alice, 273, 274
Payne, Charles, 247–48n34
Payne, Elizabeth Anne, 154, 257
Payne, Henry, 89
Payne, Margaret, 89
Payne, Mary, 89
Payne, Ruth Hawkins, 2, 319
Payne, William, 89

Pearce, Jonathan, 117
Pearl River, 10
Peaster, Margaret, 280
Pegues, Ella, 102
Pemberton, John C., 102, 106
Percy, William Alexander, 213, 215
Perry, Elizabeth, 16
Peshakova, Liba, 273
Phillips, Harriet, 124
physicians, 151
Pitard, Orell, 276
Pittman, Barbara, 293
Pittman, Paul, 301
politics, 9, 113, 243, 260–61
Pollitzer, Anita, 273
poll taxes, 203, 277
Pontotoc County, 129, 216
Porter, David D., 120
Port Gibson, Miss., 50, 104, 254
poverty: 192–93, 206, 215–16, 224;
    domesticity, 132; marriage, 57;
    parenthood, 91; race, 175, 185, 189, 239,
    253, 260
Powell, Susie V., 197, 278
Prentiss County, 129
prenuptial contracts, 57, 58–59, 62, 63, 70
Presbyterians, 41, 44, 49, 50, 295
Presley, Elvis, 222–24, 226, 228
Presley, Gladys Smith, 153, 211–29
Presley, Jesse, 222
Presley, Vernon, 222–23, 226
Presley, Vester, 228
Price, Kate Baker, 151
Price, Virginia Redditt, 163, 167–68
Pro-Family Forum, 306
Progressivism, 159–60
prostitution, 30–31, 32, 67, 68, 75n35, 122.
    See also brothels
Protestantism, 39, 40, 291; Anglicans, 45;
    Assembly of God, 217. *See also* Baptists;
    Episcopal Church; Methodists;
    Presbyterians

Stone, Hattie, 151
STOP ERA, 295–96, 306
Stratton, Joseph P., 50
Strode, Velma McEwen, 294
Student Nonviolent Coordinating Committee (SNCC), 244–45, 251–54, 260–61, 266n7, 266n12
Suarez, Matt, 253
Sullivan, Mrs. Dan E., 204
Sunflower County, 255, 261
Swain, Martha, 153
Swayze, Hannah, 42
syphilis, 151

Tarbell, Jonathan, 80
Taylor, Willie Mae Latham, 293, 295, 300
Temple, Norma, 300, 304
Temple, William, 300, 304
tenant farming, 142
tender-years doctrine, 84, 87
Tennessee Valley Authority (TVA), 153, 195–96, 199–206
Tewksbury, Martha, 68–69
Tewksbury, Timothy, 68–69
Tewksbury v. Tewksbury, 78–79
textile mills, 221, 231n37
Thomas, Lorenzo, 117, 118
Thompson, Cleopatra, 294
Thompson, Margaret Kinkhead, 157
Thompson, Martha, 120
Thomson, Rosemary, 291, 306
thrift, 113, 217, 228–29
Tichenor, Gabriel, 27, 28, 33
Tilly, Dorothy Rogers, 256, 258
Tippah County, 129
Tishomingo County, 129, 140, 202
Toms, Caroline, 276
Treaty of Pontotoc Creek, 17
Treaty of Washington, 17
Trotter, James F., 79
Troy Female Seminary, 2, 47
Tucker, Martha, 315

Tucker, Ophallon Dilworth, 313, 316
Tucker, Simon Tilghman, 313, 314, 315
Tucker, Talena, 315, 316
Tucker, Tilghman, 314–15
Tucker, Winford, 313, 315–18, 326
Tucker, Zachary, 315
Tupelo, Miss., 152, 153, 196, 200, 203, 205, 213, 216, 223, 227
Tupelo Daily Journal, 203
Tupelo Garment Company, 222
Twentieth Century Club, 271

Underwood, Felix, 149
Underwood, Sally, 16
Union County, 129, 151, 202, 319
Unionists, 174
United Church Women, 258
United Confederate Veterans (UCV), 164
United Daughters of the Confederacy (UDC), 109, 255–56
U.S. Army, 115, 118, 120
U.S. Census Bureau, 85, 193
U.S. Civil Rights Commission, 292
U.S. Department of Agriculture, 193
Usner, Daniel H., 12
U.S. Public Health Service, 149
U.S. Supreme Court, 255, 262, 290

Vardaman, James K., 91, 162
venereal disease, 68, 259
Vicksburg, Miss., 43, 109, 124, 155, 196
violence, 100, 159, 178, 186, 238, 258
virtue, 46–49, 118, 144, 213, 217, 228
vocational training, 219
Voting Rights Act of 1965, 260, 264, 292, 317

Wadsworth, James S., 113–15, 118, 121
Wakefield, Samuel, 32
Walker, Merlene, 303
Walsh, James, 26, 27
Ward, Stephen, 14

Ware, T. P., 133
War of 1812, 109
Warren, Earl, 254
Warren County, 101, 196
Warren County Fire Company, 43
washerwomen, 24, 29
Washington, Booker T., 317, 318
Washington, Miss., 2
Washington County, 40, 103
Watts, Augusta, 188
Watts, Van Buren, 188
Waveland, Miss., 252
Wayne, Michael, 72–73n13
Wayne County, 10
Weaver, William, 205
Webster County, 129
Wednesdays in Mississippi (WIMS), 153,
    257, 258, 259, 260, 292
Welter, Barbara, 39
West Point, Miss., 164
Wheeler, Charles, 320
Wheling, Mrs. M. P., 297
White, Earlene, 277
White, Mother, 40
White Citizens' Councils, 255, 256, 277,
    284n39, 301, 302
whiteness, 23, 141, 179
white supremacy doctrine, 61, 157, 178,
    203, 240–41, 251, 299
Whitfield, Henry L., 166
Wilkinson, Howard, 116
Wilkinson, Jane, 45
Wilkinson, Kate, 260
Wilkinson Circuit, 40
Willard, Emma Hart, 47
Williams, Linda, 297
Williams, Mary Ellen, 33
Williamson, Edna, 303
Williamson, Mary, 166
Wilson, Betty Rutherford, 2
Wilson, Charles Reagan, 157

Wilson, R. S., 213
Winans, William, 40, 41, 42
Winscott, James, 28
Winscott, Joseph, 26, 27
Winston County, 129, 196
Winter, William, 289
witchcraft, 7, 9
Wolf Friend, 15
Womanpower Unlimited, 257, 263
women, 81, 115; African American, 4, 116;
    Association of Southern Women for
    the Prevention of Lynching, 256; Bap-
    tist, 50; benevolent associations, 39,
    53; Business and Professional Women's
    Federation, 269, 292; Church Women
    United, 292; Commission on the
    Status of Women, 279; Coordination
    Council of Women's Organizations
    for War Services, 278–79; education,
    39, 47–48; leadership, 241, 243–45,
    251; literacy, 48; National American
    Woman Suffrage Association, 272–73;
    National Council of Catholic Women,
    258; National Council of Jewish
    Women, 258, 292; National Federation
    of Business and Professional Women's
    Clubs, 277, 281; National Women's
    Political Caucus, 282; politics, 261, 264;
    relationships with Civil War soldiers,
    97, 105, 109; rights advocates, 81, 289;
    suffrage, 43–44, 60, 153, 164; Woman-
    power Unlimited, 257, 263; Women for
    Racial and Economic Equality, 305;
    workforce, 119–20; Young Women's
    Christian Association, 258, 292. *See
    also* American Association of Univer-
    sity Women; feminists; International
    Women's Year; National Commission
    on the Observance of International
    Women's Year; National Council of
    Negro Women; National Organiza-